The House of Hemp and Butter

A volume in the NIU Series in
SLAVIC, EAST EUROPEAN, AND EURASIAN STUDIES
Edited by Christine D. Worobec

For a list of books in the series, visit our website at cornellpress.cornell.edu.

The House of Hemp and Butter

A History of Old Riga

Kevin C. O'Connor

Northern Illinois University Press
an imprint of
Cornell University Press
Ithaca and London

Copyright © 2019 by Cornell University

All rights reserved. Except for brief quotations in a review, this book, or parts thereof, must not be reproduced in any form without permission in writing from the publisher. For information, address Cornell University Press, Sage House, 512 East State Street, Ithaca, New York 14850. Visit our website at cornellpress.cornell.edu.

First published 2019 by Cornell University Press

ISBN 978-1-5017-4768-7 (cloth : alk. paper)
ISBN 978-1-5017-4770-0 (pdf)
ISBN 978-1-5017-4769-4 (epub/mobi)

Cover design by Yuni Dorr
Composed by BookComp, Inc.

Librarians: A CIP record is available with the Library of Congress.

Contents

Chapter Overview vii

Dramatis Personae ix

Noteworthy Places and Buildings xiii

Introduction 1

CHAPTER 1
Genesis: Riga before Riga 12

CHAPTER 2
Watering the Nations: Riga and the Northern Crusades 39

CHAPTER 3
Free Air in the Hanse City 69

CHAPTER 4
Master of Riga: The Archbishop, the Order, and the Rath 96

CHAPTER 5
Old Knights and New Teachings: The Reformation in Riga 128

CHAPTER 6
Upheavals: The Livonian War and the Polish Interlude 152

CHAPTER 7
Star City: The Swedish Century 184

CHAPTER 8
"This Accursed Place": The Great Northern War 224

Epilogue 259

Notes 261

Bibliography 301

Index 311

Chapter Overview

Chapter 1. Genesis: Riga before Riga.

The book opens with an origin story that introduces the watery and sandy landscape of early Riga and the pagans who lived in or near it at the close of the twelfth century. Chapter 1 considers the efforts of German merchants and Catholic missionaries to trade with and establish Christian communities among the Livish tribes who lived along the banks of the Düna River (which Latvians know as the Daugava). The chapter provides readers with a broader context for understanding these early encounters by examining western Europe's commercial and religious expansion during the Middle Ages.

Chapter 2. Watering the Nations: Riga and the Northern Crusades.

Based partly on the accounts of medieval chroniclers, chapter 2 explores the notion of Riga as a "city of God" to which thousands of monk-knights and other warriors arrived to do battle with the pagans in Livonia, which the crusaders called the "Land of Mary." Here we consider the city's role in the Baltic crusade as both a regional trading center and as a gathering point for military expeditions against pagans and Rus'.

Chapter 3. Free Air in the Hanse City.

Chapter 3 narrates Riga's history as a prosperous member of the Hanseatic League of northern trading cities. A distant outpost of the decentralized Holy Roman Empire, the "free city" of Riga became an important collecting point for primary goods from the east (Russia) destined for western European markets. Chapter 3 maps the medieval city's castles, churches, markets, and streets while exploring the roles played by Germans and "non-Germans" in the city's social and economic arrangements.

Chapter 4. Master of Riga: The Archbishop, the Order, and the Rath.

The subject of chapter 4 is Riga's unstable political dynamics, for the division of power in Riga satisfied neither the region's supreme religious authority, the Archbishop of Riga, nor the master of the Livonian Order, whose monk-knights were responsible for Livonia's defense. Least of all did the arrangement please the wealthy merchants of the Riga Town Council (Rath), an administrative body that embodied the ideal of urban self-governance. A set piece of chapter 4 is the fate of the Riga Castle, which the citizens destroyed twice during Riga's civil wars of the later Middle Ages.

Chapter 5. Old Knights and New Teachings: The Reformation in Riga.

Chapter 5 demonstrates the impact of new ideas on old arrangements in late medieval Riga. While the restlessness of the 1520s brought an end to the Catholic Church's spiritual dominion over the city of Riga, the Reformation was no impediment to Riga's growing material prosperity and in no way diminished the authority of its German elites. During an era when established authority was under challenge and neighboring dynastic states sought to expand their power and influence, it fell to the Livonian Order's long-reigning master Walter of Plettenberg to defend the feudal state and keep the peace in Riga.

Chapter 6. Upheavals: The Livonian War and the Polish Interlude.

The demise of the archbishopric and of the Livonian Order during the Livonian War (1558–1582) left Riga and the territory of Livonia vulnerable to the ambitions of aggressive regional powers. Chapter 6 examines the tumultuous era that began with the failed Muscovite advance toward Riga and that continued through four decades of Polish rule (1581–1621). This era of alien occupation and of religious and political strife is illustrated by a close examination of Riga's unique "Calendar Upheavals" of the 1590s.

Chapter 7. Star City: The Swedish Century.

For ninety years, Riga was under the dominion of the Swedish Empire, an absolutist state that relied on the Livonian port for supplies of food and for the defense of its Baltic possessions. As Riga was the empire's largest city, its most important fortress, and a significant source of income, the city underwent extensive physical renovations that strengthened its defenses and transformed its appearance. Chapter 7 demonstrates that the peace, progress, educational advances, and cultural achievements of the seventeenth century made the Swedish era into something of a "golden age" for early modern Riga.

Chapter 8. "This Accursed Place": The Great Northern War.

The concluding chapter examines the city's experience during the Great Northern War (1700–1721), whose end results were the destruction of Swedish power in the Baltic Sea and Russia's acquisition of several new ports, including Riga. Chapter 8 focuses on the actions of three powerful monarchs, Charles XII of Sweden, Augustus II of Poland-Saxony, and Peter I of Russia, as they clashed over the eastern Baltic. Its principal concern, however, is the experience of Rigans during these extraordinary times. The book ends with a scene of devastation in the starving and bombed-out city of Riga as its terrified residents surrendered to the victorious Russian state. It was in this manner that more than two centuries of tsarist dominion over Riga began in 1710.

Dramatis Personae

Individuals

Albert of Buxhoeveden (1165–1229). The third bishop of Livonia and the first bishop of Riga, Albert founded the city in 1201, secured for it exclusive trading rights, led the crusades against the pagans, and presided over the construction of early Riga.

Albert Suerbeer (ca. 1200–1273). Appointed bishop of Riga in 1253, Albert Suerbeer became the first archbishop of Riga (r. 1255–1273) and spent much of his tenure quarreling with the Livonian Order.

Bathory, Stephen (1533–1586). Bathory became Riga's first true king when the city came under Polish occupation in 1581. Rigans resisted his efforts to return Catholicism to the city and its hinterlands.

Berthold of Hanover (d. 1198). The second bishop of Livonia, Berthold died in battle with the Livs and was replaced by Albert of Buxhoeveden.

Bindenschu, Rupert (1645–1698). Riga's chief architect at the height of Swedish power, Bindenschu built the suburban Jesus Church and the Dannenstern House while also rebuilding the damaged tower of St. Peter's.

Caune, Andris (b. 1937). A Latvian archaeologist whose work has contributed immeasurably to our knowledge of early Riga.

Charles (Karl) XII (r. 1697–1718). The last Swedish ruler of Livonia, Charles XII was defeated by Peter I in the Great Northern War (1700–1721), during which he ceded Riga and other Swedish possessions to the Russian state.

Dahlberg, Erik (1625–1703). A fortification engineer and then governor of Riga during the era of Swedish rule in Riga. Known as the "Swedish Vauban," Dahlberg oversaw extensive renovations to Riga's defensive systems.

Dannenstern, Ernst Metsu von (d. 1721). Ernst Metsu was a Dutch merchant who relocated to Riga, became one its foremost merchants (and the owner of a fleet), was ennobled (von Dannenstern) by the Swedish crown, and built one of its most impressive domiciles.

Ecke, Nicholas (1541–1623). Although he was the Riga Town Council's hated burgrave during the years of Polish rule, Ecke's name is also associated with a convent built for the widows of guildsmen who had fallen on hard times.

Frederick of Perlstein (1270–1341). The long tenure (r. 1304–1341) of Archbishop Frederick, much of which he spent in Avignon waiting for an audience with the pope, was defined by his struggles with the Livonian Order.

Giese, Martin (d. 1589). Along with the wine merchant Hans Brinken, Martin Giese was one of the organizers of the Calendar Upheavals (1585–1590) that marked the early years of Polish rule in Riga.

Gustavus II Adolphus (1594–1632). Among the most revered of Sweden's early modern rulers, King Gustavus II Adolphus conquered Riga in 1621.

Henry of Livonia (ca. 1180–1259). A witness to the Northern Crusades of the thirteenth century, the monk Henry compiled a chronicle of events in early Riga and Livonia.

Knopken, Andreas (1468–1539). A pastor to Latvian and German communities in Riga, Knopken was a moderate voice of the Protestant Reformation.

Meinhard (1127–1196). The first bishop of Livonia, Meinhard was a Catholic missionary who began the conversion of the Livs of the lower Düna.

Mollin, Nicholas (1550–1625). Invited to Riga to set up a print shop, Mollin is responsible for publishing 179 books and smaller works, as well as some of the earliest depictions of the city.

Peter I, Tsar of Russia (1672–1725). Known to history as Peter the Great, this Romanov ruler left his mark on Riga by conquering the city in 1710 after a long siege. Under Russian rule, Riga was to become the empire's second most important port on the Baltic after St. Petersburg.

Plettenberg, Walter von (1450–1535). A knight of the Livonian Order, Walter of Plettenberg defeated the city of Riga to end the city's second civil war (1481–1491). Plettenberg was the order's master from 1494 to 1535 and presided over a generally peaceful era in Riga and Livonia.

Plinius, Basilius (1540–1605). Physician and author of the *Encomium to Riga* (1595), a poem to his native city.

Ramm, Nikolaus (d. 1540). A pastor at St. Jacob's who was responsible for some of the earliest translations of religious literature into Latvian.

Reuter, Johann (Jānis Reiters; ca. 1632–ca. 1697). Possibly the first academically educated Latvian, Reuter was a pastor who published many theological works and preached to nearby communities of Latvians, Finns, and Estonians.

Rodenburg, Johan van (d. 1657). This Dutchman served the Swedish crown by supervising an extensive reconstruction of Riga's system of fortifications.

Stodewescher, Silvester (d. 1479). The unsteady peace that marked the beginning of Archbishop Silvester's tenure (r. 1448–1479) fell apart in the late 1470s. Silvester's cynical dealings with the city and the knights only exacerbated the conflicts among them and contributed to a second civil war.

Straubergs, Jānis (1886–1952). A historian of Riga whose main contributions occurred during the era of the first Republic of Latvia (1919–1940), Straubergs is noted for highlighting the experience of ethnic Latvians in the city of Riga.

Tegetmeier, Silvester (d. 1552). A fiery preacher of the new Protestant doctrine during the Reformation in Riga.

Waldis, Burkard (1490–1556). Rejecting Catholicism and embracing the new Lutheran teachings while making his home in Riga, Waldis was a noted writer of fables during the age of the Renaissance and Reformation.

William of Brandenburg (1498–1563). The last archbishop of Riga (r. 1539–1561), William entertained ambitions of uniting the Prussian and Livonian territories under the house of Brandenburg but failed.

Institutions

Archbishopric of Riga. Supplanting the bishopric of Riga, the archbishopric of Riga (1255–1561) was the supreme religious authority in the Livonian lands. Frequently allying with the Riga Town Council, its quarrels with the Livonian Order resulted in two civil wars (1297–1330, 1481–1491).

Bishopric of Riga. Formed when the original bishopric of Livonia moved to Riga in 1202, the bishopric of Riga was the foremost religious authority in Riga and the Livonian lands. It was elevated to an archbishopric in 1255.

Blackheads. This fraternity of young bachelors, typically the sons of merchants and often hailing from foreign lands, was exclusive to the Livonian cities.

Burgrave. A post that was introduced after 1581 to facilitate Polish rule in Riga, the city's burgrave was also a member of the Riga Town Council.

Burgomaster. The burgomaster or *Bürgermeister* was a chief executive of the Riga Town Council. To prevent the concentration of power in any one person or family, Riga had four burgomasters (or mayors) at any one time.

Great Guild. Established in 1354 as the Merchants' Company, the Great Guild was formally called St. Mary's, and it enjoyed exclusive control over commerce in Riga.

Hanseatic League. The Hanseatic League, or Hanse, was an association of northern trading cities, ranging from London to Novgorod. Its merchants dominated the Baltic Sea trade from the thirteenth through the sixteenth centuries.

Landtag. This was an occasional assembly or diet of the leading representatives of the Livonian Confederation between 1419 and 1561.

Livonian Confederation. Founded in 1419 and dissolved in 1561, the Livonian Confederation was a loose framework that united the Livonian estates, including the Livonian Order, the cities, the archbishopric of Riga, and the other bishoprics of Livonia and Estonia.

Livonian Order. An autonomous branch of the Order of Teutonic Knights, the Livonian Order was formed in 1237 on the basis of the defunct Order of Swordbrothers. Its initial mission was to defend Livonia and convert the pagans, but its clashes with the city and the archbishop of Riga resulted in two civil wars during the Middle Ages.

Order of Swordbrothers. Founded in 1202 to provide year-round defense for the Christian outposts in Livonia, the Fratres militiæ Christi Livoniae (a.k.a. the Livonian Brothers of the Sword) was supplanted by the Livonian Order in 1237.

Order of Teutonic Knights. Based in Prussia, this crusading order was the parent organization of the Livonian Order.

Riga Town Council. Known as the Rath, the town council consisted of fourteen or sixteen wealthy merchants who ran the city's commercial and legal affairs. The town council was often in conflict with the Livonian Order, and sometimes with the archbishop in Riga. The town council maintained most of its functions during the periods of Polish (1581–1621) and Swedish (1621–1710) rule.

Small Guild. Also known as St. John's, this was the organization to which all of Riga's artisans and craftsmen belonged, each in their own fraternities of cobblers, masons, and so on. While German and Latvian laborers belonged to separate fraternities, eventually the city's Germans took exclusive control over most handicrafts.

Noteworthy Places and Buildings

Within and near Riga

Bishop's Castle. Part of the original cluster of buildings along the Riva rivulet, the building and the land around it belonged to the bishop of Riga before it was sold to the Dominican Order in 1234. The former castle is presently the site of an attractive hotel complex called Konventa sēta (Convent Yard).

Citadel. A fortress next to Riga that was constructed during the Swedish occupation in the seventeenth century. Destroyed during the Great Northern War (1700–1721), the Citadel was rebuilt by the Russians, but few of its original buildings remain.

Dannenstern House. Named after Ernst Metsu von Dannenstern, a wealthy Dutch merchant, this Baroque domicile was completed in 1696 and, although now dilapidated, at the time was one of Riga's largest and most impressive homes.

Dome Cathedral. See St. Mary's.

Dünamünde (Latv. Daugavgrīva). This refers to either of the two fortresses that were, at different times, located near the mouth of the Düna River, just north of Riga. Following a shift in the river's course in the sixteenth century, the old fort near the right bank lost its military function and a fortress was built five kilometers to the west at the river's new mouth.

House of Blackheads. Originally called the New House and erected in 1334, the building served as a meeting place for both the Great and Small Guilds, but came to be associated with the unmarried men of the fraternity of Blackheads. They became its sole tenants in 1713, by which time the building had acquired its ornate Baroque façade. The present-day edifice is a replica of the building destroyed in 1941.

Jesus Church. This was a wooden church that was located in Lastadia, just south of the old city limits.

Kobron. A seventeenth-century Swedish bastion fort located in the Überdüna district across the river from the city of Riga. This site is now occupied by Victory Park.

Kube Hill. Also known as the Old Mountain, this was an inhabited sand dune just outside the city walls. Because it loomed over the city fortifications, Kube Hill was razed in 1784 and later became the approximate location of Riga's Esplanade Park.

Lastadia. A shipbuilding area just south of Riga (today it is part of Riga's Moscow or Latgale suburb) populated by Russian merchants.

Powder Tower. Located at the site of the older Sand Tower, which guarded the main entrance to Riga, the rotund Powder Tower was built in the seventeenth century by the Swedes, who used it for storing gunpowder. Today this well-tended edifice houses the Latvian Museum of War.

Riga River. Known to Germans as the Rigebach or the Rising/Riesing, and to Latvians as the Rīdzene/Rīdziņa, the rivulet gave the medieval city its original shape and its first port. It was at "Lake Riga" that the minor tributary emptied into the Düna River that flowed past Riga to the Baltic Sea. The city's first permanent structures were erected along the Riga River.

Sand Road. Sometimes referred to as the Great Sandy Way, the Sand Road led from Riga to the lands of Russia. Although it has gone by many names, today the Sand Road is known as Brīvības iela (Freedom Street).

Sand Tower. See Powder Tower.

St. George's. Refers to the first Order Castle (Ger. Jürgenshof) that was located on the right bank of the Riga River. St. George's is also the name of the chapel that was built on the site after the castle's destruction in 1297.

St. Gertrude's Church. Located along the Sand Road in Riga's suburbs, St. Gertrude's was a wooden church that belonged to the local Latvian population. The current St. Gertrude's Church is a completely different edifice.

St. Jacob's Church. One of Riga's oldest brick churches, St. Jacob's (also known as the Church of St. James) was a Catholic house of worship that was transferred to the Lutherans during the Reformation and was attended by Riga's Latvian community.

St. John's Church. First a Catholic church and then a Lutheran one, St. John's was built on the site of the Bishop's Castle next to the Riga rivulet.

St. Mary's Church. Commonly known as the Dome (or Riga Cathedral), St. Mary's is a large church that belonged to the bishop of Riga and then (after 1255) to the archbishop of Riga.

St. Peter's Church. A large Catholic (and then Protestant) church that belonged to the citizens, St. Peter's is an iconic house of worship in the heart of Riga whose spire, at one time one of Europe's tallest, has been repeatedly destroyed and rebuilt.

Town Hall. This was where members of the Riga Town Council (Rath) held their weekly meetings. There were two town hall buildings before Riga's capitulation to Russia. Little is known of the first; the second was built in 1334 at its present location. The current edifice is a copy of the building that was erected in the eighteenth century and destroyed during World War II.

Town Hall Square. The city's main market and gathering place and originally known as the New Market Square, Town Hall Square in the Middle Ages was far smaller and busier than the broad and touristy square that was rebuilt in the 1990s.

Überdüna (Latv. Pārdaugava). Refers to the lightly inhabited district opposite Riga on the left bank of the Düna. In Swedish times, this was the location of Fort Kobron.

Outside Riga

Courland (Latv. Kurzeme). A sandy, horn-shaped region west of Riga in present-day Latvia. Also refers to a medieval bishopric.

Danzig (Pol. Gdańsk). A leading Baltic trading city whose early history bears much resemblance to that of Riga, Danzig was taken over by the Teutonic Knights in 1308 and later joined the Hanseatic League.

Dorpat (Est. Tartu). Located in present-day Estonia, northeast of Riga, this was the third-largest city in Old Livonia after Riga and Reval and also the seat of a medieval bishopric.

Kirchholm (Latv. Salaspils). Located eighteen kilometers south of Riga on the Düna River, Kirchholm was the site of an early fortified church.

Kokenhusen (Latv. Koknese). The seat of the archbishop of Riga during the later Middle Ages, its castle was destroyed during the Great Northern War and fell into ruin.

Livonia (Ger. Livland). Livonia originally refers to the lands occupied by Livish tribes at the beginning of the conquest. During the Middle Ages, "Old Livonia" came to indicate all the regions belonging to the Livonian Confederation, including Courland and Estonia. Swedish Livland included only southern Estonia and northeastern Latvia.

Lübeck. The main headquarters of the Hanseatic League, Lübeck was a German trading hub whose merchants enjoyed close connections with Riga during the Middle Ages.

Muscovy. This Russian principality united the neighboring Slavic lands and became the basis for the multinational Russian Empire. The desire of Muscovy's rulers to have direct commercial links with western Europe brought this sprawling state into direct conflict with Riga and the Livonian Confederation.

Narva. Now an Estonian city populated almost entirely by Russians, Narva was once the easternmost outpost of Old Livonia on the Russian border and the site of an imposing castle belonging to the Livonian Order.

Novgorod. A trading city of the Kievan Rus' and its hinterlands during the Middle Ages, the city of Novgorod was a member of the Hanseatic League and supplied Livonian intermediaries with furs and other goods from the forests of northeastern Europe.

Polotsk. A significant Russian trading city, which during the Middle Ages enjoyed a land connection to Riga, Polotsk stood near the border of the Livonian Confederation.

Reval (Est. Tallinn). Located on the northern coast of Estonia, Reval was the largest Livonian city after Riga and a member of the Hanseatic League.

Semigallia (Latv. Zemgale). A Latvian region located south of Riga. One of the last pagan regions to submit to the Germans, Semigallia fell into Polish hands during the Livonian War.

Treiden (Latv. Turaida). A large castle east of Riga and an important center of the archbishopric of Riga, Treiden was repeatedly taken by the knights of the Livonian Order. Like the castle at Wenden, it has been lovingly restored and is worth a visit.

Üxküll (Latv. Ikšķile). The location of a fortified church (now destroyed and submerged) and of Livonia's first bishopric, established just south of Riga on the Düna River.

Wenden (Latv. Cēsis) Located northeast of Riga, Wenden was the seat of the master of the Livonian Order for much of the fifteenth and sixteenth centuries. Partly destroyed during the Great Northern War and restored in modern times, it was one of Livonia's most impressive castles and is now among Latvia's most popular tourist destinations.

Introduction

Riga, Ryga, Rīga, Рига

My first visit to Latvia was in the summer of 2002. With a doctorate in Russian history in hand, as well as a contract with Greenwood Press to write *The History of the Baltic States* (2003),[1] I introduced myself to the region by decamping to Valmiera, a sleepy old town northeast of Riga on the Gauja River. It was while taking courses at the local college on Baltic languages and cultures that I made my initial acquaintance with Latvia and Estonia by train, bus, taxi, and thumb.

Regimented tours of Latvia's splendid Baroque palaces at Jelgava and Rundāle tested the limits of my endurance. While these old playgrounds for a vanished aristocracy have been lovingly rehabilitated for the delectation of ordinary tourists, it was Latvia's Soviet-era kitsch and medieval ruins that commanded my attention. For such a small country, Latvia has an impressive array of old castles in varying condition—a testament to the region's role in the Northern Crusades of the thirteenth century as well as to its subsequent vulnerabilities. Some, like the castles that once stood in Valmiera and Kuldīga, have been lost to war and time; a few, like the stunning fortresses at Cēsis and Turaida, have been lovingly restored and beg to be seen and enjoyed. Still more compelling is the castle at Rīga, built in 1515 near the banks of the Daugava River, where it replaced an earlier fortress destroyed in a civil war. Located at the edge of a medieval ensemble of towering church spires, the Rīga Castle anchors a skyline so iconic that even today it would be instantly recognizable to a Latvian Rip Van Winkle. Barely a decade removed from so many years of Soviet misrule, Rīga, then the resplendent and dilapidated capital city of one of Europe's youngest nation-states, immediately became my favorite travel destination in the eastern Baltic.

Local authorities put considerable time, money, and effort into sprucing up the city at the turn of the millennium: historic buildings destroyed in World War II were rebuilt in grand style, century-old *Jugendstil* (Art Nouveau) treasures were reconditioned, monuments to the great figures of Latvia's past erected and reinstalled—or, in the case of Rīga's notorious Lenin statue, removed and forgotten. Yet if the hammer and sickle have been expunged from the city's public spaces, Rīga has failed completely to eradicate its Soviet past. The Stalinist wedding-cake structure that houses the Latvian Academy of Sciences, a Soviet gift to the city dating from the 1950s, continues to cast its long shadow on the run-down Latgale (or Moscow) district, a neighborhood where many of Rīga's Russians live. It was during my first visits to the city that I encountered one monument to the Red Riflemen of World War I and another commemorating the Revolution of 1905, both located near the Daugava embankment. Directly across this wide and mighty river the Soviets built an enormous park dedicated to the Red Army's victory in World War II, known in the USSR as the Great Patriotic War. Rīga in 2002 was stately and elegant, exuberant and gentrified, shabby at the edges and still a bit Soviet. I was smitten.

Located near the mouth of one of eastern Europe's great rivers—Latvians call it the Daugava, to Germans it is the Düna, and to Russians it is the Dvina—the city of Rīga was established next to an existing settlement more than eight centuries ago by men of faith and ambition, some of whom appreciated the profits that could be had by setting up shop at the modest trading post that stood at the confluence of the Daugava and a minor river (now underground) that would give the city its name. (Henceforth the city's name will be rendered in its traditional form. It was only after 1918 that the city's Latvian spelling, Rīga, would become official.)

Missionaries and fighting men also understood Riga's potential as a religious and military center for the defense of Old Livonia, which the German settlers and crusaders called *Livland* or *Marienland*, "the Land of the Livs," or the "Land of St. Mary." Protected by a mighty wall built of brick and limestone, medieval Riga prospered as it collected the bounty of Russia's forested interior for export to the West. The city's economic function during the Middle Ages is reflected in the title I selected for this volume, *The House of Hemp and Butter*. First encountering the phrase in a collection of sixteenth-century poems that I perused while in the final stages of editing this book, I was struck by the image it conjured: "Old Riga" was the "house" from which visiting merchants obtained the primary goods—hemp, butter, wax, furs, and all kinds of goods—collected from the Russian/Belarusian interior.

If the activity at Riga's port generated wealth for some, for others it created employment: thus the city became a magnet for the ambitious and for the desperate alike, all of whom were subject in one way or another to the power of the archbishop of Riga, the knights of the Livonian Order, and the Riga Town Council (Ger. Rath). But since divided power exacerbated conflict among the men who wielded it, for Riga the Middle Ages was a time of almost ceaseless war.

Founded in 1201, Riga's life as a European city began when it became a staging point in the Baltic crusades to the pagan lands. Soon Riga became the seat of an archbishopric, making it a center of Catholic authority for three hundred years (1255–1561). Emerging as a port of regional significance, this German and Christian outpost would be repeatedly attacked and besieged by its enemies, its desperate burghers cut off from the outside world and starved for months on end on no fewer than nine occasions prior to 1710.

Its population never exceeding 15,000 souls, medieval Riga was a far smaller city than the modern capital of nearly 700,000, for during the Middle Ages the municipality's limits were defined by the walls, moats, and ramparts that remained in place until the late 1850s, when Russian authorities agreed to tear down the old fortifications and open the city up to light, air, and economic development. But in earlier years, prior to the razing of Riga's barriers and ramparts, the undefended areas outside the city were vulnerable to enemy predations and were typically burned during times of war. Sanctuary, on the other hand, was to be found within the confines of Riga's seemingly impregnable walls. But the struggles weren't always with pagans or Russians or Poles or Saxons. On two occasions, war came to Riga as a result of local conflicts between the archbishop of Riga and the Order of Livonian Knights, each of which laid claim to authority over the city. Both were swept away during the Livonian War (1558–1582), a devastating regional conflict that left many Livonian towns and castles in ruins.

Despite the metropolis's status as a free city of the decentralized Holy Roman Empire, Rigans always had to serve one or another master. If the medieval city was for centuries dominated by men of the Catholic Church and by German knights, after the Livonian War Riga came under the rule of the kings of Poland (1581–1621). It was the town's first real experience with monarchical power, but it was not to be the last, for in the midst of another great conflict the city submitted to the Swedish crown (1621–1710). The "good old Swedish times," a long period of peace and development under Stockholm's colonial rule, came to an end during the next great regional catastrophe, the Great Northern War (1700–1721). It was in the midst of that terrible conflict that Riga fell to the tsar, now desirous of a port on the Baltic and a second (after the new imperial capital of St. Petersburg) "window on the West." For the two hundred years following its capitulation in the summer of 1710, Riga would be under the dominion of the Russian Empire, then emerging as one of Europe's most formidable powers. It is this date that this book takes as its endpoint. About this decision I shall have more to say below.

It was only in the twentieth century that Riga (and Latvia) threw off its Russian occupiers, first in 1918 and again in 1991. For a brief time in between those dates, from 1941 to 1944, Rigans were subjected to the brutal policies of the Third Reich, but Riga's "liberation" by the Red Army toward the end of World War II was just the beginning of another long Russian (Soviet) occupation. The complexity of Riga's political history is appropriately illustrated by the names adorning its street signs: a change in master invariably meant new names for the city's roads. For example, today the city's main artery is called *Brīvības iela* (Freedom Street), but in the past it has also been known as *Sandstraße* (the Sand Road), Улица Ленина (Lenin Street), *Adolf-Hitler-Straße*, and Александровскій бульваръ (Alexander Boulevard). Riga's history is just that complicated.

The history of Riga is as fascinating as it is complex. Even if it was never a seat of royal power like London, Paris, or Berlin, Riga's past and present have been influenced by the same political, economic, religious, and cultural forces that have shaped a diverse continent where matters of faith, authority, and hierarchy have intermingled with those of nationality, class, and sovereignty. It might reasonably be suggested that Riga is a microcosm of northeastern Europe; yet this eclectic city of towering red-brick churches, exquisitely restored *Jugendstil* buildings, and decaying Soviet-era mass housing is in many respects *sui generis*. Riga may be familiar in its northeastern European context, yet it is also unique. Although his focus is on the modern era, the author of one recent book has gone so far as to describe Riga as "a different civilization."[2] While the contrast between the anxious and noisy city and the quiet and peaceful countryside exists everywhere, in few places is the disparity so striking as in Latvia, whose one large city seems to stand apart from the rest of a country whose very identity is rooted in nature and the countryside.

The book begins with the arrival of German missionaries in the Baltic in the late twelfth century and ends half a millennium later with Riga's capitulation to Russia at the dawn of the eighteenth century. As such, *The House of Hemp and Butter* falls well short of a complete urbanography. Despite the appearance of several English-language histories concerning specific episodes in Riga's modern history, the fact remains that the city's complete and comprehensive English-language "biography" still awaits its author.[3]

Because the city's history took a significant turn when it fell to Russia in 1710, this date seemed like a logical dividing line in the city's history. Prior to the eighteenth century Riga had been dominated by German merchants, archbishops, and knights, and then by Polish and Swedish kings. After submitting to the tsar in 1710, on the other hand, Riga's historical experience became almost entirely wrapped up with that of Russia. Another way of putting it is this: for five centuries before the Great Northern War, a generation-long conflict that fundamentally reshaped the power arrangements in northeastern Europe, the city of Riga interacted, usually from a distance, with earlier forms of a Russian state (Kievan Rus' and Muscovy)—but at no time was it ever a part of one. Beginning in the early eighteenth century, however, Riga's history became more intimately bound to that of Russia, and later to the modern Latvian state.

That being said, *The House of Hemp and Butter* is emphatically *not* about Riga's relationship with Russia—at least not directly. It is about the city that Germans and Latvians and Russians who called it their home built and repeatedly rebuilt in the wake of war and calamity. But as the life of the city was shaped by its functions and its environment, at all times I have tried to place Riga within the larger political, cultural, and religious currents taking shape throughout the continent and especially in northeastern Europe. In this sense the book might serve as a suitable text for a course on the later Middle Ages, for it narrates the early experiences of a city that stood at a crossroad between western and eastern Europe, where Latin (Catholic) and Orthodox Christianity confronted one other as well as the pagans, whom they assumed were ripe for conversion. It was in Riga above all that the goods from the forested interior were collected and weighed and loaded before being dispatched to their destinations in western Europe. Thus, *The House of Hemp and Butter* is also about the city's place in the medieval economy—and in the trans-European exchange of ideas.

While the book both directly and indirectly addresses any number of disputed issues, it is less a fundamental reimagining of Riga's past and more a work of synthesis that owes a great debt to those historians who preceded me. What I present here are stories of Riga, woven together into a chronologically ordered narrative. Telling these stories has meant keeping at least four balls in the air at the same time: an examination of Riga's German-dominated political, religious, and military institutions; sketches of the city's physical changes over the course of five hundred years; a spotlight on Riga's oppressed Latvian community; and, in every chapter, discussions of the larger Baltic and European contexts in which Rigans lived, worked, fought, and prayed. A fifth ball is the looming presence of Russia.

Chapters 1 and 2 discuss the city's founding during the Northern Crusades of the twelfth and thirteenth centuries. Here we learn about the Baltic natives, their lands, and their violent encounters with Germans and Christians who came to convert the heathen while taking control of the region's commerce. Chapters 3, 4, and 5 explore Riga's economic development, its port and urban landscape, and its internal conflicts through the era of the Reformation in the sixteenth century. The international struggles that shaped much of the Early Modern Era in Riga (the Livonian War, the Polish-Swedish War, the Great Northern War) provide the backdrop for chapters 6, 7, and 8: they aim to show how these conflicts affected Riga and its burghers. Just as the book begins with the arrival of German traders and clerics to the land of Livs, which they took for themselves even as they named it after its indigenous inhabitants, it ends some five centuries later with a scene of utter devastation as the German councilors of the besieged and bombed-out city surrendered to a new master, Tsar Peter I of Russia.

The House of Hemp and Butter is in no way intended to be a political work. While it seeks to explain the motives of the Latin Christians who conquered Livonia and established Riga as its capital, the book makes no effort to justify Catholic initiatives or to minimize the brutality of the conquest. Neither does this book argue for (or deny) the inevitability or even the viability of a Latvian nation-state: the subject is Riga, not Latvia. Least of all is this book intended to be anti-Russian, for Riga's interactions with the contemporary Russian state are well beyond its scope. However, before today's Russian Federation, before yesterday's Soviet Union, and before the Russian Empire of the Romanovs, there was a sprawling polity known as "Muscovy," and this Muscovite state pursued interests in the eastern Baltic that were hardly different from those of Poland or Sweden in the sixteenth and seventeenth centuries: all were ruled by ambitious monarchs and all saw Riga as a potentially valuable addition to their Baltic possessions. All further knew that whoever enjoyed mastery over Riga controlled much of the trade that linked the "Russian" lands to western Europe. In this contest for mastery over the eastern Baltic, the empire of the tsars was by no means special. The growing colossus was simply the winner of a long and arduous struggle.

Notes on Historiography and Proper Names

The remainder of this introduction addresses the portrayal of Riga by other historians (in other words, the city's historiography) as well as the tricky matter of rendering place and personal names in modern English. It is intended primarily for other historians who wish to understand this work in its larger scholarly context. Casual readers who are, understandably, less interested in such matters might wish to skip straight to Chapter 1.

The most significant early effort to compose a "biography" of the city was a book titled *Geschichte der Stadt Riga* (The history of the city of Riga), written by the Riga resident and teacher Constantin Mettig (1851–1914). Based on historical documents exhumed from the city archives and rich in factual materials, Mettig's informative tome suffered from a defect common to all works belonging to the *Stadtgeschichte* genre: it is a city history that is almost completely divorced from its larger European context. Mettig's subject was always German Riga and rarely Latvian Rīga. A Baltic German himself, Mettig saw little reason to devote much space to a community that during the Middle Ages had, in his view (and in the view of the city's German elite as a whole) contributed little to the city's political, religious, and cultural life.

Yet at the time of the book's publication in 1897, Riga was in the grip of rapid social and demographic change that heavily favored its Latvian community. As Riga plunged into industrialization and became the Russian Empire's third-largest city with 282,230 inhabitants (doubling to 513,451 by 1913), rural Latvians seeking employment flooded the city. In 1867 some 42.8 percent of the city's residents claimed German as their "customary language"; the remainder was comprised mostly of Russians (25.1 percent) and Latvians (23.5 percent) as well as a smattering of Poles, Lithuanians, and Jews. A census conducted thirty years later, the last one taken before the fall of the Romanovs, revealed that it was now the Latvians (45 percent) who dominated the city, while the proportion of native German-speakers and Russian-speakers had plunged to 23.8 percent and 16.1 percent respectively.[4] Although Mettig could hardly have been unaware of these developments—the city was then being deluged by Latvian peasants seeking work in Riga's new factories—this striking demographic transformation did not figure into his narrative. The Riga described by Mettig was not the modern industrial city but the far smaller town of medieval times, when it could genuinely be claimed that Riga was a "German" city in character and appearance, even if during those times some one-third of its population was comprised of Letts and Livs—people the Baltic Germans called "*Undeutsche*," or "non-Germans."

Despite its obvious omissions and biases, Mettig's book made an essential contribution to our present understanding of Riga's history. Here we might also mention early works by Wilhelm von Neumann—namely, *Das Mittelalterliche Riga* (1892) and *Riga und Reval* (1908), both of which focus on Riga's Germanic architectural heritage.[5] Scholars interested in Riga's legal history during the Middle Ages and who can read medieval Latin and Low German will be delighted at the treasures collected and edited by Jakob Napiersky (1819–1890) and Friedrich Georg von Bunge (1802–1897)—papal decrees, city laws, and so forth.[6] Another fascinating early contribution to the city's history was the work of Johann Christoph Brotze (1742–1823). A Saxon by birth but a teacher and ethnographer in eighteenth-century Riga, Brotze was the first to document the city's diverse peoples, buildings, and landscapes.[7] Yet as much as these German authors contributed to our knowledge of early Riga, none ever attempted to write anything like a proper urbanography of their city—that is, a history that places its subject within a larger international context and that stretches beyond traditional subjects like religion, politics, architecture, and war in order to grapple also with the complex themes of class, nationality, and (as far as this is possible) gender.

It was only after the establishment of the Republic of Latvia in 1918 that Latvian historians finally got their say. Now detached from the Russian Empire and released from the grip of its Baltic German ruling class, Riga (now Rīga) became the capital city of a democratic nation-state that was eager to tell its story from a distinctly Latvian point of view. The need for a Latvian history of Riga became still more critical during the 1930s, when the entire country was in the throes of "Latvianization"—a process that was analogous to similar efforts in other European countries to refashion their environments (and often their pasts) in accordance with the regime's ideological goals. Just as Latvia's interwar dictator, Kārlis Ulmanis, attempted physically to transform the city in a manner that revealed his contempt for the city's German heritage[8]—was Riga (Rīga!) not now a *Latvian* city?—so did Riga's historians seek to redress what they correctly saw as a historical void.

Let us consider, then, the beautifully illustrated book by the mathematician, historian, and city librarian Jānis Straubergs (1886–1952). Its title has the virtue of simplicity, but *Rīgas vēsture* (1937; The history of Rīga) is an idiosyncratic work whose singular contribution is its effort to restore the place of Latvians to the early history of Riga. In general, however, the Latvian historians of his era, such as Straubergs's exact contemporaries Arveds Švābe (1888–1958) and Arnolds Spekke (1887–1972), were more interested in the investigation of national history than that of Riga; in their works, the city's story is buried within the broader context of Latvia's national development.[9]

Such was also the case for the pioneering scholarship of Indriķis Šterns (1918–2005), whose historical training began during the final years of the first Latvian republic. Although his most significant works were not published until decades after World War II and were national in scope, Šterns, like Straubergs, sought to restore agency to the conquered Latvian peoples. Packed with factual information about Riga's early history, the books and articles by Šterns are essential reading for anyone interested in the environment in which the city developed during the Middle Ages.[10] Here I must also mention the exiled diplomat Alfreds Bilmanis (1886–1948) and the Melbourne-based historian Edgars Dunsdorfs (1904–2002), whose works similarly emphasized the historical roles that Latvians played in the lands that now comprise the modern country of Latvia.[11]

If Latvian history became, to an extent, the preserve of ethnic Latvian writers, this is not to suggest that German historians have lost interest in the eastern Baltic. Indeed, German scholars (as well as scholars writing in German) have sustained their fascination with medieval Livonia and have continued to write about Riga's political and commercial life, the Teutonic Order, and the history of Old Livonia.[12] The second and third chapters of *The House of Hemp and Butter* are particularly indebted to Friedrich Benninghoven's (1925–2014) detailed book on Riga's early merchants.[13] The city's submission to Poland at the end of the Livonian War is the subject of a slender volume by Wilhelm Lenz, while a doctoral dissertation by Thomas Lange focuses on the last archbishop of Riga.[14] Yet if the research on certain topics has been prodigious, scholars working on matters pertaining to Riga have shown little interest in synthesis: it was only in 2014 that a German historian, Andreas Fülberth, completed a modern urbanography of Riga.[15]

Anglophone historians have also been privy to this conversation; without their contributions, the book you are reading would not exist. Foremost among this group of scholars is William Urban (b. 1935), a prolific historian of the Northern Crusades. Urban's many monographs, notably *The Livonian Crusade* (1981), provide the necessary political and military context for appreciating Riga's position during the later Middle Ages.[16] Walther Kirchner (1905–2004) performed a similar service in his book on the Livonian War, *The Rise of the Baltic Question* (1954), published many decades ago but still of considerable value.[17]

The Anglophone community has also benefited from the translation into English of several works by contemporary scholars native to the eastern Baltic. Chapter 3 of this book has been enriched by Anu Mänd's (b. 1968) scholarship on urban culture in medieval Livonia,[18] while the influence of Ojārs Spārītis (b. 1955) can be seen in the book's many references to Riga's art, architecture, and monuments.[19] Here we must also mention Andrejs Plakans (b. 1940), a Latvian-American scholar whose books *The Latvians: A Short History* (1995) and *A Concise History of the Baltic States* (2011) are already classics in the field and are indispensable reading for anyone interested in the region's history.[20]

One should not assume that the works composed by Soviet historians, although ideologically conformist, are lacking in interest or merit. This is demonstrated most clearly by Teodors Zeids (1912–1994), whose encyclopedic compendiums dutifully conformed to the regime's political requirements but are nevertheless rich in detail; indeed, few historians have mined the available sources as thoroughly as Zeids.[21] Also of value are the many books and articles by the Latvian archaeologist Andris Caune (b. 1937), whose teams unearthed countless treasures in Riga and throughout Latvia during Soviet times and since.[22] On occasion I have also turned for answers to the Soviet-era *Encyclopedia of Riga*, even if its coverage of the city's early history is overshadowed by the modern Soviet achievements it touts.[23] About the Russian historiography of medieval and early modern Riga, there is little to say, for the Russian-language literature on Riga focuses largely on the period after 1710. That the post-Soviet literature on Riga continues to suffer from politicization merely underlines the fact that some Russian-speaking authors believe that the roles played by Russia and Russians in the city's history have been neglected or miscast.[24] Riga may have been founded by Germans and then taken over by Latvians, but the city, such authors argue, has a Russian past as well.

This brief introduction to Riga's historians merely scratches the surface, for the literature on the city's history, while scattered and requiring a reading knowledge of certain foreign languages, is not insubstantial. Its main point is that the book you are reading would not have been possible had these earlier works not existed, for this is a work of synthesis and they are its main sources.

Now we shall turn to the matter of place names and personal names. The majority of this book concerns the medieval era, when the towns of the eastern Baltic shared with western Europe both a universal medieval culture and common commercial interests. The language spoken then by the burghers of Riga and the other Livonian towns was Low German, a distinctive dialect that is used today only in parts of northern Germany and the Netherlands. Recreating a long-ago era when people spoke different languages from the ones used today and inhabited a world that was a very different world from our own presents to the writer a variety of challenges. Among these is the question of which toponyms and proper names to employ in this book. For example, is the subject of this book Riga or Rīga? While there are justifiable grounds for taking a contemporaneous approach, there is no consensus on this issue. In his essential *A Concise History of the Baltic States* (2011), Andrejs Plakans typically uses modern place names (such as "Rīga" rather than "Riga"). On the other hand, historian Andres Kasekamp "mostly used the version in official usage of the time" in his own *A History of the Baltic States* (2009).[25] Like Kasekamp's book, my own uses the historic—that is, the German—forms of Riga and other place names in Old Livonia. My reasons echo those stated by the geographer John Leighly when he was writing about the towns of medieval Livonia some eighty years ago.[26] In his insistence on using the old, German place names, Leighly stated that he aimed for historical accuracy and consistency. Here I shall do the same, for I agree with the scholar's contention that a sincere effort to be faithful to the past is best served—at least in this case—by using the place names that were most commonly (or officially) used at the time, even if such a course of action risks leaving the modern reader somewhat disoriented.

While I have made a few exceptions to this rule as needed, in general I shall speak of Riga rather than Rīga, the Düna River rather than the Daugava or Dvina, Tartu rather than Dorpat, Reval rather than Tallinn, and so on. To ease the burden on my readers, I provide contemporary names in parentheses upon first mention and again later as a reminder. I further acknowledge that the word "Livonia" itself can be confusing to the uninitiated. Depending on the circumstances, Livonia can refer strictly to the lands settled by the native Livs in what is now northern Latvia, and it can also refer to the Swedish (and then Russian) province of Livland, in Latvian known as Vidzeme (the middle land). Eventually Old Livonia or *Alt-Livland* came to include much of Estonia. The Livonian Confederation (1418–1561) refers to a series of ecclesiastical units that included nearly all of today's Latvia and Estonia. That this book generally uses the Latin word "Livonia" rather than the German *Livland* is simply a matter of convenience and consistency. The word "Livs" indicates the Finnic peoples who lived in the region; the language they spoke may be called "Livish." Since Anglophone writers have long been in the habit of using the word "Livonian" as a geographical descriptor and "Livonians" to indicate the *German* elites of Livonia, this book follows that convention.

With regard to the names of the individuals who populate this book, in many (but not all) cases I have opted for Anglicization. Thus the common German name Johann will sometimes be rendered as John, even if the Russian "Ivan," which also means John, shall remain Ivan. Likewise, the book shall refer to Albert of Buxhoeveden rather than *Albert von Bexhövede* and to Walter of Plettenburg rather than *Wolther von Plettenberg*. Since perfect consistency is not attainable in these matters and since some readers may object to my choices, the author asks for the reader's patience and indulgence. Although I may fall short in some areas, I endeavor to be the best guide to medieval Riga that the limits of my knowledge, experience, and talent will allow. If some future historian of Riga finds inspiration in these pages—and perhaps more than a little room for improvement—then I will have accomplished something significant and worthwhile.

The history of old Riga is worth knowing. Here I will show you why.

Chapter 1

Genesis: Riga before Riga

Lieli ceļi, mazi ceļi—Visi Rīgā satecēja.
Big roads, little roads—All lead to Riga.
—Ancient Latvian proverb

Riga is built on water.[1] Largely obscured by modern development, the city's aqueous environment is the legacy of an earlier geological age, when the global climate was far colder and harsher than today's. As the first intrepid bands of *homo sapiens* began to spread their genes and their languages across the Eurasian landmass, the territory that presently comprises the city of Riga was still submerged in a blanket of ice several meters thick. The enormous glacier covered a vast swath of northern Europe, from Scandinavia to what is now Berlin; but eventually the planet warmed and the ice began its slow retreat to the Baltic Sea. It was this process, beginning about ten thousand years ago, that resulted in the creation of those residual bodies of water that still cover some sixteen percent of Riga's present-day territory.

When the area's first Stone Age human inhabitants arrived at the spot that would later give birth to a city, they would have found a sandy plain that was overlaid with veins of rivers and streams, bogs and marshes.[2] Most of these waterways and wetlands have since vanished, buried beneath sand, dirt, and pavement so that Riga's citizens would come to walk over the channels they could never see. Indeed, so much water flows under Riga today that the Soviet regime's ambitious plan in the 1980s to build a metro under the city seems more fantastical than intrusive.

Riga's relationship with the waters that run past, through, and under it has given rise to many legends and sayings. "In my eyes, Riga was long extolled," goes one *daina* (a short Latvian folk song) about a peasant approaching the city; "now I see it: surrounded by sand hills, the city itself lies in water."[3] Everywhere there was water—water and sand. A mighty river, more than half a kilometer wide in some places, flowed past the city on its way to the Baltic Sea. A moat dug by medieval

Rigans provided an additional watery safeguard against invasion from the north, east, and south. And then there were the smaller channels that overlay the region's sandy topography—including a minor tributary from which the city may have derived its name. Germans knew the rivulet that wound around the edge of their bustling city as the Rigebach and later as the Rising (or Riesing). Among Latvians it acquired the nickname Rīdzene or Rīdziņa. It is commonly believed that the lost channel was the original Riga River, on whose right bank the city was founded at the dawn of the thirteenth century.

The etymology of this word continues to be debated. One intriguing (but probably incorrect) theory is that the word "Riga," or some form of it, was brought to the region by the Wends, a Slavic people who likely had been driven off the Baltic island of Rügen when the Danes conquered it in 1168.[4] Or perhaps the name was derived from the Livish word *ringa*, meaning loop.[5] It is more likely, however, that "Riga" originated from the Latvian word for threshing barn or warehouse—*rija*—a place to store the goods that were being exchanged near the river's banks. In this view, it was the Germans who replaced the softer Latvian *j* with a hard *g* and thereby gave the city what became its permanent name.[6]

Meandering along the base of a sandy hill, the Rigebach gently trickled past a hamlet of Livish farmers and craftsmen whereupon it widened into a small lake, ideal for docking the small sailing vessels that traversed the mighty Düna River linking the forested interior to the Baltic Sea.[7] It was along the Düna embankment that another Livish village emerged, less than a kilometer distant from its neighbor. A Finno-Ugric people who were related to the neighboring Estonians, the Livish peoples, or, if we go by their Latin name, the Livonians (Ger. Liven; Latv. Livi), were not alone in this unpromising environment: Cours and Wends lived nearby, and everyone lived in fear of Lithuanian raiders. The flow of peoples through this region ultimately blessed the future city with one of its distinctive characteristics: Riga is, and has always been, a city shared by people of various nationalities and languages.

Riga's founding in 1201 was no secret at the time: it is mentioned in several medieval chronicles, and it is the subject of one, *The Chronicle of Henry of Livonia*, an indispensable account—readers of this book will come to know it well—of the crusades that brought Christian missionaries and German knights to the northeast. The compilers of the partly contemporaneous *Chronicle of Novgorod*, on the other hand, overlooked the new settlement. Among the best of the genre, this Russian chronicle sketches the early history (1016–1471) of a great commercial city whose lands encroached upon those of the Estonian and Lettish (eastern Latvian) tribes.[8] The chronicle reminds us that the Rus', Slavs who were partly descended from a group of Viking conqueror-traders, were familiar with the area and its peoples.[9] Organized into a series of self-governing principalities headed by Kiev (est. 882) in the south and Novgorod (est. 862) in the north, the Kievan Rus' had long been active in the eastern Baltic, bartering their goods with the locals who inhabited the lands along the great river that flows past Riga.

The hamlet where the Livs bartered their wares was likely one of several stops the Vikings made before they headed south along the river network that led to the Black Sea, where the Norsemen exchanged their goods for eastern treasures. Among the valuables desired by these itinerant traders was amber, a hard, yellowish fossil resin that was prized in ancient times for its magnetic qualities, for its alleged medicinal value, and (especially after the Renaissance) for ornamentation.[10] As the main European source of amber is the southern shore of the Baltic Sea—this "amber coast" runs from the contemporary Latvian border with Lithuania to Jutland in the west—the Greeks and Romans were not entirely ignorant of the lands and peoples of the north. Classical authors from Herodotus to Ptolemy observed the northern "barbarians" and their lands from a distance; but it was the Roman historian Tacitus who made the first unambiguous reference to a Baltic tribe, the *Aestii* (thought to have been the Prussians) and "the sticky liquid" they gathered. "For a long time," explained the author of *Germania* (98 CE), "it lay unheeded like any other refuse of the sea, until Roman luxury made its reputation."[11]

The amber gatherers of the southern Baltic littoral were, in fact, well aware of the resin's value. Long before Roman elites became enamored with the luxuriant qualities of Baltic *glaesum*, amber had been brought to lands as distant as Egypt and Greece; the Romans simply tapped into the existing trade routes that brought the substance from the north to the south. The discovery of Roman and Byzantine coins throughout Latvia and nearby coastal lands offers further evidence of ancient commercial links between the Mediterranean world and the Baltic Sea. By the time the Norsemen began, late in the eighth century, to make their journeys down the river system that connected the Baltic to Byzantium, the routes were already well traversed. Other routes from the northerly regions to the south led from the Bay of Finland to the Volga River, home of the Bulgars and the Khazar Khaganate (near the river's mouth), and to the Islamic world.

The Düna River, then, was not the only way "from the Varangians to the Greeks." Yet few may doubt that commercial ships had been sailing past (or stopping at) Riga for many centuries—long before the Germans launched their bid to dominate the eastern Baltic and its arteries. While the Vikings, active in the area since at least the eighth century, proved capable of penetrating deep inland along the river routes using their slender wooden ships, which were long enough to carry passengers and cargo, they were unable to establish permanent colonies on the Düna. The many varieties of Viking ships would later be supplanted by larger vessels from Germany and Scandinavia—cogs (*kogge*)—whose high masts and large sails began to emerge from the spring fog with predictable regularity after 1158.

Sometimes their passengers included men of the Latin (Catholic) Church who wished to introduce the Livs and their neighbors to the Christian god. The western traders, however, were men of business, less concerned with souls and more with the profits to be earned from their exchanges with the local traders. Most important was their commerce with the Rus' merchants, who made their way to the Düna from lands as distant as Polotsk, Smolensk, and Novgorod, which were now Orthodox Christian, their princes having converted to the faith of the Byzantine Greeks. Once their transactions were concluded, the German and Scandinavian merchants then loaded their cogs with the bounty of the forested interior—fur and hides, beeswax and honey—for which they would return again the following spring.

It was on the shores of the Düna, on a field near the spot where the powerful river absorbed the trickle of the lazy Rigebach, that a young German bishop named Albert of Buxhoeveden (ca. 1165–1229) established the city of Riga in 1201. And it was near Riga, transformed into a base for German traders and pioneers whose own settlements were juridically and physically merged with those of the older Livish villages, that the first sustained encounters took place between Latin Christendom and the pagans of Livonia.

Clash of Cultures: The Crusaders

The Düna settlement's swift transformation into a trading hub, military base, and religious center was the product of human ambitions, for Riga attracted the same kinds of restless individuals who were propelling western Europe from a backwater of world civilization to its forefront during the High Middle Ages (ca. 950–1300). In Latin Christendom, and in the German lands in particular, this was a period of economic dynamism, urbanization, and expansion, the European population nearly doubling from 42 million in the year 1000 to 73 million in 1300. Paralleling this spectacular demographic growth was the process of *Ostkolonization* ("colonization of the East") that brought German culture and more advanced agriculture methods from west to east.[12]

We might call the men who sailed to Livonia—the Germans called it *Livland* or *Liefland*—pioneers. They were merchants and monks, priests and knights, craftsmen and builders. All were products of a newly energized Christian world whose expanding horizons and ideals brought its most adventurous souls into increasing contact with unfamiliar peoples and places. While outsiders had made occasional forays into Christian Europe on horseback, usually as conquerors and plunderers and sometimes as proselytizers of a foreign faith, it was now the turn of the western Europeans—Latin Christians who were convinced that they were the bearers of a higher truth—to penetrate the worlds beyond the one they knew as Christendom. It was in Europe's margins, in southern Iberia, in the Holy Land of the Near East, and in the remote eastern edge of the Baltic Sea (in German known as the *Ostsee*), that Christian settlers and soldiers confronted the Other.[13]

Some have called the deadly encounters that erupted on Europe's northeastern frontier a "clash of cultures."[14] This seems like a reasonable characterization of the violent confrontations of the twelfth and thirteenth centuries, for even if the natives of the Baltic littoral were heterogeneous and did not share a common culture to the extent that the crusaders did, what occurred was in fact a collision of two very different worlds and worldviews, in which the inequality of organization, weaponry, and technology largely determined the outcome. On one side were Latin Christians, devoted to a loving god who offered man the hope of redemption through his righteous behavior and good deeds. On the other side were the region's indigenous peoples, whom the Christians saw as tree-worshiping heathen speaking strange languages and venerating spirits connected to the natural world—and, more ominously, to the underworld. To save these accursed souls, blows must be struck. "Once the superhuman forces had been defeated," remarked historian Eric Christiansen, "the humans would be receptive to gentle words; but first things first."[15]

The Livonian enterprise brought together the ambitions and resources of men whose calling it was to save souls and other men who sought above all to earn a coin. To this mix we may add the rougher men on horseback who wielded swords to secure the region and to advance Christendom's hazy borders. It was the prospect of gaining land and status that drew the western knights to the eastern fringe of the Baltic Sea, where they built castles, did battle with pagans, and, partnering with the churchmen who carved out dioceses in the conquered lands, became the region's new rulers.

While historians of an earlier age sometimes justified these efforts as part and parcel of a Germanic civilizing mission in the east, modern scholars know full well that this brutal "clash of civilizations" resulted in many thousands of deaths, caused great devastation to the land and its peoples, and gave rise to centuries of oppression. To understand how these misfortunes came to be, and why the outside world took an increasing interest in the Baltic region after around 1000 CE, an appreciation of the changing circumstances in Christian Europe is in order. It was in this time and place that the men who did the trading, fighting, and converting developed their understanding of the world and their calling in it.

That western Europe at this time was becoming more intensively militarized has little to do with Christianity and is more likely connected to what must have been a profound sense of insecurity following the disintegration of Charlemagne's Frankish kingdom in the ninth century. Assaults on Christendom's undefended borders were launched by the Magyars (the ancestors of today's Hungarians), by Saracens (followers of Muhammad), and by Norsemen. In an age that was generally bereft of strong rulers who could command the undivided loyalty of their vassals, political power fell to western Europe's feudal lords, who conferred upon armored knights the land and status they desired in exchange for their military service. If it wasn't exactly the Hobbesian vision of "every man against every man," it was sometimes close, for after Charlemagne's grandsons partitioned the empire, warfare became endemic in much of northern Europe. The absence of centralized authority meant the proliferation of smaller centers of power whose wielders did not hesitate to resort to arms to achieve their political, economic, and religious ends.

The physical legacy of the continent's earlier militarization is evident today in the form of stone ruins that dot the European landscape. Castles proliferated in Germanic Europe, a wide swath that stretched from England to Bohemia and the eastern Baltic, with breathtaking speed. In England alone approximately five hundred castles, which the Normans used as instruments of conquest in Wales and Ireland as well as in England proper, appeared in the decades between 1066 and the early 1100s.[16] It should come as little surprise, then, that among the first stone buildings erected by the strangers who arrived in the Gulf of Riga at the end of the twelfth century were fortifications and churches, often combined in the same structure. Within a hundred years thirty castles were built in the Latvian lands alone.[17] Many were located along the strategically important Düna River, while others appeared in Courland (Latv. Kurzeme) or along a river that Germans called the Treider Aa (or Livländische Aa) and that is known today as the Gauja.[18] It is in this context that we can best appreciate Riga's early development as a frontier settlement, a commercial center, a gathering point for crusading activities, and the seat of a Catholic bishopric.

It was mostly Germans from Westphalia and Saxony who came to Riga and Livonia during the crusading era, a period that in the Baltic lands generally coincided with what nineteenth-century writers and propagandists romanticized as the Germanic *Drang nach Osten* ("drive to the East"). Perhaps a more precise term, and one less weighted by the burden of Nazi history or the suggestion of militarism, is *Ostsiedlung* ("eastern settling").[19] Like *Ostkolonization*, this term refers to the peaceful migration of Germans into central and eastern Europe, mostly at the invitation of local rulers, sometime after 1100. Drawn by the prospect of gaining farmland, employment, and wealth, waves of ordinary Germans trekked across the Saale and Elbe rivers into regions, then thinly populated with western Slavs, whom the migrants called Wends. Some of these pioneering German farmers migrated in a southeasterly direction toward Silesia and Bohemia in search of a better life. Meanwhile, itinerant merchants and resettled artisans transformed the humble urban centers of the Slavs into growing cities endowed with a German urban law code. The results of the *Ostsiedlung* were the introduction of more advanced farming methods, the stimulation of mining and other commercial enterprises, urbanization, and not least, the extension of German political, economic, and cultural influence into parts of central and eastern Europe.[20] Throughout the lands they colonized, the Germans established "linguistic islands"—German-speaking towns, villages, and farming communities—of varying sizes that in many cases retained their linguistic and cultural identities right up to the twentieth century.[21]

We may speak, then, of both the Christianization of these regions and their Germanization—less in the sense that conquered peoples became Germans (or, for that matter, Christians) and more in the sense that they eventually submitted to the imposition of Christian and German institutions. These processes took place at more or less the same time and were joined at the root. Indeed, just as ordinary German farmers and craftsmen migrated into central Europe to improve their prospects, there was a parallel series of religious-military conquests whose thrust ran along the Baltic coast north of the Polish heartland up to Courland. Unlike the peaceful German settlement of Bohemia and Silesia, the Baltic conquests were violent and were carried out mainly by crusading orders. The region's dominant branch was the Teutonic Order, founded in 1190 to provide medical care for knights injured in the Near East. After 1230 it was headquartered in Prussia, where it enjoyed the protection of the papacy and easy access to the papal court.[22] A similar order of monk-knights, the Livonian Brothers of the Sword (est. 1202), was, at least for a time, headquartered in Riga. After thirty-five years and a major defeat in 1237 it would be supplanted by a branch of the Teutonic Knights known as the Order of Livonian Knights.

About the individuals who filled the ranks of these fraternities, we may make a few general observations. First, the men who joined the knightly orders were neither wealthy aristocrats nor paupers from the margins of society. Most were noblemen from minor families who were making the best of their limited choices, for northern Europe's changing social and inheritance customs increasingly favored first-born male children. The widespread adoption of the primogeniture system in northern Europe meant that the younger sons of aristocratic families, especially those of the lower nobility, often faced the choice between a life of impoverishment at home or finding lands elsewhere to conquer. Superfluous at home, many such men sought adventure and fortune abroad. Those with ambition, military training, and a longing to see the Holy Land were often drawn to the Crusades, which provided Europe's knights with an outlet for their piety, a sense of purpose, and opportunities to enhance their dimming prospects. At last, the righteous knight would have a chance to use his training to help bring God's greater plan into reality. But if the initial purpose of the Crusades was to liberate Jerusalem from the Turks, it was not long before the crusading mentality, and the violence that invariably accompanied it, would be brought to the pagan communities of the northeast.

All manner of warfare was conducted in the name of Christianity during the Middle Ages, and while none of these battles was called a crusade at the time, and while never was there a general agreement about the precise religious objectives that justified them, the main purpose of the papacy's wars was to defend Christian communities in places where those communities were threatened. Thus the First Crusade to the Holy Land, launched by Pope Urban II in 1095, was the Catholic Church's overzealous response to the Byzantine emperor's plea for assistance in his struggle with the Seljuk Turks, who, having converted to Islam while taking control over most of Anatolia and the Near East, had cut off access to Jerusalem and now threatened the Christian city of Constantinople.

Even as historians debate the deeper roots of the crusades, one thing seems certain: the Latin (Catholic) Church, having committed itself to removing its clerics from secular influences and cleansing itself of worldly corruption, emerged from these efforts with a renewed confidence and found itself more enmeshed in secular affairs than ever before. Now behaving more like a state than a body of religious believers, and wielding sufficient influence to command a vast if disunited army, the Church penetrated ever more deeply into people's lives, in particular through its exclusive control of the sacraments through which God dispensed his grace and assured the salvation of one's soul. "Taking the cross" to faraway lands—in effect becoming a soldier of the Church—offered the hope of redeeming one's sins as well as an opportunity to see Jerusalem before joining the Holy Father in Paradise.[23]

In the Near East the crusading era lasted for two hundred years and for a time resulted in the establishment of crusader states in the Levant. Yet if the Crusades to the Holy Land were at best inconclusive—after all, the last crusader stronghold at Acre fell in 1291—Christian armies enjoyed long-term successes in other frontier areas, notably the Iberian peninsula, which underwent a centuries-long process known as the *Reconquista*: a "reconquest" of lands that had once been part of Christendom. At the opposite corner of Europe, near the eastern shores of the Baltic Sea, Christian warriors built castles and made war on the locals for the purpose of bringing Christ's love, at the point of a sword, to the pagans of the north.

The campaigns to conquer and convert the peoples of Prussia, Livonia, and Estonia were collectively known as the Northern Crusades. Authorized in 1147 by Pope Eugenius III (r. 1145–1153), roughly at the same time as the failed Second Crusade to the Holy Land, the crusades in the northeast jump-started the process of opening the lands along the Baltic rim to a Germanic and Christian influence that would last for more than seven centuries. The first of the Northern Crusades was intended to bring order to the borderland regions inhabited by the Wends, whose occasional raids, aimed principally at snatching slaves and livestock, made them an irritant to the Danes as well as to the Holy Roman Empire.[24] While the empire's Saxon rulers tried and failed to subdue the Wends through military efforts, the northern German archbishoprics of Hamburg-Bremen and Magdeburg led the efforts to convert them by peaceful means. That the two archbishoprics became the directors of the missions to the pagan lands for much of the next century underlines the fact that when it came to the eastern Baltic, local actions were of much greater significance than papal initiatives.[25] Still, it was the decisions that were made in Rome, in particular the bull issued by Pope Eugenius III, that turned a simmering frontier struggle into a full-blown crusade whose goal was to conquer and convert the pagans of northeastern Europe.[26]

Every crusade was characterized by violence and plunder, and we may presume that every crusader believed he was doing the will of the Almighty. What made the campaigns in the Wendish lands different than earlier crusades was the ideology that God's soldiers brought with them.[27] That ideology, worked out by Bernard of Clairveaux (1090–1153), in collaboration with his former student Pope Eugenius III, called for the forcible conversion of the bothersome Slavic peoples living on the empire's eastern frontier.[28] Like other Cistercian monks, Bernard was a product of the reform movement of the age, for he believed that monks should combine a life of contemplation in the abbey with work in the world to advance the goals of Christendom. Intensely devoted to combating heresy while putting forward an aggressive defense of the Church's prerogatives, the French abbot exercised little restraint when it came to the Wends: "They shall be either converted or wiped out."[29]

The inflexible belligerence typified by Bernard and amplified during the crusading era had once been only a minor thread in the thinking of Church leaders: although there were certainly exceptions, popes and theologians going back to Gregory the Great (r. 590–604) held the view that non-Christians should be converted by kindness, not by compulsion. But now the growing influence of Bernard's ideology of compulsory conversion meant that the age of (not always) peaceful coexistence with the Other was now at an end.

While conversions likely took place at the point of a sword during all crusading campaigns, Bernard's unambiguous support for the Wends' forcible conversion anticipated the crusaders' subsequent efforts in Prussia and Livonia. The long-term results were similar as well: once subdued and Christianized by the Saxons, the Wends of this region disappeared into the German ethnos—the same fate that awaited the Prussians living farther east along the Baltic's southern shores. By the end of the seventeenth century, both the Prussians and their language had disappeared.[30] Indeed, one can see in the Wendish Crusade features common to the crusades in Prussia and Livonia several decades later: not least a Christian contempt for the pagans and their beliefs, a sincere desire to share the word of

God, violence and plundering on a massive scale, and a depopulation of the lands where the fighting had taken place.

In some important ways the experience of the Crusades—a merciless struggle against an Other whose result could only be victory or death—changed those who did the crusading, for Christian crusaders adopted a mind-set that divided the world in two: Christians inhabited a world called Christendom that ought to be expanded at the expense of "heathendom." These worlds, and the people who inhabited them, were by no means equal. Thus, as a Christian presence established itself in pagan lands, the former responded to differences in traditions, speech, law, and language by asserting themselves as a privileged minority.[31] Indeed, it was not long before the strangers who arrived in the eastern Baltic erected castles for their defense and churches in which to practice their faith, all while subduing the local peoples and seizing much of the surrounding land for themselves.

Clash of Cultures: The Natives

Three hundred years before a crew of Spaniards under the command of the Italian explorer Christopher Columbus sailed across the Atlantic in 1492, knights and soldiers from Germany and Scandinavia ventured to distant lands where, like the later conquistadors, they encountered peoples who were utterly unlike them in dress, manner, and belief. Not only were the westerners entirely unfamiliar with the indigenous inhabitants of the Baltic littoral, they were also ill-equipped to distinguish between them, at least at first. Since nearly all the available documentation concerning these encounters came from the West, it is the aims and perspectives of the crusaders that are far better understood today than the lived experiences of the Baltic "natives" at the time of the conquest.

If the morally dualistic crusaders perceived this clash of cultures in "us against them" terms, it seems unlikely that the Livs and their neighbors shared a similar view of the westerners, for the region's indigenous peoples, divided by tribe, language, and local political allegiance, did not possess anything like a collective identity. Also, the Germans (and others) who appeared with increasing frequency in the 1180s and 1190s were not the first strangers they had encountered. In the eyes of the local tribes, the itinerant Christian merchants may have been little more threatening than the Lithuanians, who for decades had nurtured the lucrative habit of raiding the Livish and Latvian villages before returning to their native lands south of Riga.

This brings us to an essential point about the "clash of cultures" in the eastern Baltic: long before (and for some time after) the arrival of the crusaders, the pagans of northeastern Europe frequently clashed *with each other*. After 1200 the pagans sometimes came together to fight the crusaders, and sometimes they fought on the side of the crusaders against a known enemy. No doubt the prior existence of

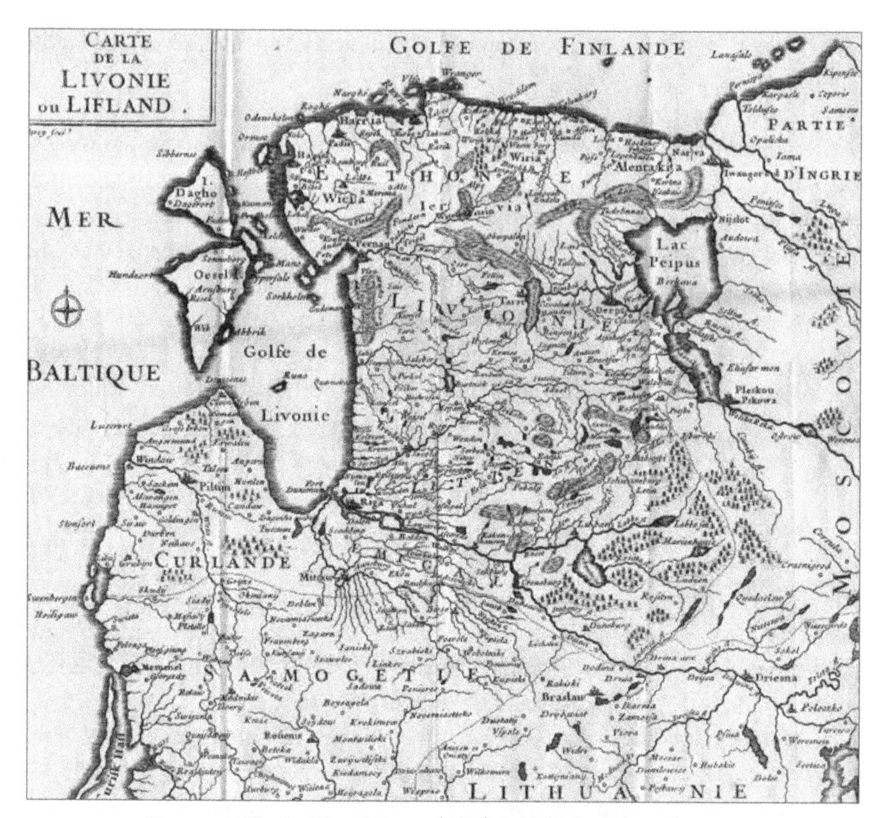

FIGURE 1. Olearius Map of Livonia (1659). Published in *Relation du voyage d'Adam Olearius en Moscovie, Tartarie et Perse: part 1*. Paris, 1659.

local conflicts made the crusaders' task easier to achieve, for the Germans were able to take advantage of the local power dynamic and either co-opt or defeat the local tribes one by one. This fact undergirds Latvia's more recent tragedies, for the thirteenth century was not the last occasion during which Latvians fought other Latvians while stronger forces reaped the benefits.

That being said, one must treat the words "Latvia" (Latvija) and "Latvians" (latvieši) with care, since these are anachronistic when used in reference to medieval Livonia and its tribal inhabitants. During the Middle Ages there was no Latvia, only *Marienland* or *Livland/Liefland*, named after the Livs, who we may assume first encountered German merchants sometime after the latter made their first journeys up the Düna River in 1158. Initially referring to the lands inhabited by the Livs, "Livonia" (in the sense of Greater Livonia or *Alt-Livland*) eventually came to include much of eastern Latvia and part of Estonia as well.

The words "Latvia" and "Latvians," on the other hand, are relatively recent inventions, coming into use only in the nineteenth century at the time of Latvia's "national awakening." Setting aside for a moment the Finno-Ugric–speaking Livs, the peoples who lived in the environs of Riga were not "Latvians" sharing a collective identity but separate tribes with their own distinctive features and customs. Although some writers refer to the polities they created as "castle districts," while others call them "kingdoms," the fact remains that at the time of the German conquest, Baltic societies were becoming increasingly complex, perhaps owing in part to some outside influences (for example, the Norsemen and the Rus'). In southeastern Latvia (Latgallia or Latgale), the most important centers were Koknese, Jersika, and Tālava, each ruled by a chieftain or king from his well-defended hill fort.[32] Turaida, known to the Germans as Treiden, was the main settlement in what is now Latvia's Vidzeme ("middle land") region, while in the southern region of Semigallia (Latv. Zemgale), the main settlements were Mežotne and Tērvete. The largest of the region's hundreds of hill forts was located at Daugmale, a Semigallian settlement on the Düna south of Riga that was likely the closest thing to what might be called a city in preconquest Latvia.[33] Since most of the political centers were located along Latvia's main rivers, they also served as river ports.

Having examined these and other sites, archaeologists have concluded that under Scandinavian influence urbanization had begun in the Latvian lands well before the arrival of the crusaders.[34] There is further evidence that the entities anchored by both these settlements and hill forts had become stable by 1000 CE, leading some scholars to speculate that it was merely a matter of time before the region would produce its own primitive states.[35] In such a view, in the course of time these Latvian entities might have united under a powerful king—like the Lithuanian tribes did under Mindaugas in the 1230s, or like the English under King Alfred in the ninth century—had it not been for the conquest. But with the German incursion and its attendant disruptions, "all chances for the indigenous population to develop were paralysed at the roots," as the Latvian historian Arnolds Spekke lamented.[36]

Of course, no one can demonstrate with any certainty that the Latvian tribal kingdoms were on track to form independent polities with their own governing elites and centralized administrations (and in any event the issue is beyond the scope of this little book on Riga). Around the year 1000 CE, there were, after all, perhaps no more than 220,000 people living in the territory of present-day Latvia, and they were divided into various kinds of units headed by kings and tribal chiefs.[37] These proto-Latvian tribes, if we may call them that, were neither politically nor culturally united, even if they spoke dialects that we may presume to have been mutually intelligible. Germans tended to refer to the Latgallians, and eventually to the other central Latvian tribes—that is, the Semigallians and Selonians—as "Letts"; the dialects they spoke were called "Lettish."[38] Also melding into the nascent Latvian nation were the Cours (Kurs, Couronians), who spoke their own distinctive dialects of a language that has changed remarkably slowly over the centuries.

Like the Old Prussians and the Lithuanians, the Latvian tribes spoke a language that descended from a common Indo-European tongue ("Old Baltic") that arrived in the region some four thousand years ago, thus making the Baltic branch the most archaic language group in Europe.[39] Gradually the separate languages spoken by Latvians and Lithuanians (and by the now-extinct Prussians) began to differentiate, starting around the time of Christ; however, each of these languages retains a lexicon that is rich in reminders of a primitive Indo-European tongue.[40]

While the Latvian language has undeniable Indo-European roots, the languages spoken by the Livs and their northerly linguistic cousins, the Estonians, belonged to the Finno-Ugric group. To the Livs, the languages spoken by the Letts and Cours were entirely unintelligible. Although the Livs belong to Latvian history and were eventually assimilated into the Latvian nation,[41] they were not "Baltic" in the linguistic sense, and they lived separately from the Latvian tribes in the preconquest era.

From the foregoing discussion it is easy to see how the words "Baltic" and "Balt" can be confusing to the uninitiated—all the more so when the word "Baltic" has a modern political meaning ("Baltic states") that is rather different from its linguistic one.[42] Long before it acquired any political or linguistic connotations, the word first appeared as a hydronym: it was the eleventh-century chronicler Adam of Bremen who first used the word "Baltic" in reference to the sea—*mare Balticum*, "the Baltic or Barbarian Sea, a day's journey from Hamburg."[43] Only in modern times was the word "Baltic" applied to the languages spoken by the peoples of Prussia, Lithuania, and Latvia.

To make matters even more confusing, the word "Balt" as an ethnic identifier appeared only in the nineteenth century and initially referred to the region's German communities—the Baltic Germans (*Deutschbalten* or *Baltendeutsche*). While today it is common in the English-speaking world to refer to the Latvians and Lithuanians as "Balts" or as "Baltic peoples," it was not long ago that the word was used to indicate the *Germans* who inhabited these lands up to World War II.

Whatever the nomenclature, one of the region's most striking features was the sheer variety of peoples occupying such a small corner of northeastern Europe. To the north of Riga were the Estonian tribes, squeezed into their present location by the encroaching eastern Slavs and the Balts, who inhabited lands in the south. To their Christian conquerors the Estonians were *Esths*; the Rus' knew them as *Chuds*. Calling themselves *Sámi*, their descendants communicate in a Finno-Ugric tongue similar to the one spoken by the Tavastians and Karelians of Finland and at one time by the Livs of Livonia. The Estonians are frequently mentioned in the Scandinavian sagas, for after the Viking Age came to an end in the eleventh century, Estonian ships were known to make occasional forays across the Baltic Sea to attack Swedish towns. Their maritime prowess, however, did little to ward off incursions from the east: by 1030 Estonians were paying tribute to Yaroslav I

(r. 1019–1054), a grand prince of the Kievan Rus', who established a fort named Yuryev on the site of a city the Estonians now call Tartu (Ger. Dorpat).

While the Rus' were sometimes able to collect their tithes from the Estonians, Latgallians, and Selonians, their attacks on the Semigallian tribes in 1106–1107—nearly a hundred years before the founding of Riga—ended in defeat. Indeed, it was then that the Russian chronicles began to record numerous conflicts with the neighboring tribes, their territories dotted with hill forts and villages, some of which were already substantial enough to be considered towns.[44] That the Russian presence in the region did not go unnoticed by the Latin Christians is clear enough, for the crusades to the Baltic region were not aimed solely at the heathen but were also intended to drive back Russian (i.e., Orthodox or Greek-rite) expansion wherever it had gained a foothold—that is, in Latgallia and parts of Estonia.[45] The strategy would eventually focus on taking possession of the Düna (Daugava) in order to compel the Rus' princes to open up their lands to the German traders.

But it was only at the end of the 1150s that visiting German merchants began to sail up the Düna, where they first encountered the Livs. Their communities, limited only to the eastern coast of the Gulf of Riga, the northern parts of the Courland peninsula, and the basins of the Düna River and Gauja River (Ger. Treider Aa), were small and politically weak at the time of the Germans' arrival; as such, they were especially vulnerable to foreign attacks. The arrival of the powerful and well-organized Germans meant that the days of the Livs, many of whom initially accepted the Germans because they brought protection from the Lithuanians, were numbered. Thanks to the region's many wars and to centuries of assimilation into the Latvian tribes, there are today only 250 people who claim Livonian ancestry.[46] Of these, none possesses native fluency, the last speaker of a Livish dialect having died in Canada in 2013.

Located west of Riga, Courland is the region that gives western Latvia its distinctive shape.[47] The name of this agriculturally rich and heavily forested peninsula is derived from its dominant population, the Couronians or Cours, a proto-Latvian tribe that also appears in the Scandinavian sagas.[48] While a large number of Couronians had, by the end of the twelfth century, united under a king who ruled with the aid of local chieftains and priests, the region was also settled by Livs, who maintained a continuous (if lightly populated) community along the northern coast almost to the end of the twentieth century. The tribes dwelling in coastal Courland, fearing the prospect of being raided or taken captive, lived from the bounty of the sea, by trading with neighbors, or by raiding them.

Written sources from the time describe the Couronians as warriors, robbers, and pirates; their raids on their neighbors were not unlike those of the Vikings, to whom they are sometimes compared. Among their victims were a Slavic people known as the Wends, from which the Venta River and the city of Ventspils, both in western Latvia, received their names.[49] The medieval chronicler Henry of Livonia

(Henricus de Lettis), a resident of early Riga and history's most important eyewitness to the Livonian Crusade, tells their story:

> The Wends, indeed, were humble and poor at that time, because they had been driven out from the Windau, a river of Kurland. They then lived on the Old Mountain [Kube Hill], next to which the city of Riga is now built. They were again put to flight by the Kurs and many of them were killed. The rest fled to the Letts and, living there with them, rejoiced at the arrival of the priest.[50]

This intriguing passage is noteworthy not least because it suggests that at the time of the Germans' arrival in Riga, the area—or at least a spot only a few hundred meters from the riverside settlements of the Livs—was also inhabited, if only transitionally, by Slavic peoples.[51] Although admittedly marginal to any serious discussion of Riga's origins, this minor fact—that Slavic peoples also inhabited the environs at the moment of the Germanic conquest—has typically been buried under the grand narrative of Latvian national history.

The relationship between the fearsome Couronians and the scattered Wends provides an example—and other examples are legion—of how the region's "natives" or "indigenous peoples" often dealt with each other in ways that were no less violent than the methods of the crusaders. The indigenous inhabitants of Europe's northeastern frontier were not—as contemporary Westerners often like to imagine of people who fall victim to more powerful intruders—noble, peace-loving innocents. More technologically advanced than the native inhabitants of North America at the same time, the Couronians and the other tribes of the eastern Baltic lived in settled communities centered around earthen and wooden castles that were erected largely to protect them *from each other*. Indeed, like the Native Americans at the time of the conquest, the Baltic tribes were plagued by internal conflicts and frequently attacked weaker neighbors.[52]

While we might imagine that the eastern Baltic tribesmen preferred to live in peace, war was their reality long before the arrival of the crusaders. What was new was the increased intensity of local warfare, for it was precisely at the moment when Christians began to arrive in the region in force that conflict among and within the various Baltic and Finno-Ugric tribes began to intensify. Thus the settlement the Germans built at the site of Riga, intended as a base for the Livonian Crusade, also became a place of refuge for natives—that is, for those who accepted the bishop's political authority and the Christian god as their Lord and Savior. Most of the Baltic and Finno-Ugric tribes, however, rejected the crusaders and remained committed to their traditional deities and spirits—and perhaps more importantly, to their independence. Determined to resist the foreigners' unwanted impositions, many Latvians and Estonians would spend decades fending off the Germans' political domination; native resistance to Christianity, however, endured for centuries.

As for the pre-Christian cosmology of the Baltic and Finno-Ugric tribes, or of their rites and rituals, little that is factually verifiable is known. This blank spot places the Balts and the neighboring Finno-Ugric peoples in a category similar to that of the druids, the priestly caste of the ancient peoples who lived in Britain. In each case many of the gaps in our factual knowledge about the customs and beliefs of these ancient peoples have been filled with imaginative fabrications and more than a little well-meaning silliness, as any outside witnesses to a contemporary druid ceremony or a Latvian summer solstice festival (Jāņi) will surely attest. What is known with some certainty is that before the arrival of the Germans the eastern Baltic had a completely rural character and that the worldview of its pagan inhabitants reflected their total immersion in the natural world. Instead of churches there were sacred groves; instead of an omniscient, universal god, there were a series of deities associated with natural phenomena.[53]

Clues about the pagans' preconquest worldview can be gleaned from Latvia's famous *dainas*. Short folk songs that are in some cases believed to be of ancient provenance, the *dainas* began to be collected and written down only in the eighteenth century and continue to influence the art, music, and modern literature of Latvia and Estonia. The *dainas* also convey the ancient traditions of the local communities regarding family, marriage, and death.[54] While the religious beliefs of the Latvian and Lithuanian tribes can be pieced together from fragmentary data so that scholars may arrive at a coherent worldview that allowed the pagans to make sense of their relationship to the natural world, to the cosmos, and to their gods and spirits, the Livs were a case apart. Given the almost total absence of a written record, evidence concerning their belief system is exceedingly thin. For the purpose of understanding the German-Christian mission in Livonia, what is most significant is not what the Livs and their neighbors actually believed—that we will never know for sure—but the way the Christians *perceived* the pagans and their customs, and the way these perceptions affected the clash of cultures that took place on the Baltic frontier in the thirteenth century. A bull issued in 1199 by Pope Innocent III that beckoned Saxon and Westphalian soldiers to come to the aid of the new church in Livonia described the Livs as "a barbarous people . . . who worship beasts, trees, waters, plants and impure spirits."[55] Likewise, Bartholomew of England, author of the encyclopedic compendium *On the Property of Things* (1240), recorded that the Livs had "peculiar religious rites, before the Germans forced them from serving demons to the faith and worship of one God. Or they honored many gods with impure and sacrilegious sacrifices, asked of demons for prophecies, made use of auguries and divinations."[56]

Christian observers viewed the pagans in the context of a Christian worldview, one that understood the world as a place created by God but haunted by the Devil and his demons. To Henry of Livonia, a monk of uncertain origin who was witness to the struggles with the pagans near Riga, these demons were the local pagan deities from which the Livs must be saved by any and all possible means.[57] Apprehending the pagans' customs with a mixture of horror, distaste, and pity, and often failing to distinguish the beliefs and customs of one tribe from another, clerics like Henry were pleased that they had begun to rid the locals of their heathen vices.[58] The Livs who accepted Christ, wrote Henry, were now God's children, and they have Him to thank for sending a shepherd, Bishop Albert, through whom "God freed his Livonian sheep and the now-baptized Letts from the jaws of the wolves."[59] Founded with the pope's blessing in 1201, the defended settlement at Riga became their refuge.

Missions to Livonia

As the most important source on early Riga and the crusading campaigns of the early thirteenth century, Henry's chronicle is in part the story of the three bishops who established a German and Christian presence in the lands near the settlement they called Riga.[60] These were, in order, Meinhard, a canon at the Segeberg Abbey who in the early 1180s traveled with German merchants to Livonia and began the conversion of the natives in Üxküll, the location of Livonia's first bishopric; Berthold of Hanover, a former Cistercian abbot who was killed in battle with the Livs in 1198; and Albert of Buxhoeveden, who moved his episcopal see from Üxküll to Riga and whom most consider the city's founder.

That these three clerics were committed to bringing the word of God to the pagans is beyond debate: only their unshakable belief in the cause could explain their willingness to face danger, hardship, and eventual death in these harsh and distant lands. But it was the merchants who came first to the eastern Baltic, and there is every reason to believe that they welcomed the Church's presence there as a civilizing force. This, as was shown by the general experience of mercantile expansion on Christendom's northern frontiers, would in turn enhance the traders' security. Indeed, the story of Riga's founding perfectly illustrates the convergence of the religious impulse and the simultaneous economic one, for parallel to the launching of a Christian universalism a web of economic relationships was being created by the continent's merchants that drew together an array of luxuries, weapons, and other goods.[61] From northern Italy, eastern France, and western Germany came textiles and wine; from England, wool; from northern Germany, beer. From the North Sea and southern Baltic coast merchants collected butter, horses, and oxen. As we have noted, long before Meinhard's passage to Livonia aboard a German trading vessel, the Russians, Danes, and Norwegians had been doing business with the locals, from whom they obtained beeswax, forest products, and hides from the Russian hinterland. In this environment the Germans were relative newcomers.

The arrival of these strangers to Livonia would be narrated by a later mayor of Riga named Francis Nienstedt (1540–1622), whose history of Livonia was based on medieval chronicles and other writings. To these we may add the influence of an oral tradition that tells us much about the views that prevailed in sixteenth-century Riga.

> In the year 1148, some also say 1158, a ship sailed from Bremen with traders and wares on the way to Visby on the island of Gotland. But a great wind drove them back, they could not stop at Gotland . . . [and] they came to Courland. Because they dared to stop at this land, thanks to God, they noticed before them some kind of smaller vessel that was sailing in the direction of the Düna. Thinking that this ship would eventually enter a port, they dared by the grace of God to follow this little ship. . . .
>
> Well, when the wild pagan peoples noticed that such a great ship had arrived such as they had never seen in their lives, they ran to the great shoals in order to take a closer look, because from afar it had seemed to them very strange. They thought about what to do with these arrivals who were as strange as their ships and about which they had never heard nor seen anything. The first nights the Christians stayed in the ship on the water and considered what to do next.
>
> In the morning, some went to the shore, and carried dark barrels to it, putting them down on the shore and placing upon it grain, beer, various food items and other things they thought the pagans could use. They waved to the pagans, and some were encouraged to come closer. Then the Christians held out their hands to the pagans and gave them sugar, figs, raisins, and so on, as gifts. They treated one another as friends, but they could not converse with each other; after that encounter they [the Christians] allowed them [the pagans] to go home, so as to report to their friends and relatives how well the Christians had supplied them.
>
> On the third day, the [Livish] warriors appeared again, and among the gifts they brought to the Christians were honey, milk, hens, eggs, poultry, and hares. The Christians accepted these with great kindness and gave them a string of hats, a string of trousers, mirrors, belts, knives, combs, and sewing needles. The friendship grew considerably and when on the fourth day the pagans appeared again, they had with them sheep, fish, flax, honey, beeswax, eggs, chickens, forest animals; these they placed on the ground and, because they could not speak to each other, indicated what they wanted to exchange by making various signs. When the Christians understood their intentions and wishes, they then examined some of the things they had brought and next to each item placed a certain amount of money [to indicate its trading value]. Since money was unknown to the pagans, they showed with signs that they are not alone and how they were willing to trade for the Christians' belongings. Then the Christians went toward their belongings, putting down and taking things away until both sides were satisfied. Then they offered each other their hands, carrying each other's goods and parting. In this manner they learned to trade with one another.[62]

And trade they did, for after 1158 (the generally accepted date) ships from Germany began to appear at the mouth of the Düna with some regularity. By the time the priest Meinhard settled near the Gulf of Riga, probably in 1184, following several earlier visits while traveling with merchants from Lübeck, the German traders had already built a modest fort at a place they called Üxküll, a name derived from the Livonian *Ikškilā*, meaning "solitary village."[63] Located on the right bank of the Düna, opposite the Semigallian port of Daugmale and approximately thirty kilometers upstream from the future site of Riga, Üxküll (now Ikšķile) was the first permanent settlement the Germans established in the region and their initial base of operations. Here the merchants enjoyed, for a time, a peaceful relationship with the Livs based on a mutually beneficial trade. Yet this minor trading post was merely a prelude to the Germans' larger ambitions of opening the river for trade with the Russians of Polotsk and beyond. Conversion of the Livs, whom the Germans recognized as having norms very different from their own when it came to matters of property, commerce, and the settlement of legal disputes, would help them to achieve their goals.[64] Thus it was in Üxküll that Meinhard saw his opportunity: he would exploit the trading peace with the Livs in order to convert them.[65]

Among the earliest mentions of Meinhard's activities in Livonia are the entries in a chronicle compiled by the Benedictine abbot Arnold of Lübeck. Written around 1210 and covering the years 1171 to 1209, *The Slavic Chronicle* chiefly concerns the ongoing struggle between the Holy Roman Empire and the Wends. The chronicle also announced the arrival of Christianity in Livonia in the form of Meinhard and his bishopric.[66]

> In the year 1186 of the incarnation the venerable Meinhard founded the Episcopal see in Livonia that was placed under the patronage of Mary, Blessed Mother of God, in a place that was called Riga. And since because of the goodness of the earth this place is abundant in many riches, it has never been lacking in servants of Christ and planters of the new church. For this land is fertile in fields, plentiful in pastures, irrigated by rivers, also sufficiently rich in fish and forested with trees.[67]

In prizing a triumphal Christian narrative over historical precision, Arnold's account is not unlike other medieval Church chronicles. It should be noted, however, that the episcopal see founded by Meinhard was initially located not in Riga, but in nearby Üxküll; it was Albert of Buxhoeveden who later transferred the bishopric to Riga and made it his base for further Christian expansion. And although it was the most successful effort to bring Christ to the peoples of the region, it was not the first: the Düna Livs, like the Latgallians of Jersika (Ger. Gerzika) further to the east, were already paying tribute to the Rus' prince of Polotsk. Some of the local tribesmen had converted to the Orthodox faith, but these were few.[68] Limited efforts in the 1170s by the Danes, whose medieval rulers sometimes entertained visions of a Baltic empire, to bring Catholicism to Estonia achieved even less success and were soon abandoned.

Nevertheless, Meinhard, possibly inspired by the missionary work of Vicelinus (Vizelin; 1086–1154), a German bishop of Oldenburg who worked to administer God's word to the Wends, decided to commit himself to the work of preaching to and baptizing the Livs. Having secured permission from Hartwig II, the influential archbishop of Hamburg-Bremen (more on him below), Meinhard was given the rank of bishop and returned to Üxküll, where German traders had already built a fort and established trade relations with the nearby Livs and Russians further inland. For the rest of his life, the modest settlement at Üxküll, where Meinhard would learn the Livish tongue and spend his days at work and in prayer—often living in fear of the increasingly hostile natives—remained the center of his missionary activity.

Having established a base for his mission, Meinhard next had to arrange an understanding with the local hegemon. Familiar with the region's power dynamics after years of seasonal trading, German merchants knew that it was risky to conduct business with the inhabitants of the Düna basin without the consent of the Rus' prince of Polotsk; so they urged the priest to waste no time in requesting permission from Prince Vladimir to convert the Livs to Latin Christianity.[69] Whether Meinhard petitioned the prince in person is unclear; whatever the case, the priest and his companions understood that the prince commanded enough respect to be able to collect tribute from the Livs in whose midst Meinhard wished to build a church.[70]

The modest ambitions of the gray-haired priest were probably not of much concern to Vladimir. Entangled in wars with other Russian principalities and thus unable to defend his subjects in the Baltic region from Lithuanian raids, Vladimir consented to Meinhard's request. Soon after, Meinhard established a stone church in Üxküll, which he dedicated to Mary. Promising to protect the small Livish community from the Lithuanian attacks that typically forced its victims to retreat into the forests, the priest proceeded to build the region's first stone castle—a fortified church—for which he employed masons from Gotland. These were the first stone buildings among the Baltic tribes, whose hilltop fortresses hitherto had consisted of wood and dirt. While it might be said that the shrewd priest had used the Germans' more advanced technology to lure the native Livs into converting to Christianity, it is likely that as the see's new bishop, Meinhard really wanted the fortified church for himself. Why else would he have volunteered to pay one-fifth of its construction cost himself?[71] A few years later, Meinhard built a similar stone fortification at a place the Germans called Holm (meaning "island") or Kirchholm, located eighteen kilometers from the future site of Riga on an island in the Düna (now mostly submerged) near a town known today as Salaspils ("island castle").[72] Writing more than seven centuries later, the Baltic German historian Constantin

Mettig, Riga's first true biographer, declared that with the building of these early structures, "so began the mission, and in such manner German life in Livonia entered the light of history."[73]

For his efforts in converting as many as half the Livs of Üxküll, Meinhard was consecrated as missionary bishop of Üxküll during a trip to Germany in 1186. While back at home, he also recruited a fresh contingent of missionaries that included monks from the Cistercian Order to augment the original Augustinian mission.[74] Meinhard's position as the supreme religious leader in all the lands inhabited by the Livs was confirmed in 1188 by Pope Clement II, who around the same time subordinated the new diocese to the metropolis of Bremen, headed by the ambitious Archbishop Hartwig II, an influential uncle of Riga's future founder, Bishop Albert of Buxhoeveden. Hartwig's goal, it seems, was to renew his see's ecclesiastical supremacy in northern Europe.[75] Although Meinhard's mission enjoyed modest initial success, the aggressive efforts of his Cistercian monks—notably the young Theodoric (Theoderich, d. 1219), who managed to convert a Livish leader named Caupo along with several others in the area around Turaida (Ger. Treiden)—aroused such hostility that sometime in the early 1190s the priest and his followers decided to give up and return to Germany. Not until the spring of 1195 did Meinhard decide once again to follow the merchants back to Gotland and thence to Livonia, where he committed himself to staying. Sadly for Meinhard, a growing opposition to him among the Livs left him a virtual prisoner in his church in Üxküll, where he fell ill waiting for help that did not arrive until after his death.

That help came in the form of God's soldiers. For decades, Danes, Swedes, and Germans had been fighting as crusaders around the fringes of the Baltic Sea with the blessing of the pope; thus it was hardly unusual that Meinhard would have sent Theodoric of Treiden to Rome to ask Pope Celestine III (r. 1191–1198) for assistance in dealing with the capricious Livs.[76] Impressed with Meinhard's work but concerned that the recent converts were turning their backs on the church, the pope ordered a crusade with the promise of full indulgences to the crusaders.[77] Theodoric then took it upon himself to organize a crusade against the pagans of Courland and sailed to Visby on the island of Gotland to recruit volunteers. What had begun as a peaceful effort to bring Christianity to the natives now gave way to more forceful methods of conversion.[78]

Although it is Albert of Buxhoeveden who is most directly associated with these early Christian and German efforts to conquer Livonia by force, it was Meinhard who first turned to the Church for military support. But the infirm priest did not live long enough to welcome that support in person, dying in 1197. Theodoric, having learned this news on his return trip to Livonia, then took the Swedes and Gotlanders he had recruited in Visby further north to Estonia, possibly in the hope that by conquering more land in the region he would be appointed the new bishop of Livonia. But after three days of plunder the Swedes decided to return home, thereby highlighting one of the problems with crusading in the Baltic: the commitment of God's soldiers to continuing the fight was always fickle, for they could simply return home.

The results of Theodoric's crusade in Estonia were meager, for the region witnessed at this moment neither a formal acceptance of Christianity nor the establishment of a permanent German settlement. Still more troubling were the circumstances faced by the bishop, Berthold of Hanover, who had been working in Livonia for some years before his consecration in 1197. Arriving in Bremen for his investiture, this former Cistercian abbot was known to be an outspoken advocate for the crusade in Livonia—a view that was given added weight by Pope Celestine's concession that participants in such a campaign would be granted indulgences equal to those who waged war for Christianity in the Holy Land.

Berthold's return to Livonia was, in fact, initially peaceful. Sailing up the Düna in the company of priests and merchants, the small convoy lacked a military force for protection. Arriving defenseless and immediately inviting the Livonian notables, both pagans and converts, to gather for a feast at Üxküll, the newly consecrated bishop may have been trying to win over the natives with a show of good will. It is also possible that Berthold was expecting to meet Theodoric and his army of crusaders, who were nowhere to be found. Most likely it was, as one historian has remarked, a "hopeful, yet calculated, move to go through the motions of giving the Livonians a last chance to receive and maintain the Christian faith peacefully" before inevitably resorting to force.[79]

While at first the apostate Livs seemed to have greeted him politely, if warily, Berthold soon realized that the tribesmen had no intention of returning to the Church. His life in danger, the bishop fled back to the merchant ships and returned to Bremen, where he asked the pope, the archbishop, and the people of Saxony for more help.[80] Relying on the financial support of Archbishop Hartwig II, who had just returned from a crusade to the Holy Land, and some of the merchants of Bremen and Lübeck, Berthold was able to assemble his army quickly. According to Arnold of Lübeck, "a great host of prelates, knights and merchants from all of Saxony, Westphalia, and Friesland—poor as well as wealthy—gathered in Lübeck, where they acquired ships, weapons and supplies, and from there they immediately continued to Livonia."[81] Thus was Meinhard's fragile but initially peaceful mission transformed into an aggressive and perpetual crusade whose end result was the German-led conquest (and incomplete conversion) of Livonia.

Berthold's fleet appeared in the Bay of Riga in July 1198. While the merchants disembarked near the mouth of the Düna with the intention of establishing a settlement in the vicinity (i.e., near the present location of Riga), Berthold and the crusaders sailed further up the river to Kirchholm (Salaspils), where they were met by a group of hostile Livs. Berthold's demand that the Livs surrender some hostages and accept the Christian faith was met with refusal. Failing to come to a peaceful agreement with the pagans, Berthold ordered his army—well-equipped with warhorses, crossbows, pikes, and iron armor—to attack the Livs, who by comparison were relatively unarmed.[82] It was in the ensuing battle—a military victory for the Christians but a disaster from the point of view of a papacy that had called upon Saxons to go to Livonia to defend and protect an isolated and vulnerable church—that Berthold perished, a lance thrust into his back, his body torn to pieces.[83] The date of his death has traditionally been given as July 24, 1198, and the place was a hill—the "old mountain" later known as Kube Hill (Ger. Kubsberg)—located just a kilometer from the future site of Riga.[84] That the crusaders won the battle—after all, 150 Livs accepted baptism after its conclusion—is easy to overlook when one considers its aftermath: the Livs simply washed off their baptism in the same waters in which they had received it. Monks who had chosen to stay behind had little choice but to abandon their churches at Üxküll and Kirchholm to the pagans, who threatened to kill any Germans who refused to leave.[85]

The story is recounted by the monk Henry, whose chronicle is a most informative source for anyone wishing to understand the ideals and clashes that gave birth to Christian Livonia and its greatest city. Comprised of a series of texts that were likely compiled for the benefit of a papal legate, William of Modena, for whom Henry served as translator in the 1220s, *The Chronicle of Henry of Livonia* describes in detail the holy wars waged against the pagans of Livonia. While written from an unmistakably clerical point of view, Henry's chronicle is an engaging and richly nuanced history of the Catholic Church's experience in the region between the 1180s and 1227. A highly observant writer, Henry hints at the conflicted aims and motives of the foreigners who sailed to the eastern Baltic, while remaining confident of God's ultimate triumph.[86] The Livs, the Cistercian lamented, were "the most perfidious, and everyone stole what his neighbor had." But now that they had been baptized through the efforts of Bishops Meinhard, Berthold, and Albert, their habits of "theft, violence, rapine, and similar things," Henry remarked with satisfaction, "were [now] forbidden."[87]

The Liv Settlements

At last we return to where this chapter began—at the site of the future city of Riga. When Germans began to arrive at the sandy and swampy lower reaches of the Düna during the second half of the twelfth century, the infertile lands they found on the riverbanks supported a paucity of human settlements. The people who lived closest to the estuary, Livs who settled in richer environs thirty kilometers further inland, used the area for fishing, cattle breeding, and beekeeping. Aware that large, foreign ships were sailing up the Düna with increasing frequency, the Livs were even more mindful of their traditional enemies, the Lithuanian tribes in particular, who would descend upon the Livish villages with little warning. The existence of more than forty hill forts in the Latvian part of the Düna valley alone—some belonging to the Livs, and others to the Latvian tribes—testifies to the fact that at the time of the Germans' arrival, no one group or tribe controlled the Düna River.[88]

Although there has been a continuous human presence in the southern Baltic littoral as a whole for some 11,000 years, the lands near the mouth of the Düna remained sparsely inhabited before the late Iron Age. Archaeological evidence suggests the existence of a settlement at Riga that predated the time of Christ, but it was not until sometime around 1000 CE that the lower Düna near Riga witnessed the appearance of permanent settlements belonging to Livish and Latvian fishermen, craftsmen, and traders. Among the most prosperous of these early settlements was the thriving Semigallian port of Daugmale, which, as the only site in preconquest Latvia that had what might be called an urban character, was located south of Riga on the river's left bank and was the city's forerunner. The Vikings who came to trade between the eighth and eleventh centuries may have set up their own colonies in the area, but these were probably gone by the time the Germans made their bid for ascendancy.

At the time of the conquest, the monk Henry tells us, the Livs lived in four distinct settlements on the Düna's right bank stretching from the Bay of Riga, at the river's mouth, to the rapids of Rumbala near the island of Dole south of Riga. Less politically advanced than the neighboring Latgallians (Letts), whose hill forts at Jersika and Koknese were governed by a lord (who in turn paid tribute to the Rus'), the Livs were free peasants who had no king, indeed no central leader of any kind, not even a central area of residence. Lacking a written language of their own, the Livs, like the Lettish tribes, left no accounts of their experience during these early years. Thus our understanding of the Livs of Riga is almost entirely derived from the archaeological record—jewelry, tools, burial grounds, building remnants—augmented only by Henry's observations.[89]

The Livish communities at the future site of Riga were modest by any standard and were of only minor regional significance before Albert chose the spot for his city. One settlement, little more than a fishing village, was located on the right bank of the Düna, approximately in the area where Latvian Riflemen Square is today.[90] A second Livish community was located near the spot where the Riga River, a minor tributary, emptied into the Düna River. While "Lake Riga" became the site of Riga's first port, it was not long before it became a stagnant tank of water filled with garbage, refuse, and sand. Having lost its original function long ago, the river was filled in and buried underground on the order of city authorities in the eighteenth century. With the exception of a small, narrow street (Rīdzenes iela) named after one of its last surviving sections, there are no visible traces of the river in the modern city. Thus the channel that gave the city its first harbor and possibly its name has, like the walls that once protected Riga from invaders, been lost. Among the few visible efforts to remind today's visitors and residents of the river's course through the city many years ago is a lawn in Liv Square, whose shape mimics the undulating surface of the river.

That the modern city of Riga lacks any clear historical markers commemorating either of Riga's Livish settlements is especially surprising when one considers the efforts in the 1930s of the authoritarian regime headed by Kārlis Ulmanis to excavate parts of the city in the hopes of erasing any doubts about the city's "Latvian" origins. While the thirteenth-century shipwreck excavated from the earth where Riga's first port once stood is now on display at the Museum of the History of Rīga and Navigation, there is nothing at the former archaeological site to indicate that this spot might be considered the actual birthplace of the city. Indeed, the thing that stands out most clearly about Albert Square, the site of the ancient Livish settlement next to the lost rivulet, is its remoteness from the busier and more attractive part of the Old Town named for the Livs. Perhaps it is more fitting that Bishop Albert's statue is located on a courtyard wall of the cathedral he established rather than on the eerily quiet square that bears his name.

In this small corner of the city, in the vicinity of present-day Kalēju, Audēju, Mārstaļu, and Alksnāju streets—now a favorite gathering place for youthful imbibers of cheap booze and beer—there once lived a tiny community of fishermen, traders, and craftsmen. Like their Lettish neighbors, the Riga Livs used pine logs felled from the nearby forests to construct their tightly spaced dwellings as well as outbuildings (for storage) and barns. With roofs made from straw and reeds, the Livs' houses typically consisted of one or two rooms with a stove in the corner that provided warmth and a cooking area.[91] In the village squares the Riga Livs conducted business with neighboring Latvian tribes, as well as with the Wends who lived on nearby Kube Hill (approximately where the Esplanade is located today). "Russian" traders (i.e., merchants from the lands of the Rus'), enjoying the protection of the prince of Polotsk, also came to the village.

Toward the end of the twelfth century, in the time of Bishop Meinhard, this modest trading community began to welcome German merchants. It is likely that the second bishop of Livonia, Berthold, who had gathered his forces there for the battle against the Livs that cost him his life, saw Riga's considerable military potential as well. Indeed, Berthold's military activities in Riga have led some historians to speculate that it was he and not Albert who was the true founder of Riga.[92] Whoever merits the title "founder"—and whatever Berthold's contributions—there can be no doubt that it was *Albert* who transformed the site into an actual city.

In its earliest years the Riga settlement was in every respect multinational, with no one tribe or nation dominating the trade on the river that flowed past it. Yet the site where Riga would be established had some disadvantages. Sand dunes created by the shifting winds rendered the area unsuitable for agriculture.

FIGURE 2. Monument to Bishop Albert of Buxhoeveden in the courtyard of the Rīga Cathedral, 2016. Photo by author.

The wind-blown sand also tended to fill up parts of the shallow and meandering Düna River, which over the centuries caused shifts in its course and hence difficulties for the larger vessels that sailed along it. It was the sand that doomed the city's first port on the Riga rivulet: the scene of much commercial activity in the thirteenth century, the harbor became unusable for the bigger ships of the fourteenth century. Once a new harbor was built on the Düna, the old port would be used only for docking smaller river vessels, such as the *strugas* arriving from the Russian lands.

Rigans have always considered the Düna a great blessing—indeed it is the reason for the city's very existence; yet it has also been the cause of many of Riga's greatest misfortunes. That the Livish villages of the twelfth century were situated only one meter above the water level of the Düna was the legacy of an earlier geological age when the area was entirely under water. Winter turns the river into a sheet of ice, which for many centuries Rigans used as a bridge between the Old Town and Pārdaugava (Ger. Überdüna) on the left bank. While spring thaws have long provided the city's inhabitants with the entertaining spectacle of watching large blocks of ice flow down the river to be disgorged into the Gulf of Riga, ice jams downstream have frequently caused the river to overflow its banks, in earlier times causing Rigans to scurry to the safety of Kube Hill. Before the construction of modern dams upstream, the specter of a major flood—something that occurred about ten times each century—was never far from the minds of Rigans.[93] The blocks of ice stuck at the estuary at the frozen Gulf of Riga were the cause of the most devastating flood in the city's history in April 1709. The river's flow to the sea severely impeded by the ice, the water rose and rose, and soon enough the walled city and its suburbs were completely submerged.

It is impossible to say how many Rigans perished that spring, just one year before the city's surrender to a Russian army headed by General Boris Sheremetev during the Great Northern War (1700–1721). Survivors of the flood then faced a cholera and typhoid epidemic that swept through the region at the same time as the city endured its ninth and most catastrophic siege, which for nearly ten months halted the deliveries of food to the starving city. Whether it was the flood, the plague, or starvation, Rigans stared into the face of Armageddon while soldiers and civilians alike died by the thousands.

Tragedy, it often seems, was written into Riga's genetic code.

Chapter 2

Watering the Nations: Riga and the Northern Crusades

Roma dictat iura, Riga vero rigat gentes.
Rome makes laws, while Riga irrigates the nations.
—The Chronicle of Henry of Livonia

At the moment that Bishop Albert settled on Riga for his Christian city, the site consisted of some minor Livish settlements surrounded by water, marshes, and sand dunes. Its inhabitants survived by fishing, by trading with seasonal visitors, and (we may presume) by hiding in the forests at the first hint of danger, for the Livish tribes were weak, divided, and easily overcome by superior forces. Indeed, the Christians from Germany and Scandinavia were hardly the first foreigners that the Riga Livs had encountered—the Lithuanians' terrifying raids gave them a certain notoriety as far away as Estonia—but it was the Christians from western Europe, and not the pagans of Lithuania, who were the best-equipped to conquer the area permanently.

The strangers' motives were clear enough, for the Riga Livs were not only pagans in need of baptism and salvation, but they also happened to occupy prime real estate, their settlements being situated near a mighty river that for centuries had carried goods from Russia to the West. It was not long before Germany's merchants and missionaries, enticed by the endless bounty of Livonia's forested interior and the prospect of converting the local pagans, identified the site's suitability as a port and as a potential center for their commercial, religious, and military activities.

While they are less well known than the bloody, often catastrophic forays to the Holy Land, the Northern Crusades have in recent times become a topic of considerable historical interest, possibly owing to their lasting effects. Not least of these was the spotty settlement of northeastern Europe by German-speaking lords, clerics, and merchants, who quickly forged a permanent relationship between northern Europe and the eastern Baltic. Now dotted with churches and monasteries, Livonia began to adopt the institutions of northwestern Europe—castles and manors, cities and guilds. By the 1230s, the growing city of Riga, with its turreted walls and church steeples that could be seen for miles in the distance, was hardly distinguishable from other northern trading cities where heavy cogs loaded and unloaded their goods at the water's edge and where the chatter of Middle Low German could be heard in the unpaved streets. But unlike Hamburg, Lübeck, or Rostock—thriving German towns at the western edge of the Baltic Sea—Riga was located in remote territory that, when the waterways froze, would be nearly closed to the outside world for months on end. Virtually surrounded by native tribes, both pagans and newly baptized converts, Riga was the center of a great missionary see and a military order dedicated to holy war. Riga was also in every respect a colonial city, dominated by strangers to the region who arrived in shiploads to make a comfortable living, conquer territory, and spread the faith.

Jerusalem on the Düna

The British writer Simon Sebag Montefiore, best known for his excursions through the whirlwind of Russian history, has also told the story of an ancient settlement that was destined to become a holy city—*the* Holy City—despite its being burdened with every possible disadvantage. "Of all the places in the world," he asks, "why Jerusalem? The site was remote from the trade routes of the Mediterranean coast; it was short of water, baked in the summer sun, chilled by winter winds, its jagged rocks blistered and inhospitable."[1]

To be sure, Montefiore's Jerusalem was advantaged by neither a favorable location nor an agreeable climate. It was the religious experience of the Hebrews, and not the fortune of geography, that launched this ancient city's rise to local, and later global, prominence. Transformed from a dusty provincial town into the capital of the Hebrews' Promised Land—the Kingdom of Israel—the Holy City became a symbol of endurance in the face of disaster, of Yahweh's special bond with his Chosen People. This sense of exceptionalism, of an exclusive and divinely sanctioned relationship between the nation and the land, was later inherited by Christian and Muslim communities, each of which has made similar claims about Jerusalem's importance to their faith. In all their visions of the Holy City, whether articulated by ancient Hebrews, medieval crusaders, or modern prophets of Zion, we witness a blurring of boundaries between the material world and the spiritual one, between the earthly city and the City of God.

Of course, Riga has never, not even at the height of the Northern Crusades, enjoyed anything like Jerusalem's unrivaled status or popular appeal. The vast majority of thirteenth-century churchmen would surely have agreed that the more important fight was in the Near East, for the thinly populated and heavily forested Livonian see was bereft of holy shrines, temples, or relics; as such it was hardly the most attractive destination for potential crusaders. While Christian soldiers who fulfilled their vows in Jerusalem, their souls heavily weighted by the burdens of sin and penance, could expect to be granted absolution, and hence salvation, the same could not be said for the men who participated in the earliest expeditions to Livonia. Crusaders in the northeast were at first granted only a limited indulgence: remission of a year's sins—a far cry from eternal salvation. That the authorities in Rome initially held the forays to the Baltic in lower esteem than they did the crusades to the Near East is amply illustrated by this disparity. Indeed, it was only under the pontificate of Honorius II (r. 1216–1227) that campaigns to the northeast were consistently placed on par with crusades to the Holy Land.[2] From this time onward, soldiers who fulfilled their vows in the eastern Baltic (which, of course, was much closer to Germany and would require a less burdensome journey) were granted the same indulgence as those who took up the cross to fight in the eastern Mediterranean.

While no marketing campaign could have succeeded in making Riga the equal of Jerusalem in the imaginations of potential recruits, nobody worked more tirelessly to lure fighting men to the northeast than Albert of Buxhoeveden, the third bishop of Livonia, his remote and fragile outpost routinely under threat of elimination. That Palestine, the subject of countless dreams and visions, would always be a more attractive draw for Christ's soldiers than mysterious, barbaric Livonia presented a formidable challenge for the young bishop, who readily responded with a compelling vision for the eastern Baltic. Promoting the idea of marching under the banner of the Virgin, of watering the Lord's vineyard with the blood of martyrs and heathen, of defending what he called the Land of Mary—*Marienland*—this, Albert surely realized, was the way to entice potential crusaders to sail across the stormy eastern sea to the shores of Livonia, where the bishop began to build his new holy city.[3] To attract Christian soldiers to Livonia and thereby turn it into a new center of power, its mysterious pagan geography needed to be sacralized, transformed into a Christian geography. In his thirty-year effort to build his new military and ecclesiastical center in Livonia, Albert cast Riga as the equal of Jerusalem.[4]

The most complete and revealing source concerning Riga's founding is Book III of Henry of Livonia's fascinating chronicle, composed a quarter century after Albert's fleet first sailed up the Düna in the summer of 1200. After some initial skirmishes between pilgrims and pagans, to which we shall return later, the Livonians

> showed to the bishop the site of the city which they call Riga. They call it Riga either from Lake Riga [i.e., the Riga River], or from irrigation, since it is irrigated both from below and from above. It is irrigated from below for, as they say, it is well

> moistened in its waters and pastures; or, since the plenary remission of sins is administered in it to sinners, the irrigation from above, that is, the kingdom of heaven is thus administered through it. Or, in other words, Riga, refreshed by the water of the new faith, waters the tribes round about through the holy font of baptism.[5]

Henry's chronicle portrays Livonia as a new "promised land" and Riga as the "City of God" (Civitus Dei). Although the Latin phrase appears only once in Henry's chronicle, it nevertheless gives us an idea of how important the monk considered the city's founding in the dual process of expanding the boundaries of Latin Christendom and converting the pagans.[6] Returning to Germany every autumn to recruit soldiers, Albert enticed potential crusaders by telling them that they were to fight for the "Land of the Blessed Virgin," and that for their efforts all their sins would be forgiven. Among his main recruiting symbols was a church dedicated to St. Mary, more commonly known as the Dome Cathedral, the construction of which began soon after the city's official founding in 1201.[7]

The product of a low-ranking aristocratic family from a town in Lower Saxony, Albert of Buxhoeveden studied at the St. Peter's school of the Bremen church, later became one of its priests, and for nearly a decade (1186–1194) was the city's mayor.[8] Named the third bishop of Livonia on March 28, 1199, by his uncle Hartwig II, the archbishop of Hamburg-Bremen (1185–1207), himself eager to secure a new ecclesiastical empire for his archdiocese, the thirty-two-year-old priest was well suited to the task that lay ahead. Possessing a respected family name, connections in high places and with merchant communities, experience as both a man of the Church and as a secular administrator, and boundless energy and ambition, Albert seemed an ideal choice to lead the Livonian mission.[9]

Entrusted by his uncle with the task of continuing the missionary work of Meinhard and Berthold, the new bishop was in no hurry to sail to Üxküll (Latv. Ikšķile), the seat of his episcopal see.[10] Before he could assume his new responsibilities, Albert first had to make the necessary preparations, not least of which were securing the support of regional rulers and recruiting a fighting force. Thus, in the winter of 1199–1200, the priest journeyed to the north German city of Magdeburg, where he sought the support of King Philip of Swabia, a contender for the throne of the Holy Roman Empire.[11] He also discussed his plans with King Knut VI of Denmark and the king's brother, Duke (and future king) Valdemar of Schleswig. Any objections they might have raised can only be guessed at. It stands to reason that they must have agreed to Albert's plans, for a crusade in the Baltic would have been unthinkable without the support of Denmark, whose rulers aspired to a Baltic empire and were enticed, once again, by the prospect of gaining Estonia.

Meanwhile, the new bishop worked to secure the cooperation of the German merchant community in Visby (est. 1163) on the island of Gotland, their support being essential for ensuring the transportation of personnel, provisions, and

FIGURE 3. Rīga Cathedral (Dome, St. Mary's) with Rīga Castle in the background, 2009. Photo by Ainars Brūvelis.

weapons to Livonia.[12] Having journeyed to Rome where he was confirmed in office by Pope Innocent III, Albert next set about gathering crusaders from Lübeck and Gotland, in the process managing to convince a handful of noblemen to accompany him on his mission to the wild lands of the northeast.

Only in July 1200, more than a year after his initial appointment to Livonia, did Albert and his men arrive in the Gulf of Riga. Dwarfing the expeditions of his predecessors, Albert's fleet consisted of twenty-three ships, several of which were capable of carrying as many as one hundred servants, pilgrims, and priests. If the size of his force has been exaggerated—Henry writes that Albert recruited five hundred men to accompany him to Livonia—even a party half that size would have been a good indicator of the bishop's intentions.[13] Persuasion was the preferred method of conversion, but Albert also had the authority to deploy force, for the thirty-nine-year-old Pope Innocent III (r. 1198–1216), believing it his duty to nurture the faithful and defend them from their enemies, had confirmed his predecessor's bull calling for a crusade in the Baltic.[14] The Livonian mission, the bull emphasized, must be defended against pagan attacks like the one that had killed Bishop Berthold.

Yet Albert, no less than his influential uncle Hartwig, nurtured greater ambitions. From the beginning it was the bishop's aim to establish some sort of territorial unit in Livonia from which to conduct the business of conversion—and perhaps of no less importance, the business of business. Realizing that whoever commanded the lower reaches of the Düna also controlled the trade route that ran southeast to Polotsk and the Russian interior, and advised by merchants who must have recognized Albert's gift for leadership, the bishop well understood the economic potential of the Livonian enterprise. While his assignment was primarily a religious one, there is every reason to believe that Albert also hoped that by providing security for the region he would be able develop commercial links between the north German cities and the Livonian lands. In this sense the bishop's goals were perfectly aligned with those of the traders. Safety for themselves and their wares was always a top concern, for merchants traveling through the eastern Baltic were vulnerable to pagan attacks, sudden and swift. There can be little doubt that the traders welcomed the arrival of those—like the new bishop of Livonia—who could establish order. Indeed, as historian Mark R. Munzinger has demonstrated, the founding of Riga was a telling example of the interaction between mercantile and missionary interests in the eastern Baltic in the thirteenth century.[15]

The fleet that Albert brought to Üxküll must have made quite an impression on the Livs, who surely noticed that the number of ships sailing up the Düna had been increasing in recent years. While the Düna Livs had from time to time endured the shock of Lithuanian raids, never before had they witnessed such a show of raw power. Failing to stop the fleet as it made its way from the Germans' island settlement at Kirchholm upstream to Üxküll, the Livs decided to made peace with the Germans—"but deceitfully," writes the chronicler Henry, "in order that they might meanwhile collect their army."[16] Meanwhile, having rescued the few priests remaining in Üxküll, Albert returned to Kirchholm, where another round of fighting broke out with the Livs. It was only with the arrival of a ship from Friesland, carrying crusaders who immediately set fire to the natives' crops, that the Livs were frightened into renewing the peace. But the matter of who was master of the downstream Düna was far from settled.

With the approach of autumn, when the German merchants traditionally returned to their homelands for the winter, Albert prepared to depart for Germany, once again to recruit more soldiers to defend his mission. Before departing he investigated another of the Livish settlements, this one located closer to the mouth of the Düna and thus a superior location from which to conduct the trade that Albert wished to monopolize. After all, the indefensible German settlement at Üxküll, the bishop realized, was ideal neither as a Catholic episcopal see (its inhabitants paid tribute to the Rus' prince of Polotsk) nor as a center for trade, since Üxküll was located forty-six kilometers from the mouth of the Düna and lacked a harbor suited for docking the Geman cogs. Instead it was the settlement the locals called *rija*, with its natural harbor and superior location, that became the base from which Albert chose to conduct his business.

Several times that summer Albert's men returned to the Riga settlement, where they spoke with tribal elders and closely inspected the harbor. To thwart any potential competition, Albert dispatched the monk Theodoric to Rome to plead his case before the pope. The Cistercian's efforts on behalf of his superior were indispensable, for he had earlier worked with Meinhard to convert the Livs of Treiden (Latv. Turaida), a settlement located northeast of Riga. Theodoric of Treiden would become Albert's main troubleshooter: not only did he get Innocent III to grant Albert permission to preach crusade (this would be necessary when the bishop returned to Saxony in the fall to recruit crusaders), he also persuaded the pope to excommunicate any Christian merchant who used the older port at Daugmale, located upstream from Riga. Instead the traders were to use the new harbor that was to be built at Riga. The document (lost long ago) that Innocent sent back with Theodoric provided the juridical basis for the city that the bishop began to build in 1201.

Two Legends of Old Riga

There are many old legends concerning the founding of Riga, and while some have a basis in fact, others are a bit more fanciful. One such legend entertains the notion that Albert established the city on the very spot where his predecessor Berthold had been killed in battle with the Livs in the summer of 1198. This is most certainly wrong, for the battle most likely took place in the vicinity of Kube Hill, a sand dune located about a kilometer from the modest settlements that Livonian and

Couronian fishermen, craftsmen, and traders had established on the right bank of the Düna River.[17] It was on the plain near the river that German Riga was to be built. Desiring a piece of land for the bishopric close to the native settlements, the bishop invited the Liv leaders—who we might imagine were by now convinced of the Germans' superior power and perhaps of their potential as allies against their rivals—to a feast, where he made them an offer they could not refuse. The details of Albert's proposal are unknown, but to be certain the natives would not renege, he took the sons of thirty of the Livs' leaders as hostages on his return trip to Germany, leaving behind a force sufficient to protect the German settlement.[18] Among the Livs who surrendered a son to the Germans that day was Caupo, the chieftain of Treiden/Turaida. Baptized nearly a decade earlier, probably by Theodoric, Caupo would become one of Albert's most reliable allies among the Livs.

A second legend concerning the founding of Riga proposes that Albert swindled the Livs by asking only for a plot of land that could be covered with an ox hide, to which the Livs are supposed to have readily agreed. The story goes that the Germans then proceeded to cut the ox hide in thin strips that they used to encircle the lands they claimed as their own.[19] While this bit of lore lacks any written evidence to support it, its apocryphal nature illustrates a deeper truth: the Germans, led by Bishop Albert, intended to secure the territory for themselves by whatever means necessary. This could be accomplished only if the surrounding areas were secured as well. The local tribes—the Livs and their neighbors—would have to be converted, even if this required the use of raw force; their surviving elites would have to be transformed into European-style nobles bound by the lord-vassal relationships common in western Europe; taxes and tithes would have to be collected; and the surrounding countryside would have to be parceled out as fiefs for the purpose of constructing a self-sustaining ecclesiastical territory in Livonia that would make the bishop less dependent on the crusader levies that brought him back to Germany nearly every year.

That the city survived beyond its first decade is a testament to the skills of its founder and lord, for it was under Bishop Albert of Buxhoeveden that the conquest of Livonia, first achieved by military force, became institutionalized.

Island of Peace

Bishop Albert's Riga was the first population center in the eastern Baltic that can truly be called a city. Its official founding as an enclosed German city—one that was built next to and then incorporated the older, non-German settlements—occurred during a wave of urbanization in Europe that swelled during the High Middle Ages. Few European cities of the time were large by modern standards. Even as the declining metropolis of Constantinople yielded its primacy to Paris, these were the only European cities whose populations exceeded 200,000. Indeed, as late as 1330, before the Black Death killed one-third of Europe's inhabitants, only nine European towns had more than 25,000 inhabitants, and of the northern German cities only Cologne and Lübeck could claim that many.[20] Riga was small even by these modest standards: a full century after Bishop Albert's death in 1229, his city on the Düna was home to no more than 6,000 or 7,000 people; as such it was at best the fiftieth largest city in Europe.[21] Yet Riga was easily the largest urban center in the whole of the eastern Baltic littoral, its founding the result of the same socioeconomic forces and personal and institutional ambitions that breathed life into a series of commercial centers in the north, notably Lübeck, Visby, and later Danzig (Pol. Gdańsk) and Reval (Est. Tallinn).

It is in this northern-European context that Riga's early history is best appreciated, for it is the story of a new settlement, established under the auspices of a feudal lord, that became a town endowed with various rights and privileges. Attracting craftsmen and merchants from Germany to settle behind its walls, Riga emerged as a self-governing polity whose administration was in the hands of its leading burghers. A refuge for Livs and Letts, as well as for some Lithuanians and a handful of Couronians and Estonians, Riga was above all a *German* city in appearance, purpose, and character. But the new city was far from Germany and its ample reserves of craftsmen and builders. The labors of such men, imported from Visby, Saxony, and elsewhere at a time when Riga's permanence was far from assured, gave the city its earliest form.

The contours of Albert's city were shaped by the two rivers that nearly encircled it and then by a brick-and-limestone wall that encased it completely. The Riga rivulet's widening near the point where it emptied into the Düna, in the area of present-day January 13th Street (13. janvāra iela), rendered it a natural port, known as Lake Riga, that measured fifty meters wide and three to five meters deep—just deep enough to allow the large merchant ships, the German cogs, to dock while their cargo was off-loaded.

If the bulge in the Riga River was the location of the country's first harbor, then it was the mighty Düna that provided the city of Riga with a broad embankment along which the city established its first hospital (St. George's) at the precise spot where the (third) Riga Castle is located today. Eventually it was on the Düna embankment that Rigans would build a second (and main) harbor to accommodate the larger ships of the fourteenth century.

Having decided to build his city at Riga, Albert now had little use for the island stations the Germans had already established at Üxküll and Kirchholm, so he invested them to a pair of minor nobles in exchange for their service. The bishop would concentrate on building his city in Riga. Merchants and craftsmen, whom Albert invited to settle there permanently, soon began to erect residential houses and farm buildings close to those of the Livs. Among the most important structures erected during the city's early years was a church (the Riga Cathedral or Dome) dedicated to the Virgin Mary, to whom Albert, having appointed his brother Engelbert as its prior, also dedicated the whole of Livonia. Such a symbol, intended to underline that it was God's will that the pagan lands should become part of Christendom, was liberally used by Albert and his successors to entice potential crusaders to sail to Livonia.

Difficult even in the best conditions, Albert's mission was made all the more arduous by the ongoing struggle between the rival Hohenstaufen and Welf families for control of the Holy Roman Empire. With Germany in a state of civil war, and thus in need of fighting men, and with the real Jerusalem beckoning, the recruitment of soldiers was perhaps Albert's greatest challenge. It was, we may be certain, his most time-consuming one, for nearly every spring the bishop would return to Germany to preach crusade and line up recruits, whom he persuaded to stay for a year in Livonia in exchange for indulgences. It was during one of Albert's absences, in 1202, that his main assistant, Theodoric, established a permanent military order to protect the Christian settlement and to assist in the conversion of the heathen—a mission that was quite different from the crusades' initial function of recapturing the Holy Places in the Levant. Within a few years, the Order of Swordbrothers (Fratres militiæ Christi Livoniae) became the most important force in Livonia after the Church itself.

Even if Theodoric's efforts were sanctioned by both the pope and Bishop Albert, who understandably wished to avoid sharing Livonia with any of the existing military orders, the creation of a crusading order was fraught with potential problems. Not least of these was the question of who would actually be in charge of the operation: would it be the bishop, or would it be the master of the order? To set matters straight at the outset, Albert insisted that the master render him an oath of loyalty.[22] The order, for its part, insisted on receiving one-third of all conquered lands. As more and more territory fell into the hands of Livonia's conquerors, and as it became ever more clear that the order's needs would not be met by the original arrangement (concluded five years after its founding), succeeding masters concluded that the deal with the region's supreme religious authority would have to be renegotiated in favor of the knights. Order castles soon dominated the Düna River valley.

In Riga the Order of Swordbrothers built its castle, initially its main base in Livonia, near the right bank of the Riga River, where it stood for nearly a century until its destruction in a war between the Livonian Order (which supplanted the Swordbrothers in 1237) and the citizens of Riga. Featuring a large conference hall and a chapel where religious services were held, the original Order Castle (Ordenschloss) was protected by the city wall that ran alongside the two rivers that defined the city's original contours. It was on the right bank of the Rigebach that the Germans built all their main structures during the city's earliest years. In addition to the first Riga Cathedral (Dome, St. Mary's), completed by 1206, the bishop also had his own castle, located adjacent to the Order Castle where St. John's Yard (Konventa sēta) is today. These were among the first masonry structures in Riga, built from dolomite and limestone that were hauled in from islands further upstream. Thus, historical sources often refer to the Order Castle in Riga as the Castle of St. George (Jürgenshof) or the White Stone Castle.[23] The Order Castle shared one of its walls with the aforementioned Bishop's Castle, which had two stories and a large yard that was delimited by its own castle wall. Like the Order Castle, the Bishop's Castle, equipped with a tower that was located near present-day Kalēju iela (Blacksmiths' Street), played an important role in the city's defense system. That system began to take shape during the city's earliest years, and it was put to its most serious test in 1210, when Couronian warriors besieged the city for several weeks.

By this time Riga had begun to assume the form it would maintain throughout the Middle Ages. That shape was defined by the city wall that ran parallel to the arching Rigebach and that soon stretched along the Düna embankment. Built of bolderstone, limestone, and bricks made in the city's kilns, the city wall, an early version of which was completed as early as 1207, made Riga into an island, entry into which could be secured only by passing through one of its gates. Built to protect its residents from outsiders, the defensive wall was one of the most striking characteristics of the medieval city. "Esthetically it made a clean break between city and countryside," historian Lewis Mumford observed of the ancient walled cities, "while socially it emphasized the difference between the insider and outsider, between the open field, subject to the depredations of wild animals, nomadic robbers, invading armies, and the fully enclosed city where one could work and sleep with a sense of utter security, even in times of military peril."[24] Thus, on the one hand, the city wall acted as a container that offered those inside it protection from outsiders; on the other hand, a completed wall acted as a magnet that drew people with skills to the city. "By means of the wall, a little town, once helpless before even a small armed force, would become a stronghold. People would flock to such islands of peace."[25]

Riga and the Crusades

Riga's earliest years were far from peaceful and secure, for the northern Jerusalem was a place to which crusaders arrived from Germany and Scandinavia to do battle with the heathen. Surrounded by snow and ice and isolated by storms, the Christian community of Riga barely survived its first winters. With the city's security dependent upon the annual influx of crusaders (and upon the uncertain loyalty of the converted local tribes), Riga's residents lived in a heightened state of vulnerability even after the construction of its earliest castles and walls. While the nearby Livish tribes were quickly subdued and converted as the crusaders established fortified positions along the Düna (Daugava) River and the Treider Aa (Gauja), the threat of a pagan invasion was never far from the minds of Rigans, even decades after the founding of their city. Indeed, the Lithuanian raids were so devastating that the sudden appearance of these warriors from the south terrorized the other pagan tribes—the Livs, Letts, and Estonians—no less than they did the Christians of Riga. The unknown author of *The Livonian Rhymed Chronicle*, written for (and probably by) the knights in Middle High German and especially important for the years 1267–1290, recounted with horror the trail of destruction emblazoned by Lithuanian warriors during a foray into Estonia:

> I am convinced the devil was leading them, for no army ever moved so arrogantly into foreign lands as did this one. They moved through Semgallia and that had never happened before. May it never happen again! They crossed the sea at Swurben, on the southern tip of Ösel,[26] which we called Easter Cape, and Perkune, their idol, made it freeze harder than it ever had before. They were daring and unrestrained. They ravaged through Ösel, robbing and burning and heeding no cries for mercy. Then they ravaged Moon, the nearby island in the sea, and as they swept across this land they were confident that no powerful forces were nearby. They turned toward Wiek[27] and covered both roads and paths with blood. The people profited little from their coming, for whenever they came they taught the people how to die—men and women, whoever could not escape them. Fearing no man's threat, they rode freely into the land of Jerwen,[28] and no one there was so powerful but that he wished himself elsewhere. The land was good and spacious and yet so lacking in forests that none of the people could escape them. They killed many noble men, who would have defended themselves well if their luck had not run out. . . . On their way home they ravaged Nurmegunde,[29] cutting down everyone they could catch, hacking many deep wounds with a free hand. They ravaged through Saccalia[30] toward the Letts.[31]

Even if we indulge the author's exaggerated contrast between the savagery of the pagans (whose feats in battle were sometimes heroic) and the heroism of the knights (who frequently behaved savagely), *The Livonian Rhymed Chronicle* conveys the dread that many early Rigans must also have felt when it came to the unexpected appearance of outsiders, especially the Lithuanians. At a time when crusading states were being established in Prussia by land and in Livonia by sea, the Lithuanian lands situated between them were protected by a forested and marshy terrain that proved impenetrable to the Christian warriors and an ideal refuge for pagan raiding parties. Better organized than the Latvian and Livonian tribes, the Lithuanians united under a ruthless tribal leader (or king) named Mindaugas (r. 1236–1263) and were spared the fate of the other pagans who succumbed to the Germanic conquest. It is no exaggeration to say that they were considered a menace by all, whether Christian or pagan.

Lithuanians were not the only threat to Albert's struggling Christian outpost: trouble could also come to Riga from Couronian raiders, rebellious Livs, or opportunistic Russians, who were still collecting tithes from tribes living north and east of the Düna. One also could not be sure about the Danes, for their kings entertained ambitions from time to time of carving out their own Baltic empire. (As discussed below, the Danes would establish a beachhead in Estonia with their founding of Reval in 1219.)

Against all these dangers Albert's holy city required protection, for only a well-defended city could provide the base that the crusaders needed to project their power into the Livonian countryside. That Albert's crusade coincided with the Fourth Crusade to the Holy Land (1202–1204) is hardly coincidental: both were products of the same nexus of power, opportunity, and greed. Pronounced by Pope Innocent III in 1202, the Fourth Crusade was the most ambitious yet conceived—or it became such when as its goal of conquering Muslim-controlled Jerusalem was diverted into an effort to unite Christendom by establishing papal control over the Byzantine Empire. No crusade did more to sully the reputation of Latin Christians, for it was the Fourth Crusade that revealed the nakedly imperialistic nature of the entire crusading enterprise. Even if the Baltic crusaders encountered no great cities like Constantinople to loot, pillage, and burn as the "Franks" had done in 1204, their holy war against the pagans was no less violent than the campaigns in Byzantium and the Levant. Like the knights who disembarked from Venice and went on to create their own Latin Empire (1204–1261) centered in Constantinople, the men who sailed to the Baltic were satisfied with nothing less than the conquest of territory. Thus did Albert unwittingly become midwife to the first successful "order state" (*Ordenstaat*)—a political lordship under the dominion of a crusading order.[32]

For thirty-five years the Order of Swordbrothers provided year-round defense of the colony while leading the charge into the Latvian and Estonian lands. While Albert made his annual journeys to Germany each spring in order to return to Riga in the fall with new recruits (who in turn would again depart for Germany after completing their year of service), it was the Swordbrothers who provided the city with its only permanent force.[33] Such men, observing the rule of the Knights Templar, taking vows of poverty, chastity, obedience, and committed to war against unbelievers, "were hardly the comfortable, pleasure-seeking nobles one might imagine," writes historian William Urban; on the contrary, it was from the poorer *ministeriales* (service) class that the bulk of the German knighthood emerged.[34] An independent religious organization that recognized no authority but that of the pope, the order consisted of knightly members who fought, a handful of priests who acted as their spiritual advisers, a servant class consisting of trained mounted warriors and infantrymen, and another category of servants that included cooks, bakers, and other helpers. The head of the order was the master:

elected by the order members for life, the order master alone took an oath of loyalty to the bishop of Riga.[35] Tension was built into this relationship from the very beginning.

In their early years the Swordbrothers were weak and few in number: at any given moment the quantity of soldiers that Albert recruited himself, as many as one thousand mailed warriors, vastly outnumbered the few dozen Swordbrothers (and their hundreds of servants) in Livonia. Yet this force of aggressive and heavily armed knights proved decisive in the battles of the early thirteenth century, and their growing thirst for territory and power clashed with the ambitions of the third bishop of Livonia.

Establishing Dominance

While Albert's achievements have been amply chronicled, they owed much to the efforts of his chief deputy, the monk Theodoric of Treiden. Not only did Theodoric, with Albert's blessing, create the Order of Swordbrothers, he also built on the bishop's orders a monastery located about four kilometers from the mouth of the Düna near its right bank.[36] Soon converted into a fortress, the monastery at Dünamünde was headed by none other than Theodoric, whom Albert appointed its abbot in 1204.

It was also Theodoric who Albert entrusted to speak to the pope on his behalf on no fewer than three different occasions. As a demonstration of the mission's success in converting the natives, on his third trip to Rome in 1203 the monk brought with him Caupo, the Livonian lord of Treiden (Turaida), where Theodoric had done some of his early missionary work and must have lived under his protection.[37] One can hardly imagine Caupo's bewilderment while traveling through Germany with Theodoric on their way to Rome to see the Holy Pontiff. After all, the chieftain had never been on a large boat and had never seen a city of any kind. Indeed, for a man who was used to living in wooden fortresses and who knew almost nothing of stone castles and churches, the splendor of Rome—or what was left of its splendor in the early thirteenth century—must have made quite an impression on him. And then to have an audience with the most powerful man in Europe while being lavished with gifts (including one hundred pieces of gold) must have confirmed his own sense of importance and likely reinforced his loyalty to Christianity and to the Germans.[38] Given Albert's strategy of trying to win over the indigenous chieftains for the purpose of transforming them into European-style vassals, a prize such as Caupo was without a doubt of great significance.

Having reported the results of the first crusades against the Livs while presenting one of their chieftains as a token of the campaigns' success, Theodoric returned with Caupo to Riga in September 1204 aboard a fleet of three ships carrying hundreds of military recruits. When they disembarked, the contingent found the newly-built city in crisis, for the Livs of Aizkraukle (Ger. Ascheraden), teaming up with a group of Samogitians (a Lithuanian tribe), had just tried, and failed, to drive the Germans out. Had it not been for the arrival of these new soldiers—or had the crusaders simply decided to sail away—Albert's beachhead in Riga might have been lost. Indeed, since the annual departure for Germany of Riga's crusaders would have left the city nearly defenseless (if only temporarily), the arrival of Theodoric's reinforcements likely saved the entire enterprise.[39]

Even with Albert's annual levy of crusaders arriving in Riga to do their year of service, in these early years the fledgling town was far from secure. Henry's chronicle mentions a serious food shortage in 1205, when Riga was saved by a priest named Daniel who arrived from Gotland with two cogs loaded with food and supplies.[40] The chronicle also recounts the many attacks on Riga during its first years, including the efforts by Jersika's King Visvaldis (Vsevolod), an Orthodox ruler who repeatedly tried to storm the German settlement in the hopes of gaining control over the Düna. His attack of 1209 ending in failure, Visvaldis saved his position by agreeing to convert to Latin Christianity and surrender two-thirds of his domain; in this way he became the bishop's vassal.[41] Likewise did Albert secure the submission of Tālava in eastern Latvia. Ceding territory and agreeing to renounce Orthodoxy in favor of Catholicism, King Tālivaldis paid for his modest holdings by rendering the bishop an annual tribute.[42]

Whether born of convenience or of compulsion, such alliances were predictably tenuous, for the use of force rarely inspires trust. A telling example of the complicated nature of the relationships between the local tribal leaders and the German invaders is the story of Vetseke, lord of Koknese (Ger. Kokenhusen), a castle mound located on the Düna some one hundred kilometers upstream from Riga. Russian sources refer to him as Vyachko and assert that he was a descendant of the royal line that goes back to Rurik, the founder of the Rus' state. Henry's chronicle suggests that Vetseke was a Livonian who had converted to Orthodoxy. Whatever his background, what is clear is that he was a vassal of the prince of Polotsk and that he tried to make himself an independent ruler in Livonia at a time when the Germans were becoming entrenched in the region. Among Vetseke's most pressing concerns were the Lithuanian raiders who terrorized the entire region up to Estonia. In 1207 the chieftain promised Bishop Albert half his lands in exchange for the Germans' help in fending off the Lithuanian threat—an arrangement that effectively made the chieftain one of the bishop's vassals. The following year, however, Vetseke quarreled with a German knight named Daniel, to whom Albert had enfeoffed the district of Lennewarden.

For a time it seemed as if the bishop had resolved the matter by providing the chieftain with a small contingent of knights and masons to help him strengthen his fort at Koknese. But Vetseke soon became wary of the Germans, now seeing them as a challenge to his authority in the region. Waiting until Albert and the three hundred soldiers who had completed their year of service boarded their ships for Dünamünde, from whence they would sail to Germany, Vetseke turned on the Germans entrusted to his care, attacking them as they quarried rocks for his fort. The message he sent to Rigans—seventeen corpses passed the city as they floated down the Düna—was unmistakable. While the lord of Koknese turned to Vladimir of Polotsk for help, Bishop Albert, delayed by a contrary wind at Dünamünde, received timely news of the planned attack and was able to convince his soldiers to renew their commitment and return to Riga to fight. Probably aware that still more crusaders were arriving to Riga, the Rus' abandoned their plan to attack the city and instead withdrew. Burning their fort at Koknese in retreat, and then doing the same to the Lettish fort at Jersika two years later, the Rus' soon departed Latgallia for good.[43]

Setting aside for the moment the frustrated ambitions of the Rus' (who collected tithes in eastern Latvia but who alone never really constituted a threat to Riga) and the terror evoked by Lithuanian raiders (who did), the most immediate danger facing the German settlement at Riga during these early years was rebellion by the local Livs, for the conversions of the Düna Livs to Christianity were always tactical and tenuous, and the Rigans could never be certain that arrangements for peace would hold for very long. Indeed, the rebellion instigated by Ako, a leader of the Düna Livs, was among the bloodiest and most consequential of these episodes.

Taking advantage of the annual departure of Albert's pilgrims, Ako of Kirchholm (Salaspils) attempted in the spring of 1206 to enlist the support of the Livs of Treiden to drive the Germans out of Riga. Ako also tried to recruit some of the neighboring Letts, but they refrained from joining the insurrection. According to the chronicler Henry, Ako and the other elders of Kirchholm had arranged a meeting at which they first tried to compel the Liv converts to renounce Christianity. The traitors' "feet were bound by ropes and they were cut through the middle. They afflicted them with the most cruel punishments, tore out their viscera and cut off their arms and legs." Then, "when this had been done, the Livonians agreed to come together as a group from all parts of their land to occupy the fort of Holm [Kirchholm]. . . . From it they were to overcome the people of Riga, who were not very numerous at the moment, and destroy Riga."[44] Rather than wait for the rebellious Livs to arrive, the Germans, together with loyal native allies in Riga, decided to take the battle to Kirchholm, where they quickly overcame the enemy. Thus did Ako's plan end in failure, his severed head sent to the bishop as a sign of the Germans' victory over the rebellious Livs.[45]

The Germans' revenge was swift and merciless, for the Rigans now called upon the forces of Viestards (or Viesturs), the Semigallian king. Having enlisted German help to defeat a Lithuanian raiding party in 1205, Viestards was now summoned to join the crusaders in taking retribution upon the Livs of Treiden. Designated commander of the German forces, the Livonian chieftain and his three thousand men destroyed Treiden, which the Semigallians thoroughly plundered before returning home with their booty. In defeat the Livs of Treiden were forced to submit to the Germans' overlordship and accept a Catholic priest. Mass conversions followed, as well as the construction of suitable houses of worship.[46]

Perhaps it was inevitable that the relationship between Viestards and his German allies would take a turn for the worse. Having secured Riga's help in another engagement with their traditional Lithuanian enemies, the Semigallians then outraged the Germans by fleeing the scene, leaving the latter to take on the entire weight of the battle. Survivors of the ordeal decamped to Riga, whose leaders, Henry reported, "decided that henceforth they ought not to confide in the multitude of the pagans nor ought they to fight with pagans against other pagans, but that they ought, hoping in the Lord, to proceed boldly against all the tribes with the now baptized Livonians and Letts."[47] The crusaders' establishment of a garrison in 1219 at the Semigallian hill fort at Mežotne (Ger. Mesothen) ruptured the relationship for good. Now that Albert had broken their treaty of friendship, Viestards allied with the Samogitians to fight the Germans. Appearing in Riga in 1225 to meet with the papal legate William of Modena, the chieftain accepted the Christians' right to preach their faith in his land but refused to become the bishop's vassal. More confrontations with the order followed, but these were inconclusive. When Viestards died in 1230, the Germans progressively seized his lands for themselves.

To many modern-day residents of Riga, the word "Viestards" signifies little more than the name of a quiet park (Viestura dārzs) located just north of Riga's Old Town; but to the crafters of the Latvian grand narrative—historians, playwrights, and poets of the nineteenth and twentieth centuries—the story of Viestards is loaded with historical significance. Even more than furnishing the story of Latvia's conquest with its earliest heroes and villains, the shards of historical evidence we have about the deeds of Visvaldis, Vetseke, Viestards, Ako, and Caupo (to this list we may add Imants, whose lance took the life of Bishop Berthold in 1198) reveal significant clues concerning the complicated nature of the Germans' relationship with the natives, and of the natives' no less complicated relationships with each other. Indeed, one must first recognize the obvious fact that the indigenous peoples of this region had their own patterns of conflict and cooperation long before the arrival of the Germans. It is likely that the appearance in the region of the Rus' and then the Germans and other Christians intensified such patterns among the pagans, or at the very least complicated them. "The enemy of my enemy is my friend" (for the time being) was the rule for all who were subsumed in the struggles of this time and place, for the clash of cultures was also a clash of interests.

Yet certain patterns were consistent as the Germans established their mastery over the region: in defeat the indigenous peoples were compelled to accept

German domination and convert, if only superficially, to Christianity, their surviving elites co-opted into the establishment imported by their new masters. First it was the neighboring Livs, and soon afterward the chiefs of the defeated Latgallian tribes were assimilated into the German-dominated power structure—that is, when they were not violently dispossessed of their lands and property. In this way the Germans made themselves masters not only of Livonia but later, by the 1230s, of Estonia and Prussia as well.

The possession of superior technology, as well as the annual influx of fighting men, certainly added to the crusaders' advantage, but the Germans possessed another asset as well: membership in a universal spiritual community. Nobody will ever know the exact reasons for Caupo's conversion or of those who followed him, but are we to dismiss the possibility that some of them might have found something appealing about the Christian god?

It was in this uncertain environment that the city of Riga was originally forged. If some of the indigenous peoples welcomed the Germans for their goods and their advanced technology, and even if some embraced the invaders' universal and loving god, the remainder had little choice but to accept the Germans' permanence, or at least to recognize their elevated position in the local power structure.

During 1207, concurrent with the baptism of the Livs and the building of the city's first walls, the Germans began to delimit parishes and build churches while also working out arrangements among themselves. Meanwhile, Albert, still needing external political backing and financial support, journeyed across Germany to the court of the Holy Roman emperor, Philip of Swabia. Arriving in February, the bishop made a gift of the conquered lands, receiving them back from the emperor as a fief. In addition, Philip, who was to fall victim to assassination the following year, promised the bishop an annual subsidy of one hundred silver marks; but, as the chronicler Henry remarked, "If only one could be rich through promises!"[48] While no money ever came, Livonia was now formally a province of the Holy Roman Empire—a German march at the eastern edge of the Baltic Sea.[49] Now an imperial prince-bishop, the emperor's vassal in temporal affairs, Albert returned to his church later that year with a sizable army and in a much stronger position.[50] Imposing heavy penalties on rebellious tribes and promising lenient treatment for loyal allies, the bishop continued to institutionalize his control over the region.

It was also in 1207 that the Swordbrothers, aspiring to the power and prestige enjoyed by the crusading orders in the Holy Land, asked the bishop for one-third of all conquests. After all, in order to increase their numbers and provide the Christian communities with year-round protection, they would need more land and rent-paying peasants to work it. Dividing the conquered territories into three parts, the region's new overlords agreed that Bishop Albert was to get the first choice (he took Caupo's former territory around Treiden) and the third, while the Swordbrothers were to receive the second part of the land already conquered, agreeing to pay the bishop "a quarter of the tithes in their areas, in recognition of their obedience to him."[51] Thus did Albert make the order the second territorial lord in Livonia, after the bishop himself, in the process introducing to the territory the feudal customs of western Europe.

Then, of course, there was the matter of carrying out the spiritual functions of his office. To help him lead the Livonian church, Albert relied on his half brother Engelbert, who left the monastery at Neumünster to become the prior of St. Mary's (the Dome) in Riga. Another brother, Rothmar, formerly a priest at Segeberg, joined the Order of Swordbrothers. In all, five of Albert's brothers and half brothers played a role in the German conquest, colonization, and administration of Livonia and Estonia.

As the conquests continued, local elites—at least those who survived the onslaught—were co-opted into the new power structure. First the crusaders established their dominion over the river valleys of the Düna and the Treider Aa (Latv. Gauja), building stone castles (these functioned as watch posts and assembly points for the armies) and demanding payments from the indigenous peoples in the form of labor, grains such as rye and barley, and other produce. Within a few years they mastered the art of fighting during the winter. Indeed, after 1207 winter campaigns became the norm: this is when the crusaders attacked, taking advantage of the frozen rivers and marshes as well as the denuded forests' inability to provide cover for raiders and fugitives. Native counterattacks followed in the summer, and soon enough another tribe or region was conquered. With the arrival of hundreds of new crusaders each year—mostly Germans, but also Danes, Swedes, Poles, and Frisians—the crusaders had the advantage of being able to replenish their forces, leaving the indigenous peoples with little choice but to submit or fight for what increasingly seemed to be a lost cause. Some, like the Livs, the Latgallians, and the Selonians, surrendered early to German demands and accepted the Christian faith; others, too distant from the order castles to be easily defeated, remained independent and pagan for decades. (Only in 1267 was Courland pacified, while the Semigallians held out until 1290.)[52]

For early Riga's modest community of German settlers, the prospect of a pagan attack must have been terrifying indeed. Consider, for example, the events of 1210, when Riga was nearly overcome by a combined assault of enemy forces. The confrontation began with a sea battle off the coast of Gotland, in which the Couronians, recalled in the Scandinavian sagas for their love of plunder, fought a contingent of crusaders, thirty of whom lost their lives.[53] As news of the Couronian victory spread, other pagans were emboldened to join the assault, including the Livs of Treiden as well as warriors from Semigallia, Lithuania, and Estonia. For two weeks that summer, the city, weakened by the absence of Albert and the soldiers who had completed their year of service and departed for Germany, was under siege. Outside the town walls Rigans and knights fought off their attackers with the aid of Caupo's forces and the Letts of Tālava (Ger. Tholowa), located northeast of Riga. On July 13, later celebrated in the Orthodox world (and Latvia) as St. Margaret's Day, the town was finally liberated as

> Caupo came into the city with all his friends and relatives and faithful Livonians. At dawn, Conrad of Uexküll came into the field next to the city with the Livonian leaders. As they made a great show with their horses and arms, all those in the city came out to greet them and great joy was manifested among them. They marched forward to meet the Kurs and, prepared either to die bravely or win, called upon them to fight.[54]

Unable to breach the city's modest defenses, the Couronians (Kurs) and their allies were compelled to retreat, at least for the time being.[55] Russians, too, were involved in the attack, but the Rigans, aware that they were surrounded by enemies, decided to pursue an understanding with Pskov in the hope that this would open a road for Rigan merchants into the Russian lands. A "perpetual peace" with the Rus' prince was at last achieved in 1212, with Albert in attendance. "[A]ll rejoiced," according to Henry of Livonia, "since they could now wage war against the Esthonians and the other pagans. And this they did."[56]

To ensure that his bishopric got its share of the conquered territories, in 1211 Albert appointed as bishop of Estonia his chief assistant Theodoric of Treiden, who clarified a new arrangement that would give each of the bishops and the order equal shares of all new conquests. In reality, however, the conquest of Estonia, where the Rus' continued to collect tribute and even converted some of the natives, did not begin in earnest for several more years. This next stage of the Baltic crusade was to be spearheaded by Denmark, a country that was at the peak of its power and once again eager to make good on its earlier claims in the region.

Personally leading the drive into Estonia was King Valdemar II (r. 1202–1241), whose 1,500 ships landed on Estonia's north coast in June of 1219. The Danes quickly seized the coastal hill fort upon which they would establish Reval (Est. Tallinn) as well as the northern Estonian ports; this meant they also controlled the flow of crusaders into the area. That Valdemar also controlled Lübeck, the crusaders' main point of departure and an important buyer of Rigan goods, gave him considerable leverage over the bishop of Riga, although it was Albert who, fearing Novgorod's ambitions in Estonia, had lobbied the Danish king to launch an invasion in the first place. With Lübeck now closed to crusaders heading to Livonia, in 1221 the bishop decided to submit, ceding his Estonian territories to the Danish king.[57]

Although the Swordbrothers were party to the jurisdictional quarrels over northern Estonia, their main efforts were concentrated on the southern interior. It was here, at the southern end of Lake Peipus, that the crusaders in 1224 established the city of Dorpat (Est. Tartu) on the site of an ancient Estonian settlement that had earlier paid tribute to the Rus'. Like Reval (Tallinn), which became a base for operations and an assembling point for German merchants traveling to Novgorod, and hence Riga's rival for the Scandinavian-Russian trade, Dorpat also became a commercial center of some importance in addition to being the seat of a bishopric. Its first prince-bishop was Hermann of Buxhoeveden, another brother upon whom Albert relied to administer his growing northeastern enterprise. During the same years that Estonia's tribes submitted to (and then rebelled against) the new authorities, the men and women who lived behind Riga's walls were building what was to become one of great trading cities of the eastern Baltic.

Albert's Riga

If early Riga was a relative island of peace, its burghers enjoying a modicum of security behind the city's brick-and-limestone walls, it was also a town in flux, for Riga's political arrangements and even its appearance evolved as its population swelled with Germans, Livs, and Latvians. Before the emergence of a town council in the 1220s (see chapter 4), Riga's administration was entirely in the hands of Bishop Albert and his officials. The fact that the city's economic center—the old market square—was located next to the Bishop's Yard attests to the unusual amount of power that the bishop, who was also able to summon Rigans to war, wielded in his city on the Düna.

It is difficult to know exactly what Riga looked like in its earliest years, as the city's appearance changed substantially during its first century. A great fire in 1215 destroyed most of the original settlement, and a second one in 1293 burned down even more of what had become by this time a much larger city that encompassed the entire peninsula formed by the Düna and Riga rivers. Each of these catastrophes afforded the bishops, the order, and Riga's citizens opportunities to start anew and reshape the city to meet its needs for defense, spiritual edification, and commerce. Thus, during these decades there were two versions of St. Mary's (Dome Cathedral), two St. Peter's churches, two Order Castles and two castles belonging to the bishop; in addition there were two Hospitals of the Holy Spirit, two market places, and two town halls.[58] Owing to the new regulations put in place in the wake of the fire of 1293, the wooden town of the early thirteenth century became a city of brick and stone during the fourteenth century, surrounded by a thick wall punctuated by more than twenty defensive towers.

Archaeological excavations reveal an early version of Riga that was little more than a modest cluster of residential and commercial structures, homes, and warehouses. The town's focal points were its castles, its houses of worship, and its main square, where citizens convened to buy and sell a range of goods and to share the news of the day. Several of the sites bearing these names still exist today; however, with the exception of St. Peter's, which has been rebuilt several times over the centuries, none has remained at its original location. Even the city's main port—originally located at the place residents called "Lake Riga," the bulge in the Rigebach that made it a natural harbor—was relocated by the end of the thirteenth century, for the old harbor had become too shallow to accommodate the increasingly large ships that docked at Riga.

Religious and administrative buildings comprised the core of the medieval city, rebuilt and expanded after the fire of 1215 to fill the whole space between the Rigebach and the Düna. It was not long before the steeples of three churches—St. Mary's and the churches dedicated to St. Peter and St. James—came to dominate the Riga skyline, beckoning merchants to the thriving port. Yet the Gothic and Romanesque churches that bear those names today look very different from these early incarnations, sharing little more than the original foundations—and not always even that. Today's Dome is a case in point: the original wooden building that was completed in 1206 burned to the ground in the fire of 1215, and with its demise went the bell that was rung to alert the townspeople in times of war. "The people," remarked the chronicler Henry, "were especially sad at the loss of the sweet-sounding war bell and at the damage done in the city. Another bell, larger than the first one, was cast."[59]

The new St. Mary's, under construction at the time of the fire, was an ambitious undertaking for such a small town. Consecrated four years earlier, the structure was built on the site of a Couronian burial ground just outside the original city walls, not far from the Düna embankment. As the settlement began to sprawl outside the old city wall, the bishop hastened to obtain this area from the Livs for the new cathedral's resident chapter.[60] Intended as a church that would impress upon both Rigans and the city's visitors the power of the bishop, the cathedral project, originally designed as a hall church similar in layout to the Lübeck Cathedral begun in 1173, was so big that most of Riga's stonemasons, supervised by builders from Gotland and Germany, were employed in its construction.[61] To its original Romanesque design and motifs later architects added other elements, including a tall tower that was built in the fifteenth century and replaced in 1776 with a more squattish one after yet another lightning strike. Over the centuries these modifications radically transformed the cathedral's appearance. While a modern visitor might think that the building has sunk into the ground, at the time of its construction the Dome stood on what was then a slight elevation. Few sites in the city serve as better reminders of the fact that present-day Riga, built and rebuilt over the centuries, sits on a cultural layer that is three to six meters deep.[62]

While the church that Albert dedicated to the Virgin was built for his bishopric, St. Peter's was built on a small elevation as a church for the townspeople, whose poor were buried in a cemetery that formed a semicircle around it. Completed sometime before 1209, and undamaged by the fire of that year, the original masonry structure was a more modest edifice than the great steepled building that has featured so prominently in the city's silhouette for the past six hundred years. Built as a small hall church with a freestanding bell tower, St. Peter's was located in a central square that was connected to the port of Riga by the Sand Road—the broadest and most important road in Riga—and at the time the only one that led into the city. A popular legend (which also happens to be true) holds that the bell tower of St. Peter's was manned by watchmen who were paid by the Riga Town Council to stand guard night and day, sounding their horns at the appearance of danger. One of the tower's two bells rang each day to signal the start of a new working day; the other "long" bell was used only for religious ceremonies. From almost the beginning, St. Peter's Church has been the beating heart of Riga's architectural and civic identity.

A third house of worship—the smallest of the three great churches showcased in Riga's remarkable skyline—was dedicated to St. James. Today this Roman Catholic cathedral (since 1923) is known as St. Jacob's, as the name for James and Jacob is the same in Latvian. First mentioned in historical sources in 1226, it was likely built as early as 1210 as a rural parish church, then located just outside the city walls.[63] Eventually St. Jacob's came to serve the city's Latvian and Livonian residents. During the Reformation, it became the first church in the city where sermons could be heard in the Latvian language.

It was in the area near St. Jacob's, annexed during Riga's mid-century expansion, that the city's "Russian" merchant community lived. Built sometime after 1212 and originally surrounded by a Russian graveyard, the first Church of St. Nicholas, which served Riga's small Orthodox population, was demolished during the war at the end of the century between the town and the Livonian Order.[64] Before the schism between the Latin and Orthodox churches became a matter of importance in northern Europe, Germans residing in Rus' cities such as Novgorod and Smolensk similarly had their own houses of worship.

It comes as no surprise that the structure that some argue is the oldest stone building in Riga started its life as a church. To be more precise, St. George's was a chapel housed within the first Order Castle on the Rigebach. Constructed between 1202 and 1209, the edifice has been repurposed many times over the centuries: during the upheavals of the Reformation, St. George's was turned into a warehouse, and more recently the space was converted into the Museum of Decorative Arts and Design. While the edifice presently houses an impressive collection of works by the founders of Latvian modernism, the unknowing visitor might be surprised to learn that the building located at Skārņu iela 10/20 was once a house of worship.

FIGURE 4. Spire of St. Peter's Church, 2016. Photo by author.

The heavy ecclesiastical presence in thirteenth-century Riga could also be seen in its four monasteries. One belonging to the Dominican Order was built on the site of Bishop Albert's original stone castle next to the Riga River. But after Albert's successor, Bishop Nicholas (r. 1229–1253), built a new residence for himself near the second Dome, he no longer needed his old estate, which in any event was uncomfortably situated next to the Swordbrothers' castle. In September 1234 Riga's new bishop handed the site over to the Dominican Order, then enjoying a growing presence in Livonia. Consecrated as the Church of St. John the Baptist and St. John the Evangelist, the new church-monastery was first mentioned in the historical record in connection with the events of 1297, the year that marked the beginning of Riga's first war with the Livonian Order (one of the central events of chapter 4).

In addition to the Dominican monastery at St. John's, thirteenth-century Riga was home to three other cloisters: a Franciscan monastery, with its own Church of St. Catherine, was founded around 1235, possibly on the site of Bishop Albert's first wooden Dome. Attached to the new red-brick Dome in another corner of the city was a monastery built around 1255, which served as the prior's residence. A cloister for girls was located in buildings that later belonged to the Church of St. James: like the Church of St. Mary Magdalene, this Cistercian nunnery at St. James's was founded in 1244.[65] Cistercians also controlled the original convent-fortress located several kilometers north of Riga at Dünamünde, which established itself as an independent power near the Bay of Riga. Exactly how many clerics there were in the city at any given time no one can say, but it would be difficult to overstate the position of priests, monks, and nuns on early Riga.

The original German city comprised a mere sixteen hectares. In the wake of its first major fire in 1215, Riga expanded to include the remaining territory on the peninsula, much of it low and wet. During Albert's episcopate the city began to approach its medieval limits, encompassing twenty-eight hectares protected by an enlarged wall. While the area near the original port on the Rigebach was the most densely inhabited part of the city, other areas that are now considered part of "Old Riga" were practically empty. The boggy area that separated the Livonian village on the Düna from the settlement next to the rivulet remained unused for a long time, but later this spot would be transformed into the center of civic life, anchored by a market place, the Town Hall (1334), and opposite that the New House (1334), later known as the House of Blackheads.[66] Another thinly inhabited area during the city's early years was the quarter delineated by today's Šķūņu iela (Shed Street), Kaļķu iela (Limestone Street), and the Rigebach, but eventually much of this area would be transformed into a warehouse district.[67] The original city's ample space for growth probably would have astonished Rigans of later ages. Indeed, it was not long before modest Riga would become one of Europe's more densely populated cities.

Considerably larger than Riga's municipal borders was the city-state's bailiwick—that is, the complex of lands under the bishop's jurisdiction. Its boundaries were determined in 1226 during the negotiations supervised by papal legate William of Modena. The bailiwick's contours ran from the Düna (Daugava) River at present-day Rumbula (near Dole Island) up to what are now called Lakes Jugla and Ķīšezers, then by Mīlgrāvis and back to the Düna. Also included within Riga's bailiwick was a great deal of land on the Düna's left bank (now known as Pārdaugava) that was not integrated into the city proper until modern times. On nearly all sides there were bogs, rivers, and impassable forests, which greatly hindered pagan attacks, especially in the springtime.

A surprising dereliction by the city's fathers was their failure to secure the mouth of the Düna River. Instead, the area remained in the hands of the Cistercians, who managed a wide range of properties in the vicinity of Riga.[68] That the papacy tasked the Cistercian abbot of the Dünamünde monastery with making sure that Albert was following orders made the former something of a rival to the bishop, but a weak one at that.[69] Riga's mistake in not securing control over this strategically priceless territory became apparent when the monks were forced in 1305 to sell their convent to the knights of the Livonian Order, which, as we shall see, would replace the original Order of Swordbrothers in 1237. With this acquisition, the order would be able to block the entry of all ships approaching the mouth of the Düna. If the brothers felt aggrieved, it would take little effort for them to bring hunger and misery to the people of Riga.

Compromise

Bishop Albert died after several months of illness in January 1229. Although he failed to fulfill his ambition of becoming an archbishop who ruled a more-or-less independent metropolis—a model employed in Cologne and in some other parts of Germany[70]—the first bishop of Riga could nevertheless lay claim to any number of accomplishments. Not only had Albert chosen the location of his military/ecclesiastical center, he had presided over its initial construction and growth. Determined to ensure that Riga alone was the great Christian trading enterprise in Livonia, he got the pope to agree to abolish trade with a competing Semigallian port farther upstream.[71] To encourage commerce in the region, in 1211 he declared that trade on the lower Düna was to be free of the sort of princely taxation that Henry the Lion had introduced in Lübeck. "Bishop Albert's privilege" ensured that the German merchants who visited Riga and other Livonian ports would be granted "eternal exemption from customs," an act in keeping with the emerging western-European idea of civic autonomy in internal affairs.[72]

When he wasn't in Germany recruiting soldiers for the crusade, the bishop was at home protecting his vulnerable flock during lean times and in the face of pagan attacks. Securing the submission of the region's Livs (even as the Latvian tribes continued to resist), Albert transformed the tribesmen into Christian allies and took many on the crusade to Estonia. Making peace with the Rus' prince of Polotsk in 1212 when war might have proved ruinous, Albert ensured that the visiting Rus' merchants would enjoy free passage on the Düna, while making certain that the Livonian enterprise would remain Latin Christian and predominantly German. Having begun the transfer of European feudal norms to the conquered lands, Albert built a solid foundation for Terra Mariana (Marienland, "the Land of Mary"), the name Pope Innocent III gave to Livonia in 1215 during the Fourth Lateran Council, which Albert himself attended.

Although Albert's realm included nearly all the territories north of the Düna that would one day become part of an independent Latvian state, the bishop of Riga was not the only power in Livonia. The Order of Swordbrothers, created to provide the colony with year-round protection, was as much a competitor as it was a partner. The problem of finding a satisfactory way to divide the conquered territories plagued the relationship between Livonia's ecclesiastical and secular rulers for decades.

Another rival for power and influence in Livonia was the city of Riga. Striving to maintain its independence from the local feudal authorities, the city, its burghers represented by a town council after 1226, typically forged tactical allegiances with one against the other. Tensions between the bishop, the order, and the city were particularly evident during Albert's final years, when the conquest of Estonia was nearly complete and a vast amount of territory fell into the hands of its Christian rulers.[73]

From 1209 the order's stronghold was a stone castle on a hill in Wenden (Latv. Cēsis), whose Slavic inhabitants, the Wends, had been defeated and converted. This position on what is now the Gauja River allowed the order to dominate the trade route to Russia militarily, politically, and economically in much the same way the Germans had obtained nearly complete control of the Düna trade route that led to Polotsk. But the Order of Swordbrothers was not satisfied with its status in conquered Livonia, for the balance of power between the bishop of Riga, the order, and the city was shaken by the Danes' involvement in the eastern Baltic. With the conquest of the Estonian lands in 1219, the earlier territorial arrangements agreed upon by the bishop and the order were called into question. The Danish king went so far as to refuse permission to Albert's brother Hermann to take up his post in Dorpat until the bishop agreed to cede to Valdemar not only Estonia but also Livonia. Having little choice but to submit, in 1221 Albert signed a contract with the Danish king that placed these territories under the jurisdiction of Denmark; however, the arrangement's collapse in subsequent years meant that Livonia would remain a semi-autonomous outpost of the Holy Roman Empire for the next three hundred years.

The Estonian issue highlights the nature of the challenges facing Albert in his last years: the Danes were now in northern Estonia; the power of the Order of

Swordbrothers increased with its acquisition of territory in southern Estonia; and Riga's citizens were alarmed at the prospect of losing their autonomy, going so far as to expel the representative dispatched by Valdemar to supervise the city's government.[74] The good news, at least for the crusaders, was the end of any immediate prospect of Orthodox/Russian expansion into the Baltic area, for in 1223 the great Mongol invasion began in the lands of the Rus', devastating Kiev and many other principalities. Even as the Russian threat abated, however, Livonia's internal conflicts were so significant as to require outside intervention, which Albert requested of Rome. This came in the form of the aforementioned William of Modena, the pope's Italian vice-chancellor and chief troubleshooter. Already prominent in Prussian ecclesiastical affairs, William was now designated Pope Honorius's papal legate to Livonia, enjoying the full power to represent the pontiff.

Arriving in Riga in late 1225, William, an able diplomat and reputedly a man of great integrity, was authorized to settle the ongoing dispute between the bishop and the order. It was William, we may recall, who determined the territorial arrangements that governed the city; the papal legate also had the authority to raise Riga's status to that of an archbishopric, which would have liberated the prelate from the supervision of the archbishopric of Hamburg-Bremen while at the same time enhancing Albert's position in Livonia and Estonia. But William chose not to use this mandate, and Bishop Albert never achieved his likely goal of creating a more-or-less independent metropolis headed by an archbishop.[75]

Of particular concern to the legate was the Christians' treatment of the local tribes, who under Albert's strict rule were subject to burdensome tithes and tributes. For this and for depriving converts of their properties in Riga, the crusaders had been reprimanded on several occasions by both Pope Innocent III—who had repudiated the idea of conversion by the sword—and then by Pope Honorius III. In 1224 it was the turn of Emperor Frederick II (r. 1220–1250) to chastise the lords of Prussia, Livonia, and Estonia for molesting the converted inhabitants, whom he now declared under his protection.[76] Now William of Modena, speaking on the pope's behalf, was warning the Germans not to impose "any harsh, unbearable burden upon the shoulders of the converts." Ill treatment of the new converts, William believed, would cause them to have a negative view of the Christians and their faith, which he thought should bring the converts greater peace, justice, and fairness. Eschewing violence in favor of love and restraint, the Germans were to "bring in Christian customs and abolish pagan rites by assiduously teaching the faith of Christ, and to teach and instruct them both by their words and by their good examples."[77] The legate's admonishments having no more impact than Emperor Frederick II's "Baltic Manifesto" or Pope Gregory IX's protective bull of 1227, the atrocities continued unabated.[78] The ensuing decades, writes Mara Kalnins, were to witness "a systematic brutality that would crush the last sparks of freedom in the native Baltic peoples."[79]

It was in the diplomatic arena that William of Modena enjoyed his greatest success, for the legate proved able to arrange a series of compromises on boundaries, overlapping ecclesiastical and territorial jurisdictions, taxes, and other matters. But even someone with William's impressive skills could not resolve the basic problem: who was to be master in Livonia? Placing Estonia directly under the control of the papacy and appointing his own vice-legate as governor, William attempted to remove Estonia as an object of contention. But the vice-legate simply turned the disputed territory over to the Order of Swordbrothers. That the transaction enhanced the knights' position at the expense of the bishop of Riga was perhaps balanced by the decision of the Holy Roman emperor in December 1225 to recognize Albert and his brother Hermann, the bishop of Dorpat, as princes of the empire, thereby confirming their status. While many individuals and institutions had a stake in *Terra Mariana*, none had yet emerged as its undisputed master.

It might be argued that the greatest beneficiaries of the legate's intervention in Livonia were the citizens of Riga. In 1226, the same year that the Riga Town Council (Rath) is first mentioned in the historical record, William of Modena elevated Riga's status to that of a city-state, granting the city one-third of all future conquests and forcing Bishop Albert to cede to Rigans lands around the city.[80]

During his year-long stay in Riga, the legate also helped shape the city's laws on citizenship: henceforth everyone who had settled down in the city to live permanently—a minority of the town's inhabitants at any given time in those days, for its earliest merchants, crusaders, and builders arrived and departed on a seasonal basis—could become citizens by paying the city half a silver mark, equivalent to about four ounces of silver.[81] Although Riga's relatively liberal citizenship policy did not legally exclude the former pagans, in practice few peasants of Livonia could afford what to them would surely have been an exorbitant sum. But since the city needed builders and porters as well as dock and warehouse workers, its "non-Germans" would be tolerated as an unskilled labor force without the right of citizenship, excluded from the privilege of holding real estate.

But could the knights of the order be citizens of Riga? Yes, ruled the legate, and not only that, one or two brothers would henceforth be allowed to participate in meetings of the town council.[82]

By the time William completed his mission in Livonia (he would return again in 1234 to settle another round of disputes), the situation had more or less stabilized: a balance had been established between the power of the Church and that of the order, and Riga's status as a city-state within the Holy Roman Empire had been confirmed. Now that the crusaders had conquered the entirety of Estonia, an important chapter in the history of what has become known as the Northern Crusades came to an end. Thus Henry closes out his chronicle with the baptism of the defeated inhabitants of the Estonian island of Ösel (now Saaremaa).

> Thus does Riga always water the nations. Thus did she water Oesel in the middle of the sea. By washing she purges sin and grants the kingdom of the skies. She furnishes both the higher and the lower irrigation. These gifts of God are our delight. The glory of God, of our Lord Jesus Christ, and of the Blessed Virgin Mary gives such joy to His Rigan servants on Oesel. To vanquish rebels, to baptize those who come voluntarily and humbly, to receive hostages and tribute, to free all the Christian captives, to return with victory—what kinds have hitherto been unable to do, the Blessed Virgin quickly and easily accomplishes through her Rigan servants to the honor of Her name. When this is finished, when it is all done, when all the people are baptized, when Tharapita [an Estonian deity] is thrown out, when Pharaoh is drowned, when captives are freed, return with joy, O Rigans! Brilliantly triumphal victory always follows you. Glory be to the Lord, praise to God beyond the stars.[83]

Affirming the crusaders' sense of historical mission and approving whatever methods were necessary to secure the natives' conversion, Henry's position on the Livonian mission could hardly be more plain, for it was the chronicler's goal to provide proof of a divinely ordered destiny, to demonstrate that it was God's will that the natives be baptized even under threat of death.[84] And so the fighting continued, the blood of its countless victims absorbed into the same earth that gave rise to the churches and castles that soon came to dominate the Land of Mary.

Chapter 3

Free Air in the Hanse City

Stadtluft macht frei nach Jahr und Tag.
The city air makes you free after a year and a day.[1]

A visitor sojourning in Riga for any length of time will surely come to recognize a red-brick ensemble that is located about two hundred meters from the Düna embankment. This is the Riga Dome, a building project launched by Bishop Albert of Buxhoeveden in 1211 on the site of a pre-Christian cemetery that belonged to an indigenous tribe. Still one of Riga's most distinctive landmarks, the Dome, formally known as St. Mary's, is among the largest churches in the eastern Baltic region and for more than three hundred years was the seat of an archdiocese.

Circling just around the corner from the Dome's main entrance, the curious visitor encounters another red-brick building (it was once the cathedral's chapter house) which accommodates a wonderful little institution dedicated to the city's history. This is the Museum of the History of Rīga and Navigation. Established at a different location in the 1770s and later moved to the Dome complex, the museum is the first of its kind in the Baltic region and one of the oldest in Europe.

Among the museum's many archaeological and historical treasures is a weather-beaten wooden likeness of a very large man with a small boy on his shoulder. This is Big Christopher (Latv. Lielais Kristaps), the patron of Latvian seafarers. Standing at the edge of the Düna (Daugava) embankment, Big Christopher was thought to protect the city from floods and other natural disasters; as such, he is considered one of the great "legends" of Old Riga.[2]

Only a few steps from Christopher and the Christ child, who rests on his shoulders, the visitor encounters the remains of a medieval ship that for centuries had lain buried under the city. Excavated in 1938 from the riverbed of the vanished Riga River, the ancient vessel measures 14.3 meters (about forty-seven feet) in length, with a width of nearly five meters (sixteen feet) and a carrying capacity of thirty tons.[3] This single-masted oaken vessel was typical of the ships that crossed the Baltic Sea at the end of the twelfth century and as such is a telling example of Riga's growing significance after 1200.

It was just around this time that a new kind of ship began to appear in the Baltic. This was the German cog, a larger vessel that was first constructed in the shipyards of Lübeck. With a flat bottom and a far greater carrying capacity of 100 to 200 tons, the cog was more suitable for transporting bulk goods from the eastern Baltic to ports in northwestern Europe.[4] Since larger ships meant lower shipping costs, the profits for the men who made their living exchanging goods on the rim of the Baltic Sea became all the greater. Indeed, the technical superiority and the vastly greater holding capacity of the German cog goes far in explaining the quasi monopoly in northern cities enjoyed for nearly three hundred years by the port cities of the Hanseatic League.

Ideally situated to profit from a growing East-West trade, Riga was a model Hanse city whose leading merchants enjoyed relative wealth and considerable influence on civic life. If war was always accompanied by the plundering of the countryside, shortages for the cities, and hunger (especially for the poor), peace, on the other hand, was usually followed by prosperity. Few benefited from extended periods of quiet more than Riga's industrious and haughty merchants, who naturally preferred to conduct their business without the interference of quarrelsome priests and knights. Their struggles are the subject of chapter 4.

Even in the best of times, wealthy traders never comprised anything more than a small minority of the city's growing population.[5] While it is true that many of Riga's earliest residents came by ship from Germany to conduct business with other traders and that others were summoned to preach the word of God, hundreds were lured to the new city by the prospect of finding work as builders and craftsmen. Peasants from the nearby countryside came to Riga in search of the freedom and opportunities that could be found only in the region's few towns. Forming the bulk of the city's lower classes, these "non-Germans" (*Undeutsche*) shared Riga's narrow streets and its "free air" with their social superiors, but found themselves increasingly excluded from its civic and social life. Multinational though it was, Riga was in most respects a typical German Hanse city in which business was the order of the day, but order was necessary for the conduct of business.

Riga and the Hanse

From its humble beginnings as a loose association of German merchants, the Hanseatic League coalesced into a commercial and defensive confederation of market towns that came to dominate the North and Baltic seas.[6] Reaching the height of its power in the fifteenth century, the Hanse, a word that suggests the concept of "fellowship," at that time controlled the commerce of eighty towns and perhaps one thousand ships. Among the most important of these towns was

Visby, a city on the island of Gotland that might be considered "the mother of Riga and of the Livonian towns in general."[7] An old Norse trading and manufacturing center, Visby was taken over by German traders who then laid down the laws followed by merchants in Riga, Reval, Danzig, and the other new trading centers that were being set up in the eastern Baltic. In this way the seeds of European urbanism that germinated in Visby were transplanted across the eastern Baltic. Like Bergen, Bruges, and London in the west, the great Rus' city of Novgorod, the network's eastern pole, also became a Hanse town where Germans had their own commercial quarter in St. Peter's Yard, the *Peterhof.*

If Novgorod is still admired for its ancient churches of white limestone topped by their glimmering onion-dome cupolas, the northern German town of Lübeck, located some 1,500 miles west of Novgorod, was characterized by its red-brick buildings, pointy towers, and curved walls. This was the Hanse merchants' main meeting place and the capital of a trading empire that stretched from southern England to northern Russia. Founded in the middle of the twelfth century and declared a free imperial city in 1226, Lübeck was liberated from obligations to any feudal lords other than the German emperor and thereafter developed as an autonomous part of the Holy Roman Empire. Since the creation of urban charters and legal codes was one of the signature achievements of the medieval *Ostsiedlung*—that is, the Germanic colonization of parts of eastern Europe—Lübeck law was soon exported to dozens of cities then sprouting in Germany and beyond. The law code of Hamburg was based on the customs of Lübeck; and it was the alliance of the two cities after 1241 that marked the origin of the Hanseatic League.[8] After concluding similar arrangements with Lübeck and Visby, Riga copied the Hamburg law code for its own use in 1291. Other Livonian townships—Dorpat, Wenden, Wolmar, Windau, and so on—soon adopted the Riga law for their themselves. In such manner did Riga law become the common urban legal code in medieval and early-modern Livonia.[9]

As the largest city in the Baltic, with some 40,000 inhabitants in 1300, Lübeck became the coast's central hub and Lübeck sea law became the common denominator in the Hanseatic world. To the courts of Lübeck fell the task of enforcing the rules that governed the northern trade, now in the hands of a brotherhood of merchants who spoke a Middle Low German dialect that was becoming common in the cities of the Baltic littoral as far to the east as Narva.[10] Growing from a series of alliances into a full-fledged trading empire, the league jealously guarded its monopoly against all competitors, including the Danish pirates with whom the Hanse frequently warred. After the fifteenth century the main threat to the Hanse were enterprising Dutch (and later English) merchants, who would soon shatter the Hanse's commercial dominance of northern Europe.

Even if the larger Livonian centers shared more in common with each other than they did with the cities of northern Germany, with which they lacked a continuous land connection, nearly all the significant Baltic cities were members of the Hanseatic alliance.[11] Originally conquered by Denmark but increasingly settled by Germans from Saxony and Westphalia, the Hanse town of Reval was important as the assembly point for men and ships making the journey to Novgorod by way of Narva, Lake Lagoda, and the Neva River—a route that long predated the Hanse. By virtue of its location on the north Estonian coast, Reval also profited from trade with Sweden and Finland. To the southeast of Reval was a third important Livonian Hanse city. This was Dorpat, situated on the overland trade route to Pskov and thence to Novgorod, a city that played an important role as the main entry point for Russian goods bound for Riga during the winter.

Owing to these connections, Riga, easily the largest of the Livonian settlements, became a vital hub of an East-West trading system that linked the Russian hinterlands to the markets of western Europe. Although modest and impoverished by Mediterranean standards, the cities of Riga, Reval, and Dorpat would come to dominate the smaller Livonian towns. Eventually the general pattern would be for ships to sail from the Baltic ports to Bergen laden with grain, beer, and goods from the forested interior; in Bergen the vessels would be loaded with dried cod to be sold in England or Flanders; the main cargo on the return to the Baltic would consist of salt and cloth. The Livonian towns' proximity to Russia meant that their ports and warehouses would be filled with products from the eastern forests—furs, beeswax, and honey—that were destined for the markets of western Europe.

Riga's potential for regional primacy was obvious from the start to the city's founder, Bishop Albert of Buxhoeveden, who worked to ensure that the trade route along the Düna to Polotsk and Vitebsk would be directly controlled by the new city. German traders used to visiting the older Semigallian port just upstream from Riga were henceforth compelled to traffic their goods solely through Riga, whose defenders and merchants secured control of the Düna nearly as far as Russian Polotsk. In 1229 Riga's diplomats also managed to ensure for its traders free dealings in Vitebsk and Smolensk.[12] That the mutual trading rules determined at this time by the German and Russian merchants remained in force for nearly two centuries testifies to the enduring nature of the system.

But if the German traders ("Latins") were mere "guests" in the Russian lands—just as "Russian" and all foreign traders were regarded as guests in Riga—it was the Germans, forming a small minority of Livonia's population, who controlled its towns, its trade routes, and its religious life. Being the first of the pagan tribes to succumb to the region's new overlords, the Livs who had formerly paid tribute to the Rus' ruler of Polotsk were now under the protection of German emigrants who erected an ethnically heterogeneous and politically disunited crusader state with Riga as its capital. Over the decades the submission of the Livs was followed by that of the neighboring Latvian tribes—the Latgallians and Selonians, and later the Couronians and Semigallians. Hundreds of the conquered came to Riga to make their homes, where they lived alongside a superior number of German emigrants and a handful of Slavs and Lithuanians, each group occupying its own separate part of the city.

With the capture of the Semigallians' last stronghold in Sidrabene in 1290, the Livonian Crusade came to an end. Now that competing trade centers such as Jersika, located on the route to Polotsk, were abolished, and the walled and well-defended city of Riga was made secure from outside threats, business boomed. From the Russian lands came forest products. Beeswax, honey, and furs comprised well over half the value of items exported through Riga to the West during the thirteenth century. Trapped mainly in the Novgorodian lands, the fur-bearing creatures of northern Russia's seemingly endless forests—ermine, otter, marten, sable ("black gold")—brought great profits to the merchant while satisfying the wearer's need for warmth and status. Still greater was Europe's demand for the cheaper furs harvested from squirrels: they occupied first place among the fur items exported through the port of Riga.

But it was not always so. Before the rise of shipping in the Baltic area, Rus' traders principally sold their wares to markets in the Byzantine south (via Kiev to Constantinople) and in the east, where their buyers were the Volga Bulgars. By the thirteenth century these routes and markets had become obstructed by the ongoing wars between the Byzantine Empire and the encroaching Turks. As western European markets began to replace the ones that had been disrupted, the Rus' came to depend on the surging commerce of the Baltic Sea. So did western Europeans, especially the wealthy and status-conscious, who liked to sew the Russian furs—the softer and silkier the better—into the linings of their outer garments or use them to make coats, cloaks, caps, hats, and gloves. The aristocracy's demand for gray squirrels could be satisfied only by the Rus' of Novgorod, who collected their pelts as tribute from nearby tribes.[13]

To obtain these products, and others such as honey and wax, twice a year merchants from the Livonian towns set out for Novgorod ("New Town"), the bustling and unusually literate city of 15,000 that was as famous for its commercial ethos as it was for its gleaming Byzantine-style churches.[14] In the summer months the merchants took the sea route. During winter they traveled to Novgorod by land. At the peak of the trading season, as many as two hundred Germans—the merchants and their assistants and servants—could be found in their compound in Novgorod, where they were subject to their own rules and regulations and where they inspected, purchased, and sorted their merchandise. In their yard, known as the *Peterhof*, the Germans bound the furs in bundles of forty and packed them in barrels containing between 5,000 and 10,000 pelts. Purchases made in the winter were then stored and shipped the following spring.[15]

To appreciate the importance of the fur trade to Riga's early merchants, we may consider several examples. One concerns the plight of the seven Rigan traders who were robbed on the road between Novgorod and Pskov in the year 1292.[16] While hold-ups like this were not unusual, what matters here is the fact that the brigands got away with no fewer than 20,000 pelts and thirty *birkavs* of wax.[17] Far more voluminous—and perhaps this tells us something about the explosive growth in the fur trade during the fourteenth century—was the cargo of a ship belonging to Engelbrecht Bonnit: sailing from Riga to Flanders in 1403, it carried more than 200,000 fur pelts.[18] More than twice as many pelts were shipped from Riga to Bruges in 1405.[19] Of the wholesale transactions conducted by a business operated by Engelbrecht Witte, a full 60 percent (in terms of overall value) were comprised of the furs that he exported through Riga.[20] In the eyes of Livonia's merchants, fur was money; in terms of sheer volume, however, nothing could top beeswax, which probably comprised more than 80 percent of Riga's exports by weight during the first half of the fourteenth century.[21] Even if the data on Riga's medieval trade are fragmentary, it is clear that the value of Riga's exports to the West always exceeded that of its imports.

Before Riga's merchants could sell their Russian treasures to Europe, they first had to get them to the port of Riga. Traders using the Düna accomplished this using rafts and barges, which were better able to navigate the river's many rapids than were larger vessels. Although these barges and rafts were typically powered by oars, sometimes they were dragged by horses or by Russian trackers.[22] Thus from the Rus' towns where they were collected, such as Vitebsk and Polotsk, the wax, furs, and other forest goods destined for markets in western Europe were sent downriver to the port of Riga, where the merchandise was unloaded by Latvian and Livonian laborers. Service occupations such as these, like carrying salt and beer through the city, or piloting small vessels on the lower reaches of the Düna, were the exclusive preserve of "non-Germans," a term that the Germans of Riga and used in reference to residents who spoke an indigenous language. Likewise, when Riga's merchants took the land route to Pskov during the winter, they similarly employed non-Germans to haul their merchandise in convoys of sleds. While at this time a fairly substantial number of non-Germans were able to make a living in Riga from retail and petty trading, wholesale commerce was strictly for the German merchants and their "guests."[23]

Once weighed, the goods were transported to a nearby warehouse for storage. Then at some point the merchandise would be transferred to a larger vessel that was likely owned by a merchant from Lübeck or another Hanseatic city (or later Holland), for Riga did not have its own fleet of seagoing vessels. After it was loaded and conditions on the sea were judged to be fair, the ship carried the merchandise of perhaps dozens of merchants to the port of Lübeck in a journey lasting more than two weeks. Often the passage took longer, depending on the weather and the size of the vessel, which might make three or four passages between Lübeck and Riga in one trading season. Once the ship had docked at Lübeck and the merchandise was unloaded, the goods were taken across Danish Jutland by land to Hamburg and thence by ship once again to North Sea ports like Bruges or London. The additional legs added several more weeks to the journey: as a result, the goods that were loaded onto a merchant vessel at the port of Riga might not arrive at their final destination in the West for two months.[24]

For a telling example of the way Riga's merchants organized their trade operations, we might consider the activities of Heinrich Gendena. In the spring of 1455, this enterprising merchant did business with at least ten trade partners, including "companions" in Lübeck, Bruges, Danzig, and Riga. Gendena also partnered with the master (*Ordensmeister*) of the Livonian Order, to whom he sold, for a handsome profit, large quantities of hops he had purchased in Danzig. From the master the merchant purchased Prussian flax, while the order further relied upon Gendena to use his contacts in Lübeck to obtain high-quality cod.[25] Indeed, it was not unusual for Riga's wholesalers to arrange complex transitions involving a variety of partners not only in the German lands, but in Flanders and Prussia as well. The favored currency among Riga's traders at this time was the Lübeck mark (valued slightly higher than Riga's mark), but guldens of all kinds were also welcome: Rhenish gulden, for example, could be exchanged at a rate of two Rigan marks for one gulden.[26]

For the river trade with Russia, and also for the local transshipment of merchandise, Livonia's merchants used barges and rafts. However, in the difficult journey across the Baltic Sea, the traders' goods were transported in larger, sturdier vessels. As noted, cogs had become standard by the fourteenth century, but these were eventually supplanted by larger ships like the hulk (*holk*), some of which had a carrying capacity of more than five hundred tons—more than twice what even the largest cog could hold. By the sixteenth century, the caravel, first developed by the Portuguese to explore the west African coast, would also begin to appear in the Baltic Sea.

Travel by sea was always hazardous, and much time could be lost at Riga and other ports while merchants waited for a favorable wind. Since losses due to storms, shipwrecks, and piracy were both common and expected, Hanse merchants took measures to protect themselves and their wares. One way the traders tried to limit their risk of loss was by spreading consignments across several vessels, with each ship carrying the merchandise of several if not dozens of traders.[27] Thus when two of the three ships from Riga bound for Bruges were seized by English pirates in 1404, the losses were shared by fifty-four merchants.[28] Being sensible people who understood the value of cooperation, merchants also tended to travel in groups, for convoys enjoyed greater protection against pirates than ships traveling individually.[29] Winter months, when conditions became more difficult and the northern ports froze, were mostly idle at Riga's harbor, for Hanse cities limited overseas trade to nine months each year. This old custom was codified in 1403 by the Hanse diet, which decreed that navigation was to be prohibited between November 22 (St. Martin's Day) and February 22 (St. Peter's Day),[30] according to the old Julian calendar that remained in effect in Riga through 1918.[31]

Riga's traders had a localized set of problems as well. An early concern was the deteriorating condition of the original port on the Riga River (a.k.a. Rigebach, Riesing, "Lake Riga"). It was not long before a new port was constructed on the Düna opposite the older port, which had become too shallow to accommodate the increasingly large ships that carried goods from Riga to markets in the West. Paved in stages during the course of the fifteenth century, the Düna port gradually replaced "Lake Riga" as the city's main import-export facility, while the older port continued to be used for off-loading local goods. These typically arrived in smaller vessels that, sometime in the fourteenth century, began to be constructed in a shipyard just south of the old port in what was then called Lastadia, where the Latgale (or Moscow) suburb is today.[32]

Another concern of Riga's merchants was winter, which can feel excruciatingly long in northern Europe and which was a rawer experience for anyone who lived in the later Middle Ages, not least because the temperature was lower in those times than it is today. That the Düna was transformed into a sheet of ice each winter rendered the Riga port inaccessible for nearly four months each year—a challenge not only for Riga's traders but for anyone hoping to travel after mid-November or before mid-April. Moreover, the Düna's shallowness in some places made it difficult for larger ships coming from the West to reach their destination. Thus another precaution undertaken by Riga's merchants, beginning around the end of the fifteenth century, was to dock the larger seagoing vessels at the monastery-fortress at Dünamünde, located near the mouth of the Düna, before transporting the merchandise destined for Riga onto smaller boats and barges.[33]

What did those great vessels sailing from the West bring to Livonia? The weightiest and most voluminous commodity by far was salt, necessary for preserving dried herring and butter, but unavailable in eastern Europe. Used as ballast, most of the salt brought to Riga (and thence to Russia) came from southwestern France. Among the other goods unloaded at the port of Riga were Flemish and English textiles, as well as the metals (especially silver) that were rare in the Russian lands. At times the Hanse tried to prevent its merchants from purchasing the Russian goods with silver or with any metal that could be used in the production of armaments; however, precious metals were particularly valued in Novgorod and it seems that such regulations were not especially difficult to circumvent. Indeed, it was almost exclusively with silver that the Teutonic Order, which emerged as a commercial power in its own right, purchased its goods from the Rus'.[34]

It was through the Livonian ports, and through Riga above all, that Western goods—textiles, wine and beer, glass and paper, and later silks and colonial goods—found their way to the Russian cities. Through their trade contacts in Riga and the other Livonian trading towns, the Russian merchants were able to obtain spices from southeast Asia like pepper, ginger, saffron, and cloves, as well as dried southern fruits like figs and raisins.[35] A growing dependence on the German traders, however, rankled the businessmen of Novgorod and the other Rus' cities, for during a period of Russian weakness and disunity (i.e., the period from the Mongol invasions of the 1230s through the rise of Muscovy in the fifteenth century), the Germans had secured their positions in the Russian trade and become the indispensable middlemen in the commerce of the northeast. In 1346 the Hanseatic League granted Riga, as well as the towns of Reval and Pernau (Est. Pärnu), the right of emporium. This entitled a city to demand that all goods destined for Russia be unloaded, weighed, and reloaded when passing through the city. As the law required a four-day waiting period before goods could be reloaded for sale in Russia, its intention was to encourage foreign traders to sell their products to middlemen in the Livonian towns.

As the German traders secured for themselves a monopoly on Russia's trade with the West, Russian merchants grew frustrated. The complaints that Polotsk, Pskov, and Smolensk sent to Riga's town council often focused on unfair treatment and abuse—as, for example, the ears of several Polotskian traders were hacked off in Riga, or when Rigans violently shaved a Russian's beard.[36] Germans, meanwhile, complained about the prevalence of cheating on weights and measures. As tensions rose between the Russians and their German counterparts, Rigans conducting business in the Russian cities faced the threat of having their goods confiscated and their trading privileges abrogated. By the time the Russian authorities decided in 1494 to close the *Peterhof*, then the German *kontor* in Novgorod, only forty-nine German traders were to be found. All of them were imprisoned and later released.[37]

As the biggest urban center in all Livonia, Riga was also a significant consumer of goods in its own right. Its population steadily rising to 8,000 or more by the year 1500,[38] the Düna metropolis was a user of resources supplied by neighboring farms as well as a consumer of goods imported from the West. But unlike in the Russian lands or in western cities, where Rigan merchants dealt almost exclusively with other traders, in Riga's hinterlands the city's agents conducted business directly with the local producers. To Riga the Latvian and Livish peasants brought flax and hemp, grain, meat, chicken, butter, dried fish, honey, wax, and an array of other agricultural goods. In the city the local peasants purchased everyday items the German merchants had obtained from western Europe, the Russian lands, and southern Estonia.[39]

The relationship was, of course, entirely colonial, for Riga's merchants tried to gain maximum benefit from a peasant economy that during the sixteenth century was increasingly shaped by serfdom. Indeed, it was the serf economy of northeastern Europe that in the Late Middle Ages began to determine the composition of Riga's exports to western markets, increasingly dominated by flax, hemp, and grains. Later it was lumber products, with Dutch traders emerging as important buyers of resin, pitch, and ash, as well as blocks of oak. All were needed to build the great fleets that came to dominate the Baltic trade as it passed from the Hanse to Holland.[40]

Behind the Walls

In good times visitors to Old Riga would have found a flourishing city of the northern German type so familiar to Hanse traders. Guests entered through one of the gates that punctured an imposing brick-and-limestone wall—just under two meters thick and up to nine meters high—that surrounded nearly the entirety of the peninsula.[41] Manned by guards who opened them just before sunrise and closed them every evening after sunset, the gates acted as a screen to filter out undesirables and as a means of keeping track of who was in the city and who had left it.

The main gate after around 1330, when it first appears in the historical record, was by the Sand Tower, which led to the city's main streets, the Sand Road[42] and Market Street.[43] Rebuilt and massively expanded during the Swedish era, and known today as the Powder Tower,[44] the imposing, cylindrical edifice was one of more than two dozen towers of varying shapes and sizes—circular, semi-circular, and square—built into the city wall at intervals of up to one hundred meters.

Some received their name from the nearest street (Butcher's Tower) or church (Jacob's Tower). A few, like the Salt or Weighing Tower, went by two or more names or were simply known by their appearance (e.g., the Gray Tower). One of the city's largest round towers was known as Sundern Tower, originally named after a city councilman, Hermann of Sundern, who owned property in the area around the time it was built in the fifteenth century. But, as with many place-names in the city, its original meaning changed over the years. For example, the word "Sünder" being German for "sinner," the nearby street eventually became known as Sinners' Street[45] and the tower likewise became Sinners' Tower.[46] As the centuries passed, some of the old towers acquired new functions: Sundern or Sinner's Tower became a grain warehouse, and later in the seventeenth century it began to be used as a water tower. The strongest and largest of Riga's towers was known in German as the *Marstallthurm*,[47] a name that for centuries was associated with the nearby city stables but in fact originated from the name of an early councilman (Marscalcus).[48] Located near the entrance to the original port on the Riga rivulet, the round 4.6-meter-thick tower, once Riga's largest and strongest, was demolished at the end of the seventeenth century.

Visible from a distance, Riga's magnificent towers were the focal points of the city's fortification system, which by the end of the sixteenth century extended more than three kilometers around the city and was one of the strongest on the Baltic Sea coast. When danger approached, the entire population would be mobilized in the city's defense. That every German citizen of Riga was obliged to own a set of armor or pay a penalty of three marks indicates that this was a civic responsibility that mattered.[49] One tower might be defended by fishermen or boatmen, who were responsible for its upkeep; another by shoemakers. There were also specially trained detachments of archers who manned the towers that protruded from the city wall, enabling them to flank any enemies who had managed to cross the river or the moat. In peacetime the city used the towers as warehouses, gigantic containers for holding grain, gunpowder, and war materials. Maintaining the system was one of the town council's highest priorities, and it was also one of the city's most burdensome expenses.

Such expenses grew precipitously during the fifteenth and sixteenth centuries, for the increased use of gunpowder weaponry eventually rendered the walls and towers insufficient for the city's defense and compelled its leaders to make costly improvements. To minimize the damage wrought by heavy cannonballs, in the 1530s the town council ordered the erection of earthen fortifications beyond the old town walls, for the new ramparts would better absorb the force of cannon shot better than the brittle old walls. But building ramparts and digging deep ditches in front of them were not insignificant challenges, for Riga was surrounded by marshland, especially between Jacob's Gate and the second Order Castle that was built on the banks of the Düna after 1330. In some places the ramparts were not high enough and remained unfinished for a long time. It was only after the city came under Swedish rule in the seventeenth century that Riga's fortification system could truly be considered comprehensive.

Behind Riga's brick-and-limestone walls was an ethnically mixed population whose lives were regulated by a social hierarchy that determined the status and rights enjoyed by each of the city's inhabitants. Germans, who comprised about two-thirds of the city during the Middle Ages, originally lived in the defended semicircle along the right bank of the Riga River, a short distance from the port where goods were collected for exchange. Soon the Germanic settlers spread to other parts of a city that grew by annexing adjacent areas and extending the city's walls around them. Livs originally tended to congregate closer to the Düna in the area where the Dome complex is located today and in the suburbs outside the walls.[50] Like the Latvian tribes, the Livs were consigned to certain low-status occupations that typically involved loading, unloading, and transporting merchandise. Russian traders had a quarter in the northern part of the city that was annexed in 1234. This *Russche dorp* ("Russian village") is in the area of today's Trokšņu iela (Noisy Street), where the Swedish Gate has stood since the 1690s.[51] The presence of these Slavic traders is confirmed by the use of Russian weights and measuring systems in Riga, for German traders frequently measured their goods in *poods*, and some even spoke a smattering of Russian—a skill that was later frowned upon by the Hanseatic League.[52] Also living in the city was a small number of Lithuanians, their numbers spiking in the years after 1298, when Riga hosted a Lithuanian garrison during its war against the Livonian Order.

By the time Riga's first civil war ended in 1330 (see chapter 4), the heart of Riga's civic life was the central square that began to develop once the city had expanded its territory beyond St. Peter's. There, near the church in an open space that became known as Town Hall Square,[53] a new market place was established that was better suited to meeting the needs of a growing merchant community.[54] If the street network was not especially dense at this time, getting around was easy enough, for the main roads all led to the New Market Square.[55] As in all the German colonial towns into which the open rectangular square was introduced, Riga's market place had a utilitarian function: it was the focal point of urban activity.[56] On the edges were not the monumental and representative buildings that would later arrive with the Renaissance, but rather butchers' shops, bakeries, breweries, and trading houses.[57] It was for these activities that many of Old Riga's forty or so streets were named, if only informally.

After 1334 the market square was also the location of the new Town Hall, equipped with a bell tower that warned Rigans of dangers like insurrection or invasion. This was above all a civic building: it was while standing on the Town Hall balcony that a councilman read a series of rules and decrees (*Bursprake*n) to the citizens who assembled in the square each year on September 29, the Christian feast day of Michaelmas that signified the end of the harvest. Horse stalls, all kinds of booths and huts, the city scales, and a mint were all located near the Town Hall, which even had its own wine cellar.[58] It was behind the Town Hall that many of the city's councilors and merchants made their homes.[59]

As in other Hanse cities, Riga's main square, much smaller during the Middle Ages than today, was also a theater for the townsfolk—a space where celebrations for the people took place during holidays, on market days, or when fairs came to town. On this cobbled square (sometime after 1413 the area became the first part of the town to be paved with stones) the townsfolk of Riga assembled for entertainment. During the extravagant Carnival celebrations that took place every February or March, the men and women of Riga observed plays based on biblical themes and enactments of scenes from the lives of saints. Early on the performers were typically monks, who would take the time to explain the performance to onlookers before attending to the practical matter of collecting donations; but eventually the square became a popular place for secular productions put on by laypeople as well. As Riga entered the later Middle Ages, the market square would attract performers of all kinds—conjurers, rope-walkers, and traveling comedians.[60] For entertainers such as these, a stop at distant Riga might be one of many on the Baltic coast.

No less entertaining, if only in the crudest way, were the gruesome public punishments inflicted upon those found guilty of some sort of crime. On such occasions, witnesses would be summoned (after 1480) to the square by the ringing of the "poor sinners' bell" located outside St. Jacob's Church. Later, during the witch scares of the sixteenth and seventeenth centuries, people suspected of having sold their souls to the Devil were taken to the main square to be tried, condemned, and burned on a bonfire. No less often the accused, mostly women, were subjected to the "water ordeal": their hands and feet bound, the accused were thrown into a Düna channel then known as a "judgment ditch," whereby those whom the water accepted (i.e., those who drowned) were proclaimed innocent.[61]

While the central square was the city's main scene of power and authority, where justice was carried out and lawbreakers were punished, the growing city was nevertheless bound to spill outside its constricting walls, where Riga's non-Germans toiled in the city's shipyards, kilns, and gardens. The city's first major suburb was located outside the wall behind the Rigebach, in what was then called Rigeholm (Riga's islet), now known as the Moscow suburb.[62] Accessible from the walled city by a bridge over the Rigebach outside the Stable Gate (Ger. Marstalporte), at first Rigeholm was the location of the city's vegetable gardens before it was transformed into a center for shipbuilding known as Lastadia, first mentioned in historical sources in 1348 and now the location of the present-day Central Market.[63] It was probably around this time that main port was moved to the Düna embankment, a location better suited to accommodate the increasingly large ships that sailed to Livonia. Thus the Düna port, paved during the fifteenth century, fully replaced "Lake Riga" as an import/export harbor, while the latter continued to serve as a facility for the transport of local goods.

The Guilds

Like the Prussian towns and the other Livonian centers, Riga was now a part of Germanic Europe, where craftsmen and merchants organized themselves into guilds whose development was closely tied to that of the towns. If the Riga Town Council (Rath) was the city's government, then the guilds were its leading civic associations.[64] Over the years the urban guilds or brotherhoods acquired a monopoly over all the trades in town so that they might limit competition and regulate the number of people who could practice a particular trade. Seventy crafts enjoyed official recognition during the fourteenth century; later more than one hundred crafts would have their own organizations.[65] In addition to regulating the quality of goods produced by their craftsmen, the guilds also offered their members support and protection at a time when cities had few other social resources. Crucial to the city's social life, the guilds dispensed charity, buried the members' dead, provided welfare for widows and orphans, held Mass for the deceased, and organized weddings for the betrothed.[66]

Two overarching guilds in particular dominated the affairs of medieval Rigans: the Great Guild (Grosse Gilde) and the Small Guild (Kleine Gilde). Established in 1354 as the Merchants' Company, the Great Guild (the term first occurs in 1399) was formally called St. Mary's. Not only was it Riga's most notable civic institution, it was also its most exclusive. From the beginning the Great Guild refused admission to non-Germans and to all who provided auxiliary services. Endeavoring to maintain its independence from the town council, the Great Guild forbade its members from bringing internal disputes before city authorities. The amount of self-regulation in early Riga—by the traders, the craft guilds, the monastic knights, and the archbishopric—would astonish modern peoples accustomed to the pervasiveness of centralized authority.

Alongside Riga's Great Guild, the merchants had a second organization, the Brotherhood of Blackheads (Schwarzenhäupter). The name for this fraternity, established only in the cities of Livonia, was derived from its patron saint Mauritius, who commonly appears as a North African Moor. This is the "blackhead" who was depicted on the portal of the New House, which after 1334 stood opposite the Town Hall built at the same time.[67] Like St. Nicholas and St. Anne, St. Mauritius was a patron to Lübeck merchants and sailors who undertook trade voyages to the eastern Baltic. First mentioned in historical sources in 1416, although certainly much older than that (a chapter in Reval dates to 1399), the brotherhood consisted of foreign traders and journeymen merchants, typically sons of Great Guild members.[68] Less than thirty years of age, such men had not yet acquired a household or established a family life. For many young merchants, joining the Blackheads was a rite of passage before their eventual marriage and admission to the Great Guild, where they would remain for the rest of their lives. The similarities between the Blackheads fraternities and associations called King Arthur's Courts (Artushöfe) in Prussia were so great that the House of Blackheads in Riga was often called by that name. Although they were not citizens, the Blackheads enjoyed close relations with the Great Guild, with whose members they jointly celebrated holidays. For many years they even shared the same headquarters.

Despite their itinerant status, the Blackheads were not exempt from civic duties. Above all, they were expected to participate in the defense of the city in case of attack. A principally German fraternity that also welcomed Swedes, Dutchmen, Englishmen, and other foreign traders, the society remained in existence until the Baltic Germans, summoned to the Reich by Adolf Hitler, en masse abandoned Latvia and its capital city in 1939.

Institutions like the Blackheads fraternity were common in all the major towns of the Baltic Sea. Reval, Dorpat, and even Novgorod each had its own chapter. No less organized were the associations created by Livonia's craftsmen, whose social status was distinctly below that of the exclusive merchant guild. Formally known as St. John's, the overarching craftsmen's organization was commonly called the

FIGURE 5. House of Blackheads and statue of Roland, 2010. Photo by Nikater.

Small Guild, due to the size of its meeting quarters.[69] Anyone who produced particular artisanal products—leather, shoes, iron goods, and so on—was obligated to join the corresponding guild, which in turn assured that its members had an equal chance to earn a living by eliminating all outside competition, limiting the number of workshops, and stipulating both the price and quality of their products.[70]

While little is known about the origins of the city's first craftsmen organizations, what's certain is that such bodies were modeled on European patterns. Like the accomplished and independent artisans of Germany's towns and cities, the master craftsmen of Riga enjoyed a privileged existence that was envied by men positioned farther down the social ladder. Not the least of these privileges was a certain contentment with one's station in life, for in social terms the master craftsman, who owned his own shop, tools, and home, stood head and shoulders above the people who worked for him. These included Riga's journeymen, who labored for years under different masters, at times in faraway Germany, in the hopes of someday becoming masters themselves. Journeymen had their own brotherhoods within the Small Guild, as the statutes for vocational associations of bakers, blacksmiths, and other brotherhoods attest.

Whatever autonomy journeymen had once enjoyed gradually narrowed. By the end of the Middle Ages, Riga's journeymen artisans were not even allowed to meet in the absence of the master.[71] But at least the journeyman's position was better than that of the apprentice, who stood at the bottom of a workshop's hierarchy while being taught how to make shoes, forge metal, or bake bread. Enjoying few rights and condemned to what amounted to a semi-voluntary indentured servitude, the lives of the young apprentices were shaped by their total dependence on the master and on wages that were barely enough to sustain themselves even in good times.

Festivals and Celebrations

The same institutions that supervised commerce, labor, and production also controlled Riga's social life. It was the guilds and brotherhoods that arranged the city's banquets, holidays, and ceremonies, for the sharing of common meals and the enjoyment of great festivals reinforced the corporate identity of the city elite. The most splendidly celebrated occasions in Riga during the later Middle Ages were Christmas and Carnival, as well as Pentecost and Martinmas.[72] Such occasions for merrymaking were distinguished from the many other holidays and festivities by the use of the German word "*drunke*," a "drinking feast" that could last for days on end. As the historian Anu Mänd has shown, the word is connected most closely with Christmas and Carnival, winter holidays so similar in their merrymaking as to appear almost identical in their scale, expense, and traditions.[73]

If the word "*drunke*" conjures images of a boozy binge with besotted bachelors and bumblers shambling from one beer cellar to the next until they could stagger no more, the reality is less awful (or amusing). Not only were the alcoholic beverages of the Middle Ages less intoxicating than their modern counterparts, the festivities usually didn't begin until late in the afternoon; thus a brother who managed to achieve sobriety might choose to use the day to conduct his business.[74] In some respects the festivals *were* business. These were, after all, the principal gatherings of Riga's most important civic and social organizations. On the morning of Ash Wednesday, after more than a week of eating, drinking, and dancing, the Blackheads would hold their general assembly (*steven*) at which the statutes were read, new regulations were added, and new members were admitted.[75] On this occasion the fraternity's leaders would also collect any outstanding fines and try to resolve their members' complaints and quarrels.

So seriously did the city take its major festivals that its unmarried men—dozens of Riga's most eligible bachelors—were compelled to attend. "I ask you to listen!" cried the Blackheads' alderman as the festival preparations entered their final stage. "Whoever is a Black Head or intends to become one, should come tomorrow at twelve, and take the *drunke* seriously." And serious it was: facing fines for absenteeism, the vast majority of guild members joined in the celebrations. Yet the guild leaders were determined to keep the *drunke* an orderly affair, levying fines—usually payable in cash, but also in wax or even in beer—for verbal insults and physical altercations, for gambling, for spilling or splashing beer, for dumping it on another person's head, or, most indecently of all, for vomiting in the guildhall. Although plentiful and relatively cheap, the beer imported from cities like Hamburg, Wismar, and Danzig (there were also the substandard local ales quaffed by Rigans) was the main expense of the *drunke*.[76]

Since maintaining their traditions was of particular importance to Riga's burghers, over time the customs associated with festival regulations were written down in an effort to maintain continuity with the past and to affirm the group identities of the city's leading civic associations. Detailed Carnival regulations from the early 1500s provide a reliable indication of how elaborately staged the Blackheads' celebrations had become by the later Middle Ages. The preparations would commence on a Monday at seven in the morning, as a banner displaying the Blackheads' coat of arms was set up in front of their imposing new fraternity house at the edge of Riga's central square. The beating heart of Riga's social life, the market square would soon be buzzing with Rigans of all social classes. The next two days were typically spent getting ready for the *drunke*, as the brothers "tasted" the locally brewed beer, making sure it was up to snuff, and decorated the feast hall. On Wednesday at noon the Carnival *drunke* would be announced with the rolling of drums and the bleating of horns. While the food and beverages were being prepared, servants laid the celebrants' silver goblets upon the feast table, after which the alderman would deliver his speech and welcome the fraternity's guests. The following day the brothers would assemble on horseback in front of their New House ("King Arthur's Court"), where the parade was to begin. From there the brothers, led by hired musicians, would ride out of the city through the Sand Gate, only to be "fetched in"—that is, returned in a festival parade—sometime later in a manner intended to suggest that law and order was now being reestablished amid the wild atmosphere of Carnival.[77] In the afternoon the men jousted at the market square near Town Hall, with the feasting and dancing (sword-dancing was a favorite) continuing into the evening at the New House.

Then the indoor celebrations would spill into the street, whose squares were lit with burning leaves as the Blackheads paraded to the Town Hall and to the New House where the Great Guild met.[78] Since the buildings belonging to Riga's most important civic institutions were all located on or near the market square in the center of the city, the well-to-do revelers, nearly all of whom were Germans, would not have had occasion to pass through the smellier and noisier neighborhoods on the city's margins where Riga's butchers[79] and weavers[80] plied their trades. Nor would the procession have taken the pageant to the port area neighborhood[81] where the modest homes of the Latvian salt and beer porters and warehouse attendants were located. The parade route also steered clear of the archbishop's area, dominated by the Dome Cathedral complex. Nor would the revelers have approached the Order Castle that was built on the Düna embankment to replace the original castle the townsmen destroyed during a war in 1297.

While it is unfortunate that the Latvians and others who worked for pay were excluded from the revelries (and from almost everything else), there was food, beer, and entertainment aplenty to satisfy Riga's upper crust and their guests. These were typically traders and ship captains, and occasionally noblemen, who hailed from foreign Hanseatic towns and had to spend the winter in Riga. A wonderful example is the lavish pageant the town council held during Carnival in 1495 for Walter of Plettenberg (Wolter von Plettenberg; 1450–1535), a commander of the Livonian Order who had defeated the city in a war in 1491 and was subsequently elected the order's master. Accompanied by an entourage of armed men that numbered in the hundreds, the master, who at the time resided in Wenden, was feted like a monarch in what was a major event in the life of the city. Rigans held blazing torches made from expensive beeswax in front of the knight as he entered through one of its gates. The Blackheads reportedly danced for the master; town councilors paid him homage.[82] Order masters were also frequent guests of the town council at Christmas—at least during the years before 1484 when the master's residence was located in Riga. Thus, the festivals were excellent opportunities for Riga's leading citizens to practice the art of diplomacy with their distinguished guests, with whom they shared a table that was well stocked with foreign wines, wild game (a food for aristocrats during the Middle Ages), and all manner of exotic fruits and spices.

Such extravagances would hardly have been possible had it not been for the commercial explosion of the fifteenth and sixteenth centuries, and with it, Riga's expanding trade links.[83] When they could, Riga's burghers drank expensive claret, a spiced wine connected above all with the Christmas celebrations; otherwise they were happy to quaff the cheaper wine that Riga imported from the Rhine valley. On certain feast days, Riga's leading citizens sank their teeth into specially prepared hunks of beef, oxen, mutton, chicken, ham, or tongue. On designated fasting days they ate fresh fish, including pike, salmon, and carp. Enhanced, depending on availability, with colonial spices such as saffron, pepper, cumin, cloves, nutmeg, and cinnamon, the main dishes were typically accompanied by condiments like onions, vinegar, mustard, and horseradish. Rolls and sweetbreads were ubiquitous at Riga's feast tables, while sugar was commonly used in desserts, confectioneries, and condiments.

Fashions and tastes are prone to change, but one thing remained consistent over the centuries, and that was that the grander luxuries were reserved for the men. On the days when female guests were invited to attend, particularly those occasions dedicated to dancing, only apples, nuts, and cakes were served as refreshments, along with butter and cheese.[84]

Religious prescriptions also affected what was available on feast tables on any given day of the *drunke*. But it seems that nobody, aside from the clerics (who, if so moved, might have ensured that only proper feast dishes were served on the appropriate days) seemed to mind the extraordinary array of luxury items that well-to-do Rigans and their guests consumed during the major holidays. Eating well, like being clad in silks and fur-lined coats, wearing gold ornaments, and dwelling in a well-tended and spacious home, was just one of the ways that members of the wealthier upper crust distinguished themselves from Riga's downtrodden non-Germans, themselves clad in homespun clothing made from linen and similarly cheap materials that ensured they would never be mistaken for Riga's elites.[85] Merchants and Blackheads further indulged in games such as dice and cards that were condemned by the Church and by their own guilds and brotherhoods, but such amusements were undoubtedly an important aspect of the main festivals.[86]

One thing that all of Riga's celebrants could agree upon was beer, as the city's beer cellars remained open late into the evening of the *drunke*. Concluding the Carnival *drunke* on the first Tuesday of Lent after eight days of celebrating, the Blackheads' alderman would announce that "no one is to leave here, until the beer is finished."[87]

It is worth noting that amusements enjoyed by well-to-do Rigans and their distinguished guests—competitions and war games, jousting and sword-dancing—were accessible only to a privileged minority, for these pastimes existed at the intersection between the urban culture of the Livonian cities and the knightly ranks of European society. If one ponders Riga's particular ethnic and social environment, wherein an exclusively German elite ruled over a non-German underclass, it makes perfect sense that the town's urban elite would have identified with a landed aristocracy consisting almost entirely of Germans who, even if small in number, thoroughly dominated a countryside populated by Latvian peasants. The adoption of courtly customs suggests a growing self-consciousness on the part of Riga's German merchants, for to behave in the manner of a knight, and to live as well as a nobleman, were signs of pride and prestige.[88] It was not long before Riga's bourgeoisie would adopt coats of arms and other affectations of the highborn.

Another winter holiday custom that commands our attention is the tradition of carrying trees or branches—a practice that had become common in the Livonian cities in the decades before the Reformation swept through the region in the 1520s. Tourist literature in Riga informs modern visitors that this is where the decorated Christmas tree was born. Indeed, there is even a commemorative marker in Town Hall Square indicating the alleged location of Riga's first "Christmas tree." If this claim adds a splash of color to Riga's history, it is nevertheless clearly a stretch, for trees, notably maypoles, had a role in festivals at other times of the year as well, and not only in Riga.

Perhaps one of the most illuminating aspects of these festivities is how they demonstrate the close relations enjoyed by members of the city's leading associations, as the visiting and receiving of guests was one of the most important aspects of these urban celebrations. Members of both guilds as well as the Blackheads regularly participated in processions such as Corpus Christi, a feast held in late May or June that began to be celebrated in Riga in the 1320s. On this occasion members holding candles called "guild's lights" (*gildestaven lichte*) marched one after another in succession, with those occupying the city's most prestigious positions in the rear, closest to the Host borne by the clergy.[89] Another tradition of the Blackheads in Riga was to invite clergymen to the dinners that were served near the end of the major festivals—perhaps as a means of maintaining good relations with Riga's spiritual authorities, and perhaps to obtain pardon for the sins committed at the *drunke*. Indeed, at eight or nine o'clock the following morning the brothers were expected to show up for Mass at the Dominican church (which, of course, many overslept) before assembling at their house to hold the closing general assembly.[90]

The celebrations described here were the preserve of an urban elite, for as the distance between the merchant and craft guilds grew, Riga's artisans were excluded from the great festivals as the old communitarian traditions gave way to increasingly rigid patterns of inclusion and exclusion. Nevertheless, the artisanal guilds continued to hold feasts that were connected to their annual meetings, which usually took place around Easter and Michaelmas.[91] About the celebrations put on by the poorer *Undeutsche*, there is very little in the way of written evidence, for the city's lower classes did not draw up regulations for their festivals like the Blackheads did. It is clear enough that Riga's Latvian communities maintained their devotion to traditional holidays such as Jāņi (June 24), the summer solstice festival that is connected to St. John the Baptist.[92] While the Catholic priests recoiled from the strange rituals and practices they witnessed on such occasions—these must have smacked of the locals' residual paganism mixed with Christian traditions—the fact is that the St. John's Day celebrations were important to nearly all the city's residents. That said, it should always be remembered that even if the town's ordinary residents—Latvians and Livs, Russians and low-status Germans—shared Riga's streets and squares with the city's well-to-do burghers, their social lives rarely overlapped.

Deutsche and *Undeutsche*

Anu Mänd's lively investigation of the theater of drinking festivals in Riga and the other Livonian cities illustrates a common problem when it comes to studying urban life during the Middle Ages: ordinary residents appear at the edges of history much as they do at the margins of medieval towns, for the focus is almost always on the wealthy few who dominated a city's economic, political, and cultural life. Indeed, the names that appear in Riga's trade registers and debtor's books come not from the abundant ranks of the poor, but from the city's more prosperous households—the same families that enjoyed membership in the Great Guild and whose leaders were elected to the town council. But if in good times money flowed into the busy port, Riga's inhabitants did not share equally in the prosperity. That many of the town's more affluent citizens had the means to employ servants or that Riga's master craftsmen were able to take on plenty of apprentices owes much to the paltry wages they offered; even by the standards of the time, wages in Riga were low.[93]

Every medieval city had its working poor: they tended to live in modest homes behind the larger facilities (the port, civic buildings) or in the ramshackle suburbs that spilled beyond the city walls. Every city also harbored an underclass of marginalized peoples like beggars and lepers, orphans and prostitutes, who tended to live in the city's undesirable peripheral districts. Particularly grievous was the fate of peasant girls who fled the countryside only to arrive in Riga with no skills or trade. If some managed to obtain a position with a German merchant as his handmaiden, they ran the risk of also becoming the object of his lust. The most unfortunate among them ended up working in one of the city's three brothels, for even if prostitution was reviled, it was legal just the same.[94]

Exercising no power and often dependent on charity, Riga's unfortunates—overwhelmingly non-Germans—were nevertheless recognized as having a place in the life of the city. The task of feeding the needy fell in part to charitable associations called Table Guilds (Tafelgilde), whose members usually belonged either to the Great or the Small Guild. But it was the Church that provided the poor with houses of worship, hospitals for the care of the sick, and almshouses for the destitute. Some of Riga's charitable institutions were founded by wealthy individuals or by the city itself. A few, like St. George's and the Hospital of the Holy Spirit, became important landowners in their own right.[95]

Throughout the medieval world, care of the sick, the elderly, and the "shamefaced" poor—people who had fallen into poverty through no fault of their own—was regarded as an obligation of Christian charity, not least because paupers repaid donors' alms by praying for the salvation of their souls.[96] In the later Middle Ages, however, the concept of "dishonorability" came increasingly into use for the purpose of exclusion in what had become a rigidly hierarchical society dominated by those who possessed wealth and power. Perhaps no medieval institution was more responsible for this development than the guilds, which, in an effort to stave off competition, began to hold honorable birth as a precondition for membership.[97] Thus the illegitimate children of prostitutes, street sweepers, latrine cleaners, and similarly disadvantaged peoples faced a socially and legally acceptable form of discrimination that relegated many unfortunates to the ranks of a perpetual underclass. Given the almost total social separation between Germans and non-Germans (the latter comprised about one-third of the city's population in 1450) and the clear advantages that the former enjoyed over the latter, it is no exaggeration to say that Latvians themselves, a minority at any given time, comprised the lion's share of Riga's underclass.

The initiative for these constraints, possibly influenced by the plague epidemic, came mainly from the guilds, which sought to limit the number and type of people who could become members. While Riga's ruling class did not want or need Latvians to conduct overseas trade—this was the preserve of Germans—those same traders welcomed the annual flow of peasants from the nearby countryside to do the strenuous work of off-loading the goods that arrived in Riga each spring.[98] But if the city dwellers allowed some peasants to settle in the town to do physical labor, once in the city those same enterprising peasants—safe from the power of the nobility once they had lived in Riga for a year and a day—became an economic threat as they began to learn new trades and crafts.

Unwilling to tolerate this competition, Riga's craft guilds placed limits on them, so that by the end of the fourteenth century the lines between the city's *Deutsche* and *Undeutsche* had begun to harden.[99] Already in 1354 the traders had separated from the craftsmen: their rules would not allow non-Germans to be members of the merchants' guild. Then it was the turn of the artisanal guilds: in 1375 master coopers were forbidden from taking non-Germans as apprentice coopers. A similar prohibition was extended to linen bleachers in 1390, followed by tailors, cobblers, and so on.[100] Although they were permitted to organize their own brotherhoods or "guilds" (*Zünfte*), Riga's transport workers, salt porters, bathhouse owners, fishermen, and people who labored in other auxiliary services—that is, non-Germans—were similarly excluded from the Small Guild, which meant that they did not enjoy the same legal rights as the city's German burghers.

Thus a whole series of occupations that were once permitted to non-Germans incrementally became closed off. For example, during the city's early years it was permissible for any householder to brew beer—a vital component of Rigans' diet—for personal use or for sale. However, as the potential for making profits by selling beer for export to Danzig, Königsberg, and other Prussian cities became increasingly evident, regulations went into effect in 1384 that not only banned imported beer but also prohibited non-Germans from brewing beer or even making honey.[101] While the locals were allowed to continue to ply their traditional trades—tending to the port, unloading goods, filling barrels, driving in the piles upon which houses were built, and so on—barriers to social mobility had hardened by the end of the fourteenth century. This is not to say that Latvians had no opportunity to improve their lot, but if one did manage to move up, he was no longer *undeutsch* but German, having invisibly assimilated the Germans' language, dress, manners, and customs.

Meanwhile, as the number of Latvians escaping an encroaching serfdom to breathe Riga's "free air" swelled, their position in the city worsened. Some became coachmen and domestic servants, but most were relegated to physically demanding trades such as masonry and carpentry, and later to the pounding (scutching) and weaving of hemp and flax. Although allowed to join brotherhoods that were organized by occupation (beer and wine carriers, porters, and so on), after 1469 non-Germans were no longer allowed to acquire real estate (even if wealthier Latvians got around this) and they now enjoyed fewer rights than Riga's free citizens.[102] Denied the right to obtain homes or buildings within the city walls, lacking citizenship or a collective identity, and exerting no political influence whatsoever, the position of Latvians in Riga would remain largely unaltered until the abolition of serfdom in the nineteenth century.

It was sometimes possible, nevertheless, for Germans and non-Germans to find common ground. Documents from the late fifteenth century indicate that a few high-ranking Germans—wealthy merchants, town councilors, and even clergymen—began to join the ranks of the brotherhoods of porters, a phenomenon common to other Hanse cities. Perhaps the most prominent example is John (Johann) Schöning (d. 1502). Arriving in Livonia in 1458, this enterprising trader became a Riga town councilor in the 1470s and later served as one of its four burgomasters, or chief executives.[103] In 1486 Schöning, a German, joined the porters' guild. Thus, for a time and in a limited way, the brotherhood of beer porters, with an average membership of some two hundred people (including some women) at that time, united the city's socially marginal non-German population with an element of its German elite. Such was the case until the Reformation decimated the power of this guild. While its German and non-German members did not enjoy the same standing before the law, all conspired to keep undesirables such as dishonest people and "openly loose women" out of their organizations.[104]

Members of the auxiliary crafts were obligated to carry out certain responsibilities to the city. Above all, the Letts and Livs were expected to contribute to Riga's maintenance and security as a firefighting force. Supplied with hooks, buckets, and other firefighting equipment, members of the auxiliary crafts were Riga's first firefighters.[105] As the wooden city was repeatedly ravaged by fire during its first century (1215, 1264, 1272, 1293, and 1297), in the wake of the great fire of 1293, the city issued its first building regulations, which now required Rigans to erect buildings of stone and brick within the city walls. The new regulations also encouraged uniformity by setting a maximum height and length for new houses: henceforth the closely built houses were to be a maximum of twenty-four feet high and the facades facing the street no more than fifty feet long.[106] While some of the sacral architecture of this period has survived, sometimes only in fragments, none of the domiciles, meeting halls, and warehouses built in the fourteenth and fifteenth centuries remain today.

Riga's buildings and streets were laid out much like those of other northern European cities of the time. Burghers acquired plots of land in long narrow strips that stretched from one street to the one behind it. Traditionally, the front of a building would face the street, while the cattle sheds (many homeowners in medieval Riga kept cattle), stables, coach houses, and servants' quarters were located in a yard that was accessible through the back streets.[107] Such was the arrangement of the houses belonging to the well-to-do on Wealthy Street:[108] its yards with pigsties faced a back street that, suitably enough, became known as Pig Street,[109] to which the socially marginal were consigned to live among rows of unattractive warehouses. Although few street names were fixed, by the beginning of the sixteenth century, nearly all the streets that exist in Old Riga today had already been formed.

The most common type of house for prosperous Germans in medieval Riga was a combination of dwelling house and warehouse, with high, steep gables that faced the street and spacious attics that were used as storerooms. Typical of Hanseatic commercial culture, Riga's houses were arranged in such a way that goods stored up above could be retrieved easily by pulling them down with a winch attached to the beams of the roof. While a typical craftsman might have a one-story attic, the city's merchants required more space for storing bulk items like flax and hemp for export. By the later Middle Ages their attics could reach four or five stories.

By this time a prosperous burgher's house would also have been distinguished by its entrance: above a Gothic portal, for example, one might encounter a proprietary mark that was carved on a slab of stone—a representation of wheat, a scene from the Bible, a relief of the Virgin Mary or one of the other saints, a coat of

FIGURE 6. The Three Brothers, 2016. Late medieval dwelling houses at 17, 19, and 21 Mazā Pils Street. Photo by Guntars Mednis.

arms. Not only did these function as "addresses," some identified the owner's line of work as a baker, a master craftsman, or a merchant.

All of Riga's earliest dwellings have been lost to time, with only a few examples from the later Middle Ages remaining. Dating to the late fifteenth century, 17 Mazā Pils iela is the oldest of Riga's famous "Three Brothers" and a typical dwelling house of the late Middle Ages. Several stories high and possessing a façade decorated with a stepped gable, the building's main hall was probably used as a shop and an office, while the "kitchen" in the building's rear did double duty as a bedroom for apprentices and servants. Storerooms on the upper floor might at times have been converted into bedrooms and living areas. But with renovations altering the building's appearance and even its function (by 1697 there was a bakery in the house), it is difficult to know exactly what the building looked like at any point in time. That it was a middle-class dwelling that was passed from one German to the next, generation after generation, there can be little doubt. Servants, typically fugitive peasants with few alternatives, also lived in such houses—in the master's attic or basement—but that was because city regulations prohibited servants from living outside the dwellings of their masters.

Like Amsterdam, which would emerge as one of Europe's most dynamic cities after 1500, medieval Riga was a work in progress, if only on a smaller scale more suited to the lightly inhabited eastern Baltic. Where fires destroyed buildings and property, Riga's citizens rebuilt them. Where embankments eroded, Rigans shored them up. For example, as the port on the Riga River became polluted with waste and debris, rendering it increasingly unusable, the issue was taken up by the town council, which in 1352–1353 allocated eleven marks for oak logs and piles to reinforce the deteriorating embankment. Further reinforcements were carried out in the fifteenth century to prevent the base of the city wall from leaching in the spring when the Düna tended to overflow.

The old port by the Riga rivulet was also improved: extending the reinforcements closer to the middle of the riverbed gave dock workers a wider area along the embankment where they could unload their goods. As we have noted, by the end of the fourteenth century the main port—one better able to accommodate the larger cogs and hulks arriving from western Europe—had been relocated to the Düna, while the older facility on the Rigebach continued to serve as a winter port and place for boat mooring. As it filled up with garbage, stones, and bricks, "Lake Riga" became a public nuisance, a tank of standing water whose foul odor exacerbated what was becoming an increasingly congested and noxious urban environment.[110]

Town councilor Tönnies Frölich was all too familiar with the Rigebach's sorry condition, for it was his charge to oversee the difficult job of broadening and deepening the channel. "In 1610 I began to clean the Riga, starting from the Düna, through the vaults, advancing from the Düna up to the inner ramparts, and it was hard work." Here the city's workmen came upon the oaken piles that indicated the exact location of what may have been Riga's original Livish fortress, buried in the earth.[111] Later, during the dictatorship of Kārlis Ulmanis (1934–1940), the work of uncovering the remnants of Riga's ancient past would fall to Latvian archaeologists. Rauls Šnore headed the team that in 1938 unearthed a thirteenth-century shipwreck in a part of the city known today as Albert Square. As noted at the chapter's beginning, the ship's remnants are housed in the Rīga Museum of History and Navigation, where they testify to the city's importance in the growing Baltic trade of the later Middle Ages.

Why the city's reigning authorities have never bothered to commemorate the site of Riga's original port—the birthplace of the medieval city, now entombed in a sarcophagus of cement and cobblestone—remains an unsolved mystery.

Chapter 4

Master of Riga: The Archbishop, the Order, and the Rath

Mit namen Riga heisst die statt
da ist ein weiser kluger rath,
darzu ein erbar gmeine,
die leben stets in einigkeit,
sind unverzagt in lieb und leid
widerzustehen dem feinde.

The city is called Riga
It has a wise and sound council
For that reason
they always live in unity
They are undaunted in love and song
resisting the enemy.[1]

This chapter begins with a modest challenge. I invite the reader to thumb through the index of whatever general history of the Middle Ages that happens to be at hand and scan it for the word "Riga." Perhaps your text offers one or two references to Livonia's largest urban center, if only in passing. It is just as likely, as I have discovered on many occasions, that the text overlooks the city altogether.

Even as Riga guarded a major trade artery, converted the pagans, and collected the treasures of the Russian forest, the bustling port is entirely absent from *A Distant Mirror* (1980), Barbara Tuchman's haunting tome about the crises of the later Middle Ages. The historian's focus, of course, was not on the lands and peoples of northeastern Europe, but rather on that part of the continent that is traditionally identified as the "West"—that is, the lands from the eastern Atlantic and the North Sea to the western Mediterranean. So remote from the major centers of royal power were the smaller, nonroyal cities of Danzig, Riga, and Reval that this Pulitzer Prize–winning historian concluded they were hardly worth mentioning at all.

The customary emphasis on the western part of the continent is understandable, for the economic and intellectual recovery of the High Middle Ages was distinctly more prominent in the West. While Flanders and Florence surged ahead, the "other Europe" fell behind and was gradually swallowed by the Ottoman, Polish, and Muscovite states. So distant was Riga from the main centers of European civilization that it might as well have been located in Muscovite Russia, whose reputation for barbarism, whether warranted or not, was well known in the West.

Terra incognita to all but the most knowledgeable European travelers, medieval Riga was a modest frontier outpost of the decentralized Holy Roman Empire, a polity that granted considerable autonomy to its "free cities" (*Freie Städte*). As a rule, the free cities were initially subject to a prince-bishop, but over time tended to secure greater independence from their feudal lords. Originally placed under the authority of Bishop Albert of Buxhoeveden, during its first century Livonia's largest settlement developed its own institutions of self-government—notably, the Riga Town Council (Rath) that made law and administered the city's affairs. However, the town's pretensions to autonomy clashed with the ambitions of the region's other great feudal lord, the Order of Swordbrothers (and then its successor, the Livonian Order). The burning question of who possessed ultimate authority—who was master of Riga?—bedeviled the city from the beginning.

Balance of Power

Early Riga was in most respects a typical Germanic city with the usual urban hierarchies and institutions of self-governance. It was also a town of immigrants, dominated by Germans who comprised the political class, the priesthood, and the merchant class as well. The struggles that shaped medieval Riga, then, were not between Germans and "non-Germans" (that was to come later), but among rival institutions that were populated largely by Germans.

Staking its claim to power first was the city's ecclesiastical authority—the bishop of Riga, and then, after 1255, the archbishop of Riga, who reigned over his walled residence within the city and over a cathedral where he received oaths from his vassals and the clergy. The archbishopric was also in possession of various castles and properties throughout the conquered territories. From Emperor Philip II, Bishop Albert of Buxhoeveden received the title of margrave; the appointment made the city's first ruler the ninety-fourth prince-bishop of the Holy Roman Empire.[2] Some twenty men, nearly all of whom were Germans (and none even remotely Latvian), served as archbishop of Riga up to 1563. But as the archbishop exercised little influence outside his see and was often unsafe within it,

Riga's prelates tended to sojourn in the papal curia in Avignon or Rome during the troubled fourteenth century.[3]

Aiding the archbishop were the twelve canons and the provost of the Riga Cathedral (Dome) chapter. They advised their superior and governed the diocese during his frequent and often prolonged absences. The canons also had the right to elect a candidate for a vacant archbishopric, their choice being subject to papal confirmation. Originally belonging to the Premonstratensian Order, in 1373 the Riga canons adopted the Augustinian rule and exchanged their white habit for a black one—a decision that offended the Livonian Order, whose habit was white. As it was the order's intention to incorporate the archbishopric by enticing or compelling the canons of the Riga Cathedral to become members of the order, the clerics' provocative act of adopting a black habit inaugurated nearly eighty years of litigation at the papal curia.[4]

The archbishop remained legally sovereign in Riga until 1330, the end of Riga's first civil war, and his spiritual authority went unchallenged in the areas under his jurisdiction until Luther's call reached the eastern Baltic in the 1520s. But the prelate's temporal powers over the 18,000-square kilometers of territory that he ruled, and hence his ability to impose his will on Riga or to defend his interests where they clashed with those of the knights, were limited first by the agreements that papal legate William of Modena hashed out with local authorities during the time of Bishop Albert (see chapter 2), and after that by the archbishops' progressively declining influence over their vassals, who sometimes challenged the prelate's authority. Whatever the disputes between the city and the archbishop of Riga, the latter usually supported the burghers' rights against the claims of the order.

A second center of power in medieval Riga was the Order Castle that belonged first to the Livonian Brothers of the Sword and then after 1237 to its successor organization, the Livonian Order. As the region's best-organized fighting power, the order provided the 67,000 square kilometers of territory (including lands in Estonia) that it ruled with the military shield upon which the maintenance of internal order depended. However, the order's ambition to create a unified Livonian state under its undivided authority clashed with the prerogatives of Riga's weak archbishops and its troublesome burghers, who resolved to resist all encroachments on their autonomy and who demonstrated little interest in crusading. Indeed, early defense treaties between the city and the Swordbrothers (1226) and later the Livonian Order (1255) made participation in the expeditions to the pagan lands optional for the burghers of Riga.

Still, Riga's Germans, much like the citizen-warriors of the ancient Greek *polis*, were required to own armor or to serve as a guard during times of danger—even if the well-heeled could afford to send a proxy in their stead.[5] Far from being sword-happy warriors, Riga's leading citizens were above all men of business, some of whom enjoyed citizenship in other towns as well. Preferring concord and commerce to the disruptions of a perpetual crusade, Rigans resented the order's interference in the city's trade with the Orthodox peoples of Russia and with the heathen Lithuanians, for they were Riga's main sources of supply.

While the order and the archbishop continued to insist on their feudal rights vis-à-vis the city—a resolve that typically brought them into direct conflict with each other—Riga comported itself in a fashion befitting a "free city" of the empire. That is to say that Riga behaved as an independent power led by its thriving merchant class, who dominated all the city's political, commercial, and social organizations—most notably the Rath, or town council.

That foreign traders initially exercised the greatest influence in Riga's civic life is evident from the city documents of the thirteenth century, which demonstrate the connections that early Rath members had with foreign lands (such as Johannes de Horehusen and Tidericus de Berewich, among others).[6] Indeed, Riga's liberal terms for citizenship attracted waves of new settlers during its early years. Of these, the most numerous were artisans who found the lack of competition in Livonian towns congenial. Although the average Hanseatic merchant, at least during the thirteenth century, was an itinerant trader, in the course of time visiting merchants also began to adopt Riga as a permanent home. No longer on the road, the settled merchant managed his own firm, while his most respected peers assumed positions of status, responsibility, and influence. Like Germans in other northern cities during the later Middle Ages, the burghers of Riga expected that they would be left alone to handle their own affairs without the interference of the local feudal lords.

The wealthiest Rigans formed what would later be called the patriciate—a hereditary estate of long-distance merchants who modeled their way of life on that of the landed nobility, whom they envied for their titles and privileges. It was through the Rath, and after 1354 through the Great Guild as well, that the patricians exercised their power. But only the most influential and oldest families were represented in the town council, whose twelve councilors (soon increased to sixteen and later, for a time, to twenty) gathered on Fridays to conduct their closed meetings. Of these councilors, two, and later four, enjoyed the status of burgomaster (*Bürgermeister*), a word that literally means "master of the citizens" but is usually understood as "mayor." Of these men, and they were always men and nearly always German, one took the role of chief executive. Although in later years the Rath would become the preserve of a few wealthy families whose seats passed from a deceased patrician to a living relative, this was far less the case early on: up through the end of the fifteenth century some 410 men hailing from three hundred different families served as councilors.[7]

While the archbishop dealt mainly with matters involving the Church, and the order mainly with matters of defense, the Rath controlled all activities involving property. The city supplemented its revenues through income from the imposition of taxes and tolls as well as property rentals (such as the towers in the town walls and the city vegetable gardens) and its oversight of a wide range of business and industrial enterprises (the market place, brick and lime kilns, a shipyard, tanneries, and so forth). Here we might add that the town council also functioned as a bank, lending money at interest to Riga's citizens as well as to the knights of the order. The city's main financial burdens included the maintenance of walls, buildings, and facilities; salaries for city employees and laborers; and sending delegations to other Livonian and Hanse towns. Defensive needs also required considerable outlays, especially during times of war. The purchase of copious amounts of beer and wine (which the Rath stored in its own cellar) added to the city's financial burdens, for the procuring of alcohol drained some 3 percent of the city's treasury in the years 1405–1474.[8]

First appearing in 1221, Riga's coat of arms exemplified the city's power arrangement. Impressed onto the silver marks that Riga used as its currency, the coat of arms depicts a city wall, a symbol of urban independence, with two towers and open gates. At the top are two keys, symbolizing the city's patron, St. Peter; between them stands a cross that symbolized Riga's obedience to the bishop. Although modified many times over the course of nearly eight centuries and many transfers of power, one or another version of the seal may still be spotted in the older parts of Riga, a compelling reminder of the city's historic autonomy.

The arrangement between the city's earliest spiritual, administrative, and military authorities was repeatedly tested and recalibrated, for each side hoped to exploit its rival's weaknesses in order to gain the upper hand. For Riga's merchants, the main threat was the Livonian Order, whose possession of a line of castles and vast material resources gave it a military potential unmatched in the region. The order was also the city's commercial rival—even if the scale of its mercantile activities was dwarfed by that of both the parent branch in Prussia and by Riga's great traders. Increasingly engaged in both local and long-distance commerce, the brethren of the Livonian Order were Riga's competitors for markets, especially in the grain trade. Sometimes they partnered with the Livonian (including Rigan) merchants, from whom the order purchased everything "from salt to roof tiles and from cloth to armor."[9] On occasion the grand master (*Hochmeister*) in Prussia was called upon to advocate for the interests of the Livonian merchants; likewise, it was not unusual for Riga or the other Livonian towns to lend money to the Livonian master (*Ordensmeister*) to pay for mercenaries and other expenses.[10] In disputes with pirates on the Baltic Sea and for help in recovering stolen goods, the cities, including Riga, would turn to the Livonian master—a telling example of the merchants' dependence on the order for protection.[11] One way to characterize the intercourse between Riga's enterprising traders and the querulous Livonian knights is to say that the two groups behaved in ways that were alternately antagonistic and codependent. In other words, their relationship, like that of any uneasy marriage, was complicated.

While the knights' ties with the city of Riga were more troubled than they were with Reval and the other Livonian centers, the fact remains that some of the knights and citizens shared personal and commercial bonds, and that these connections often smoothed the wheels of diplomacy. If the historiography of medieval Livonia tends to be dominated by the struggles between the order, the prelates, and the cities (political history, after all, has always focused on conflict), it should also be remembered that war was expensive business and that Riga and the order resorted to arms only when efforts at mediation failed.

The usual course of action for the Rath during times of crisis was to ally with the archbishop against the order. Yet this relationship, too, was burdened with mistrust, for the archbishop's interference in the city's secular affairs offended the sensibilities of Riga's burghers. In cases of conflict the archbishop or the Dome chapter could seek outside help: they might, for example, ask the papacy to issue an interdict on the city that suspended the public celebration of religious rites like marriage and baptism. The town council, on the other hand, had no say at all in religious affairs, lacking a voice even on the matter of priestly appointments to St. Peter's Church, the church of Riga's citizens. An unsteady balance between the city's spiritual authorities, its well-to-do burghers, and the knights upon whom all relied for protection satisfied no one for very long, for each sought to improve its position in Livonia and to assert its mastery over the Düna metropolis.

The Livonian Order

Livonia's military forces faced enormous difficulties from the beginning of the occupation. Founded in 1202 as the region's first permanent military force, the Order of Swordbrothers failed to survive beyond its thirty-fifth birthday and was replaced by a successor organization, the Livonian Order (discussed below). A main problem facing Livonia's defenders was the Swordbrothers' inability to recruit enough soldiers to man its many castles, for usually were there no more than two hundred brothers in Livonia at any one time. A related issue was financial, hence the order's habitual need to expand its holdings in the hope of increasing the number of tribute payers and warriors.

As a result, the Order of Swordbrothers was almost always embroiled in conflict. And it was not only resisting pagans with whom the knights clashed: order masters quarreled with the papacy (which tried to restrain the knights), with the bishop of Riga (over the Livonian territories), with the king of Denmark (over Estonia), with the Russians (who had claims in the region), and with the Lithuanians (with whom the knights frequently warred). Yet the castles belonging to the order were Livonia's first line of defense, and as long as the territory was threatened by pagans and schismatics, its arrogance would have to be tolerated.

Haughty and contemptuous of their rivals, the Swordbrothers were no strangers to hardship. "[T]hey kept watch, fasted and seldom rested," observed one chronicler, who was likely a knight himself. "Their sufferings were great."[12] In their cloister-castles they followed the Rule of the Templars, which required the knights to eat common meals, to live modestly and frugally, and to obey the master unequivocally. Still more austere were their fighting conditions, for the forested and sometimes swampy terrain was more favorable to the kind of warfare practiced by the natives, who used it as cover from which to conduct their raids. Even after a region had been secured, knights cloistered in frontier castles faced the possibility that seemingly conquered peoples might rebel at any time. An Estonian insurrection in 1223, for example, cost the order one third of its men. But it was the Battle of Saule (Lith. Šiauliai) that lay bare the order's weaknesses and augured its dissolution.

The battle's origins lay in a papal bull issued by Pope Gregory IX (r. 1227–1241) in February 1236 that called for a crusade in Lithuania. In strategic terms, however, the goal was to annex the lands that lay between the conquered Livonian and Prussian territories and thereby create a land bridge along the Baltic coast that would connect the two crusader states. Responding to the pope's call, in September a contingent of some two thousand crusaders sailed from Holstein. Upon arriving in Livonia, they immediately demanded to be led into battle. Although the Swordbrothers, having already conquered Estonia, were mostly interested in expanding their holdings along the Düna in what is today southeastern Latvia, Master Volquin (r. 1209–1236) found himself under pressure to act. Mobilizing a force of crusaders and allied natives, mostly Estonians, the master led his men into the swamps of Samogitia (Lith. Žemaitija), located south of Riga in northern Lithuania. If the exact site of the battle is uncertain, the outcome raises few doubts, for the encounter was a disaster for the order and for the entire crusading enterprise in northeastern Europe. Bearing in mind that medieval chroniclers typically exaggerated the scale of such battles, the author of the *Livonian Rhymed Chronicle* nevertheless indicated that Volquin and fifty or sixty of his knights—about half the Swordbrothers—perished that day, as did many others.[13] Soldiers and knights attempting to flee to the safety of Riga were allegedly slaughtered by Semigallian forces, who, like their Samogitian cousins, continued to resist the spread of German and Christian power.

Fatally weakened by the debacle in Samogitia, the Order of Swordbrothers was dissolved on papal orders, its surviving knights absorbed by the new Livonian Order. Created in May 1237, the Livonian Order was an autonomous branch of the Order of Teutonic Knights (formed in Acre around 1190), sharing the parent organization's rules and statutes. It was then that the Teutonic Order, having established an *Ordenstaat* in Prussia in 1230, introduced its distinctive habit—a white robe emblazoned with a red cross and sword—into Livonia. Following the dissolution of the Order of Swordbrothers in the spring of 1237, Hermann Balk, then the provincial master of in Prussia, rode into Riga and installed his own men to command the stone castles that the defunct Swordbrothers had built. Thus to their own *Ordenstaat* in Prussia, the Teutonic Knights now added Livonia and southern Estonia.[14] In principle, the grand master in Marienburg, a town that would soon witness the rise of what would become the world's largest brick castle, was responsible for the entire region from Prussia to Estonia; in practice, however, the order's Livonian branch was mostly left to its own devices under the direction of its own provincial master.

Meanwhile, the fighting continued. Although the crusaders refused to abandon the cause in the south—there were many battles to come with the Semigallians and Lithuanians—another possibility for evangelizing the Latin (Catholic) faith in northeastern Europe appeared in the shattered lands of the Orthodox Rus', which had just been overrun by the invading Mongols. Among the few Russian cities to escape Mongol terror were the northern cities of Pskov and Novgorod, but they too were forced to pay tribute to the Mongol khan, who cared little what faith his subjects practiced as long as they paid their annual tithes in people and goods. In the eastern Baltic the Latin forces (the Teutonic Knights, the Swedes, and the Danes) saw a new opportunity: they would exploit Russia's weakness to wage a war on Orthodoxy.

Fought in the autumn of 1240, the first battles with the Rus' brought victory to the Teutonic Knights and their allies and auxiliaries, who together succeeded in taking (if only temporarily) Pskov, Izborsk, and Koporye. The key to the crusaders' plans was the anticipated defeat of Novgorod, a city believed to be so powerful that it was known as Lord Novgorod the Great. At the moment, however, the interests of commerce took a back seat to the matter of power.

It was not until early April of 1242 that the struggle came to a head, for it was then that the knights and their auxiliaries—mostly Estonian infantrymen, led by Albert of Buxhoeveden's brother Hermann, the prince-bishop of Dorpat—fought the Rus' on the thin ice that still covered the southern end of Lake Peipus. Even if Sergei Eisenstein's classic film *Alexander Nevsky* (1938) wildly exaggerates the scale and significance of the famous "Battle on the Ice," it is true that the Russian forces were victorious (even if the margin of victory was not as great as the film suggests) and that many order brothers drowned that day.[15]

Despite this setback in the east, the 1240s and the 1250s were mostly successful for the Baltic crusaders: territories were gained, power was consolidated, and thousands were introduced to the Christian god, even as the natives clung to their old spirits, customs, and outlooks. Although the knights had few compunctions about the use of force, this is not to say that all conversions occurred at the point of a sword, for peaceful conversions were common as well—even if they often failed to stick.

Even the defiant Lithuanians, as they resisted the order's advances and raided its newly Christianized territories, learned to negotiate with their Christian adversaries in a language all could understand. Thus the shrewd tribal ruler Mindaugas (1203–1263), at last persuaded that the god of the Christians was militarily superior to the pagan gods, accepted Christianity from the Germans and was recognized as the king of Lithuania, receiving his crown from Pope Innocent IV in 1253. Agreeing to a tactical alliance with the order, Mindaugas ceded to it some of his westernmost lands, while also granting commercial privileges to the merchants of Riga, for Lithuania's rulers were coming to understand the value of developing commercial relations with the outside world.[16] A calculated flirtation with Christianity was sometimes a means to that end. Indeed, Lithuania's road to salvation was far from a straight path, for Mindaugas's relatives rejected the Christian faith and killed their king in 1263—and with that the crusader campaigns against the Lithuanians resumed. Another century would pass before Lithuania would be fully integrated into the Christian world.

Archbishop of Riga: Albert Suerbeer Confronts the Order

It was just at the time of Mindaugas's conversion that a vacancy appeared in the diocese of Riga with the passing of its second bishop, Nicholas I (r. 1230–1253). An uncontroversial figure whose main imprint on the city was his purchase of the area near the Düna embankment where he had the new Dome (St. Mary's) complex built, Nicholas managed to maintain a policy of peaceful coexistence with the Livonian Order for sixteen years until his death in 1253. But unlike the mild Nicholas, who had been proposed by Riga's canons, the third bishop of Riga, Albert Suerbeer (r. 1253–1273), was a papal appointee who did not hesitate to take advantage of the order's troubles as it battled once again with the seemingly unconquerable Lithuanians. The order, Suerbeer was convinced, must be tamed.

Albert and the order had been on a collision course long before the priest's appointment to Riga. Passed over as a candidate for Riga's bishopric in 1230, Suerbeer developed a reputation for toughness during his tenure in Ireland as archbishop of Armagh (1240–1245), and it was this reputation, that of an inflexible supporter of papal power against secular authority, that he brought to Prussia when he was appointed its archbishop in 1246. Suerbeer's propensity to wield his power by seizing taxes and excommunicating offending knights irritated the order's leadership, who warned him to stay away. As the conflict between Suerbeer and the knights escalated, the pope decided to dispatch the cleric to Livonia, assigning him the coveted Riga bishopric in 1253. Soon afterward, in exchange for Suerbeer's promise to stop harassing the order, Riga's status was elevated to an archbishopric. Under this arrangement, Suerbeer, confirmed in his post by Pope Alexander IV in January 1255, exercised religious control over both Livonia and Prussia. In secular matters, however, the bishoprics of Courland, Dorpat, and Ösel-Wiek[17] conducted themselves as small states whose interests did not always coincide with those of the archbishop of Riga.

Nevertheless, the archbishop, like the pontiffs of this time, remained convinced that it was he, the Church's highest representative, who had ultimate authority, both religious and temporal, in the areas under his jurisdiction. Even the master of the Livonian Order was subordinate, if only nominally, to the archbishop's temporal jurisdiction in the lands he ruled. When the order refused the archbishop's demand that its officers render their personal fealty and present him with gifts as tokens of their submission, Albert Suerbeer levied taxes on its property in Riga.[18] Each side brought its complaints to the pope, who, along with the German emperor, remained the Livonian principalities' nominal overlord, but neither the archbishop nor the master were appeased.

Having received little satisfaction from Rome, Suerbeer responded to the order's acts of intimidation and harassment by hatching a conspiracy with the goal of eliminating, or at least severely weakening, his rival. The plan involved the services of a poor but ambitious German nobleman, Count Gunzelin of Schwerin, who in the summer or fall of 1267 sailed with a contingent of crusaders to Riga with the intention of fighting a winter campaign near Novgorod. The first thing Gunzelin did upon arriving in Riga was to meet with the archbishop. While their conversation has not been recorded, it seems certain that they made a pact to attack the knights and seize their properties, which would have allowed the count to satisfy his ambitions of becoming a great landowner. Suerbeer, on the other hand, would be rid of his most powerful competitor. But when Gunzelin returned to Germany to recruit more soldiers, Suerbeer's scheme unraveled. Catching wind of his plans, the order kidnapped the archbishop, giving him only bread to eat and water to drink until he chose to submit. Finally capitulating in December 1268, Suerbeer dismissed Gunzelin, agreed not to complain to the pope about his imprisonment, and was allowed to return to Riga.[19]

Here was the first major confrontation—in fact, the first act of violence—between the archbishop of Riga and the Livonian Order. And it was the knights who prevailed, for the helpless prelate had been left to fend for himself. Understanding that the order was the only force capable of defending Livonia's vulnerable frontiers against the Lithuanians and Russians, it appears that the papal curia lacked an appetite for intervening in the complicated affairs of this distant see. The papacy's unwillingness (or inability) to act left Suerbeer, the titular ruler of the eastern Baltic, with little choice but to recognize the order's authority in Livonia. His power thus weakened, the archbishop died a few years later. His successors, John I (of Lune) and John II (of Vechta) were feeble and unable to resist the order's demands that they surrender some of the archbishopric's castles. It was during this period, more precisely in 1274, that the order obtained from the Holy Roman emperor a charter that allowed it (fictitiously) to claim lordship over the city.[20] The order's advantageous position vis-à-vis the city was further buttressed by its brutal victory over the Semigallians in 1290, an event that brought to a close the crusade in Livonia.[21] Consolidating its holdings along the Düna, the order was in a position to strangle Riga's trade if it so desired.

By the end of Riga's first century, the young city had assumed the shape that defined it for the remainder of the Middle Ages. Walls with gates now enclosed the entire peninsula, sealing its residents off from the outside world. Much the same could be said of the order knights: when they were not off fighting crusades, the brothers isolated themselves in St. George's (Jürgenshof), the order's fortified convent on the right bank of the Riga River (Rigebach) that wrapped around the city. Modern archaeological excavations on the site known today as the Convent Yard, now a swanky hotel complex, reveal the remnants of a modest castle that was built in the Romanesque style, with an inner yard, a protective wall, and at least three or four buildings along this wall. This first Order Castle would be destroyed in an all-out war (discussed below) between the city and the knights.

Archaeologists have also located the exact site of Riga's first port, a narrow strip along the Rigebach embankment where goods were off-loaded and the business of the day was carried out. As sand, wood chips, waste, and other materials filled up the river bed, the town council repeatedly voted to reinforce and extend the wharf deeper into "Lake Riga" so as to give its dock workers more space to carry out their work. A more intractable problem, at least until the construction of modern dams in the twentieth century, was the flooding that resulted when ice floes dammed the Düna just before the great river emptied into the Bay of Riga. In an effort to shore up the river banks so as to protect the city from the devastating floods that greeted many an April, in 1296 Rigans constructed a bridge across the Rigebach that would allow them to obtain earth, stones, wood, and other raw materials from Rigeholm, located outside the walled city. When it became apparent that the bridge could also have a military function—that it could block shipping access to the Order Castle—the knights destroyed it under cover of darkness. Each side prepared for combat.[22]

Late in the spring of 1297, Rigans began to notice a stream of men and hardware flowing into the white castle on the Rigebach. Although allowed to maintain no more than fifty knights in its fortress, the order brought up to five hundred war servants into the city, accompanied by a stone-throwing machine and other war materials.[23] Just as Riga's burghers had begun a few years earlier to replace the old city wall with a new one more than twenty feet high, now the order began to construct a wall that would connect its castle with two of its towers in the city's fortification system.[24] Having demolished the bridge, the order ignored Rigans' complaints and proceeded to place various obstacles in the way of their trade routes. The city was nearly isolated, with no Hanse allies it could count on: Lübeck was not about to risk its profits for Riga; Visby was being eyed by Sweden's rulers. Nor could Reval, which also traded with Russia, be considered a reliable ally, for it stood to benefit from Riga's adversity.[25]

Closer to home, Riga's natural allies were the prelates—the archbishop and his canons. Selected by Riga's canons in 1295 to head the archbishopric, John III (Johannes von Schwerin) was an avowed enemy of the order and therefore a friend of the city. Yet it may well have been his absence from Riga (the new archbishop was in Flanders being treated for a broken leg) that emboldened the knights in the months leading up to the confrontation.[26] The complicated story of this triad—the powerful and aggressive Livonian Order, Riga's politically ambitious but militarily impotent prelates, and the city's independent-minded citizens—unfolds like a television serial drama with a changing cast of colorful and sometimes duplicitous characters (including a few Lithuanian grand dukes) whose motives are not always clear and who sometimes behaved very badly indeed.[27] The plot is a question: who is to be the master of Riga?

Riga's First Civil War, 1297–1330

The atmosphere in Riga grew thick with tension as the order collected its forces in the summer of 1297. A truce between the city and the knights dampened passions for a time, but the peace was broken when some burghers who had gathered before the Order Castle were attacked with a volley of arrows, killing one and injuring several others. As the panicked citizens began to shoot back, the knights sprayed flaming arrows onto some of the Rigans' houses. Working tirelessly to stop the fire from spreading, the burghers scrambled to save their possessions as the flames consumed their city.[28] It was with a victory for the order that the pilot episode of Riga's first civil war concluded.

The story resumed on September 30 (old style),[29] the day after the Michaelmas celebrations that marked the end of the harvest. Aware that there weren't many knights in the city, Rigans burst into the Order Castle and captured dozens of order brothers, whom they allegedly either beheaded or dragged to the gallows and hanged.[30] The object of their wrath was the castle: when all was said and done, all that remained of St. George's was its chapel—now the location of the city's Museum of Decorative Arts and Design.

Once again in control of their own city, Rigans welcomed the archbishop's return from Flanders. The first thing the prelate did was to arrange a truce; then he dashed off a report to Rome in which he blamed the knights for what had happened. Meanwhile, an enraged Master Bruno ordered his knights to ravage the area around the city: Riga would be starved into submission. Eyewitnesses reported that the knights burned down manors and homes, destroyed the Rigans' orchards and vegetable gardens, drove off their livestock, and hindered nearby peasants from selling their surpluses in the city.[31]

Having eluded the order's blockade, the archbishop set out for his castle northeast of Riga at Treiden (Latv. Turaida), where he hoped to organize a resistance. Born of desperation, the plan collapsed when the knights took the castle and captured the archbishop, whom they mounted on a tiny horse—probably intended to humiliate him—and brought him to their castle at nearby Wenden (Cēsis). There the archbishop was thrown into a chamber and placed on a diet of bread and water for thirty-three days while the knights seized the archbishop's treasury and church ornaments. To these thefts the knights added the archbishop's seal, which they used to prepare the documents they would force him to sign. The knights even seized the lands of the cathedral canons when they rejected the order's conditions.[32]

Disgusted by these outrages, the pope summoned the order's leaders to Rome to explain themselves. But exactly what Boniface VIII (r. 1294–1303) could have done to alleviate the situation in Livonia was unclear, for the order was near and Rome was too distant and too distracted by problems within the Church to impose its will in this faraway corner of northeastern Europe.

A truce negotiated by the Hanse cities lifted the order's blockade of Riga on November 11, but it lasted only through the first week of January 1298.[33] At this moment, the story introduces a new character—the Lithuanian grand duke Vytenis (r. 1295–1316). The ruler of a growing realm that had turned its back on the Christian faith after the death of Mindaugus in 1263, Vytenis spent the first years of his reign defending Samogitia from the Teutonic Knights, whose audacious raids were met with fierce pagan resistance. By allying with the Lithuanians for help against the order, the Christians of Riga certainly took an unusual step; yet this decision only underlines the city's desperation at a moment of crisis. Vytenis, of course, had his own motives for coming to the aid of Riga. After all, the city was a leading buyer of Lithuania's grain, furs, wax, and honey—and the order's actions now threatened the commercial traffic upon which Lithuania was now dependent. That the pagan grand duke offered the archbishop the services of a Lithuanian garrison to fend off the order may seem incongruous, but awkward alliances such as this are far from rare in the annals of international diplomacy.

Vytenis must have known that having his pagan army encamped near the city of Riga would sit well neither with its Christian burghers nor with the cathedral canons, so the grand duke sweetened his proposal by making a vague offer of converting to Latin Christianity. The prospect of military cooperation between Riga and the pagans no doubt astonished and angered the order. Yet the allure of converting the Lithuanians, no matter what their offenses, must have been tantalizing to the archbishop of Riga. But even if Vytenis was committed to protecting

Lithuania's profitable trade with Riga's merchants, the grand duke, it seems, had no real intention of accepting Christ.[34] Expansion and consolidation, not salvation, were the grand duke's main concerns.

With a Lithuanian garrison now ensconced in a fortress just outside the city, Rigans imported siege machines and other equipment as they prepared for battle. Together the Lithuanian and Rigan forces fought campaigns against the order in the spring of 1298, although not always successfully. In June, the order won a great battle near Wenden, killing hundreds of pagans and freeing several thousand Christians whom the Lithuanians had captured in Estonia. The victory must have been bittersweet, for despite routing its enemies, the order lost twenty-four brothers that day, including Master Bruno, and, sources claim, hundreds of its servants.[35] Later that month, the order welcomed reinforcements from Prussia. Together the knights set out in the direction of Riga, just outside of which stood the New Mill, an order castle the Rigans and their Lithuanian allies had placed under siege. Although the Rigan forces managed to raze the fort, victory went to the order, whose soldiers invaded the city on June 29, St. Peter's Day.[36] Both sides suffered heavy losses, including the deaths of four members of the Riga Town Council.[37] As one chronicler put it: "In the city of Riga there were many widows, and many Lithuanians lost their husbands."[38] Enjoying the upper hand, the knights of the order proposed peace talks, while Archbishop John III, released from captivity, rushed to Rome to plead his case.

Rigans waited for a resolution that would humble the order, but Pope Boniface VIII was uninterested in listening to the litigants' testimony, for concerns closer to home, notably his struggles with King Philip IV of France, competed for his attention. The fact of the matter was that the pope saw no alternative to the order ruling in Livonia: who else, after all, would defend these lands from the pagans? The papal ruling of December 1299 brought about a temporary peace, but it failed to resolve the outstanding issues. That the knights won the right to remain in the city deprived Riga's burghers of a total victory; yet the knights were also compelled to make concessions. Between the city and the property of the order, the latter was to construct, at its own expense, a wall nine feet high with only a single, small gate through which the knights could leave and return. In the castle the order could keep no more than twenty brothers and no more than fifty could attend its meetings in Riga, which could take place only once a year. The bridge over the Rigebach—the ostensible cause of the conflict—would remain; however, the order's vessels were free to pass through it in order to reach the Düna.[39]

Concluding they could no longer live in the center of Riga, the brothers sold their ruined castle to the city for one thousand marks.[40] The papacy also forced the order to surrender the castles and estates it had taken from previous archbishops. These were handed over to Isarnus (r. 1300–1302), a placeholder appointed by Pope Boniface VIII following the death of Archbishop John III in 1300. For a moment it seemed as if a fair settlement might be achievable—Isarnus enjoyed good relationships with both the order and the citizens of Riga—but the new archbishop's tenure was brief. After two years Isarnus was transferred to Lund, leaving a dangerous vacancy in Riga. The death of Pope Boniface in October 1303, after being kidnapped and briefly held by his enemies, meant that there was also a vacancy in Rome that the order could exploit to its advantage.[41]

The order hurriedly consolidated its position, engineering a series of alliances that were directed against Riga and its archbishop. In February 1304, Master Gottfried of Rogga (r. 1298–1307) forced treaties of alliance on the Estonian bishoprics of Dorpat and Ösel–Wiek; similar treaties were imposed on the local knights. Of more immediate danger to Riga was the forced sale in May 1305 of the Cistercian cloister at Dünamünde on what was then the Düna's right bank just north of the city near the Bay of Riga.[42] Converting the damaged monastery into a fort that stood at the gateway between the Düna River and the Baltic Sea, the knights placed themselves in a perfect position to choke off Riga's trade with the outside world. Defying an earlier agreement, the order further reinforced its position on the upstream Düna by seizing the archbishop's castles at Kokenhusen and Lennewarden. Goods that were floated downriver on vessels destined for Riga were easily confiscated by the order, whose knights added to the unease by harassing the city's fishermen on the Düna and on nearby rivers and lakes. Sometimes the knights robbed Riga's traders on the overland routes as well.[43] Just as the Teutonic Order was forcing the Prussian cities into submission, the goal of the Livonian Order was to squeeze the Rigans until they recognized its full authority.

Under the circumstances there was little more that Riga's prelates could do other than hope for an audience with the pope. But the papacy was of little help to Riga, for in the wake of the disputed election of Pope Clement V (r. 1305–1314), a Frenchman who had much experience at the papal court, the curia was moved to Avignon in France, where it remained for most of the fourteenth century. Riga's archbishops likewise spent much of the century in exile, for the order's hostility made it nearly impossible for any archbishop to stay in the city for very long. During these years, then, the Church would not be much of a factor in the struggle: the locals would have to settle their disputes among themselves.

Thus Riga turned once again to the pagan Lithuanians, whose resentment of the crusading orders grew as the knights disrupted the grand duchy's trade with Riga and continued to build castles opposite the pagans' own fortifications on the Nemunas and Jura rivers. Lithuanian forces pushed back by attacking territories claimed by the knights in Prussia and Livonia.

Seeing in him a possible ally against the knightly orders, Grand Duke Vytenis drew closer to Riga's new archbishop, Frederick of Perlstein (Friedrich von Perlstein; r. 1304–1341). A well-connected Bohemian of noble lineage and a Franciscan monk who had studied at the University of Bologna, the cleric arrived in his diocese too late to prevent the sale of the strategically important Dünamünde convent-castle to the Livonian Order. If Perlstein's thirty-seven-year reign was defined by any single issue, it was the ongoing struggle between the archbishop and the city of Riga on one side, and the armed knights on the other. For three years, from 1307 to 1310, the archbishop waited in Avignon, anxious to present his case against the order, but the Avignon popes changed frequently during these years, as did the papacy's priorities. Competing with crises closer to home, problems in a peripheral region like Livonia often had to wait.

While Frederick waited, Rigans heard news of another Baltic city that stood in the way of the crusaders' ambitions. This was Danzig, an emerging hub near the Pomerelian coast that drew from the Polish hinterland and was therefore coveted by its predatory neighbors. Indeed, Danzig was Poland's only possible port to the Baltic. If the aim of the Livonian Order was to unite Livonia, including the city of Riga, under its rule, then the goal of the Teutonic Order was to do the same in Prussia and Danzig. This meant preventing its competitors—namely, Brandenburg and the growing Polish state—from taking the Pomerelian coast and its cities. This, the knights believed, would require the use of brute force: the Teutonic Order must drive the Brandenburgers out of Danzig, take control of the town, and incorporate it into the order's growing territory. Forcing their way into the city on November 12, 1308, the knights mercilessly burned down the burghers' houses and executed resisters. By the next morning the bodies of hundreds of Danzig's merchants and artisans lay in the streets. Afterward, the order saw to it that the city's walls were razed. Many years would pass before Danzig recovered from the shock and destruction.

Rigans would have been correct to take the bloodbath—legend had it that 10,000 people were slaughtered, an obviously inflated figure—as a warning. The Danzig massacre did not escape the notice of the seriously ill Pope Clement V, whose papal bull of June 1310 contained a scathing denunciation of the order.[44] To say that the crusading orders were sometimes an embarrassment to the papacy as well as a threat to fellow Christians would be an understatement. Indeed, the criminal activities of the Knights Templar were so notorious that in late 1307 many of the order's members in France were arrested and tortured into giving confessions; some were burned at the stake, their properties confiscated. In 1312, the same year Archbishop Frederick sailed once again to Avignon (he would not return to Riga for twelve years), the pope disbanded the Templars.

Yet when it came to both the Teutonic Order in Prussia and to its Livonian branch, the papacy, perhaps partly influenced by the order's immense wealth, was reluctant to take punitive measures. Although they were quickly rescinded, there were interdicts and excommunications in 1311 and 1312; some at the time thought that Clement V might dissolve the Livonian Order as he had the Templars.[45] Unable to count on the troubled papacy for help, Frederick of

Perlstein effectively lost control over a diocese that he managed for years at a stretch from Avignon, where the learned archbishop compiled an extensive library as he waited to plead his case.

Catastrophe came to Livonia in 1315, a year that witnessed the first in a series of bad harvests that sent prices skyrocketing as a famine of Biblical proportions—in some places it lasted a full seven years—descended upon a swath of territory that stretched from the British Isles to the eastern Baltic. The rains and flooding left the crops and pastures under water while the grain rotted, good agricultural land was despoiled, and yields plummeted. Everywhere the demographic growth that had helped propel Europe out of its backwardness came to an end as millions perished from hunger and disease. In Livonia it was said—although we must make allowance for the possibility that the chroniclers exaggerated their reports in an effort to convey the very real horrors of the time—that mothers ate their babies, while graves were opened under the cover of darkness in a macabre effort to obtain flesh to sustain the survivors, now reduced to walking skeletons.[46]

An unusually severe winter compounded the misery: with the Baltic Sea frozen over, hundreds of ships were immobilized as cities waited for deliveries of food.[47] As the price of grain skyrocketed, hoarding and speculation drove the cost of food higher still. While rural beggars massed near the towns in the hopes of receiving alms, many cities responded to the crisis by limiting the admission of new citizens to their already weakened communities. Riga, where grain was stored in warehouses for just such emergencies, was better off than the surrounding countryside, but food supplies were dwindling just the same. Yet while Master Gerhard II (r. 1307–1322) had opened up the order's grain stores to the needy in the Prussian cities as an act of Christian charity,[48] the knight was merciless when it came to Riga: forbidding merchant vessels from sailing past the order's castle at Dünamünde, Master Gerhard intended to force the city to submit. To the master's cruelty the starving Rigans responded by storming and burning the fortress in April 1316. With river traffic open once again, the grain ships could proceed to Riga.[49]

As the hunger crisis passed, Clement's successor, John XXII (r. 1316–1324), summoned Gerhard and some other order leaders to testify in Avignon. Although it had taken many years, the Rigan suit was at last concluded in May 1319, the pope now admonishing the knights not to interfere with Riga's commercial affairs. The order was nevertheless allowed to keep its fortress at the mouth of the Düna—a reminder to Rigans that their fate rested on the whims of the order master.

Riga's Lithuanian allies also became weary of their long struggle with the order, for the conflict was a distraction that hindered the grand duchy from achieving its greater aim of expansion in the east. This was the ambition of Grand Duke Gediminas (r. 1316–1341), an enormously successful ruler who married his children into the leading dynasties of eastern Europe and in such manner—accompanied by the occasional use of force—absorbed Polish areas as well as vast stretches of Rus' territory. In order to pursue these aims in the east, Gediminas needed peace and commerce with the West—hence his letter to Pope John XXII of 1322 in which the grand duke not only complained about the abuses of the knights but also announced his readiness to make peace and to welcome the Catholic faith into his realm. With Lithuania appearing to be on the brink, at last, of conversion, the pope was ready to listen.

The resulting Vilnius Treaty of 1323 ended the Livonian Order's war with Lithuania, even if the Prussian branch was not bound to it.[50] The document also guaranteed safe passage for Catholics in the grand duke's territories and offered legal protections to Rigan merchants who conducted business there. But once again the Lithuanian leader seems to have misled the hopeful Christians. Irritated that Gediminas had rejected their offer of baptism, the knights resumed their harassment of the grand duchy. The order also targeted Rigan craftsmen and merchants traveling through the lands between, hoping that such acts of intimidation would compel Riga to surrender some of its Livonian territories.[51]

Riga's anxious burghers took matters into their own hands. On the night of June 23, 1328, they again attacked the order fortress at Dünamünde. Unable to capture it, they succeeded in razing it to the ground. The next spring the Rigans sent four envoys to Gediminas, for the burghers once again needed a contingent of Lithuanian forces to garrison the city. In exchange, Riga offered to hand over to Lithuania some of the archdiocese's castles and fortifications. Gediminas having accepted these terms, the knights discovered the plan and immediately seized four of the five forts.[52]

By this time the Livonian Order's new provincial master was Eberhard of Monheim (Eberhard von Munheim; r. 1328–1340), a proud and capable knight who considered himself Riga's mortal enemy. In October 1329 his soldiers set upon Riga from all sides, blockading the city by land and by sea and causing the poorer residents to die of hunger. The Rigans sent envoys to their Hanse allies, but no help came as the order's forces gathered around the city. Belying the order's well-earned reputation for barbarism and cruelty, on several occasions its forces opened the city's gates to allow Riga's most destitute inhabitants to search for food, wherever they could obtain it.[53] By the early spring of 1330, conditions had become unbearable, and Riga's mayor, John of Fellin (Johann von Fellin), decided to convene an assembly of the city's notables for consultation. The canons were nowhere to be found. Nor was there any food, the mayor reported, for the city stores contained only three and one-half *lasts* of grain.[54] Surrender or death were the only options remaining.

On March 20, Riga's humbled councilors fell on their knees before the master, surrendering to the order's authority all the city's properties, begging only for their lives and freedom. The knights immediately took the Sand Tower and the Holy Spirit Tower and all the city walls between these towers.[55] According to the terms of surrender, signed ten days later, Riga's burghers were to rebuild the order's destroyed castle, which the knights naturally intended to use to control the flow of traffic on the Düna and thereby dominate the city. Compelled to abandon the city's alliance with the Lithuanians, Riga's magistrates were furthermore required to swear an oath of allegiance to the master, and Riga's citizens were expected to assist in the order's wars, either in the field or by making financial contributions.[56] As the winner of the struggle (for the time being), the knights would retain the right to participate in sessions of the town council, and their properties—now augmented by the acquisition of fields, pastures, and meadows in the surrounding areas—were freed from city taxes.[57] The order's triumph nearly total, there could be little doubt now about who was master of Riga.

On June 13, 1330, Eberhard of Monheim laid the foundation stone for the new Order Castle on a spot where there had earlier stood the city's hospital, its stables, a lime kiln, and a horse-operated mill.[58] Large and imposing, the convent-style castle on the Düna embankment, finally completed in 1354, consisted of four blocks surrounding a courtyard. The new fortress was built in a way that isolated it from the city both juridically—the property belonged to the order and was outside the town council's jurisdiction—and physically, for the fortress was to be surrounded by a wide moat, with a drawbridge providing the only access to the city.[59]

Until the new castle could be completed, the most visible symbol of Riga's humiliation was the fifty-foot gap that was torn into the city walls through which the master and his retinue would enter; the order, after all, must have its victory parade. In the final analysis, however, Riga was given basically the same kind of deal that the Teutonic Order had forced on the Prussian cities like Danzig, whereby it lost many of its privileges and became dependent on the order.[60] But unlike the slaughter in Danzig, there were no massacres in Riga, and the city walls, aside from the notable gap, continued to stand as a defiant reminder of the city's former sovereignty.

The humbling of the city underlined the impotence of the archbishop of Riga. Frederick of Perlstein would continue to make his complaints to the pope, but even if he so desired there was little the pontiff could do from Avignon to make the knights surrender their victory. Indeed, it was the first anti-pope, Nicholas V (r. 1328–1333), who confirmed that victory by recognizing the order's supremacy over the archbishop. Riga's fickle canons also saw little choice but to come to an agreement with the order, and so they abandoned their impotent prelate. Even Riga's burghers recognized the futility of further struggle and soon normalized their relations with the knights, while Archbishop Frederick spent the remainder of his life in Avignon, wandering the corridors of its newly built palaces, reading his many books, and praying for assistance that would never arrive.[61]

An Unsteady Peace, 1330–1481

When the fighting ended in 1330, the forces commanded by Master Mondheim occupied the entire city of Riga. But even as the order's growing wealth and military effectiveness increased its power and independence, the knights' political struggles with the archbishop and the Rath continued for many more decades without resolution.

Having capitulated to the order, then nearing the peak of its power, the city openly disdained the settlement that had ended Riga's first civil war by conducting its policies almost as if it had never been defeated in the first place. But if Riga's defiance tested the order's tolerance, the knights were undeterred, for the realization of their goal of building a unified order state in Livonia on the Prussian model required the submission of Livonia's largest city. Such a plan would also require the resources that the order could expect to gain from further conquests. Prompted to intervene in Estonia to quell a peasant revolt known as the St. George's Day Uprising (1343–1345), the order next purchased the region from Denmark, whose ruler was happy to unload the troublesome province.[62] The acquisition of more territory and power feeding their arrogance, the knights went on the offensive in Lithuania, where they scored their greatest victories in decades.

Barely distracted from its political goals by the arrival of the plague in 1351—its catastrophic effects were hardly any different in Livonia than elsewhere, the notable exception being the lack of Jews upon which to blame it—the order also maintained pressure on the archbishopric to accept its dominion over Livonia. The archbishops saw things differently, for it was their goal to reestablish their authority over the order, whose master was expected to render homage to the archbishop. As each side tried to assert its hegemony over the Livonian territories, and over Riga, the order strengthened its hold on the neighboring bishoprics of Dorpat and Ösel-Wiek. It also adopted a new strategy for bringing the archbishop of Riga to heel: now the knights hoped to persuade or to compel Riga's canons to enter the order, with the expectation that in time the chapter would be transformed into one of its convents. In this way the order could influence the selection of new archbishops, who in turn would be expected to be loyal to it.[63] Riga's prelates continued to complain about the knights' misconduct, but the papacy, still exiled in Avignon, had bigger fish to fry, not the least of which was the Hundred Years' War (1337–1453), a multigenerational conflict between England and France for the throne of western Europe's largest kingdom.

Efforts by Archbishop Fromhold (r. 1348–1369) to strengthen the Church's position in Riga were met with ambivalence by the burghers, who enjoyed full municipal rights and economic freedom under the order's dominion. Aiming for the restoration of his sovereign rights in Riga, the archbishop personally took his case to the papal curia. But it was only in 1359, the same year that the order took seven of the archbishop's castles, thereby depriving him of much-needed tax revenue, that the papacy at last issued its ruling on Riga. Imposing an interdict that prevented the knights from participating in certain Church rituals, Pope Innocent VI declared that all arrangements in Riga were to revert to what they had been before the city's defeat in 1330: dominion over Riga (apart from its castle) should be returned to the archbishopric.[64]

Shrugging off the papacy's unenforceable interdict, the knights simply refused to give up the city. Only after stories of the order's misbehavior reached Emperor Charles IV (r. 1355–1378)—a close friend of the pope and a man whose authority they could not ignore—were the knights willing to enter into a more accommodating relationship with the archbishop.[65] Meeting in Danzig with the bishops and lords, as well as with delegates from Riga and some other Baltic cities, the order's representatives agreed to recognize the archbishop's equivalent power in the Livonian lands and would not ask for any feudal vows. The Danzig Treaty of 1366 thus appeared to restore the old balance of power in Riga, with both the order (which retained the right to exact military service from Riga's burghers) and the archbishop agreeing to observe the city's historic rights and privileges.[66]

Although far from ideal, at least from the knights' perspective, this compromise arrangement in fact relieved the order of a headache that had been distracting it from achieving the more important goal of territorial unification. With the Danzig Treaty in place, the Livonian Order, along with its parent organization in Prussia, could now focus its energies on defeating Lithuanian Samogitia, whose conquest would provide the crusader states with a corridor connecting the Livonian territories to the lands of the Teutonic Order in Prussia. Having reached its territorial limits by the end of the century, the Teutonic Order consolidated its authority throughout Prussia, where its monopoly on the lucrative amber trade yielded a hefty income that covered the bulk of the order's expenses.[67] Henceforth the order's actions were largely defensive, aimed at keeping what had been acquired.[68]

If the crusading orders of northeastern Europe were now at the peak of their might, the position of the Church's leading representative in Livonia was far less secure, for the Papal Schism (1378–1417) deprived the weakened archbishop of the full authority of the papacy. Indeed, during this period no fewer than three men claimed the papal throne at any one time. In such circumstances, what was decreed by one pope could simply be annulled by another. The implications for Riga's prelates were obvious: in any confrontation with the order, the archbishop would be on his own.

Developments in Lithuania reveal another aspect of the shifting regional power dynamics, for its nobility was at last prepared to convert to Christianity. If sincere, such a move would undermine the order's very *raison d'être*. The Lithuanians' acceptance of Latin Christianity was a prerequisite for the Union of Krewo (1385), a political marriage that united the sprawling grand duchy with the Polish kingdom.

While such a combination would be better positioned to check the emerging Muscovite state in the east, it might also prove able to hinder the order's ambitions in the Baltic. Indeed, it was in the Polish-Lithuanian lands that the order confronted its greatest challenges during the early decades of the fifteenth century. The thorniest problem facing the knights was Samogitia, where pagan uprisings broke out in 1401–1404 and again in 1409. Another Samogitian rebellion in 1410 drew the knights into battle with Poland-Lithuania.

We may trace the beginning of the order's century-long decline to this very moment, when the Germans confronted their enemies at the Battle of Tannenberg.[69] Thousands of the order's servants fell to a combined army of Poles, Lithuanians, Czechs, and others, while most of its leaders, including the grand master himself, were killed or taken prisoner. In symbolic terms, Tannenberg was a German Alamo, where defeat gave rise to nationalist myths about Germany's destiny in the east.[70] But first there was humiliation, as the order was compelled to return its Samogitian conquests in defeat.

Another battle in 1435, this time at Wilkomierz (Lith. Ukmergė) yielded a similar outcome, with Polish forces once again routing the knights of the Livonian Order. From these setbacks neither of the crusading orders would recover. No longer would the monk-knights be able to interfere in the internal affairs of Poland and Lithuania or expand their territorial holdings. The days of the crusading orders in northeastern Europe were numbered.

But even in defeat the order never lost sight of the city of Riga, over which its master sought unfettered dominion. As noted, this objective was closely tied to the knights' main goal, which was the creation of a unified *Ordenstaat* under the grand master in Prussia. Facilitating the knights' advancement toward that goal was the papal decree of March 1394, which sanctioned the order's demand that all future archbishops of Riga be members of the order.[71] That the dress of Riga's canons was to be changed from the Augustinian black to the white of the knights gave symbolic recognition to the fact that the archdiocese was well on its way to being incorporated.

Some archbishops, like John V Wallenrode (Johann von Wallenrode; r. 1395–1418), were willing to work peaceably with the knights. Becoming the first archbishop to join the order, Wallenrode was content to make his career in the diplomatic arena and spent little time in Livonia.[72] His successor, John VI Ambundii (Johann Ambundii von Schwan; r. 1418–1424), also took a conciliatory approach, at least initially. Promising that he would join the order himself, the young archbishop, aged thirty-four at the time of his appointment, agreed to allow the Riga chapter to be converted into one of its convents. Yet when it came to the city itself, the archbishop behaved with surprising independence. Responding to the burghers' concerns about the order's plans to build fortifications in places that threatened them, John VI took the side of the citizens and requested that the pope remove the authority of the order in his diocese.[73] The pope's ruling came down in December 1422: the Riga chapter, with its seat in the Dome Cathedral, was to be freed from its subjection to the order.[74]

Yet the burghers were far from a unified body when it came to the order: while some recognized the knights' irreplaceable role in regional defense and chose to accept the order's impositions, others hated the order, seeing it as a threat both to their freedom and their profits. The fact that few of the knights enjoyed long-standing connections to the "Land of Mary" may have played into the burghers' suspicions, for only a few were native to Livonia.[75] That the spread of plague had turned Livonia into a scene of devastation and massive depopulation surely added to the tensions among the contestants for power.

A scene in the Dome in November 1423, when Master Siegfried Lander of Spanheim (r. 1415–1424) threatened the town council with violence, underlines the gravity of the conflict. While the Rath accused the order of harassing Riga's merchants and of being in contempt of Riga's own laws, Master Siegfried directed his ire at those treacherous councilors who had turned for help to John VI, whose sympathies were clearly with Riga's burghers. Knowing that it would not take long for the order to bring its forces from its many other castles to Riga, the citizens expected an attack at any moment.[76] By the end of 1424, however, both the master and the archbishop were dead and a major confrontation between the city and the order had been averted.[77] But the release that same year of a papal bull recognizing the archbishop as the sole spiritual and temporal ruler of Riga rendered inevitable further clashes between the archbishop, the citizens, and the knights.[78]

Indeed, the harassment continued: merchants who had dared to venture beyond the city walls to procure or sell their wares sometimes encountered knights who would sequester their goods for themselves. Also subject to the knights' provocations were the canons of the Riga Cathedral: in 1428 the Teutonic Order in Prussia saw to it that several of Riga's canons were murdered as they journeyed to Rome.[79] So dangerous was it for the archbishops who clashed with the order that most of the men appointed to the Riga archbishopric in fact spent little time in Livonia during these years. John V Wallenrode, for example, was in Riga so rarely that his quarter-century tenure was of almost no consequence for Rigan politics. Given the papacy's inability to exert its influence on such a distant and problematic region (gradually Poland would emerge as the archbishopric's nominal protector), an appointment to the Riga archbishopric wasn't much of a stepping stone for a man of ambition. Nor was the neglected archdiocese an undemanding sinecure awarded for a lifetime of service, as the Prussian native John VI Ambundii quickly discovered.

While John VI never was able to come to an agreement with the order, the archbishop could claim one significant achievement, and that was the founding of the Livonian Confederation, a mechanism he hoped would bring order to the troubled region. Lasting from 1419 until 1562, this feudal creation was the closest thing to a functioning state that had ever existed in the territory of "Old Livonia." The confederation included the domains belonging to the Archbishop of Riga and to the bishoprics of Courland, Dorpat (in Estonia), and Ösel-Wiek (Estonia's Saare, Hiuu, and Lääne counties), each of which were also lords of the order's fiefs on their territories. The lion's share of the confederation's power and territory, however, belonged to the Livonian Order, whose main castles were located along the Düna at Riga, Kreuzburg (now Krustpils), and Dünaburg (Daugavpils); on the Treider Aa at Wenden (Cēsis); and at Windau (Ventspils) in Courland.

The convening in 1419 of a *Landtag*—a diet of Livonia's upper classes representing the nobility, church, and cities—was an attempt to stabilize the Livonian lands and to secure the rights of its estates and cities, but the Livonian Confederation fell well short of a fully unified territorial state. Its weak structure and sporadic activities—instead of meeting annually, the estates convened at moments of crisis—left it at a disadvantage in a part of the world that its neighbors increasingly viewed as up for grabs, for Lithuania, Poland, Sweden, and Muscovy were doing exactly what Livonian had failed to do, and that was to create unified (if not actually centralized) states that were capable of summoning the resources necessary for waging war. By the middle of the sixteenth century, feudal Livonia and its greatest city would find themselves surrounded by a series of hungrily formidable powers.

It was for this reason above all—to unify the Livonian territories against potential aggressors like Poland-Lithuania and, soon enough, Muscovy—that the grand masters in Prussia insisted that all future archbishops be members of the Teutonic Order. Henning Scharpenberg was such a member; yet the archbishop was also a confident upholder of Church prerogatives. It was during Scharpenburg's tenure (1424–1448) that a twelve-year truce was concluded in 1435. Here the order conceded that it would not compel the Riga clergy to wear its habit as long as the archbishop agreed not to interfere with the order's exercise of its sovereign rights.[80] That this peace coincided with the order's defeat at the Battle of Wilkomierz is no coincidence, for at this moment the order simply had too many problems to expend its energies on Riga.[81]

The uncertain peace unraveled during the tenure of Archbishop Silvester Stodewescher (r. 1448–1479). A chancellor and chaplain to Grand Master Conrad of Erlichshausen in Prussia, Silvester became the Teutonic Order's candidate for the Riga archbishopric after Scharpenberg's death in 1448. Entering the city in grand style after a glorious procession through his archdiocese, the insecure Silvester tried to win his subjects over with feasts and festivals, but he failed miserably, for the burghers knew that he was a member of the reviled order.[82] Yet his appointment turned out to be the master's great mistake, for, like his predecessor, Silvester immediately reneged on an earlier promise that future canons in Riga wear a white habit with a red cross—the same as that worn by the knights.[83]

The double-dealing Silvester also got the Livonian Confederation to agree to a new power-sharing arrangement that would place the city of Riga under his direct control; that way the archbishop could claim that he was watching over the citizenry and preventing them from organizing. Bearing in mind how the Teutonic Order was struggling with the Prussian cities, which in 1448 had organized themselves into the Prussian Confederation under the leadership of Danzig, we can better appreciate Riga's circumstances at this time. At a moment when Riga was giving indications of its intent to join an existing coalition of Prussian cities that were then uniting against the order—indeed, the fear was growing that Riga might soon stand at the head of an alliance of Livonian cities—Archbishop Silvester and the Livonian Order entered into an arrangement known as the Treaty of Kirchholm (Latv. Salaspils) in the autumn of 1452.

Orchestrated by the archbishop without the knowledge of Riga's burghers, the treaty took city leaders by surprise. Accused of violating its agreements with both the archbishop and the order, the city would now have to swear fealty to both. In addition to paying the master a thousand Rhenish gulden, Riga was compelled to surrender its biggest and most powerful cannon, known as the Lion, and to relinquish lands just outside its eastern wall.[84] The city's submission was accompanied by the usual pageantry, as witnessed by a later burgomaster named Melchior Fuchs (1603–1678):

> Soon thereafter the two lords made their entry into the city. The council and all the citizens were required to greet them, some on horseback, and bring them in as if in a [Roman] Triumph. The canons, monks, priests, and lay and student choirs had to march from the harbor gate to the cathedral singing "*Tue est potential, tuum Regnum Domine*" ("Thine is the power, thine is the kingdom, O Lord").[85]

An act of capitulation was more than the laying down of arms: it was a theatrical performance that required the participation of the city's spiritual and temporal leaders, who were expected to take public oaths to their sovereign(s). As we shall see, Rigans would stage similar displays of submission in later years when the city acceded to Polish (1581), Swedish (1621), and, finally, Russian (1710) power.

For the crusading orders, Riga's capitulation of 1452 came not a moment too soon, for the anticipated rebellion of the Prussian cities turned out to be only two years away. This was the Thirteen Years' War (1454–1467). Attempting to break free from the Teutonic Order, Danzig and the other Prussian cities turned to Poland, whose ruler, King Casimir IV Jagiellon, was only too happy to take the separatist areas under his protection.[86] The temptation of Riga's leaders to join the Prussian rebellion in order to secure the city's independence from the Livonian Order must have been irresistible. Yet on this crucial matter the burghers were divided. While Archbishop Silvester renewed his ties with vassals who had earlier been won over by the order master and urged the burghers of Riga to prepare for war with the knights, the pragmatic town council balked, for it was more interested in pursuing conciliatory measures. But if some were willing to purchase peace at almost any price, others, especially the long-distance merchants who dominated Riga's guilds, were prepared to fight, believing that the order's possession of the fortress at the mouth of the Düna was a greater threat to Riga than the power of the archbishop. To this the Machiavellian archbishop, fully appreciating the order's suddenly weakened position as it struggled with the Prussian cities, responded that Rigans would be permitted to raze the order fortress at Dünamünde if they would recognize him as their sole sovereign. But it was only when he promised to revise the Kirchholm Treaty so that what was taken from Riga (including territories in Courland, Semigallia, and the Estonian island of Ösel) would be returned to it, did the archbishop manage to win over the Rath.[87] Riga would resist the order.

In a public ceremony held in March 1454, Riga's officials tore up and then burned the treaty they had been forced to sign only sixteen months earlier. What followed was the first direct confrontation between the city and one of its feudal lords in nearly 125 years. While Master John of Mengden (Johann Ostfhoff von Mengede; r. 1450–1469) collected his troops around the city, the burghers went on the attack that summer. Their focus was the Order Castle in Riga, but its thick and imposing towers withstood the blows of the city's modest artillery.[88] Silvester and the priests of the Riga Cathedral also joined the struggle: in a daring and solemn procession, the armor-clad archbishop and ten of his canons rode their horses to the Town Hall, where the prelate released the councilors from their oaths to the order while assuring them of his protection in good and bad times.[89] But as his holdings outside Riga slipped from his hands into those of the knights, the archbishop was forced to surrender, his secret negotiations with the master leaving Riga's burghers in disgust. The war was over in only six days. With Riga restored to the order's control, the Livonian knights could now run off to Prussia to rein in the rebellious cities; afterward they would be redeployed to the Russian frontier.

The main players in the struggle over Riga have thus far included leading citizens, the crusading orders of northeastern Europe, the archbishops of Riga (backed by a weak papacy), and at the periphery the sprawling Polish-Lithuanian state. To this cast of characters we may now add Muscovy, which in 1471 gave notice of its ambitions by overrunning the old trading city of Novgorod and then annexing it a few years later. Now focused on "gathering" the lands that had succumbed to Lithuania in earlier times while casting off what was left of the Golden Horde in the south, Muscovite rulers would next launch a drive toward the Baltic Sea. The undeniable threat posed by this aggressively expansionist state became an obsession of Livonia's military defenders.

But, first things first: the treacherous archbishop must be brought to heel and Livonia's divided lands unified. This was the intention of Bernd von der Borch, who in 1471 was the Teutonic Order's second-highest representative in Livonia when he led a conspiracy against the reigning provincial master, John Wolthuss of Herse. Imprisoning him at his castle at Wenden on the charges of corruption and mismanagement, Bernd assumed the master's office (r. 1472–1483) and then moved its seat to Riga, thereby making himself a direct threat to the burghers. The game of intrigue thus renewed, the new order master fomented dissension among Riga's burghers by insisting that the closed meetings of the town council, a body that had always been dominated by wealthy merchants, be opened up to members of the Small Guild of artisans and craftsmen.[90]

When negotiations failed to achieve any result, the prelate began to gather allies, looking to foreign powers for assistance—Lithuania and Poland, Sweden, Denmark, and the Hanse cities. Silvester also turned to the papacy, which in December 1474 (a famine year) issued a bull that granted the archbishop temporal power over the city.[91] But since the order and the burghers simply ignored his coup, the archbishop unsheathed the sword of excommunication, wielding it against the master, his castellans, the Rath, and the aldermen of the guilds. A ban and interdict fell over the town on June 26, 1477: church bells went silent, altars were draped in black, stones were laid in front of the church doors, priests were unable to perform their work. For nearly five months the dead were buried without last rites, confessions were no longer heard, and the betrothed remained unmarried.[92]

It would be difficult to overstate the impact that the archbishop's actions had on the lives of ordinary Rigans. As God-fearing Catholics, the burghers saw the interdict as a threat to their mortal souls, for to be buried without church ceremonies was, in effect, to be damned. One may suppose that such a fate befell John (Johann) Soltrump, one of Riga's beloved burgomasters, when he died in 1477. While his son Reinhold, a vicar and a collector of books and art, would later become known for his illuminated manuscripts,[93] John Soltrump enjoyed great respect among the burghers for leading the fight against the archbishop; now the people of Riga insisted on giving him a proper ceremony at St. Peter's. Silvester's punishment was swift: not only were penalties imposed on all who had participated in the church burial, but the deceased mayor's corpse was ordered to be exhumed and buried in an open space.[94]

Bombarded with complaints from Riga and the order, Pope Sixtus IV (r. 1471–1484) excommunicated the prelate and lifted his interdict over the city. In no time at all did the archbishop's power over his bishops and priests evaporate, while the citizens liberated themselves from Silvester's authority. Captured by the knights and imprisoned at his former castle at Kokenhusen, the archbishop died in the summer of 1479. While the knights and burghers alike were relieved to be rid of this meddlesome priest, the archbishopric itself would remain intact for another eighty years.

It was at the height of the confusion in Riga that the Muscovite Grand Duke Ivan III (not to be confused with his more famous and "terrible" grandson Ivan

IV) undertook his second campaign against the Novgorod Republic, now wont of both leadership and allies. Facing a large army equipped with cannons and other firearms, and familiar with the effects of artillery assaults from the attacks by the Teutonic Knights on its outlying castles, Novgorod surrendered without a fight.[95] Thousands of the grand prince's opponents were executed or exiled, while the bell that called meetings of the *veche* (assembly) was transported to Moscow. Although for the time being a few German merchants were allowed to conduct their affairs as before in their yard, the *Peterhof*, they were now placed under surveillance as relations between Muscovy and Livonia deteriorated.[96] More alarming still was the news that forces from Pskov had marched on the bishopric of Dorpat and devastated the Estonian lands, which the Russians plundered for five weeks.[97] Would Riga be next?

In the face of foreign invasion, civil conflict, and general turmoil, it was the master of the Livonian Order, and not the archbishop of Riga, whom many came to see as the man who would unify the fractured territories of Livonia.

The Second Civil War, 1481–1491

As events turned out, Master Bernd would not be that man. Having disposed of a rebellious archbishop while extracting oaths from the prelate's former vassals, Bernd von der Borch next put Riga's canons in their place. Although free to walk the city streets during daylight hours, so long as they made no trouble, at night they were locked in a tower. Then there was the matter of replacing Archbishop Silvester. The papacy's decision to appoint the outsider Stephan Grube (r. 1480–1483) affronted the master, who resolved never to allow the archbishop to enter the city gates.

Concerned that a potentially disruptive prelate might assume (and use) the powers of his office and enraged at the city's continued defiance, Master Bernd, whom Frederick III (r. 1452–1493) had recently appointed a prince of the Holy Roman Empire, had an alternative candidate in mind. Surrounding himself with witnesses, the master ordered his cousin to kneel before him: Simon von der Borch was now to be the archbishop of Riga.[98] But it was one thing for the aging knight to make an illegal appointment that lacked the backing of the papacy; any attempt to enforce it—to compel Riga to obey—was certain to bring the order into direct conflict with the city.

That was to come soon enough, for with another skirmish at Dünamünde in 1481 and the looming threat of an order blockade, the city began to mobilize its forces. That autumn Master Bernd wrote to Reval with the news that Rigans had besieged the Order Castle in their city and were preparing to attack it.[99] Not only did the master insist that the knights of Reval take part in the campaign against Riga, he further called upon its burghers to join the battle. Whether the Revalians fought against Riga is unclear: there is far more evidence of solidarity between the two Hanseatic towns than of conflict. But even if Reval supported the order's cause—which was, above all, unity in the face of the Russian threat—its citizens were mostly interested in peace and the commerce. Later, despite the blockade, the Estonian town would send its ships to Riga, smuggle goods to the beleaguered city, and help mediate the conflict between Riga and the order.[100] But first there would be a confrontation on the Düna.

That day arrived on December 19, when the defenders of Riga, possessing a giant mortar cast with the inscription "I am called the Raven and upon whatever I lay an egg, that breaks in two," fired on the Order Castle and set its stables on fire. The order's counterattack focused on high points in the city like church towers that could serve as observation points for artillerymen. In such manner did St. Jacob's fall victim to the fighting, its roof shattered by the order's own cannon called the Lion.[101] Unable to destroy the Order Castle, Rigans took the battle to the open field, torching the order's manors and taking a series of castles, including Dünamünde, which the city's traders and craftsmen besieged for four weeks before finally capturing it.[102] But even this achievement did not spare the city from further sorrow, for Riga, although victorious on the battlefields of Livonia, was now haunted by hunger and disease.

While Riga struggled with the knights, papal appointee Stephan Grube was completing his dangerous journey across Poland and Lithuania, for the lands belonging to the order were closed to him. On April 20, 1482, the town council sent one its leading members, Hermann Helewegh, to Vilnius to welcome the archbishop, whom the burgomaster hoped would be as much a friend to the city as he was anathema to the order.[103] The following summer the prelate arrived in Riga, where he was excitedly greeted by the citizens. One of the archbishop's first acts was to confirm the city's ancient rights—an unmistakable gesture of good will toward, if not solidarity with, its anxious burghers.[104]

Grube's tenure was brief, for the archbishop's earthly life ended late in 1483. Then it was the turn of the aging and sick Master Bernd, the knight who not only had failed to unify Livonia but who had also suffered the disgrace of papal excommunication. Now under the command of John Freitag (Johann Freitag von Loringhoven; r. 1484–1491), the knights gathered their forces from the other Livonian convents and once again besieged the city. The citizens responded in kind. Capturing thousands of enemy forces encamped outside the city, the armed burghers pounded the order castle with their modest artillery; trapped inside were dozens of sick and wounded men left to conserve dwindling supplies of food and ammunition while waiting out an assault that went on for days and weeks and months.[105]

On March 22, 1484, the order's damaged castle at Dünamünde fell to the Rigans. Two months later it was the turn of the order's castle in Riga, where only ten healthy knights remained. On May 18 the knights surrendered their fortress, but they were permitted to leave with half their treasure, the other half being used to pay Riga's mercenaries. Three days later the demolition began. Everyone, young and old, German and non-German, was granted the right to tear down the Riga Castle and take away building materials to use for their homes and shops. When the largest tower collapsed on August 15, Rigans completely leveled the fortress. Whatever bricks remained were collected by beggars to be sold on the banks of the Düna.

The guns had gone silent, but the knights had not given up the struggle for Riga. If the papacy was, at best, ambivalent about the order, at least it still enjoyed the support of Emperor Frederick III, who conferred to its master sovereign rights over the archbishop and the other Livonian bishops. Acknowledging the realities of the situation, the pope too advised Rigans to recognize the master's supremacy.[106]

Thus did the order manage to install its own candidate at the head of the Riga archdiocese. This was Michael Hildebrand (r. 1484–1509), a canon at Reval and a former secretary for the order. Attempting to convince Rigans to accept an appointment they resented, the order relaxed its efforts to force the Dome chapter to become one of its convents.[107] But since the carrot failed to achieve its goal, the order again resorted to the stick as it blockaded the city and confiscated goods and properties belonging to Riga's merchants.

Looking abroad for help, the city's exceptional mayor, John Schöning,[108] secured a Swedish promise of four thousand troops, expecting that these forces would do more than break the siege of Riga: it was hoped that the Swedes would take advantage of the order's weakened condition and conquer all Livonia. To the mayor's surprise and disappointment, however, only two hundred Swedes arrived, and their purpose was not to destroy the order but to prop it up so that they might stand together against Russia, which threatened Sweden's possessions in Finland. Some of the visiting Swedes attended the *Landtag* of March 1486 at which the Rigans decided at last to recognize the new archbishop. In exchange, the citizens were awarded a contract that detailed all the city had won since the war had begun.[109]

Unable to leave well enough alone, Master John Freitag blocked the mouth of the Düna in order to prevent Riga from being aided by the Swedes. When he ordered the city to rebuild the order's destroyed castle in Riga and the ruined castle at nearby Dünamünde, the burghers simply ignored his commands. But when the order declared war on the city on September 30, 1489, the new archbishop took flight.

The campaign was led by the order's new *Landmarschall*, Walter of Plettenberg. Convinced that the order, whose holdings stretched along the entire southern coast of the Baltic Sea, could outlast a city that was completely dependent on trade, Plettenberg rigorously enforced the blockade while gathering his land forces to join the war on Riga. Its own resources running dry, Riga struggled to pay the mercenary troops upon which it now depended for security. With the trading season about to begin and deliveries needing to be made, the beleaguered city was forced to submit at last.

On March 30, 1491, Riga's weary leaders stood before the order master and the archbishop with lowered heads—this was their moment of reconciliation after a decade of civil war—as the councilors listened to the peace terms. The demands were, in fact, rather mild, for the order's goal was not to destroy the city but to use it for the defense of Livonia. Taking an oath of allegiance to the order, Riga's leaders agreed to renounce their arrangement with the Swedes and to return all prisoners. Captured forts were to be handed back along with all the order's property that the city had obtained during war. Riga must also within six years rebuild the order's destroyed castles in Riga Dünamünde.[110]

Years passed before construction work on the new castle got off the ground. At last completed in 1515, the restored Riga Castle was equipped with towers at every corner, reinforced cellars that could provide shelter for people and cattle in times of danger, living rooms and dining rooms for the master, and a chapel for worship. Although built on the foundations of its predecessor, the new castle was generally regarded as inferior—smaller, less stately, less imposing. While the castle was being rebuilt, the order master resettled in Wenden, located some eighty kilometers to the northeast of Riga in the strategically important corridor of order-controlled territories between the Livonian capital and Estonia.

Even if Wenden and not Riga was to be the primary residence of all the Livonian masters until the order's dissolution, there was now little question as to who possessed ultimate authority over the city. If the restoration of the Kirchholm Treaty of 1452 meant that Riga was again nominally subject to two masters, the burgomasters now swore their oaths directly to the master and not to the archbishop. Changes to the city's coat of arms made the new arrangements evident to all: while the walls with the raised gates (symbolizing the city's independence) and the crossed keys (symbolizing St. Peter's patronage of the city) remained, the cross of the order now appeared above them both.

The real master of Livonia, and of the city of Riga, was Walter of Plettenberg. Elected *Ordensmeister* in 1494, the victorious knight was welcomed like a king when he and his large retinue of 450 horses and armored men entered Riga on a Friday in February 1495. The event was recorded by burgomaster John Schöning:

> On the following Saturday, he came to the town hall, and then all of us paid homage to him and swore him [an oath of fealty] according to the pact of Kirchholm. . . . He gave me a beautiful book [decorated] with a sapphire, and we gave him three

> kinds of spices: ginger, *barkenrutt*, and *kruserkrum*, and we presented him with claret, malmsey, and Rhine wine; and sent one *Ahm* of Rhine wine, one *Last* of beer, one *Last* of oats, and 4 *wreven* of bread for him into the castle. After eight days he was here again and stayed gladly with us during the *Fastelabend*.[111] The Blackheads danced for him, and our ladies joined him on *Fastelabend*. May God give us a long life, concord and grace. Amen.[112]

Whether he truly enjoyed the festivities in Riga no one knows, but there can be little doubt that Plettenberg took a sober view of the challenges facing the divided Livonian Confederation. A strong, vibrant, and well-defended Riga, the knight knew well, was essential to the region's prosperity and security. But to make Livonia defensible in the face of Muscovite aggression was no simple task. Fortifications could be strengthened, but the order's reliance on fewer than two hundred aging knights, a tiny minority of whom were born in (or had much attachment to) Livonia, to lead the country's defense was hardly a winning strategy. A dependence on foreign mercenaries—notoriously unreliable soldiers who fought for pay and who had little stake in the outcome—became inevitable. At a time when its neighbors were centralizing their states and modernizing their armies, the feudal Livonian Confederation had become a living anachronism.

Chapter 5

Old Knights and New Teachings: The Reformation in Riga

Iesim, brāļi, mēs uz Rīgu,
Rīgā laba dzīvošanas
Sarkans alus, brandavīns
Daiļas pašas nesējiņas

Let us go, brothers, to Riga,
In Riga a good life awaits
The ruby beer and brandy wine
Beautiful are their bringers[1]

—Latvian folk song

First came the good times, then the bad. The first half of the sixteenth century was an especially pleasant time for the burghers of Riga and the other Livonian towns, for it was one of those rare stretches when the contestants for power managed to avoid open conflict, even as each prepared for the trials that inevitably lay ahead. In this age of cultural revival, geographical discovery, overseas colonization, and growing international trade, the Livonian capital prospered like never before. But while Livonia's neighbors busied themselves with modernizing their military forces and centralizing (to an extent) their governments, this loosely organized and ethnically diverse crusader state remained disunited and decentralized, barely able to mount a credible defense against outside threats. The realities of the Livonian Confederation's internal weaknesses—the sporadic meetings of its diet (*Landtag*) were what passed for "government"—were obvious to all, not least the rulers of Poland, Muscovy, and Sweden.

Having subdued Riga in 1491 and with Livonia now at peace, the knights of the Livonian Order, now dependent on the thousands of mercenaries it hired for pay during times of war, were concerned above all with the emergence of a powerful Muscovite state in the east whose rulers yearned for a Russian outlet to the Baltic Sea. As long as they made no trouble, Riga's burghers could be left in peace. With the order master away at his castle at Wenden—that is, when he and his knights were not fending off the Russians—the citizens were free to manage their own affairs with only a minimum of outside interference. Muscovy's disruptive potential, however, was a reality that even the people of Riga, even in this age of peace and relative plenty, could not safely ignore.

Yet Riga's domestic tranquility would first be put to the test not by the Russians, but by the newly-liberated disciples of an enraged German friar, for in the 1520s the Protestant Reformation would shake the Livonian capital to its foundations. Once the movement had smashed the old ecclesiastical order in Germany and northern Europe, it then swept through the eastern Baltic, where it aimed its fire at the Catholic Church and its foremost representatives, its bishops and archbishops. Striking the Livonian cities during a time of peace with Muscovy, its rulers then distracted by other concerns, the Reformation ignited a series of urban upheavals that gave the era its well-deserved reputation for rebellion, disorder, and spiritual enlightenment. As the Church's authority collapsed, so did that of the archbishop of Riga—even if, as we shall see, the new circumstances in no way hindered the political aspirations of William of Brandenburg, the last man to hold the office.

The religious disturbances of the early Reformation aside, the six decades before the outbreak of the Livonian War (1558–1582) were for Riga the most fortunate of the entire medieval era. While the town council continued to perform its traditional functions of overseeing the city's financial affairs, administering justice, and maintaining the city's infrastructure and defense, ships of all sizes continued to drop anchor in the Düna River at a walled city that visiting merchants called the "house of hemp and butter."[2] It was at Riga's busy harbor that dockworkers of Latvian origin loaded and unloaded goods arriving from the Russian and Belarusian lands, Lithuania, and western Europe, while German merchants counted their profits and lived a good life that was reflected in their large, orderly homes and the clothing (hats and coats made from sable or bear fur) and adornments (precious metals and jewels) that they alone were allowed to wear.

In western Europe this was a period of religious warfare, overseas conquest, skyrocketing inflation, spiritual fervor, artistic achievement, and general unrest; but for the nearly ten thousand men and women who made their homes in Riga, the early sixteenth century was in many respects a most congenial time to have lived.

Confronting Muscovy

That Old Livonia and its greatest city now enjoyed a prolonged period of tranquility owes much to the man who had defeated the city in 1491. Born in Westphalia in 1450 to a family of noble lineage, Walter of Plettenberg (Wolter von Plettenberg) enjoyed family connections in Livonia that allowed him to enter the Teutonic Order at the age of fourteen. The man who would become the German emperor's appointed prince of Livonia (1526–1535) spent his early years in castles near the Russian border, notably Narva, at a time when the grand prince of Muscovy was mostly concerned with the Tatar threat in the south. By 1482, when Plettenberg was appointed commander (*Vogt*) of the castle at Rositten (Latv. Rēzekne) in what is today eastern Latvia, the power arrangement in northeastern Europe was shaken by the ambitions of Muscovy, which proclaimed itself the center of Orthodoxy after the Byzantine Empire's final collapse in 1453. The idea of Moscow as a "Third Rome"—"two Romes had fallen," a monk named Filofei wrote seventy years after the surrender of Constantinople, "the Third stands and there shall be no Fourth"—would later be handily deployed by Russia's rulers to legitimize all actions in defense of the faith and to justify their enhanced powers.[3]

With the glittering cupolas of its newly built churches rising behind the brick walls of a reconstructed Kremlin ("fortress inside a city"), replete with palaces and bridges, moats and dams, the wooden city of Moscow enjoyed a new prosperity that was buoyed by the industry of its townsmen, now numbering between 50,000 and 100,000, and in no small measure by the taxes it collected from the territories it annexed.[4] Having defeated and subjugated the great trading city of Novgorod in 1478, followed by Tver' in 1485, the Muscovite ruler Ivan III (the Great), the first to call himself "Grand Prince of All Russia" (Великий князь всея Руси) and on occasion even "tsar," continued his predecessors' quest to reunify the Russian lands, shattered after the Mongol invasions of the thirteenth century. Such a policy of relentless territorial expansion brought the Muscovites to the shores of the Baltic and White Seas, thereby bolstering the Russians' strategic position. Allowing a truce with Livonia to lapse, in 1492 the grand prince provocatively established the Ivangorod ("Ivan's town") fortress directly opposite the Livonian (now Estonian) border town of Narva. Its purpose was not only to establish the direct trade links with western Europe that would allow Muscovy to circumvent the Livonian ports, but also to prevent Sweden, which had territorial interests on the Russian periphery (Finland and Karelia), from establishing a connection to the territories of the Livonian Order. Such an alliance would threaten Muscovy's inexorable drive to the Baltic.

Quarrels between the Livonian and Russian cities usually had their origins in business: one advantage-seeking trader might swindle another; sometimes an insult or mishap would escalate to the level of violence. But the real issues at stake were power and wealth: the Livonian traders wanted to keep what they had already secured for themselves, and the Russians wanted more. That the Livonian towns pursued increasingly exclusionary policies that permitted them to be the sole intermediaries in Russia's commerce with the West frustrated the Russians, for after

FIGURE 7. Livonia in 1500 (Greenwood Press / ABC-CLIO).

1346 Novgorod's trade with Europe was limited only to Riga, Reval, and Pernau. Further efforts to ward off unwanted competition followed, including the ban on "guests" trading with guests (*Gasthandlersverbot*) that Riga introduced in 1460.

Such limitations could work both ways: sometimes it was the Germans who faced restrictions. In 1450, for example, Germans working in Polotsk were forbidden from having taverns and from selling beer, mead, and wine. The following year, German traders, including those from Riga, were prohibited from going to Vitebsk and Smolensk.[5] Why, the Muscovites wanted to know, shouldn't Russians be able to sell their own goods to buyers in the West without having to go through the Livonian (German) intermediaries?

The limitations imposed upon the Russian trade sometimes complicated relations among the Livonian cities. The merchants of Reval and Pernau were understandably displeased when they saw Riga's traders ignoring the existing prohibitions against selling metals (copper, lead, brass, tin) and other war materials (saltpeter, sulfur) to Russian buyers. Likewise, so incensed were the merchants of Narva when they found Rigans selling cloth and purchasing wax in neighboring Ivangorod that they fired off complaints to Reval's town council, which shared these concerns about Riga's encroachment.[6] Years later it was a moralizing minister from Reval—one Balthasar Russow—who laid the blame for the coming troubles squarely on the shoulders of the Livonian traders: while the merchants grew complacent, enjoying their profits and indulging in all kinds of fun and games, in the east the Muscovite threat loomed virtually unchecked.[7]

Safe in his palace within the Kremlin walls, the Muscovite ruler Ivan III, the "gatherer of the Russian lands," contemplated his realm's landlocked position and the alleged mistreatment of Russian traders in the Livonian towns. While the Livonian merchants complained about counterfeit goods and the more restrictive trade practices being introduced in Novgorod, still worse was to come: in the autumn of 1494 the Muscovite ruler abruptly arrested the Germans, confiscated their goods, and closed their offices.[8] Meanwhile, the Russians solidified their position on the Livonian border, along which they maintained a series of fortresses—the castle at Ivangorod across the river from Livonian Narva (now in Estonia) being a case in point. But when the Swedes conquered and burned Ivangorod in 1496, the setback for the Muscovites was only temporary. Committed to maintaining their Baltic foothold, the Russians simply rebuilt their fortress as a large, quadrilateral structure and extended it toward the Livonian border.[9]

What was Ivan's game? Was his closure of Novgorod's *Peterhof* part of a plan, as Russian and Soviet historians have contended, to breach the Livonian trade barrier and establish direct links with Western merchants? Or was it, as Western historians have emphasized, a matter of an ambitious and hostile ruler of an expanding kingdom trying to impose his will upon the foreign merchants who traded in his domains?[10] Certainly Ivan understood the value of trade and wanted to further it; no doubt he also knew that his actions against the Germans in Novgorod would provoke the Livonian cities. Both Riga and Reval arrested the Russian guests who were visiting their cities; later, however, they were repatriated, and Ivan responded in kind, releasing his German hostages with the exception of four Revalers.[11] Apart from Pskov, which remained partly independent of Muscovy and thus was able to continue trading with Dorpat, direct commerce between Russians and Hanse towns in the rest of Livonia ceased for some time.[12]

The disruption of normal trade relations only added to the growing unease. The prospect of a Muscovite conquest of Livonia also had implications for the Polish-Lithuanian state, which would then be rendered vulnerable to attack not only from the east but from the north as well. Such a proposition was not merely theoretical, for Muscovite rulers had long harbored resentments against the Grand Duchy of Lithuania (GDL) for having engorged itself on territories that had once been part of Kievan Rus'. That these lands were inhabited primarily by Orthodox

Slavs lent credence to the Muscovites' contention that an injustice had been done that could be corrected only by themselves.[13]

The battles of 1492–1494 resulted in a stinging defeat for the GDL, for the encroaching Muscovites forced Lithuania to cede significant amounts of territory—and not for the last time. Since Lithuania could not expect any support from Poland (now preoccupied with the Tatars and the Ottoman Empire) or from its sometime ally Novgorod (conquered by Muscovy), the GDL looked to its former nemesis, the Livonian Order, for help against the Muscovites. Such an alliance was anathema to the Kremlin, whose masters would continue to do everything in their power to drive a wedge between Livonia and the grand duchy.

Another war over Lithuania was unavoidable. Presented with evidence that its Orthodox subjects were being persecuted—which is to say that Catholic authorities were trying to convert the Orthodox faithful—Ivan III had all the pretext he would need to launch an attack on Lithuania, some of whose princes were then defecting and transferring their allegiance to the Muscovite ruler. Ivan's plan was simple and audacious: he would liberate the lands that had been "subjugated" by Lithuania and thereby reclaim his "patrimony."[14] Following a series of threatening exchanges between the grand prince and Muscovy's ambassadors to Lithuania, Russian forces appeared in Lithuania in May 1500, seizing the town of Bryansk and nearby districts as a prelude to an advance on Smolensk. By the end of the summer, Ivan III held in his grasp the districts watered by the upper reaches of the western Düna and Dnieper rivers. As one historian has noted, "It looked as though the conquest of the old Kievan state by Moscow was merely a question of time."[15] As much as Alexander, Lithuania's grand duke (r. 1492–1506), might have hoped to stave off another confrontation with the tsar's armies, it is difficult to imagine how any diplomatic solution was going to prevent the Muscovites, now allied with the Crimean Tatars in the south, from pushing farther west.

As the new century dawned, the Livonians made ready for what they too must have seen as an inevitable clash with the eastern giant. Their greatest (and most obvious) challenge was the lack of military resources, for the knights had aged, the burghers of the Livonian towns increasingly shirked their military duties, support from the order's Prussian branch was doubtful (indeed, the Prussians were asking for contributions from the Livonian towns), and mercenary forces were both unreliable and expensive. As cavalrymen armed with swords and halberds, Riga's burghers were once reluctant participants in the order's campaigns; but the new type of warfare, conducted with firearms and cannons, was at this point beyond the Livonians' capabilities and carried within it a greater capacity for destruction. In the anticipated confrontation with Muscovy, Livonia would require outside assistance. A treaty concluded with the Lithuanians in 1501 reflected these calculations: the order, the Livonian cities, and the Lithuanian grand duke would unite their forces in a planned attack on the Russians.

Yet when the decisive hour arrived, the Lithuanians were nowhere to be found, for just at that moment a succession crisis in Poland intervened. Hurrying to Cracow upon the death of his brother, the alert Grand Duke Alexander, the fourth son of Casimir IV Jagiellon, sought to ensure his own succession to the Polish throne. To that end the grand duke needed to avoid another disastrous confrontation with Muscovy. (The plan worked: Alexander got his crown and held onto it until his death in 1506.) Left in the lurch by the Lithuanians, Master Plettenberg learned a powerful lesson: Livonia should not count on outside support in times of peril.[16] Mercenary armies, on the other hand, could be bought for a price if the prospect of victory was good.

From Lübeck thousands of volunteers poured into Livonia, whose military commanders took the battle to the Siritsa River, near the western approach to Pskov. There, on August 27, 1501 (old style), they were met by a far greater force of Muscovites and Pskovians. Although victory that day went to the Livonians, the Russians won a great victory near Dorpat in November, allegedly killing or taking prisoner some forty thousand inhabitants of Livonia against negligible Russian losses.[17] Even if the Livonians were not forced to cede any territories as yet, each side continued to attack each other's lands through the winter. Already weakened by a series of harvest failures, eastern Livonia was ravaged by plunder and then by plague.[18] Now reduced to "a loose association of mutually exclusive interests,"[19] the Livonian Confederation banned grain exports—a blow to the merchants and to the revenue stream necessary for the recruitment of mercenaries—and nearly collapsed, held up by little more than the personality of Walter of Plettenberg, the last great knight of the Livonian Order.

Disregarding his countrymen's pleas to make peace with the Russians, Plettenberg took back the initiative and confronted Livonia's most formidable enemy at the Battle of Smolin on September 13, 1502. Although again outnumbered by their enemies, the Livonians "won" the battle, if only in the sense that they prevented the Muscovites from taking (for the time being) the fortress-city of Smolensk. Both sides suffered heavy losses, leaving neither in a position to pursue the other. It was during these campaigns that the Muscovites developed a reputation for the most barbaric cruelty.[20] Indeed, propaganda pamphlets that accused the Muscovites and Tatars of committing unspeakable atrocities against babies and women were distributed throughout Germany in order to raise money for Livonia's defense.[21]

Unable to mount another military campaign, the Muscovites agreed to a six-year peace (March 1503 to March 1509) that restored the *status quo antebellum* and allowed them to focus on Lithuania, which was forced to concede its eastern territories. Livonia, on the other hand, emerged from the battle territorially intact. Over the centuries the clash at Smolin was to become a cornerstone of Latvian political mythology, celebrated by historians and nationalists as a local victory over the mighty eastern giant. Little did anyone realize at the time that this battle would be the swan song of the Livonian Order.

The policies of Vasili III, who assumed the Muscovite throne in 1505, were entirely consistent with those of his father, Ivan III. During his twenty-eight-year reign, Vasili would annex, one after another, the last remaining autonomous provinces on the Muscovite frontier, including Volokolamsk, Ryazan, and Novgorod-Seversky, a territory in present-day Ukraine. Capturing Pskov in 1510 and (at last!) Smolensk in 1514, the Muscovites encroached upon the Livonian territories and finally succeeded in opening the gateway to the GDL, which became their main focus. As for Livonia, Vasili kept up the pressure by shifting from military to commercial operations, leaving the Russian trade in the Livonian towns at a standstill.

The treaty that ended the war between the Muscovites and the order obliged the Livonian cities to abstain from making alliances with other powers directed at Muscovy. Once the Livonian-Lithuanian alliance was broken off, the Livonian merchants were again admitted to their office in Novgorod; in return, the Russian churches and quarters in German towns were restored and merchants on both sides were guaranteed safe travel without hindrance.[22] That the embassies sent to Moscow to conclude this agreement were compelled to follow a humiliating set of protocols that included kissing the cross as proof of their honesty and knocking their heads on the ground as a sign of their obedience—much as Russian princes once did before the Mongol khan—augured poorly for the future, for this became standard practice.[23]

For the time being, the Livonians enjoyed some breathing space, not least because the Muscovites were still contending with the Lithuanians and Tatars. However, Vasili III's conquest of Pskov—a bridge to the West that had long depended on Muscovy's help for its defense—meant that Muscovy was now Old Livonia's immediate neighbor. While the aging German knights stood guard in their renovated castles near the Russian border, the burghers of Riga enjoyed a period of internal peace that was interrupted only after the Holy Roman Empire—and much of northern Europe—had become a religious battlefield.

The New Teachings

Although it took more than twenty years, by 1515 the citizens of Riga had completed the reconstruction of the hated Order Castle, destroyed in the upheavals of the 1480s. But since the order needed Riga to be strong and prosperous in the face of the looming Muscovite threat, its enforcement of the peace terms was lax. As the years passed the city's quarrels with the order receded into the background as a new generation adapted to the city's power arrangements and enjoyed the financial rewards of a booming global economy. With Walter of Plettenberg more than eighty kilometers away in Wenden (Cēsis), the master's official residence during much of this period, Riga's citizens could be forgiven for thinking that theirs was a truly independent city whose blossoming trade with Lithuania and Pskov brought profits to its merchants and employment to its laborers. Old traditions carried on: never once during this period of peace did the master's representatives challenge the Rath's decisions and laws.

Yet if Rigans now accepted the dominance of the order—upon whom else could they rely to defend Livonia?—their growing resentment of the clerics (there were by now perhaps one hundred priests in Riga, not including monks and nuns) helped set the stage for the events to come. That the city's schools, attended almost exclusively by the sons of Riga's well-to-do German merchants, remained under the control of the archbishop was one source of popular resentment: the Dome chapter even maintained the right to select the rector of the school at St. Peter's, a church that, like St. Jacob's (the church of the city's Latvians), was under the authority of the city rather than the archbishop.[24] While the Catholic Church had sorely neglected the spiritual life of the peasants, its hold on Livonia's cities seemed unshakable—that is, until the writings of an Augustinian monk by the name of Martin Luther took the eastern Baltic by storm. Priests lamented that pagan traditions continued to flourish in the countryside; in the city of Riga, thousands flocked to the new teachings.

At the moment that Luther's message arrived in Riga, the reigning archbishop was the reputedly mild Jasper Linde (r. 1509–1524), whose promotion was preceded by more than twenty years of service in the Riga Cathedral. In contrast to previous archbishops, whose confrontations with the order courted threats to their personal safety (and to the safety of Riga's canons), Jasper ruled his diocese in peaceful times and managed to maintain a good relationship with Walter of Plettenberg and the Livonian Order. Reputed to be a humanist and a scholar, the archbishop traveled throughout the countryside, where he lectured the German faithful—especially the semiliterate priests who had arrived in Livonia only to find that the locals spoke strange languages that were too troublesome to learn—on their responsibilities to the peasants.[25] But if Riga's now aged and sick archbishop rejected Luther's "protestant" doctrine—namely that personal salvation is achieved through God's grace alone, and not through "good works" that required the mediation of priests, and that all Christians are "priests" in the eyes of God—there was little he could do to prevent its spread in the city of Riga, for it was to Riga that traders and priests arriving to Livonia brought the news of the day. And it was from Riga, already a hub of the Baltic book trade, that Luther's challenge radiated throughout the Livonian territories.[26]

The new teachings found a ready audience in much of northern Europe. Indeed, it was in those lands where a yearning for spiritual nourishment paralleled a growing resentment against authority—in particular, that of the Catholic Church and its popes—that the Reformation found its most ardent followers. Many Christians were outraged by clerical abuses such as the selling of indulgences. While their money donations to the Church purportedly reduced the amount of time that penitents would spend in Purgatory, any visitor to the newly splendorous city of Rome during the pontificates of Julius II (r. 1503–1513) and Leo X (r. 1513–1519) could see for himself just how such monies were being spent. Having made such a journey himself in 1513, Luther's disenchantment with the Eternal City turned into loathing by the time he returned to Germany.

It was Luther's denial of the Church's authority to remit sins that drove his famous act of nailing his *95 Theses* to the church door at Wittenberg on November 1, 1517. This provocation was likely intended as a means of continuing a discussion begun by the Bohemian priest Jan Hus, a reformer who used his pulpit to denounce the moral failings of priests, bishops, and even popes.[27] Although burned at the stake for heresy in 1415, Hus's ideas inspired a violent "protestant" resistance in the Bohemian lands, and his teachings, especially the notion that the Church is more than its priests and bishops—that it is the entire body of believers—not only inspired the young Martin Luther but were also well known in Riga. That Rigans were receptive to Luther's message is hardly a wonder, for by the early 1500s many burghers longed for the city's deliverance from clerical domination. What was true of Riga applied to the rest of northern Europe: no longer would the old hierarchies remain unchallenged.

While Luther's doctrine found supporters in the Baltic port of Danzig as early as 1518—indeed, the Reformation's political repercussions in the Prussian cities were almost immediately evident—several years would pass before the movement touched the lives of ordinary Rigans. Yet from nearly the moment the burghers began to embrace the new teachings, the pulpits of the city churches of St. Peter's and St. Jacob's became open to men who would preach them. The first, but hardly the most radical, was Andreas Knopken (1468–1539), a lay preacher who first arrived in Riga in 1517, where he preached in the old way to the Latvian fraternities of beer porters and other transport workers.[28] It was only after returning to Germany to study at the university in Frankfurt an der Oder that Knopken was first exposed to Luther's doctrine. Outraged by the events that led to Luther's *Letter to the Christian Nobility of the German Nation* (1520), which had been sent to Knopken by his friend Philip Melanchthon (one of Luther's collaborators), Knopken returned to Riga in the summer of 1521 and immediately committed himself to denouncing the abuses of an institution to which he had devoted his life. Soon the evangelical movement would enjoy the support of Riga's young burgomaster, Konrad Durkop, as well as the Rath's secretary, John Lohmüller, who contacted Luther in the summer of 1522, assuring him that Riga was taking the lead in Livonia and imploring him to send an encouraging greeting to the brethren of his city. Luther's reply, *To the Christians of Riga, Reval, and Dorpat*, synthesized for the struggling new evangelicals the essence of the Christian faith.

As Rome's spiritual authority slipped away and the burghers of the Livonian cities embraced the Lutheran reforms, the archbishop's initial response was to turn to Walter of Plettenberg, the enforcer of Livonia's fragile peace. Eschewing a violent approach to the problem, the order master instead favored a public disputation like those that were then being arranged in many other countries. Attended by Durkop and other councilors, the disputation took place at St. Peter's on June 12, 1522. There the able Knopken refuted his opponents' attacks and proved to the congregants' evident satisfaction that his doctrine was compatible with scripture. Together with the city's guilds, the Rath appointed Knopken archdeacon at the enormous St. Peter's Church, where he preached the reformed faith until his death in 1539.[29]

On October 23, 1522, the fifty-three-year-old pastor, by now a conservative Lutheran theologian and a relatively moderate voice in the growing demands for reform, delivered his first Lutheran sermon at St. Peter's. Those that followed, accompanied by lectures to the citizens on Paul's Epistle to the Romans ("He who through faith is righteous shall live"), proved popular with Riga's civic leaders, themselves eager to escape the control of the Church—and of the order. Soon the scholarly priest wrote a commentary on them that was published in Wittenberg (Riga did not yet have its own printing presses) and became widely read in Livonia.[30]

While Knopken preached the Gospel at St. Peter's, on November 30 Silvester Tegetmeier (d. 1552) of Rostock took a position at St. Jacob's. When the Reformation spread to Livonia's other cities, it was the fiery Tegetmeier who traveled throughout the region and brought the previously distant figure of Jesus closer to the hearts of his parishioners. Supporting Riga's craftsmen and petty traders against the authority of the town council, as always dominated by the city's wealthiest merchants, Tegetmeier represented a strain of the movement that blended a theological revolution with a passion for economic and political justice. Violence was sometimes the result. Indeed, when Luther's letter of encouragement and advice to the Christians of Livonia arrived in Riga in August 1523, more disorder followed in the Livonian cities. But since neither Archbishop Jasper nor Master Walter of Plettenberg were willing to intervene, churchmen of a more conservative bent had no place to turn. The temperate archbishop died in the middle of the storm, in the summer of 1524, while Tegetmeier remained at the pulpit of St. Jacob's (until 1542) and then of St. Peter's until his death in 1552.

As the new teachings swept through the cities of Livonia, it was Catholic clerics who bore the brunt of popular anxiety. Neither priests nor monks nor nuns, all agents of an increasingly despised institution, were spared the burghers' contempt. Some faced banishment. Indeed, when the Franciscan and Dominican monks, carrying relics and church flags, made their annual procession through the suburbs on Good Friday of April 1523, the citizens simply locked the city gates, allegedly leaving the brothers little choice but to march some one hundred kilometers to the archbishop's residence at Kokenhusen (Latv. Koknese) to find shelter. No doubt this pleased the knights of the order, whose commander in Riga, Hermann Houte, encouraged such disorders and even sent the Blackheads a symbolic whip to indicate that the detested monks should be driven from the city.[31] "This dangerous disease," the knight suggested, "must be cured through violent remedies."[32]

A wave of iconoclasm rolled through the Livonian cities during the early months of 1524, bringing hooliganism and destruction to the churches of Riga. The objects of popular wrath were the icons and altars that adorned the church interiors—many of which had been paid for by wealthy burghers seeking absolution for their sins through their donations to the Church. Although critical of luxury and unnecessary expenditure, Luther himself didn't see such images as inherently problematic (nor, for that matter, was Luther pushing for political change in Livonia); it was the misguided desire to gain salvation by endowing sculptures and images that he considered corrupt.[33] Whatever the motives behind the attacks, the iconoclastic events in Riga were entirely spontaneous acts of the population. Luther had already condemned similar acts that had taken place two years earlier in the Wittenberg parish church, and soon enough the confiscated images were returned to their churches. But the excesses were greater in Riga, where the newly emboldened reformers tore the icons and altars from the mounts of all the city's churches, confiscating some and smashing others to pieces. Most shocking of all was the riot that broke out on August 8, 1524, when the mob dragged a venerated image of the Virgin Mary from the high altar of St. Peter's to the Düna River, where they subjected it to an ordeal by water. It would be hard to imagine a more appropriate illustration of the link between the iconoclasm of the early Reformation and popular anxieties about witchcraft.[34]

Agitated Rigans—and not only Rigans, for the city always housed a number of temporary residents, such as the young men of the Blackheads fraternity—attacked the archbishop's own cathedral, St. Mary's (the Dome), destroying the interior of Livonia's most important religious building. Catholic services ceased to be heard in St. Mary's, now under a Protestant occupation. Once popular passions abated, the former cathedral was transformed into a parish church, its school reorganized as a Lutheran school. Also repurposed was the Dome's Franciscan monastery: it was from the books and manuscripts the monks left behind that one of northern Europe's first public libraries (*Bibliotheca Rigensis*) was created in 1524 on the initiative of councilor Paul Dreiling.[35] But if the monastery courtyard was now a marketplace, at least St. Mary's itself remained a church. The alternative was sometimes less dignified: after its seizure by the town council, St. John's—a Dominican church that only decades earlier had been razed and rebuilt with a tall, slender tower, large windows, and pointed arches—suffered the insult of being turned into a horse stable and barn, and shortly after that into an armory. Sadder still was the fate of St. George's, a chapel that had been built on the site of the first Order Castle in Riga, for it was turned into a warehouse for flax, hemp, hides, and other goods that came to the city. Never again would St. George's be used as a church.[36]

Similar actions took place throughout Germany, Switzerland, and the Low Countries, where the iconoclasts were for the most part the town rabble, a handful of fanatics, and clamorous youth.[37] Thus it should come as little surprise that in Riga the most active participants in the pogroms were the unmarried men of the Blackheads fraternity, nearly all of whom were newcomers—typically the privileged sons of established Hanse merchants.[38] But it was also the case that ordinary Rigans, among them Latvian artisans and laborers, took part in the disorders.[39] While historians of the Reformation correctly emphasize the sense of liberation and excitement that accompanied the destruction, often left understated is the fact that the early Reformation was, to a large extent, writes Diarmaid MacCulloch, "a movement of the young," now acting out "their sense of their personal liberation from a deception."[40]

Catholic leaders struggled in vain against the rising tide. John Blankenfeld, then the bishop of Dorpat but already entertaining grander ambitions, tried to stop the Reformation's spread, forbidding priests to preach reformist doctrines from their pulpits and personally burning a copy of *The Babylonian Captivity of the Church* (1520). It seems likely that such actions got the attention of Rome and led to Blankenfeld's appointment as archbishop of Riga in early 1524, but this decision only inflamed the unrest.[41] His successor, Thomas Schöning (r. 1528–1539), the stout and conservative son of a famous mayor, struggled to protect the Church in Riga, but concluded that his chances of avoiding a dangerous conflict with both the city and the order were best realized by moving his main residence to the archbishop's palace at Kokenhusen.

While the violence in Riga and the other Livonian cities paled in comparison to the mayhem that was unleashed within Germany, the attacks on icons and church property destabilized both the Livonian Confederation and Catholicism's position within it. Not wanting to take sides in a quarrel that could tear the country apart and deliver it into the hands of the Muscovites, Master Walter of Plettenberg, now an elderly man in his seventies, open to moderate reform but concerned that he might find himself in the line of fire, took a position of benevolent neutrality. Faithful to both the Livonian Order and the Catholic Church, and disturbed by the actions of radical Protestants in Riga, Dorpat, and Reval, Plettenberg found himself in the position of supporting the Reformation in order to secure greater independence from the archbishop—the same reason that Rigans now made common cause with the order. Understanding the need to maintain stability while at the same time giving vent to popular frustrations, Plettenberg promised to protect the city from any efforts by the archbishop to reimpose Catholicism.

Plettenberg's Dilemma

The story of the Reformation in Riga is also the saga, replete with all manner of destruction and carnage, of Christian Europe leaving the Middle Ages behind and entering a new epoch of humanism, science, and discovery. At the moment when all the old certainties were coming apart, traditional ties now torn asunder, the beleaguered Emperor Charles V (r. 1519–1556), in collaboration with a weakened papacy, struggled to hold their crumbling world together. During the three years (1519–1522) that the Portuguese explorer Ferdinand Magellan devoted to circumnavigating the globe, the German friar Martin Luther completed his transition from inconvenient heretic to dangerous competitor. It was during these years that the Lutheran Church was born. By the time Giovanni da Verrazano set his gaze on the island of Manhattan in the summer of 1524, the papacy's ideal of a united Christendom was more divorced from reality than ever before. The situation within Livonia's precarious borders reflected the sudden onslaught, for the sense of Christian unity that had for more than a century sustained the Livonian Confederation, that loosely organized complex of territories and bishoprics shared by the order and the Catholic Church, was shattered. The obsolescence of the feudal state was apparent even to the knights themselves: even at the time it was obvious that the ramshackle Livonian Confederation might simply implode.

One option for Walter of Plettenberg was to follow the example of Albert of Brandenburg (1490–1568), the last grand master of the Teutonic Knights. For years Albert had been methodically working to unify under his rule the entirety of Prussia, then split between the crusader state in the east and Royal Prussia, a smaller Polish possession (since 1466) in the west. But such ambitions brought him into conflict with his uncle, King Sigismund I ("the Old," r. 1506–1548) of Poland. Although Albert showed little interest in Protestantism at first, after a personal meeting with Luther, he came to see the potential benefits of turning his ecclesiastical estate into a secular and dynastic one. After converting to Lutheranism, the margrave offered his lands to Sigismund, who reluctantly sanctioned the agreement and bestowed East Prussia upon his nephew as a fief, for this seemed like the only way to prevent Albert from tearing *all* of Prussia away from the kingdom. Thus did Albert of Brandenburg become the ruler of a hereditary dukedom, his acquiescent knights transformed into hereditary nobles. Confirmed by the Treaty of Cracow on April 8, 1525, the arrangement left Albert as the secular ruler of an East Prussian state. This, as we shall see, was only the beginning of his audacious plans in northeastern Europe.

What, then, of Livonia? There a *Landtag* and the citizens of Riga and Reval encouraged a similar course of action. Letters from Riga's town secretary, John Lohmüller, to the Livonian *Landmarschall* and to the bishop of Samland (Prussia) urged the order to take power from the bishoprics and rule Livonia on its own.[42]

While deposing the archbishop of Riga and setting up a secular Livonian state might have proved tempting to Plettenberg, his sense of duty—that is, his responsibility to defend a united Livonia as a loyal Catholic—eclipsed any personal ambitions he might have entertained. Even if Plettenberg, a true believer in medieval ideas about a universal Christian empire, had followed Albert's lead and established a secularized state, the knight was surely aware that Livonia was unable to defend itself from a potential Muscovite attack on its own and that the fractured polity would need the protection of a powerful overlord.[43] If, on the one hand, the collapse of the Teutonic Order in Prussia had freed the Livonian knights from subjection to a distant and neglectful parent organization, on the other hand, it had rendered the teetering Livonian Confederation more vulnerable to Muscovy's ambitions.

It was John Blankenfeld's secret talks with Muscovy that spurred Plettenberg to have the archbishop arrested at the end of 1525 on suspicion of treason.[44] Even if the charges were dropped and the two were soon reconciled, the prelate was finished as a political power, for the bishops had placed themselves under the protection of the master.[45] Compelled to sign a treaty with the Livonian Order that made it responsible for the administration of his lands, the archbishop kept his titles and the spiritual functions of his office but died soon after.[46] His successor, Thomas Schöning, held the office from 1528 until his own death in 1539.

Further undercutting the archbishop's authority was Plettenberg's agreement with Riga. On September 21, 1525, the master annulled the Treaty of Kirchholm, which for nearly three-quarters of a century had guaranteed the sovereign rights in Riga of both the archbishop and the order master. Waiving his rights over the city and surrendering one of his estates to the town council, the elderly knight guaranteed the city's complete religious freedom. Under Plettenberg's watch, no restrictions would be placed on Lutheranism in Riga.[47]

How differently it might all have turned out had Plettenberg opted to follow the path of Albert of Prussia, who, as we have seen, had boldly secularized the Teutonic Order's holdings in Prussia and become a Protestant duke. But Plettenberg, a faithful Catholic to the end, remained committed to keeping intact both the Livonian Confederation and the knightly order over which he had presided since 1494. To the burghers of Riga and Reval, the master promised his military protection; there would not, however, be a new state as in Prussia. Yet it was with the support of both the *Landtag* and the German emperor that Plettenberg in 1526 acquired the rank of an imperial prince that made him the secular ruler of Livonia as a vassal of Holy Roman Emperor Charles V, an avowed enemy of Luther.

Plettenberg's final achievement was a treaty with Muscovy. Signed in 1531, the nonaggression pact was to endure for more than twenty years. Four years after its conclusion, the knight who saved Livonia from itself died in his castle at Wenden at the age of eighty-five.[48] By the time of his passing, Plettenberg's likeness, a solemn figure clad in armor and in a mantle bearing the cross of the Livonian

Order, had been installed over the north gate of the rebuilt Riga Castle next to a figure of the Holy Virgin, the order's patroness.[49] Somewhat less devoted to the Catholic faith or to the institution of the Church were Plettenberg's successors, who were content to divide among themselves the monasteries and other Church properties of Courland, Livonia, and Estonia.

If Walter of Plettenberg remained loyal to Rome and to the Livonian Order—despite the fact that with the conversion of the pagans of northeastern Europe, it had long ago lost its *raison d'être*—his counterpart in Prussia, Duke Albert of Brandenburg, entertained still greater ambitions. Having become one of northeastern Europe's most prominent Protestants, Albert began to work on a plan to place his brother William into power in Livonia by having him installed as the coadjutor (the assistant and presumed successor) to the archbishop of Riga. The duke's real goal, to create a Livonian principality headed by a close relative on the model of Albert's own East Prussian duchy, seems clear enough, for with a member of the house of Brandenburg ruling in both Prussia and Livonia, the stage would be set for the unification of the two states under a Brandenburg dynasty that enjoyed Polish protection.[50]

Alas, Albert would prove unable to bring his audacious project to fruition. Not only would the two polities never be united, after the outbreak of war in 1558 the Livonian territories would be taken over by Muscovy, Sweden, Denmark, and Poland as the helpless and friendless Confederation was wiped from the map. Nevertheless, it was Albert's brother William of Brandenburg (Wilhelm von Brandenburg), a nominal Catholic, who ended up becoming Schöning's successor and, as events turned out, the last archbishop of Riga (r. 1539–1561).

Relations between the town council and the young archbishop, now residing in Kokenhusen, where he plotted the secularization of his office and Livonia's submission to Poland, were fraught from the beginning. Although nearly all properties in Riga formerly belonging to the Catholic Church had been turned over to the Protestants, Archbishop William refused to surrender his political influence within the city, clinging to his feudal rights in Riga even as the Rath refused to render its usual oath.[51] It was only in 1546, according to an arrangement made by the *Landtag* in Wolmar, that the archbishop agreed to recognize Protestantism's victory.[52] His one personal triumph was minor: while the negotiations of late 1551 over Church property relieved the archbishop of the Dome's properties, he would hold onto the church itself, selling it and other clerical properties back to the city for a sum of 18,000 marks, equivalent to about 3.6 tons of silver.[53]

Reformed Riga

Throughout the German lands, the early Reformation was associated with violence and disorder as thousands of armed farmers, now suddenly imbued with a sense of their own power, attacked manors and killed noblemen in the summer of

1525. Nothing comparable to the Peasants' War took place in Livonia, where the violence was almost exclusively an urban phenomenon and was largely confined to the spasms of 1524–1526.

From Riga, the new faith spread throughout Livonia. But while the burghers of Dorpat and Pernau embraced the Protestant teachings and turned against the Catholic clerics, the landed nobility, like the Order of Livonian Knights, remained loyal to Rome and its representatives—at least for the time being. The arrival of Lutheranism to the cities triggered urban upheaval, but the countryside remained undisturbed, for despite their earlier conversion to Catholicism, the majority of Latvian peasants remained largely indifferent to Christianity in any form (the Jesuits' efforts during the Polish era notwithstanding) until the Swedish reforms of the seventeenth century. In the meantime, the principle of tolerance became widely accepted: while neither side accepted the correctness of the other, the Catholic and Lutheran confessions enjoyed equal standing within the Livonian Confederation and a major conflict was avoided.

In Riga, there was little question about the outcome: there the Reformation's result was an unequivocal victory for Lutheran Protestantism. It might also be said that this was a triumph for education, for the institutions that previously had been open only to a narrow segment of the population now became available to a wider public. No longer under the control of the archbishop, the school at St. Peter's Church came under the management of the town council, which sought to promote a secular education that could furnish the sons of Riga's traders with basic writing and record-keeping skills suitable to young men of their class.[54] In 1528 the council took control of the Dome School, where it established a three-year curriculum (five years after 1588) that encouraged the learning of grammar, mathematics, and languages such as Latin, Greek, and even the basics of Hebrew. But unlike the school at St. Peter's, the Dome School's main task was to prepare Rigans to study at foreign universities like Rostock, Heidelberg, Wittenberg, Margburg, Erfurt, and Leiden.[55] While the Reformation was certainly a time of upheaval, it was also an era when public libraries and medical institutions were being built, as well as shelters for the old, the sick, and the orphaned.

Historians of an earlier age typically portrayed the Reformation in Riga and the other Livonian towns as a largely German affair.[56] Yet few today would dare to downplay the role of Latvians in the movement.[57] It was Latvian porters who were the first people to whom Knopken preached, and then it was the members of the other Latvian craft guilds—the brotherhoods of warehouse workers, fishermen, and so on, always had a religious character—who joined the earliest Lutheran congregations. By 1527 the Latvians who had guild altars at the Lutheranized churches of St. Peter's and St. Jacob's had united into a single congregation at St. Jacob's.[58] It was not long before the German pastors realized that the old problem of the Latvians' residual paganism could perhaps be overcome by preaching to them in the Latvian language, and in this way they might be won over to Christianity. Still, many years would pass before such pastors were able to offer comprehensive church services in Latvian.[59]

As Latvian refugees from the surrounding countryside continued to stream into Riga in the hopes of escaping the barbarities of serfdom (i.e., forced labor, corporal punishment, sexual abuse, geographical immobility) and breathing the city's "free air," authorities began to set up the earliest schools for Latvian children. The first such school was established at St. Jacob's, a church where Latvian Lutherans were free to worship and sing spiritual songs in their own language.[60] While such schools were hardly intended to prepare Latvians for studying at a university—such a novelty was practically unheard of in the sixteenth century—the Latvian boys who attended these institutions at least received a rudimentary education that allowed them to learn the hymns and better participate in Lutheran church services.[61]

Latvians who hoped that they would at last enjoy some influence over civic affairs were to be disappointed, for even if the Reformation had freed the burghers from the Church's spiritual shackles, it had strengthened the town council, as usual comprised exclusively of wealthy Germans. The Reformation also enlarged the role of the now completely secularized and Germanized guilds in the city's administration. For example, it was now the responsibility of the Great Guild to oversee the construction of the new ramparts outside the city walls.[62]

On the other hand, the timely arrival of Protestantism, with its emphasis on making the word of God accessible to people in their own languages, may have averted the assimilation of the Latvian people into the German ethnos. This was the fate of the Old Prussians, who suffered grievously at the hands of the crusaders, their residual populations eventually falling victim (like the Livs of eastern Latvia) to the plagues of the early eighteenth century. Although we may be certain that very few peasants could read Latvian (or any other language), it was with the translations of religious literature during the Reformation that the Latvian language finally emerged in written form. It was not long before Lutheran pastors began to focus on spreading the word of God to the locals in a language they could understand.

Among such preachers was Nikolaus Ramm (d. 1540). This native Rigan, for sixteen years (1524–1540) the pastor for the Latvian congregation at St. Jacob's, is believed to have translated various religious writings into Latvian, Livonian, and Estonian.[63] It has been alleged that these were among the Lutheran books that were packed in a barrel destined for Riga before being confiscated by the Catholic town council of Lübeck in 1525, but nobody knows for certain since none of the expropriated works survived.[64]

Another important early Latvianizer was Ramm's successor at St. Jacob's, Johannes Eck (d. 1552), a German who is believed to have translated Riga-made hymnals from Low German into Latvian in the 1530s.[65] While it is possible that on occasion a monk or priest of Latvian origin could be found in the city before these times, it was only after the arrival of Lutheranism that non-Germans, if only a few, began to join the ranks of the Livonian clergy.

For the most part, however, the language of the Reformation in Riga was German, and it was in a Low German dialect that the increasingly literate burghers of Riga challenged old ideas and postulated new ones. For insight into the humanistic thrust of the Reformation era in Riga, we might consider the life of Burkard Waldis (1490–1556), a monk and tinsmith whose story illustrates the perils and passions of the times.[66] A native of Hesse in Germany, Waldis arrived in Riga in 1522, where his entry into a Franciscan convent coincided with the furor over Luther's new teachings. These, as we have seen, were quickly embraced by the city's patricians and guilds but were met with trepidation by the archbishop of Riga, who at that time was the innocuous Jasper Linde. Seeking the help of the emperor and the pope, in the spring of 1523 the aged archbishop dispatched Waldis and two other monks on a journey to Italy that transformed the young cleric forever. At the time of his departure, he was a faithful and devout son of the old Church, but it was another man who returned to Riga, for the trip to Rome had shaken Waldis's monkish devotion. Having seen for himself the magnificence and splendor of the Eternal City, Waldis shuddered at the immoral and frivolous behavior of the local clergy. The return trip through Nuremberg only reinforced his insights; and although he returned to Riga in 1524 with a contempt for the papacy, the city's Protestant authorities promptly imprisoned Waldis in a dungeon.

These biographical details underline the astonishing speed at which Riga's spiritual order was turned upside down during the early years of the Reformation. By the time Waldis was released from detention he had abandoned the Franciscans and converted to Lutheranism. Soon afterward he married (unhappily) and became a tinsmith, a profession at which he succeeded magnificently. But his rising influence and prestige afforded the curious craftsman the opportunity for further travel abroad and encounters with people from all walks of life. Such experiences provided him with the insights into human nature that inform the four hundred Aesopian fables that he published in his maturity. Many of these stories, composed in a Middle Low German dialect that was then common along the southern shores of the Baltic Sea, were recast as anti-Catholic polemics, as was his version of the annual Shrovetide play, *The Prodigal Son*, performed in Riga's market square on February 27, 1527.

It was on the strength of his fables that Waldis has come to be known as one of the great unsung humanists of the northern Renaissance—or at the very least a significant Protestant polemicist of local renown. Yet his restless nature made further confrontations with authority inevitable. Joining a conspiracy organized by town secretary John Lohmüller (who had been one of the catalysts of the Reformation in Riga) and directed against the Livonian Knights, Waldis was jailed around

Christmas in 1536 on charges of engaging in un-Christian practices, mutiny, and rebellion. Released in the summer of 1540, his business destroyed and his health ruined, Waldis, along with several brothers who had joined him in Riga, returned to his homeland, where he resumed his literary activities with renewed fervor. It was to a mayor of Riga that he dedicated the stock of fables on which he had begun to work while living in that city; but it was in Hesse that he finished the work of translating the ancient tales from Latin into German. While the works of the brave and pious Burkard Waldis are underappreciated in the English-speaking world, the vicissitudes of his life help us to paint a more vivid picture of the Reformation's impact on the city of Riga.

The victory of Protestantism in Riga was nearly total. The principle of religious freedom had been established, the Catholic Church was forced to surrender its properties in the city, and the ruling elites throughout Livonia eventually embraced the new teachings. It was not long, however, before the movement took a more conservative turn that coincided with the arrival in 1527 of John (Johann) Briesmann (1488–1549), a disciple of Luther who brought a return of some of the Catholic Church's more ornate rituals and ceremonies to Riga and the other Livonian towns. But this hardly constituted a return of the Catholic Church. Indeed, it was Briesmann, who had earlier been instrumental in converting Königsberg (Kaliningrad today) and East Prussia, who introduced an evangelical church organization in Livonia's larger urban centers.[67] But, having issued church regulations (1530) for Riga, Reval, and Dorpat, Lutherans failed to do the same in the rest of Livonia. That Luther's message had failed to reach Livonia's rural peoples during the early Reformation may help to explain why there were no Latvian peasant uprisings as there had been in Germany; but the fact that there *were* rural uprisings in neighboring Estonia only demonstrates the complexity and irregularities of the Reformation.

A telling manifestation of the Reformation's puritanical bent in Riga could be seen in the efforts of Protestants to cleanse their city of certain moral evils: for if the world was about to end, as many people believed at the time, then it was essential to make the world's condition during its Last Days correspond as closely as possible to what they believed was desired by God.[68] To take one of the most egregious examples of evangelical austerity, Protestant authorities in Riga banned the celebration of certain holidays, including the pre-Lenten Carnival festivities, during which people ran about in disguises and indulged their appetite for food and drink (see chapter 3).[69] Eventually the urge to purify softened: within fifty years of the iconoclast riots of 1524–1526, Lutheran churches along the Baltic coast were once again adorned with splendid altars and pulpits decorated with religious images.[70] As elsewhere in Europe, the rational (humanistic scholarship) coexisted with the irrational (attacks on witches); catechisms were printed and reprinted as the culture of the sermon, then the most common form of education in the Protestant world, emerged alongside the singing of hymns in the vernacular.

Although Catholic and Protestant communities in Riga, and elsewhere in Livonia, remained unreconciled for many years, Catholic congregations and institutions gradually learned to coexist beside Lutheran ones, and vice versa.[71] By the time the Wolmar *Landtag* declared religious freedom throughout Livonia in 1554, a new normal had settled over the city. The following year marked the official end of religious struggle within the Holy Roman Empire with the conclusion of the Treaty of Augsburg, to which a representative of the Livonian Order affixed his signature. It was with this document that the legal division of Christendom within the empire's sprawling territories was made permanent, each prince enjoying the right to choose the religion for the territory he ruled.

At a time when Europe was in crisis—the wars of religion would continue for more than a century—life went on in Riga, and in Livonia, with Catholics and Protestants learning to tolerate one another. It was a time when beer was plentiful and tournaments and entertainments of all kind abounded. But if preachers were scandalized by the moral laxity they saw all around them, even the most appalled among them would have found it difficult to deny that this was a mostly peaceful and pleasant era for Livonia and for Riga. But small feudal states like Livonia were becoming an anachronism. Surrounded by great powers, Livonia enjoyed an unusual period of calm before the unleashing of a great storm.

Years of Peace

Elsewhere in northern Europe, Luther's teachings incited peasant revolts, the dramatic uprisings of the Anabaptists, and wars of liberation that were directed against the Catholic hierarchy and that in turn helped spur the creation of modern, national states. This was not the case in Livonia, a distant outpost of a German "empire"—that is, the Holy Roman Empire—that had been dealt a blow from which it would never recover. In Prussia, the Teutonic Knights abandoned the emperor and, as we have seen, submitted to the Polish crown. If corresponding changes were inevitable in Livonia, Courland, and Estonia, for the time being their fragile confederation remained a political vacuum at the crossroad of a booming regional trading system. The feudal state's obvious weaknesses only whetted the appetites of its better-organized and more-powerful neighbors.

Nevertheless, from the time of the Livonian victory over Muscovy at the Battle of Smolin in 1502 until the outbreak of the Livonian War in 1558, Riga enjoyed a highly favorable set of external and internal conditions that allowed its citizens to enjoy the full reward of their labors. Peasants entered through the city gates to sell vegetables, butter, and eggs in the local markets, while at Riga's busy port Latvian dockworkers loaded goods from the Lithuanian and Belarusian interior onto ships that were bound for the Baltic Sea. Of course, not everyone shared equally in the city's prosperity, but for many Rigans, these were indeed the best of times.

Riga's good fortune in the early decades of the sixteenth century, like that enjoyed by every European center of trade, was closely connected to the surge in global commerce unleashed during the "age of exploration." With Western powers such as Portugal and Holland taking over the trade routes that connected Europe to East Asia, much-desired colonial goods flowed into the port of Riga as trade blossomed the world over. Laden with salt used as ballast, the heavy wooden ships from western Europe still carried traditional products like wine, silk, and cloth across the Baltic; now these vessels additionally transported sugar, pepper, and spices.[72]

No country benefited from this spike in global exchange more than Holland, for by the middle of the sixteenth century Dutch cities had become "money-making engines without parallel in Europe."[73] The ascendancy of Dutch commerce in the Baltic region meant that it was the cities of the Netherlands (and of England) that became the leading markets for the construction materials now being exported by Riga—ash, planks, and pitch. Goods such as these came from the forests of Russia, the Belarusian lands, and Lithuania, but it was the merchants of Danzig, Riga, and other Baltic cities who controlled their export.[74] The types of goods that passed through Riga are reflected in the inventory of four Dutch ships, each of which had been detained sometime between 1510 and 1520 en route to Holland: comprising about four-fifths of the absolute value of the goods on these ships were goods from the forests of eastern Europe; the remainder consisted of leather, grain, linen, and hemp.[75]

Trade relations also blossomed with England, a maritime country whose economic wellbeing was entirely dependent upon overseas commerce; but it was only after being handled by middlemen and taxed that the goods of northeastern Europe arrived in English ports. Aiming to circumvent the Sound (Öresund), the straight that separates Sweden from Denmark (whose authorities collected duties from all the ships that passed through it),[76] the English discovered a new route to Muscovy, which they viewed as a potential market for English cloth. For those willing to endure the stormy northern passage to Russia, discovered by Sir Hugh Willoughby and Richard Chancellor in 1553, the White Sea route offered the advantage of evading the Sound dues and bypassing the middlemen who controlled the export of Russian goods. So invested in this enterprise did the Muscovy Company (est. 1555) become that a port for the English trade in Russia was established at Archangel (Rus. Arkhangelsk) in 1584. But even if the great dreams of England's rulers and merchants never really panned out and the northern passage to Russia failed to develop as a major trade route, the Livonian cities (and the declining Hanse) saw the new route as a serious threat to their livelihood.[77]

Despite occasional downturns owing to the impact of local and continental wars, trade in northern Europe surged during the sixteenth century. If in earlier times peoples living in the more developed parts of Europe considered the eastern Baltic a backwater, it was impossible now to deny the importance of the primary goods that were collected in the Livonian cities for delivery to the West. For the enterprising, and above all for those who enjoyed legal and military protection, the superior profit margins offered by the Baltic trade were there for the taking.

Riga's economic character during the sixteenth century was only superficially different from the one it had developed during the Middle Ages. One long-standing pattern that advantaged Riga's great traders, and those of the eastern Baltic in general, was the emphasis on exports: since the value of Riga's exports to the West was always greater than the value of the goods Europe sent to Riga, Westerners had to pay the difference with silver and gold obtained from the New World. While this had long been the case, what changed was the "price revolution" of the 1530s–40s that triggered a doubling or tripling of the prices that western Europe paid for Baltic grain, linen, and hemp.[78] In such manner, significant quantities of precious metals made their way into the hands of Riga's merchants. Rigans then used the same silver to pay for the Muscovite goods, despite Hanseatic bans on sending precious metals to Russia that were intended to prevent exactly that outcome.

Also consistent with Riga's earlier character was the continued role of the town council in regulating the city's commercial affairs. Its authority buttressed by the archbishop's exile to Kokenhusen and the order master's decision to live in Wenden, the town council continued to issue ordinances that regulated the activities of some 150 to 200 merchants who had acquired membership in the Great Guild.[79] Mentioned in the city's taxpayer list from the middle of the sixteenth century were 353 householders who alone enjoyed the right to enter into commercial transactions and take a seat in the Rath.[80] Standing together in opposition to the activities of foreigners and "guests"—that is, traders from other Hanse cities, the Dutch, and the Russians, all of whom were subject to a ban (1460) on trading with each other—Riga's merchants were typically divided among themselves: while the great trading families dominated the city's commerce, the rights of journeymen traders, such as the unmarried men of the Blackheads fraternity, remained limited. And as we have already noted, within Riga the rights of non-Germans—that is, the Letts and Livs who made Riga their home—were steadily curtailed as prohibitions against guild membership and real estate ownership went into effect during the course of the fifteenth century. (See chapter 3.)

Yet the divisions among Rigans were not always as sharply defined in reality as the decrees and ordinances of the time might suggest. Indeed, the historian of eastern Europe (or, if one prefers, northeast central Europe) must always be wary against oversimplifications of class and nationality, for even if there was growing discrimination against and exploitation of Riga's Latvians, the city was home to some wealthy Latvians—and it was also home to many poor Germans. Whatever their internal divisions, for Rigans and the burghers of the other Livonian cities, this was a time of peace, plenty, and relative security.

The contrast with the worsening conditions in the countryside could hardly have been more stark. If the mounted noblemen were freed from the need to wage war and were transformed into country squires, their good fortune came at the expense of the Latvian peasants: oppressed from the very beginning of German rule, the rural *Undeutsche* were now enserfed, their hereditary rights revoked. In most cases, their lands were either expropriated by the order or enfeoffed to one of the master's vassals. Sometimes farmers who were unable to pay their debts—typically due to bad harvests, famine, or increasingly onerous duties—simply abandoned their lands and migrated to Riga or one of the other Livonian towns, much to the annoyance of the German squires. Others offered their labors to a lord they believed to be less demanding. By 1500 a series of statutes had been introduced that legalized what had already been underway for decades: the permanent attachment of the peasantry to the land. As their condition deteriorated, the peasants lost their freedom even to sell their surpluses in urban markets. In times of war, it was not unusual for the exhausted peasants to harbor and supply invading forces who promised something better.

Although peace reigned for the time being, Riga's prosperous burghers had known the catastrophic effects of war and were always preparing for the next one. Indeed, the decades after Riga's civil war of the 1490s were a time of rebuilding as the city fortified itself against outside attack. The Order Castle in Riga was rebuilt; the height of the city walls was increased and cannon platforms were added; the city's towers and gates were strengthened. The burghers also began to work on constructing new ramparts outside the city walls—a response to the increasing importance of firearms. By 1552 the earthen fortifications between the Sand Tower and the mouth of the Rigebach, the stagnant and stinking rivulet that wound around the city before merging with the Düna, had been completed, now reaching a height of eight to eleven meters. (As the old brick and limestone walls lost their original defensive significance, residents began to build their dwellings into them on both sides.) Running along a distance of two hundred meters from the old city walls, the new ramparts were built by sweating Latvian laborers who drove in the piles while standing waist high in mud, for in front of the ramparts they had also built a moat.[81]

Not even these expensive efforts to fortify the city's defenses against potential enemies were enough. Riga would be spared from a direct Muscovite assault during the calamitous Livonian War, but when the victorious Stephen Bathory entered the city to take possession of it in the spring of 1582, the king of Poland simply crossed the shallow ditch on horseback.

Chapter 6

Upheavals: The Livonian War and the Polish Interlude

From Riga to Dorpat, not a single dog was heard to bark, nor a cock to crow.
—Unattributed[1]

Many hidden cannons are kept at the ready
peering through the teeth of the mighty wall.
—Basilius Plinius (1595)

Barely a century after the invention of Europe's first printing press by the German blacksmith Johannes Gutenberg, one of the first images of Riga appeared on the pages of the hugely popular tome *Cosmographia*.[2] Published in 1550 in Basel, Switzerland, by the cartographer and explorer Sebastian Münster, the book featured dozens of woodcuts and maps and was reprinted in numerous languages. Few publications did more to contribute to the growing interest in world geography during the "age of exploration."

Appearing during an unusually peaceful period just before calamity struck the region, Münster's panorama presents an image of a tranquil and prosperous city not unlike other north German towns of the time. Dominating the skyline are the towering spires of St. Peter's, St. Mary's (Der Thum), and St. Jacob's. Although rebuilt in various styles and heights in the wake of misfortune, these stately old churches, now romantic symbols of Riga's medieval past, formed a distinctive silhouette that was as recognizable in the sixteenth century as it is today. On the far left, just outside the walled city, stood the castle that belonged to the Order of Livonian Knights—one of perhaps sixty such fortifications it maintained throughout Old Livonia (including Estonia).[3] Rebuilt after the civil war that closed the fifteenth century, this third Riga Castle, currently the official residence of Latvia's president, was part of an extensive defensive system that ringed the city and that

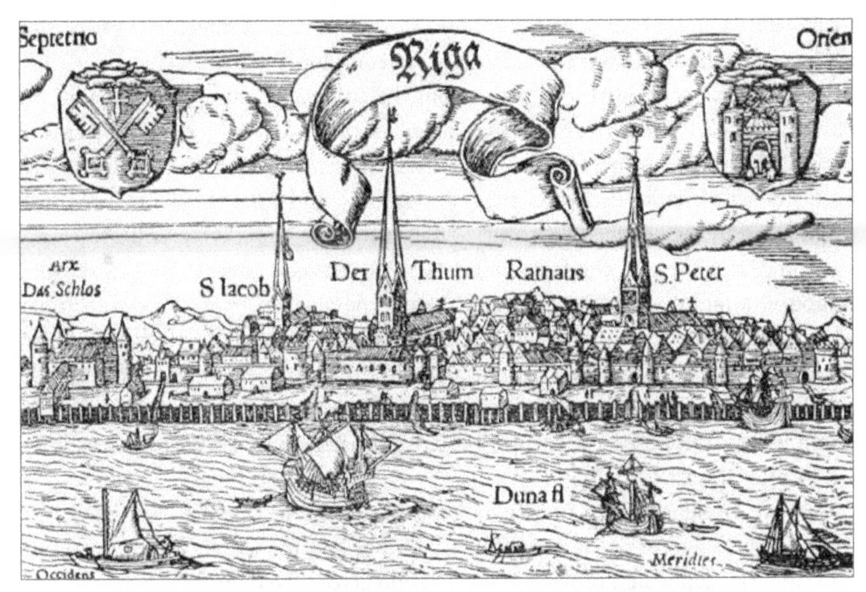

FIGURE 8. Riga in 1547. Sebastian Münster, *Cosmographia* (Basel, 1550). From the Mechanical Curator collection, released to Wikimedia Commons by the British Library.

included a high, thick wall built of limestone and bricks and two dozen towers of varying shapes and sizes. Behind the castle stands Kube Hill, an inhabited sand dune whose height exceeded that of the town walls. For that reason, the "old mountain" was later razed on the orders of Russian imperial authorities, who appreciated the hill's potential value to anyone who might wish to attack the city.

Yet the Münster panorama offers few hints about the construction projects of the era; nor would readers have been informed of the great fire that destroyed the Dome's 140-meter tower (then the world's tallest) in April 1547. But it was just at the time when western Europeans were getting their first glimpse of Riga on the pages of *Cosmographia* that the city's old defensive system was being upgraded with an outer shell consisting of ramparts and ravelins and bastions—necessary to meet the requirements of a "gunpowder revolution" that was radically changing both the experience of war and the preparations required for it.

Encompassing a somewhat larger territory than the area delimited by its thirteenth-century walls, during these years the inner city expanded from twenty-eight to thirty-five hectares; not until the walls were razed in the nineteenth century would these territorial limits be exceeded. Outside the defended city were the unplanned suburbs, where modest wooden homes and manor houses were built and then, in response to an encroaching enemy, burned to the ground. The city's Polish rulers (1581–1621) supervised still further improvements in Riga's fortifications, but it was only under Swedish rule in the seventeenth century, the subject of chapter 7, that the new system was completed and perfected.

If the Münster print reveals little about the changing nature of warfare at the dawn of the early modern era, it nevertheless portrays a densely developed city of modest size. Behind the town wall that lines the embankment, clusters of closely built houses obscure a maze of narrow, winding, and uncobbled streets—most originating in the thirteenth century—that has been remarkably well preserved into modern times. In the foreground near the embankment there is a slaughterhouse, a tannery, and storehouses.[4] The scene also shows a half-dozen ships anchored in the middle of the Düna River, the source of Riga's wealth and also one of the city's greatest anxieties, for not only did the Düna deliver goods from both the east and the west, the mighty river, measuring some seven hundred meters in width where it flows past Riga, also brought disaster about once every decade in the form of devastating floods.

A more mundane concern was simply getting across the channel—accomplished easily enough during the winter simply by traversing the ice. In warmer weather Latvian ferrymen would provide transportation across the river, for it was not until 1701, during the Great Northern War, that a floating bridge was assembled on the orders of Sweden's King Charles XII. The Swedes' floating bridge was to connect the city to the sparsely populated and undeveloped Überdüna (Latv. Pārdaugava) region on the river's left bank, which in turn linked Riga to the town of Mitau (now Jelgava) in Courland.[5]

A later version of this "floating bridge" was considered one of the "three miracles" of old Riga. Another was the bell of St. Jacob's Church, forged in 1480 and emblazoned with the words "God please save us from Russians, Floods and Plagues." It was the ringing of this bell that invited the public to attend beheadings at the main square. Although this particular spectacle came to an end in 1863 when the post of public executioner was abolished, the bell remained in place until 1915 when it, together with the bells of all of Riga's churches as well as many other metal statues and industrial items, was evacuated to wartime Russia.[6] It was only in 2001, as Rigans celebrated the city's eight-hundredth anniversary, that the bell was at last restored to St. Jacob's.[7]

Riga's third "miracle" was a multicolored sculpture that stood in a small hut near one of the moorings on the Düna embankment. This was Big Christopher, whom we first met in chapter 3 as a rough-hewn giant with a walking stick in one hand, a lantern in the other, and a little boy perched on his left shoulder. First appearing sometime around 1510, Christopher was for centuries adored by Rigans, who created legends that depicted him as a boatman who protected the city from misfortune. It was said that the big man could ward off floods, ensure safe sailing, and even cure sickness. To that end the burghers decorated their beloved statue with ribbons, colored yarn, and garlands of flowers. Once these objects had touched Christopher, it was believed that they could then be used to cure the various illnesses and ailments suffered by ordinary Rigans.

But there is more to the legend, for Rigans also told a story of how Christopher heard the cries of a drowning child, jumped into the water and saved him. According to local lore, he then placed the Christ child on his shoulder and took him to his hut. After putting the boy and himself to sleep, Big Christopher awoke to find a pile of gold. It was with this money that the city of Riga was said to have been built.[8]

To this bit of lore we might add another old legend that illustrates Riga's endless cycles of construction and rebuilding. In a popular variant, a voice from the Düna—it might be a fish, or perhaps a sea monster—is periodically heard to ask if the city is finished ("*Ist Riga fertig?*" / "*Vai Rīga jau gatava?*"). Every time this occurs, which might be every New Year's Eve or perhaps once a century (depending on the teller of the story), a voice responds that Riga is not yet completed—for if somebody at some point affirms that it is in fact finished, then the city together with its inhabitants will be submerged into the waters of the Düna.

Exactly when this popular folk legend originated is anyone's guess: variants of this story have been told for centuries. The essential truth it conveys, that Riga will never be completed, was borne out by the city's experience during the troubled transition from the feudal age of knights and vassals to an early modern era characterized by religious diversity and increasingly centralized states. As Riga adapted to the new conditions, its burghers did what they had always done: they rebuilt their city.

Earlier we saw how the damaged city recovered after the civil war of the 1480s as its leading citizens attempted to cast off the domination of Riga's spiritual rulers while embracing the new teachings of Martin Luther. But the city's relative good fortune during the first half of the sixteenth century became imperiled during the Livonian War (1558–1582), a catastrophe that began with a Muscovite invasion and ended with victories for Poland and Sweden, each of which obtained pieces of the shattered Livonian Confederation for itself. Whatever the disagreements among the great powers of the Baltic Sea, all understood that a secure and prosperous Riga would add considerably to the fortunes of whomever controlled it.

The Peace Unravels

A fateful decision by the archbishop of Riga, William of Brandenburg (r. 1539–1561), tested the fragile peace, and soon enough Livonia was at arms. The fact that the archbishop's brother Albert, a former grand master of the Teutonic Order, now ruled eastern Prussia as its hereditary duke (see chapter 5) lent some credibility to the concern that the House of Hohenzollern harbored grander ambitions in the eastern Baltic.

Indeed, the prelate's decision was fraught with implications. Having ruled his diocese for seventeen years and now approaching old age, William had resolved to appoint the eighteen-year-old Prince Christopher of Mecklenburg as his coadjutor and, it would seem, his hereditary successor. In the works for several years but only announced in 1556, the scheme violated an earlier agreement that forbade the appointment of foreign princes as archbishops, bishops, or coadjutors, for such a blatant move in the direction of hereditary monarchy would imperil the rights and privileges of the Livonian aristocracy. The nobles, of course, were also aware that Prince Christopher's cousin was King Sigismund II Augustus (r. 1548–1569) of Poland, who did little to hide his preference for resolving the Livonian problem by incorporating the region into Poland-Lithuania.[9] Even the archbishop's own chapter condemned the move, viewing it as an act of treason. In June of that year, open warfare broke out between the plotting archbishop and the knights of the Livonian Order.[10]

If the Livonian Confederation now teetered on the edge of chaos, the final push into the abyss was the sudden death of Master Heinrich of Galen (r. 1551–1557) and his replacement by his coadjutor William of Fürstenberg (Johann Wilhelm von Fürstenberg), a fifty-seven-year-old Westphalian who had previously held many posts in Livonia and Estonia. Seizing and imprisoning both the archbishop and his coadjutor, it was Fürstenberg's intention to annex the archbishop's lands, thereby settling the Livonian question in favor of the order.[11] Outraged by the master's poor treatment of his cousins, King Sigismund II Augustus demanded their liberation and the reinstallation of William of Brandenburg at the head of the archbishopric of Riga, which the Polish king now regarded as an independent principality friendly to Poland. To ensure an outcome favorable to his interests, the Polish king, the nominal protector of the Riga archbishopric for more than two hundred years, poised his armies for an attack on Livonia. Agreed to by Charles V's younger brother Ferdinand, who was also the emperor's representative in Germany, the ploy succeeded flawlessly. His own forces dwarfed by those of the Polish king, the grand master reluctantly agreed, after a delay of six months, to reinstate the archbishop. At this point, there was little that Fürstenberg could do other than accept the military alliance imposed upon him by the king of Poland, then acting in his capacity as grand duke of Lithuania.

Concluded in September 1557, the Treaty of Poswol imposed a Polish protectorate upon Livonia and gave Sigismund II Augustus the right to assert himself in Livonia's internal affairs and thereby gradually extend his influence. As such, the agreement, combined with the coming war, rendered inevitable Riga's later incorporation into the Polish-Lithuanian Commonwealth (it would be established in 1569). That the Polish-Livonian alliance was directed against Muscovy was clear to all, not least to Tsar Ivan IV, whose earlier agreement with the Livonians, signed in 1554, included a pledge by the knights that they would refrain from allying with the Lithuanians, whose dynastic links with the Polish state were then being strengthened. "When the Muscovite learned that Livonia was not allowed to make war against the King of Poland," wrote Johannes Renner, an observer of Livonia's destruction in the years that followed, "he recalled his secret hatred against Livonia and thought now to act and seize the prize."[12]

The Livonian War and the Demise of the Order

Like so many conflicts that have raged across the Latvian and Estonian lands, the generation-long Livonian War left vast stretches of territory in ruins and exerted a profound influence on the course of Riga's history.[13] Even if all the major Baltic powers—Russia, Denmark, Sweden, and Poland—saw in it an opportunity to acquire territory in Livonia and thereby bolster their strategic and economic position, the war's outbreak was entirely the product of one man's ambitions and resentments, and that was the Muscovite ruler Ivan IV (r. 1547–1584).

Whether or not Ivan the Terrible[14] was genuinely insane or merely a temperamental tyrant, there can be little doubt that this complicated individual was an able statesman—at least during the first half of his eventful reign—who exerted a tremendous influence on the course of Russian history.[15] Inheriting a landlocked Muscovite state when he assumed the full powers of the throne in 1547 at the age of sixteen, Ivan would go on to conquer the Tatar states of Kazan (1552) and Astrakhan (1556), to which he later added the Mongol-Turkic Khanate of Sibir (1582), thereby opening up the boundless expanses of northern Asia to Russian colonization. Despite the difficulties and tragedies of his age, and these were many, the first "tsar of all the Russias" transformed a relatively isolated Muscovite state into a multiethnic entity comprising some 5.4 million square kilometers.

Ivan's invasion of Livonia was not unexpected. It was only three years into his reign, in 1550, that the Muscovite ruler first gave notice of his desire for Russian control over its commercial relations with the West, then consistently obstructed by the German merchants of Livonia. Unlike the future Peter the Great, a subject of chapter 8, Ivan appears to have had little personal interest in the sea. He was, however, sensitive to the fact that Russia's trade went through potentially hostile territory. Moreover, his country was dependent on its trade partners for munitions and precious metals.[16] Some of his concerns were shared by England, with which the Muscovites sought a closer commercial and diplomatic relationship at this time. If Ivan's later proposal of marriage to Queen Elizabeth was rejected out of hand, by the 1550s the two countries had established direct trade links through the aegis of the Muscovy Company. Each hoped that the Arctic route, with its terminus in Archangel, would prove less cumbersome and more mutually profitable than going through Livonia. Border conflicts with Sweden in 1555–1557 provide another example of Ivan's concerns about his western neighbors and his apparent desire for a direct outlet to the Baltic Sea.

But it was the Livonian towns' rejection of his demand for tribute—an imposition premised on an ancestor's collection of tribute from Dorpat in the eleventh century—that triggered the war that broke out in January 1558. A report to the German emperor underlined the urgency of the threat to Riga and its fortress near the river's mouth at Dünamünde. "As soon as the Grand Prince [of Muscovy] wins this castle, the people of Riga will not be able to use the sea, and [the city] will be landlocked," declared Heinrich von Staden, a self-described "adventurer" in the court of Ivan IV.[17] Attempting to persuade the emperor to ally with Poland and Sweden and jointly launch an invasion of Russia, von Staden hoped that a victory over Muscovy would restore the region to the Teutonic Order, on whose behalf he acted as a spy while ostensibly in the service of the tsar. No such invasion was ever to take place; it was the Russians alone who took the offensive.

With Narva and Dorpat under Muscovite attack, a *Landtag* convened in March to deliberate on defense and to consider what could be done to appease the tsar. Resolving to collect the required tribute and send it to Moscow, which would mean acknowledging that they were his subjects, Livonia's leaders hoped for peace, but the capricious Ivan soon changed his mind. Even as Riga's hopeful (or miserly) leaders dismissed the soldiers who had been placed on alert—in such manner Riga's wealthy traders would thereby be relieved of what some considered an unnecessary expense—the tsar rejected the Livonian tribute and canceled peace negotiations. Narva fell on May 11, Dorpat at the end of July, as the entire region reeled from the shock. Everywhere, the chroniclers wrote, the Muscovites behaved atrociously. The tsar's Khalmyks and Tatars plundered and pillaged, terrorizing the peasants even as they assured them that they would remain unharmed as long as they acknowledged the grand prince as their lord. Under such circumstances, some of the locals were moved to place themselves under Muscovite suzerainty.[18] Having intimidated their ruling elites into abandoning any resistance, Ivan IV then imposed lenient terms on the defeated cities.

The tsar's motivations for the attack have long been debated. Was his main aim to establish direct contact with western Europe for trade?[19] Was the Muscovite ruler reacting to Livonia's alliance with Poland? Was the war, as the tsar himself stated, really about his hereditary rights in Livonia[20] or the desire to protect the region's Orthodox churches?[21] Or was it a simple matter of Muscovite territorial expansion?—a "progressive" development in the view of Marxist-Leninist historians. Even if it was a combination of several or all these factors, it is clear that the tsar's military goal was to conquer not only Narva and Dorpat, but also Reval and Riga, the most important centers for Russia's trade in the Baltic. Ivan timed his attack well, for Poland was bound to a truce with Muscovy until 1562; moreover, its ruler was distracted by a war with the Turks and thus was not in a position to offer immediate aid to Livonia, whose regular forces were modest by comparison and were capable only of fighting a defensive war.

At the time of the invasion, the combined armies of the Livonian Confederation numbered about seven thousand men. Three thousand of these were under the Livonian master (only 150 to 200 of these men were actual knights of the order, who served principally as officers, not as soldiers); another two thousand men belonged to the Archbishop of Riga, to which we may add another two thousand trained infantrymen from Riga, Reval, and Dorpat.[22] But modern artillery was in short supply, the geriatric knights of the order were hardly in a condition to take the field, and the local gentry who provided the cavalry force had grown soft on their estates and were inexperienced in the art of war.

If the Muscovites enjoyed far superior numbers, a variety of problems and conflicts—drought, famine, treason, the death of the tsar's first wife, and a war with the Crimean Tatars, to name a few—prevented them from following up on their victories. As is typically the case when a power vacuum emerges in a troubled region, neighboring actors were eventually sucked in and the entire region became a battleground.[23] The Livonian Confederation, a holdover from a bygone era, an outpost of a declining empire that was helpless to defend it, was doomed: the future would belong to the centralized dynastic state.

The unpreparedness, or perhaps the unwillingness, of the Livonian estates to fight against what they knew to be Russia's stronger forces only hastened Livonia's inevitable demise. As the Muscovites besieged the Estonian coastal city of Reval, located some 280 kilometers north of Riga, its burghers placed themselves under the protection of the Danish king, Frederick II. His temptation to intervene in Livonia is understandable, for the Danes shared with the Swedes a desire to break up the Hanseatic League's maritime monopoly.[24] But Denmark was only a minor and fleeting player in the conflict, unable to provide Reval with its protection. Instead it was Sweden, buoyed by its new and powerful navy, that in 1561 staked its claim as the protector of Reval and its hinterlands. Consolidating its position in northern Estonia, Sweden immediately became a formidable contestant in the struggle over Livonia. But Sweden's gains would be contested by Poland, even if the Polish state's powerful *Sejm*, or assembly of notables, was not especially keen on getting militarily involved in Livonia.

Indeed, for Poland-Lithuania, the Livonian issue represented something of a pickle. The Grand Duchy of Lithuania (GDL), by far the territorially larger but politically the junior partner in its sometimes testy relationship with the Kingdom of Poland, saw the rich lands of the Düna as an inherent part of Lithuania. A Lithuanian occupation of these lands would offer the GDL a chance to strengthen its independence from Poland—an outcome the Polish aristocrats in the *Sejm* wished to block. On the other hand, Sigismund II Augustus, the German ruler of Poland from 1548 to 1572, could easily imagine the profits to be gained from a Polish-Lithuanian occupation of Livonia (and Riga)—all the better if such a move might block Muscovy's economic and political development.[25] Like his Swedish counterpart, Eric XIV (r. 1560–1568), Sigismund intended to fill the void in Livonia to his country's advantage, but for that he would require the approval of the fractious *Sejm* and the cooperation of the Lithuanian magnates.

Reval, as we have noted, had fallen in the initial attack, and so had Dorpat. A German chronicler named Johannes Renner was convinced that the enemy could have conquered the entire country had he pressed his attack, so great was the panic in Livonia.[26] But the city of Riga, the key to controlling the Livonian territories, remained unscathed.

A second round of fighting began in January 1559, when the tsar's forces renewed their attack. Taking advantage of the frozen rivers that connected the Baltic Sea to the hinterlands, the Muscovite-Tatar armies drove deep into Courland and approached the walls of Riga, encircling the city for three days and nights while the suburbs, including the wooden St. Gertrude's Church, were burned to the ground.[27] "In the sand dunes around Dünamünde," located just north of Riga, "they piteously slew a great number of people."[28]

Riga itself appeared to be next in line. The city's chief magistrate, Jürgen Padel (1505–1571), gives vent to the disquiet of Riga's burghers in the following passage:

> This fine town and the whole country is now abandoned by the Holy Roman Empire and the Germanic peoples, . . . and left in the possession of non-German barbarians (*barbarisch Unteutschen*) who never had a high opinion of the Germans and who have always tried everything possible and with all available means, as those who live among them well know, and who never wanted or aimed at anything else but to harm German blood.[29]

The assault exposed the weakness of German rule in Livonia: if the estates were unwilling or unable to defend the Estonian cities, what chance did Riga have against such "barbarians"? While the citizens' anxieties were grounded in the terrible realities of the Livonian War and in their neighbors' actual experiences with the Muscovite armies, the publication of an anti-Russian leaflet in Nuremberg in 1561 surely fanned the flames of the hysteria: soon making the rounds in Livonia, it showed the invaders torturing the Christians of Livonia. If the alleged brutality of the invaders has been debated, there is little doubt that many noncombatants were killed in the attack and that much of the countryside was left in ruins. Like a passing storm, however, the winter campaign ended quickly, and the tsar unexpectedly withdrew his forces in order to deal with the Crimean Tatars in the south. To this end, Ivan was willing to sign a six-month truce with the Livonians that would allow the Muscovites to focus on the southern threat. Nevertheless, the tsar insisted on the fulfillment of his three principal demands: recognition of himself as lord of Livonia (including Estonia); the restoration of old Orthodox churches in Riga, Dorpat, and Reval to the local Russian communities; and free trade for Russian merchants without the requirement of going through Livonian intermediaries.

Knowing the inadequacy of their combined forces, in the run-up to the attack the Livonians began to seek outside help. Riga and Reval turned to their Hanse allies. The order's appeals for assistance were brought to the attention of Ferdinand I (r. 1558–1564), but the feckless emperor still hoped that his best tool was not force but persuasion.[30] The king of Poland, on the other hand, desirous of Livonia's castles as a first line of defense against Muscovy, offered to bring the territory under his royal protection provided the estates submit to his suzerainty. Intense negotiations followed, the archbishop expressing his hope for a partial subjection that would not violate the Livonians' oaths to the Empire.[31]

A letter from a German prisoner in Russia to the provost of the Riga Cathedral, written in 1560, conveys the frustrations of the moment. In it the prisoner laments how "this dreadful war has lasted three years now. The enemy has neither been seriously opposed nor has peace been negotiated. Once a year a delegation arrives, but what does it achieve? . . . And where is the empire that is supposed to defend the poor country?" Especially galling to the author were the Hanse traders who continued to trade with the enemy at Narva, an old Livonian port that was now in Muscovite hands: "In sum, one does not know who is one's enemy, who is his friend."[32] Mutual suspicion grew among the knights: all were on the lookout for treason.

Despite Emperor Ferdinand's ambivalence, northern Germany remained a principal source of aid to Livonia. Enlisted by the Livonian Order, thousands of mercenaries sailed from Lübeck to Riga in groups of one hundred to three hundred, armed with spears, halberds, and muskets.[33] From the town of Kolberg in Pomerania came two medium-sized cannons and half a ton of gunpowder.[34] Yet even these additional resources fell short of the challenge when hostilities resumed in November 1559. In the only important campaign of 1560, the order was defeated and its former master, the aged William of Fürstenberg, who the previous autumn had abdicated in favor of the much younger Gotthard Kettler (Goedert Keteler; 1517–1587), was taken prisoner by the Muscovites. Respected by Ivan, the pro-Russian Fürstenberg was reportedly well treated by his Muscovite captors,[35] but once again the Russians failed to follow up on their successes, leaving Riga, Reval (which had not yet submitted to Sweden), and most of the country in between these cities under the weakened rule of the Livonian Order.

This pause by the Russians allowed Sweden and Poland-Lithuania to raise their profiles in the region. In June 1561 Reval submitted to Eric XIV, who also dispatched his agents to Riga to negotiate (to no avail) on the king's behalf. The competition from Sweden impelled the rulers of Poland-Lithuania, still hoping at this point to avoid a confrontation with Muscovy, to redouble their efforts in Livonia; but the independent-minded burghers of Riga, although terrified that they might come under Muscovite control and be forced to change their religion, remained wary of all suitors—including the ardently Catholic Polish state. Indeed, Riga's initial experiences with Poland were disappointing, for it had sent no aid at all during the first Russian attack. This did not stop the foresighted Kettler from turning to Poland's Sigismund II Augustus for help, for in the chaos of the invasion the new order master would come to see an opportunity: he would preserve the disintegrating Livonian state by making himself its king under Polish protection.

A movement in this direction was the compromise agreement signed in August 1559 that established Polish suzerainty in the Livonian lands, which meant that they were now under the king's protection. Believing the choice lay between acceding to Poland-Lithuania or surrendering to Muscovite rule, both the order master and the archbishop of Riga, still William of Brandenburg, urged the Livonians to accept the arrangement.[36] While the Treaty of Vilnius committed the order to handing over a series of border castles to the Polish king, then acting in his capacity as the grand duke of Lithuania, the fortresses could later be repurchased by the order.[37] A similar lien was placed on castles belonging to the archbishop.

Lithuanian troops began to appear in Livonia the following summer. The prospect of foreign soldiers entering their city, sufficient in number to be disruptive but too few to counter a determined Muscovite assault, sat poorly with the burghers of Riga. The arrival of General Gregory Chodkiewicz[38] confirmed the citizens' worst fears: politically and personally close to the Polish king, the Lithuanian magnate inspected the environment and immediately ordered that his soldiers be quartered in the Riga Castle, where the Polish king's representative would also reside. The affronted Rath rejected Chodkiewicz's demand out of hand, as did the order master: the foreign troops, Kettler insisted, should be deployed only against the enemy and must not be stationed inside the city. The looting and generally poor behavior exhibited by Polish-Lithuanian soldiers only added to Rigans' concerns about the looming prospect of being incorporated into the GDL.[39]

While in the course of events King Sigismund II Augustus became intent on securing the full submission of the Livonian estates, his attention was initially focused on the lucrative and strategically valuable port of Riga. But to take the city in hand would require the acquiescence of its patricians, still committed to the oaths they had taken to Emperor Ferdinand I. The matter was settled by the *Landtag* that convened in Riga in November 1560. With Kettler's assurance that by accepting Polish occupation the city would not be withdrawing its obedience to the Empire, Riga reluctantly accepted the Polish-Lithuanian troops. In exchange for his protection, the king of Poland was to take custody of the nearby castles at Dünamünde, Neuermühlen, and Kirchholm, plus several more in Courland.[40] There was, however, one significant caveat: not more than two hundred knights should be allowed in Riga and its castle (far fewer than the six thousand proposed by Poles), and even then only in the most extreme circumstances.[41]

It was not long before the king of Poland became displeased with this compromise arrangement, for the situation in Livonia was fraught with anxiety and the Rigans were being difficult. Some in the king's circle whispered that the burghers secretly supported the Russians. The agreement likewise dissatisfied Sigismund's military leader, Nicholas ("the Black") Radziwill, a magnate from one of the GDL's most powerful families, who served as the Lithuanian grand chancellor.[42] Desiring nothing less than complete control for Poland-Lithuania, Radziwill declared that Riga too must submit to royal power in the manner of Danzig and the Prussian cities.[43]

To expedite the matter, in June 1561 the king dispatched Radziwill to Riga to demand that the endangered cities be placed directly under his dominion. Reval, after all, had just submitted to the rising Kingdom of Sweden, which now controlled most of Estonia. Arriving in Riga with several thousand cavalrymen, the Lithuanian prince peacefully made camp at Keller Field near Riga and stayed there for several weeks. The chronicle of the observant Balthasar Russow tells us that during the time of his encampment, Radziwill

> entered Riga in August in a most splendid and majestic procession. He rode through the city accompanied by many men of foreign nations: Armenians, Turks, Tartars, Podolskians [*sic*] (*Podollier*), Russians and Wallachians (*Wallachen*), along with many Germans, Poles and Lithuanians. Many a pious heart in Riga was amazed as they saw these various foreign nations and peoples, each in their own costumes, with their own weapon, escutcheons and music. They saw their own distress in the fact that such bizarre, strange and barbarian nations and peoples were in their fatherland, treading the streets of the Christian city of Riga. If the sight of these peoples, riding amiably through the city of Riga, brought sorrow and dismay to everyone, what dismay and terror would there be if one saw them at war, besieging, conquering and ruling a Christian city?[44]

The following month Radziwill gave a public speech at Riga's Town Hall, where he reiterated the Polish king's position. Rigans, however, remained unconvinced, believing that their walled and well-defended city was not threatened in the same way that the countryside and the smaller towns were. Moreover, having just freed themselves from Catholic domination, the Protestants of Riga, comprising by far the majority of the city's population, intended to keep their hard-won religious liberty. To many, the notion of coming under Polish (and Catholic) rule was little more attractive than the prospect of having to convert to Orthodoxy under Russian rule. Exasperated by Riga's refusal to submit, Radziwill turned to the order and its reigning (and last) master.

Gotthard Kettler was prepared for this moment. Formerly a devout Catholic, Kettler had converted to Protestantism during a stay in Germany in 1553–1554 and returned to Livonia convinced of Luther's correctness. Having developed a plan for secularizing the Livonian state, he convinced his knights, enticed by the prospect of becoming hereditary landholders, to support it. By the time autumn turned to winter, Radziwill and the Polish authorities, as well as the Livonian estates, had all signed on—or almost all. Continuing to hold out against Polish demands, Riga was not a party to the ceremony that took place in Vilnius on November 28, 1561, when the order master and the archbishop formally submitted to the Polish king and ceded to him their territories.[45]

The formal act of surrender took place on March 5, 1562. In a magnificent ceremony staged in front of the Riga Castle, Master Kettler swore an oath of allegiance before Radziwill and symbolically handed over to him all the privileges he had enjoyed in Riga, surrendering to the king's representative the keys to the castles and to the city gates. Ten days later, the Livonian Order, its anachronistic nature reflected in its elderly membership, was finally dissolved. One could say that this moment, marking the end of the Confederation, was for Livonia the symbolic conclusion of the Middle Ages, reminders of which can still be seen in the castle ruins scattered all over modern Latvia and Estonia; it was precisely at this time that some of these castles were being destroyed.

For Kettler, however, this was not the end, but a new beginning.[46] Having surrendered his territories to the King of Poland, Kettler received part of them back as a fief in the form of the Duchy of Courland and Semigallia (Kurzeme and Zemgale), which included territories west and south of Riga. These would remain in his family for the next 175 years. It was in his capacity as duke of Courland that Kettler came back into possession of the region's castles and of the city keys of Riga.[47] But, unlike Kettler's knights, the citizens of Riga had yet to be convinced of the necessity to submit to Poland. Negotiations would drag on for another twenty years.

From 1561 to 1581, when the beleaguered city finally acceded to Polish rule, Riga enjoyed the status of a "free imperial city" of the Holy Roman Empire, even as it also came under Polish protection. Allowed to forge its own currency, the city continued to use the Riga mark—also half-marks, thalers (worth 4.5 marks), schillings, and pfennigs—minted according to the same rules as in the days of the Livonian Confederation. On the obverse side of Riga's coins, the standard inscription remained an image of Riga's coat of arms, typically represented as a stone portal with two flagged towers, the two crossed keys of St. Peter (representing the pope's patronage), and a small cross above them both. Around the edges of Riga's coins were engraved the words CIVITATIS RIGENSIS.

The Free City of Riga, 1561 to 1581

Although little more than a sideshow to the rest of Europe, which remained poorly informed about events in the northeast, the Livonian War continued to rage, its complexities no less bewildering to the diplomats of the time than they are to readers today. None of the Baltic powers could afford to stand completely aside, so great was the temptation to expand into (or block one's enemies in) a troubled region that had become a political vacuum.

Despite its timid initial foray into Livonian politics at the outset of the conflict, Denmark opted to stay out, leaving most of Estonia in the hands of Sweden. This rising Baltic power turned out to be one of the war's main beneficiaries, having agreed to a treaty of friendship with Muscovy in 1564 that allowed Russia to keep Narva and, in principle, the bulk of Livonia, while the tsar renounced his claims to those parts of Estonia that had come under Swedish rule.

Having launched the war to begin with, Muscovy was now hobbled by internal conflicts that prevented its unhinged autocrat from securing his territorial claims. Possibly suffering from a nervous breakdown after the death of his wife and the desertion to Lithuania of some of his leading boyars, the Russian ruler now focused his will on persecuting his enemies during the time of the *oprichnina*.[48] Only in 1577 would Ivan IV be in a position to mount another major offensive, briefly taking all the lands north of the Düna save Riga (which remained an imperial "free city" under Polish protection) and Reval (under Swedish rule). However, a rout at the hands of Polish-Lithuanian forces at the Battle of Wenden (Cēsis) in 1578 ended the tsar's dream of establishing dominion over Livonia.

In Riga the sense of uncertainty was exacerbated by the death in February 1563 of William of Brandenburg, a frustrated schemer who had held the office of archbishop of Riga for more than twenty years. Hoping to subdue the proud and independent city, the king of Poland—the deceased archbishop's cousin—wasted little time in claiming authority over the vacant see. But the curia was seized by the burghers of Riga, who then refused to hand it over to Kettler, the king's vassal and his chief administrator in Livonia. Resist as it might, the Riga chapter eventually found that it too had little choice but to acknowledge the reality of Polish power. In 1566 the archbishopric's lands were secularized and turned over to Poland, which now had another lever with which to exert its influence on the city of Riga.[49] While the rest of Livonia north of the Düna, a region that became known as Inflanty, had been directly incorporated into the GDL in 1564, discussions about Riga's potential legal status within the structure of the Polish-Lithuanian state continued through the 1570s.

Kettler's replacement as Livonia's chief administrator was General Jan Chodkiewicz. Assuming this post in 1566, the region's new governor was given instructions to subdue the city of Riga. When persuasion failed, Chodkiewicz resorted to force. Establishing a blockhouse garrison at the mouth of the Düna and demanding customs for all ships seeking passage to Riga, Chodkiewicz briefly managed to cut the city off from its maritime lifeline. Having made his point and having achieved little in doing so, Chodkiewicz soon abandoned this expensive and needless enterprise, for his show of power had failed to persuade the Rigans. Although concerned that the war might come directly to their city, the burghers stuck to their demands that Poland confirm without conditions Riga's ancient privileges that it assure local control over military matters, and that the king guarantee the city that there would be minimal outside interference in its internal affairs.[50]

The death of Sigismund II Augustus in mid-1572 postponed the realization of Poland's external goals for several more years and afforded Riga some breathing space. Not until the election in 1576 of the Transylvanian prince Stephen Bathory (r. 1576–1586) was the Polish-Lithuanian Commonwealth (Rzeczpospolita), the sprawling, multiethnic polity that came into existence following the formal act of union in 1569, in a position to return in a serious way to the Livonian problem, and to Riga. Unsuccessful in his struggle with a rebellious Danzig, which in 1577 not only resisted a Polish siege but managed to broaden its autonomy, Bathory approached Riga cautiously, knowing that Polish expansion into Livonia could create still more problems with his unruly Polish and Lithuanian nobles. After concluding an informal alliance with Sweden that would allow their combined forces to defeat the Muscovites at the Battle of Wenden (1578), and terminating the unpopular administration of Chodkiewicz, whom he replaced with the young Prince Radziwill (a Protestant), Bathory opened another round of negotiations with Riga's town council.

Outside the defended city of Riga, the fighting took its toll on the countryside while the peasantry succumbed to hunger and disease by the thousands. "From Riga to Dorpat, not a single dog was heard to bark, nor a cock to crow."[51] Especially ravaged were the Estonian lands, whose estimated population of 250,000 in 1558 was reduced to perhaps 70,000 by 1625 in the wake of another war—this one between Poland and Sweden.[52] Adding to the misery was the outbreak of plague—first in the autumn of 1578 and then again in the summer of 1579—which took far more lives than the fighting did.[53] During the worst years of the Livonian War, business slowed to a crawl at the port of Riga: in the year 1580 only 89 ships sailing from Riga passed through the Sound on their way to the Atlantic ports, less than half the number of ships which had made the same passage only five years earlier, when 202 ships from Riga paid Sound dues.[54]

Despite the many hardships in Livonia, Polish power surged during the Bathory years. Having expelled the Russians from Livonia, Polish forces, supplied by Riga and including Rigan military detachments, laid siege to Pskov in 1579, while Sweden took Narva in 1581.[55] In early 1581 Rigans dispatched an embassy to negotiate once again with the king of Poland in the hope of securing an arrangement that would sustain Riga's religious freedom and, as much as possible, its independence. But the Rath's position was as weak as the king's was strong, leaving Riga's ruling class of wealthy merchants with little choice but to accede to Bathory's demand for full control over the Düna port.

At last the city's fate was decided on January 14, 1581 by the Treaty of Drohiczyn, which formalized Riga's submission to the Polish king. A related document was the Treaty of Yam-Zapolski, concluded exactly a year and a day later, for this agreement ended the war and compelled Russia, in the wake of its heroic defense of Pskov, to retreat from Livonia in favor of Poland. Formerly a "free city" of the Holy Roman Empire, settled, built, and governed by German colonizers, Riga was now to be, in effect, a colony of the Polish-Lithuanian Commonwealth. Placed under a unified administration overseen by a Polish governor (*Statthalter*) in Riga, Livonia and its greatest city were leaving the Middle Ages behind. The beginning of the early modern era, well under way in western Europe, was to bring a new set of challenges for a city whose citizens yearned for a return to peace, prosperity, and self-rule.

The Calendar Upheavals

Having dominated the region for more than three centuries, the Baltic Germans were only peripheral players in the war over Old Livonia, now divided between Swedish Estonia (Estland) in the north and Polish Inflanty in eastern Latvia and southwestern Estonia. By following the Prussian example of paying homage to the Polish king, the Baltic German elites were able to preserve their influence in Livonia throughout the era of Polish rule and beyond. Riga's Rath, or town council, continued to exercise its administrative and judicial powers while the Livonian nobility enjoyed civil and criminal jurisdiction over their peasants.[56]

Yet it was with some trepidation that the Protestants of Riga accepted the rule of Stephen Bathory, for the burghers had every reason to fear that their new sovereign's religious policies would relegate the Lutheran faith to the position of, at best, a merely tolerated belief. Conflicts over religion would be inevitable. Although they took care to erect a special triumphal arch to welcome their savior—Riga's first king—the city's German elite was no less shocked by Bathory's entry into the city in April 1582 than it had been by that of Nicholas Radziwill twenty years earlier.

Still more unsettling to the burghers of Riga was the encroachment of the Muscovites, who had earned a reputation for unspeakable cruelty as they destroyed the city of Dorpat and ravaged the Livonian countryside during the war's early campaigns. But at least the conflict had come to a decisive conclusion as Ivan IV, who personally led his soldiers into battle, accepted his defeat and retreated to the east. While the Commonwealth's protective embrace may have spared Riga from the anticipated evils of Muscovite rule, the prospect of permanent subjection to Poland brought its own concerns—in particular, the likelihood that Catholicism would be reimposed on the city. By no means far-fetched, such fears were given further credence when the king appointed as Riga's governor the Lithuanian nobleman George Radziwill, a former Calvinist who had earlier converted to Catholicism.[57]

Consecrated as a bishop at age twenty-three and then as a cardinal, Radziwill enjoyed close ties with the Society of Jesus, whose priests, known as Jesuits, aimed to reform the Catholic Church from within and to turn back the advance of Protestantism. It should come as little surprise then, that "anti-Polish sentiments accompanied this forced political marriage from the beginning."[58]

Even if Bathory had assured Rigans that he would respect their ancient privileges (preserved in the *Privilegium Stephaneum*), the king had every intention of returning Livonia to the Catholic fold, believing this to be his right by virtue of conquest. Bathory's main focus was Riga, which under Polish dominion immediately became a center of pro-Catholic propaganda. The king's insistence on the return of several churches that had gone over to Protestantism in the 1520s added to the mistrust. Although Bathory did not demand the reestablishment of the defunct archbishopric, one way he attempted to facilitate the Counter Reformation in Riga was by bringing Jesuits to the city (they were awarded St. Jacob's Church) and by allowing them to found their own college (located in the former Mary Magdalene cloister) with its own library and hospital.[59] To the objections of Rigans, who suggested that the Catholics take one of the Russian churches instead, the Polish king responded with arrogance and disdain. "Many citizens," recalled the chronicler Balthasar Russow, "felt like prisoners."[60]

Tensions were greatest during the early years of Polish rule. Yet even if Bathory's introduction of a new calendar in Riga was the proximate cause of the unrest that followed, the troubles of the 1580s were also a product of Riga's simmering internal conflicts. Indeed, the events known as the Calendar Upheavals (1584–1589) were not simply a matter of popular anti-Catholic feeling but were the culmination of a decades-long struggle between the town council and both the city's guilds. These were the Great Guild, whose members consisted exclusively of long-distance merchants, and the Small Guild, the overarching organization for the many smaller brotherhoods of craftsmen and lesser merchants. While historians continue to debate the meaning and historical significance of the Calendar Upheavals, the record of events is clear enough: for five years the city was torn apart by what Riga's citizens perceived to be an abrogation of the Polish king's assurance of religious freedom.

Elsewhere in Europe, the introduction of the new calendar had taken place with little fanfare, for Pope Gregory XIII (r. 1572–1585) was simply addressing two very real problems. The first, explained the historian Daniel Boorstin, was that "the vernal equinox, which traditionally marks the beginning of spring in the northern hemisphere, had moved back from March 21 to May 11. Farmers could no longer rely on the calendar for the planting and gathering of their crops, merchants could not depend on the calendar in signing contracts for the delivery of seasonal products."[61] The errors in the Julian calendar also had religious implications, for the spring equinox was tied to the date of Easter, which over the centuries had drifted; thus when the Gregorian calendar was introduced by papal bull on February 24, 1582, the Vatican's goal was to bring the date for the celebration of Easter back to the time of the year when the early Church had celebrated it. The new calendar was implemented the following autumn: Thursday, October 4 in the old Julian calendar was to be followed by Friday, October 15 in the new Gregorian one. The decree applied everywhere, including the city of Riga, but the town council, concerned about the potential political implications during a period of growing unease, thought it best not to introduce the reform at that moment.

When, after two years had passed, Bathory insisted on the calendar's adoption, threatening the Rath with a fine of 10,000 gold ducats for disobedience, the city patricians finally relented. Ignoring the objections of the outraged citizenry, in December 1584 the city's hated burgomaster, Nicholas Ecke (Nicolaus Eck; 1541–1623), a German who also served as the Polish king's representative, or burgrave, in Riga, introduced posters announcing that the new calendar was now in force. Opponents argued that the Gregorian calendar was an instrument of Catholic propaganda, but the town council now agreed that the Christmas holiday celebrations would be observed in Riga in the new style.

The calendar decree was bound to offend the sensibilities of Riga's Protestant burghers, especially as it came on top of a decision to hand over the church of St. Jacob to the Jesuits for the popular Christmas eve services. In response, a mob descended upon the red-brick basilica, destroying its icons and pelting the Jesuits with stones.[62] News of the arrest and execution of the rector of the Dome School, Heinrich Müller, an active opponent of the Jesuit college and of the calendar reform, only inflamed the unrest. Incited to seize the Town Hall, the mob proceeded to plunder the homes of the councilors—including the one belonging to Ecke, who sought refuge in the former Order Castle on the Düna embankment just outside the walled city.[63] In the melee a few people were even murdered.

While order was soon restored and an agreement reached between the loyalist town council and what some historians call the "urban opposition," the events at St. Jacob's were just the beginning of a larger contest that was not only a religious conflict between Catholicism and Protestantism but also a political struggle between the Rath, backed by the power of the Polish state, and the guilds, which felt the erosion of their power and influence.

Soviet historians have portrayed the Calendar Upheavals as another manifestation of an ongoing class struggle, and in this they were not incorrect; indeed, even non-Marxist historians—including the Riga burgrave (from 1590 to 1621) and chronicler Francis Nienstedt (Franz Nyenstede; 1540–1622), who resisted the upheavals—have emphasized the social aspects of the struggle, for the broader economic changes of the period benefited the great traders at the expense of the craftsmen and petty merchants of the Small Guild.[64] If for a time these antagonisms had lain dormant due to the larger concerns raised by Ivan the Terrible's invasion and the quarter-century of war that followed, the introduction of strong state authority brought these simmering tensions to a boil. Such conflicts between opposition groups and city elites were not unusual in the towns of Prussia and the Netherlands during this period; indeed, the phenomenon in Riga perfectly conforms to the social, economic, and political patterns of the late sixteenth century.[65]

The opposition's main figure was Martin Giese (d. 1589), a young lawyer and a secretary of the Great Guild of merchants. Having organized a council of sixteen men—a body that paralleled and supplanted the town council—Giese managed to make himself into what was, for all intents and purposes, the city's dictator. Another opposition leader was the wine merchant Hans Brinken, who would ultimately share the same grisly fate as Giese. Ordering the closing of the city gates so as to prevent the council's reinforcements from getting into the city and seizing its treasury, Giese claimed that his beef was not with the Polish king but with the town councilors. If Giese's declaration that he would not interfere with the activities of the Jesuits was intended to mollify his opponents, this assurance was immediately contradicted by laws that forbade Jesuit processions in Riga.[66] Curtailing the administrative authority of the Rath (leaving it only with judicial functions) and that of the burgrave, Giese also repealed the new calendar.

As the opposition's attitudes radicalized, so too did its propensity for taking punitive measures: some of Giese's enemies were expelled from the city, while two of the city's councilors were arrested and sentenced to death in the summer of 1586. A few escaped to Warsaw, where they convinced the king that the riots were in fact a revolution directed against Polish power.[67] Responding to the crisis in Riga, Bathory declared Giese and Brinken outlaws and demanded their arrest while he ordered the assembly of his military forces in the districts outside the city.

Looking for help in Germany and Sweden (and finding that none was forthcoming), Giese returned to the city shortly after the king's death on December 2, 1586. But Bathory's successor, Sigismund III Vasa (r. 1587–1632), a devout Catholic and the son of a Swedish king, was no friend to the rebels, for the king immediately positioned himself on the side of the town council. So alarmed was Sigismund by the actions of the opposition that he closed Riga off from the source of its export goods up the Düna—a move that cost both the city and the crown much of their income.[68] For the next two years, however, it was Giese and the radicalized citizenry who held full power in Riga, from which the Jesuits were finally banned. (They would return to the city after the upheavals subsided.) Yet if Giese's tyranny eventually alienated some of Riga's burghers, their efforts to remove him from the leadership of the Great Guild produced no immediate result.[69]

Only in the summer of 1589 did the upheavals finally end, thanks in part to the arrival of Polish mercenaries who for some time had been encamped northeast of Riga in preparation for an attack on the city. As the Polish forces marched into the market square in June, the opposition, confronted with a show of overwhelming force as it barricaded itself in St. Peter's, was compelled to enter into negotiations with the king's ambassador, the Lithuanian Grand Chancellor Lew Sapieha. At a session of the town council held on July 22, Sapieha confirmed the city's privileges and its religious freedom, while at the same time demanding the return to the Catholics of St. Jacob's, seized by Protestants following the expulsion of the Jesuits. Also appearing at the session were the leaders of the urban opposition, Giese and Brinken, who apparently took Polish guarantees of their safety at face value. The ruse worked, and the two were arrested on the spot. Following a quick trial, their sentences were carried out in the Town Hall Square on August 2, 1589. Also punished were many of the rioters, although their penalties usually amounted to expulsions and money fines.

In the final analysis, the upheavals accomplished almost nothing. The St. Severin Treaty concluded later that month restored to the Rath all its previous functions, while the guilds, the opposition's main bases, lost much of their power and influence. The fact that elders from both guilds would now be admitted to the town council did little to mitigate the reality that this outcome was, in fact, a nearly complete victory for Riga's patriciate and for the Polish state; ordinary citizens had no more voice in city governance than they did before the upheavals.[70]

But what of the calendar whose introduction precipitated the upheavals of the 1580s? In the end, Riga won the right to keep the old Julian calendar. It was not until 1919, after another great war—*the* Great War—and the creation of a Latvian state, that the citizens of Riga switched to the Gregorian calendar and in this sense joined the modern world.

Nationality and Culture under Polish Rule

The legal basis of Polish rule in Livonia was the *Privilegium Stephaneum* of January 1582. Its fifty-eight paragraphs confirmed Riga's "ancient liberties," among the most significant of which was the monopoly enjoyed by the city's merchants as trade intermediaries on the Düna River. Indeed, the great concern of Riga's merchants was that the Polish government might deny them rights upon which their material well-being had been based for more than three centuries. Yet it was only in the political arena that the city's liberties were circumscribed, for the oath of loyalty to the Polish king forbade those actions it deemed contrary to the interests of the Commonwealth.

The Rath, still comprised of fourteen or sixteen of Riga's leading citizens (typically drawn from the better-educated members of the Great Guild), continued to perform its traditional functions of overseeing matters concerning property, trade, and the enforcement of law. When a vacancy occurred, it was typically filled by the sons or relatives of existing council members.[71] Overseeing the work of the town council were four burgomasters, from whom Polish authorities selected one to be the burgrave. In this manner, and through the collection of portage—a new tax on the goods that Riga imported and exported—the Polish-Lithuanian Commonwealth dominated Riga for nearly forty years. Five of these were shaken by the Calendar Upheavals, and twenty-one with the disruptions caused by the Polish-Swedish War. By then the relatively good times of the early sixteenth century, when Riga was an inviting and prosperous "free city" under the loose jurisdiction of the German emperor, were but a distant memory.

Riga (Ryga, in Polish) groaned under Polish rule, for the long and bitter struggle over Livonia had left the city in poor financial condition, and now the city found itself subject to an alien method of government that was ill-suited to the preferences of its independent-minded burghers. In protecting Riga, the Commonwealth, now at the peak of its power, acted as a bulwark against Muscovite predations; at the same time, the Polish state exploited Riga with its collection of portage, two-thirds of which were sent to the city's new overlords and one-third to Riga. Part of this income fell into the pockets of Lithuania's magnates and another part went to the king of Poland. The remainder was used to improve Riga's fortifications, maintain its churches and schools, and pay its officials. Particularly objectionable was the establishment of tax collection points on the routes that led to Riga, such as those along the Düna at Lennewarden, Kokenhusen, and Dünaburg.[72] Such impositions, the Rigans complained, only hindered Riga's trading economy and redirected the flow of goods to Prussian Königsberg[73] and the ports of Courland and Estonia.

Rigans further complained about looting by Polish soldiers and the Polish landlords' habit of exporting their goods along illegal routes in an effort to bypass Rigan intermediaries. Perhaps the most painful point for Riga's traders was the granting to Dorpat (Tartu) of special rights as a transit center for goods from Russia to Inflanty—that is, to the Latvian lands north of the Düna that Poland had acquired during the Livonian War. Not only did this policy have the effect of redirecting Russian goods to Swedish-held Pernau (Pärnu) and Narva, but, Riga's traders selflessly countered, it also reduced the king's income from portage.[74]

The difficulties endured by Riga's great and petty merchants, who at the time collectively comprised perhaps 20 percent of the city's population, were further complicated by Poland's intervention in Russia during the latter's "Time of Troubles" (1598–1613), for the aggressively Catholic King Sigismund III Vasa was bent on exploiting Muscovy's internal disorders with the intention of extending Polish and Catholic influence into what had been historically Orthodox lands. During the peaceful 1590s, the high point of Polish rule in Livonia, Rigans enjoyed connections with Pskov and other "Muscovite" cities, encouraged by the tsarist government to bring their goods to Moscow where a small German colony remained. In wartime, however, the Polish state forbade Rigans from trading with the Muscovites, thereby depriving Riga of an important source of income.

Meanwhile, in Riga itself, Russian traders continued to face the usual limitations on their activities, frequently complaining about being forbidden from enjoying direct trade links with other guests in the city. To these laments they added another: that the chapel in the city's Russian quarter, the church of St. Nicholas, had been seized by the city's Protestants. Teodors Zeids, a generally reliable (if ideologically conformist) Soviet historian of Riga, noted how Riga's Protestants struggled with this modest center of Orthodoxy no less fervently than they did with the Catholics and Jesuits.[75]

Then there were Riga's far larger contingents of Letts and Livs—"non-Germans" who were traditionally employed in service occupations that involved the transportation, loading, and off-loading of goods. One might reasonably suspect that the Latvian communities of Riga, wherein the Livs gradually assimilated into the numerically superior Lettish peoples, were no more satisfied with their relative circumstances than was the city's tiny Russian community. Having grown to perhaps 40 percent of the city's population by the last quarter of the sixteenth century and largely inhabiting the wooden houses located in the belt between the city's brick walls and its new earthen ramparts, Riga's non-Germans continued to face restrictions in employment. A number of crafts, then under the supervision of the Small Guild, were simply closed off to them. (See chapter 3.)

While the city's subjection to Polish power didn't necessarily worsen the lot of the *Undeutsche*, the fact is that the flight of peasants to Riga during the Livonian War meant that there were now a lot more Latvians living just outside the city walls. Ordinances on clothing introduced in 1598 were intended to sharpen the distinctions between Riga's German and non-German residents: forbidden to adorn themselves with certain kinds of cloth or jewelry, Latvians were legally bound to wear clothes of a peasant character that underlined their subservient position in the city's social hierarchy.[76] It might be argued that such distinctions strengthened the cohesion of the Latvian community, for the social separation of German and non-German was near total, each community living in separate parts of the city, engaged in legally and socially distinct occupations, and speaking different languages.

The Polish era undoubtedly facilitated the growth of a distinctive sense of identity among the Baltic Germans. If foreign rule reinforced the Germans' sense of community, Poland's assurances that the incorporated territories could keep their own laws, their local administrations, and their existing network of social and economic relations reinforced the status and traditions of their elite citizens.[77] Yet the Baltic Germans did not suffer from complete cultural isolation, for the Germans of Riga enjoyed close connections to the German communities of central and western Europe. It was common, for example, for the sons of Riga's wealthy merchants to study at universities in Germany before returning home to make their fortunes and contribute to the city's vibrant social life.

A notable example of the city's cultural flowering at the height of Polish rule is the figure of David Hilchen (1561–1610), a Riga native who played a pivotal role in the negotiations that brought an end to the Calendar Upheavals of the 1580s. Having received his legal training in various universities in Germany, where he established connections with the highest representatives of the Polish and Lithuanian nobility, Hilchen returned to the city during the upheavals and became a leader in the city government. Although many Rigans suspected him of being overly servile to Polish authority, it was Hilchen, as the town council's secretary and the son-in-law of the burgrave Francis Nienstedt, who helped found an orphanage as well as a shelter for the widows of Riga's craftsmen (Ecke's Convent).[78] Another institution associated with Hilchen's cultural activities was the city library (*Bibliotheca Rigensis*), established on the basis of the books confiscated from Catholic monasteries and schools during the Reformation.[79]

Perhaps most consequential of all was the young councilor's invitation to Nicholas Mollin (Nikolaus Mollin; 1550–1625), a Flemish woodcarver and typographer, to set up a shop in Riga. At the moment of Mollin's arrival in 1588, there were well over a thousand printing presses working in Europe and more than sixty in the Dutch city of Leiden. In many regions, however, typography was still in an early stage of development: permanent shops had only recently been established in the English university towns of Cambridge (1583) and Oxford (1585), and it would take nearly another half century before Reval (1633) acquired its own printing presses.[80] In Polish Livonia, then, Mollin, was a pioneer: appointed Riga's official book printer at an annual salary of one hundred thalers, the typographer went on to produce 179 books and smaller works while living in the city, 92 of which have been preserved. The dominant language of Mollin's press was Latin, then enjoying a belated literary presence in a city that was only just beginning to set up Latin schools. This was the language of nearly two-thirds (126) of his books, a quarter (48) were in German, and three were in Latvian, whose life as a written language was only just beginning.[81] Mollin's printing house also produced some of the earliest views of the bustling town, including a detailed panorama from the year 1612 that provided admiring readers with a detailed depiction of the city's topography, its mighty walls and spires, and the many vessels of all sizes that called on the port of Riga.[82]

As was common everywhere in Europe at this time, most of the works produced in Mollin's busy print shop were religious in nature.[83] It is in this light that we may consider the most prolific Livonian author of the era, Hermann Samson (1579–1643), who is credited with some sixty-five publications in German and Latin. Educated as a youth at the Riga Dome school, Samson went on to study theology at the universities at Rostock and Wittenberg before returning to Riga to become a school inspector and a pastor at the Dome and St. Peter's. During these years, the same period that saw the transition from Polish to Swedish rule, Samson was a leader of Lutheran life in Riga who preached (in German) against the perils of false belief. Although a compilation of his sermons on witchcraft was published as a handbook, this did not, as far as we know, inspire any witch hunts in Riga. Nevertheless, Samson's body of work was dominated by the struggle with his religious adversaries, for this was a time when the Jesuits, with whom Samson conducted a vigorous academic debate, enjoyed a privileged position in Riga and the doctrine of Calvinism was making temporary inroads in Livonia.[84]

Mollin's printing house also published some of Riga's earliest humanist literature, including verses by the Prussian poet Daniel Hermann (1543–1601), who spent the last twenty years of his life in the city. It was in Riga that Hermann was married and buried and where his three poetry collections were published posthumously.[85]

But if Daniel Hermann's works remain obscure to modern readers, the *Encomium Rigae* (Encomium to Riga) by Basilius Plinius[86] (ca. 1540–1605) still enjoys some popular renown. Published in Leipzig in 1595, a time between the wars and upheavals when Riga was internally at peace and its merchants enjoyed a renewed prosperity, Plinius's long poem is a love letter to his native city. It was from a distance of many kilometers that the physician, following the conventions of other writers who praised their cities, composed this glowing, if not strictly truthful, description of Riga and its environs.

Plinius's Riga was a city that had been saved from the Russians by King Stephen Bathory ("As avenger, you lifted our land from that bloody embrace and saved our people from the yoke of eternal slavery") and was capably overseen by the pro-Polish burgrave Nicholas Ecke ("What the luminous father of the Heliads is in the heavens, you are to my country"), in whose hands the municipality remained steadfast in its devotion to peace and justice ("Impervious to corruption, beyond reach to the conqueror, she stands by her laws, steady in her course"). Indeed, amid "all the horrors of this world," the Riga of the preacher's son Basilius Plinius persevered as a bastion of piety and purity, its markets overflowing with goods from the countryside ("fruit, or loaves risen white as snow, or rolls stuffed full of savory meats"), its streets graced by the world's most beautiful women ("daughters lovely enough to be fit bridesmaids for the gods").[87]

It was perhaps his gratitude for the opportunity, financed by the city, to pursue his medical studies in Leipzig that accounts for Plinius's unusual admiration for both Bathory and the widely despised Ecke (who, we may recall, took the Polish side during the Calendar Upheavals), for the bulk of Riga's Baltic German upper crust resented Polish rule and associated it with a distinctly un-Teutonic barbarism. It nevertheless seems reasonable to remember the Polish era, especially the 1590s, as a time, however brief, of cultural blossoming before another extended period of war. More than ever before, foreigners came to Riga to trade, to work, to build—although rarely to settle permanently. Experienced Italian engineers, for example, supervised the modifications to the defensive system praised by Plinius, to which Stephen Bathory demanded the improvement of its previously inadequate and unfinished earthen ramparts. ("O Rome, so many conquerors could

FIGURE 9. Riga in 1572. Georg Braun and Franz Hohenberg: Civitates Orbis Terrarum, 1581.

FIGURE 10. Riga embankment in 2016. On the left is the Riga Castle. To the right of the Riga Cathedral (center) is St. Peter's Church. Photo by author.

not have sacked you had you been ringed by defenses like ours," declared the poet with the optimism of the besotted.) It is possible that foreign engineers were employed to construct the city's oldest dikes: the first, on the city's northern side (now Sarkandaugava), was built in the area of the city pastures (Ganību dambis); a second, John's Dam (Inču dambis), was built in 1600 to protect the Moscow suburb on the city's southern side from flooding.[88] But it was to the fortification system that the city's Polish rulers devoted the greater part of their attention and resources. Improved with an eye to withstanding the advances in artillery that characterized sixteenth-century warfare, Riga's defenses would be put to the test during yet another devastating Baltic war.

The Swedish-Polish War, 1600–1629

The inevitable next war was always on the minds of Riga's Polish rulers, who appreciated the city's attraction to potential enemies and realized that if it were to be snatched away in the next round of fighting, then in all likelihood the Commonwealth's possessions in Inflanty would disappear along with it. To make Riga an impregnable fortress became an obsession of the Poles, and then later of the city's Swedish masters.

The weakest section of the old defensive system was around the Sand Tower (it is now called the Powder Tower), whose gate had provided the main entrance into the city from the east until that time. The problem was less the tower itself than the nearby sand dune known as Kubsberg (Kube Hill), the "old mountain" from which Poland's enemies, should they get close enough to Riga's walls, could comfortably view the city and threaten it with cannons. To thwart this possibility, in 1601 Riga built next to the tower an additional fortification for the placement of guns. Positioned at the same height as the adjacent city wall, this was the circular roundel (or rondel). By 1612 five such roundels were created by the other city gates, while additional fortifications were built in the shape of a half-moon between the Sand and Jacob gates on the city's eastern side. The entire inner-city fortification system was also ringed by a water-filled canal, a moat that provided Riga with an additional protective layer.

Further insurance against outside attack was provided by the new Dünamünde fortress (Pol. Dynemunt), which defended the city from enemies who would arrive by sea. Built by the Poles during the Livonian War, the new fortress replaced a ruined order castle of the same name that for centuries had guarded the mouth of the Düna River but was rendered obsolete by a recent change in the channel's course. It was at the river's new mouth, located five kilometers west of the old one, that the new fortress (today known as Daugavgrīva) was built.[89] To patrol the Düna where it flowed past the city, the city stationed a modest fleet of small warships near the Rigebach, the stagnant rivulet that looped around the medieval city.

The anchor of the city's defensive system remained the Riga Castle, completed for the Livonian Order in 1515 and still standing near the water's edge more than five centuries later. During the era of Polish rule, the castle housed some three hundred cavalrymen along with several cannons that could be deployed against an approaching enemy. Opposite Riga, on the other side of the Düna, the Poles erected blockhouses with earthen defensive walls. The most prominent structure in this vicinity remained the Red Tower, an older structure that was made of red bricks in the Gothic style. Featured prominently in the bottom right of Mollin's panorama of 1612, this landmark's military value declined after the Swedes built the far larger Fort Kobron complex in the vicinity (see chapter 7).[90]

The origins of the renewed confrontations between Sweden and Poland are closely related to the events of 1600. This was when Sigismund III Vasa, as he was known to his Polish subjects, was driven from the Swedish throne, usurped unconstitutionally by his uncle, a duke who would later take the title Charles IX (r. 1604–1611).[91] The ensuing war, then, was the product of a dynastic struggle with confessional overtones, for Sigismund, a Catholic who was educated by Jesuits, was the son of a Swedish king and his Polish wife; as such he was viewed by his Swedish subjects, and by his Protestant uncle, as an instrument of the Counter Reformation. It was in the hopes of bringing resolution to the rivalry between Sweden and Poland over Estonia, then in Swedish hands, that Sigismund had earlier (in 1587) been elected king of Poland, for the Polish nobility expected that Sweden would consequently cede this territory to the Commonwealth.[92]

When the Swedish *Riksdag* balked, Sigismund simply overruled it, announcing in March 1600 to the Polish *Sejm* his intention to incorporate Estonia into the Polish-Lithuanian Commonwealth. To forestall this outcome, his treasonous uncle marched an army from Reval to the Polish-occupied territories in southern Estonia and Livonia.[93] Few could have foreseen that the resulting war would transform the impoverished Kingdom of Sweden into a vast Baltic empire with Riga as its leading economic center and its most important military supply point.

At the time of the attack, Sweden was far from the prosperous state it would later become: the Scandinavian kingdom was, in fact, a poor and thinly populated country (perhaps 1.25 million people lived in Sweden-Finland) on the margins of Europe, its rulers aspiring to control the flow of trade between the eastern and western edges of the Baltic Sea, then still largely in the hands of Hanse and Dutch merchants. Although rich in copper and iron, Sweden was commercially weak, with few towns of any significance aside from Stockholm—and even that city housed significantly fewer people than Riga at the beginning of the seventeenth century. However, since the kingdom was poorly situated for defense, unable to defend its own territory effectively, its rulers chose instead to take the fight to enemy soil. By transforming its nobility into a military service class—such men would have a material stake in the development of the military state—and by focusing on easy pickings abroad, the Swedes sought to compensate for their internal weaknesses through expansion.[94]

Duke Charles launched his first attack on Riga from Estonia in the middle of August in the year 1601. As neither this foray nor a more serious clash at the end of the month yielded the desired fruit, the Swedish duke paused. Sick and lacking food and warm clothing as autumn approached, many of his soldiers retreated to Estonia. Those who remained behind laid siege to the city, whose leaders decided to burn the suburbs that were inhabited by Riga's poorest (mostly Latvian) inhabitants. The early years of the seventeenth century were difficult all over northern Europe: a crop failure in 1601–1602, to which we may add a decade-long Swedish blockade of their city, only compounded Rigans' hunger and misery. That winter the city streets were littered with the bodies of the starved and frozen, typically peasants who had only recently arrived from the countryside and who had left their kin behind to subsist, as best as they could, on whatever dogs, rats, and tree bark remained.[95] Perturbed by the economic disruptions and the widespread looting by Polish-Lithuanian troops, Riga's councilors hoped to obtain peace and even established contact with Swedish authorities. Sigismund, however, refused to negotiate with his allegedly cruel and vindictive uncle.[96]

The war's most dramatic confrontation, the Battle of Kirchholm (Latv. Salaspils), took place in 1605, when the Swedish navy sailed up the Düna carrying its forces as well as a few thousand German and Dutch mercenaries. Arriving in August, one part of the army began to destroy the area around Riga, burning what remained of its suburbs and destroying the city's mills and (once again) the wooden St. Gertrude's Church as the Swedes prepared a major offensive against the city. On September 13 Charles himself appeared in the Swedish camp outside Riga—just at the moment when Polish reinforcements began to approach the city from the upstream Düna. On the rainy night of September 16, one part of Charles's army left its well-fortified camp and advanced on Kirchholm, located on the Düna southeast of Riga; another three thousand men were left behind to hold the siege.

The confrontation took place on a battlefield that stretched over the entire eighteen kilometers between Kirchholm and the borders of modern Riga. Lasting a mere twenty minutes, the bloody clash was a boon to Poland and a disaster for the advancing Swedes. Although enjoying an overwhelming numerical advantage, Swedish forces were lured into an open field by Jan Karol Chodkiewicz, the Great Hetman of Lithuania and the commander of the Polish-Lithuanian army. "The road to Riga," the military historian Robert I. Frost would remark centuries later, "was littered with the bodies of the Swedish cavalry." Indeed, only one-third of Sweden's original force managed to reach their ships in the Bay of Riga, while many others drowned trying to cross the Düna. "The burghers of Riga, who had to bury the dead, recorded the bodies which were thrown into mass graves. Two separate sources record 8,983 and 8,918 corpses, representing over 82 per cent of the Swedish forces."[97] Polish-Lithuanian losses numbered in the hundreds.

With this catastrophe, the second Swedish attempt to capture Riga came to a dismal conclusion. However, the blockade of the city, which had begun in 1601, remained in effect, for Charles IX's goal was not only to stop sea traffic with the besieged city but also to redirect to Swedish ports the goods carried by arriving merchant ships; in this way, the duke would be able to increase the crown's revenues and supply his own troops. Ships from Holland, a country that was deeply invested in the Livonian trade, tried to break the blockade, but to no avail: in 1608–1609 alone, the Swedish navy captured as many as eighteen Dutch ships.[98]

With the Commonwealth engulfed in internal unrest—this was partly a consequence of Poland's failed intervention in Muscovy during its "Time of Troubles"—Sigismund was unable to consolidate his victory at Kirchholm. His dream of transforming the failing Muscovite state into a Polish dependency now in tatters, the king presided over a series of failures in northeastern Europe that afforded Charles IX the opportunity to continue to work on Riga. The latter's goal of conquering the city came closer to being realized when in July 1608 Swedish forces captured the Polish fortress at Dünamünde, which immediately became an essential support point for his blockade of the city.

But setbacks soon followed. In March 1609 the Swedes lost possession of Pernau, a port town located on Estonia's west coast. Dünamünde surrendered to Poland on September 29. In an effort to break the siege and reestablish normal commercial relations with western Europe, Riga's councilors established contacts with Denmark—but then naturally denied having done so when word of their treachery got to the Polish king. By the end of the century's first decade, Danish warships began to accompany the merchant vessels that approached the Bay of Riga from western Europe. Although the convoys were allowed to proceed this time, it was not long before Sweden was at war with Denmark as well.[99]

Unlike the armed conflicts of the twentieth century, waged by centralized states with mass armies intent on securing the total defeat of a hated enemy, the wars of medieval and early modern times were typically on-again, off-again affairs that might drag on for years or even decades. Theaters would change as frequently as a state's allies and objectives; decisive outcomes were elusive, partial victories more common. Indeed, for both Sweden and Poland, the war in Livonia became a secondary issue when each found itself drawn into Muscovy's civil war. The Swedes exploited Russian weakness to strengthen their position along the common border with Russia (Kexholm, Karelia, Ingria), while the Polish king tried, unsuccessfully, to install his son Ladislas on the Muscovite throne. Alone and isolated, Sweden now fought its war with Poland largely on Russian soil.

By the time the coarse and unpopular Charles IX died in November 1611, Sweden's wars in the eastern Baltic—with Poland, with Denmark, and then with

Russia—had ground to a halt. But the conclusion of the advantageous Treaty of Stolbovo with Russia in 1617, signed while the Polish-Lithuanian Commonwealth squared off against the Ottoman Empire in the south, would allow Sweden, now aligned (temporarily) with Muscovy, to renew its operations against the Poles. Under his able command, Sweden's endeavors in northeastern Europe became above all a struggle for the port of Riga.

Yet it would be another four years before the aim of conquering Riga was realized under the leadership of Gustavus II Adolphus (r. 1611–1632), a man of erudition and ambition who some believe to have been the greatest monarch of the age. Well-educated in languages and history, highly trained in the military arts (he had commanded his own armies since the age of sixteen), and devoutly Lutheran, Gustavus pursued a path of modernization and centralization that transformed his once-peripheral kingdom into a great power—and a Baltic empire.[100] At the time of his coronation in 1611, the war in the Baltic had been languishing for years, but the Treaty of Stolbovo gave Sweden a free hand to realize its goals in Livonia. Gustavus's seizure of Dünaburg on the upper Düna brought Swedish forces within striking distance of Riga, whose capture would deny Sigismund a port from which he might launch a legitimist invasion of Sweden.[101] A temporary peace with Poland in 1618–1620 allowed Sweden to rebuild its fleet and improve the quality of its artillery, while the Commonwealth, its treasury drained by so many years of war, had to maintain readiness in case of yet another clash with Turks and Tatars in the south.

The Swedes were well positioned for an assault on Riga, having also captured the Polish fortress at Dünamünde, located only ten kilometers downstream from Riga at the mouth of the Düna River. But it was only in the summer of 1621 that the Swedish king, at the head of a combined operation requiring the efforts of 18,000 soldiers and 158 ships (nearly the entire Swedish navy), was fully prepared to launch a major assault on the city, itself defended by fifty cannons and a garrison of 334 professional soldiers, who were supported by a citizen militia of 1,900 Germans and Latvians.[102] Practically abandoned by the Commonwealth, which was then deploying the bulk of its forces against the Turks in the south, Riga came under a long artillery barrage that capped many years of hunger and suffering. Here we may cite a report from the town council to Riga's Lithuanian governor:

> The situation in Livonia is very regrettable, as battles, fires and destruction have devastated her. The King's soldiers, even though they are few, seek only food for themselves . . . Despair has taken hold of the farmer . . . The greatest part of the province has been turned into a desert of ruins, the work on the land has stopped.[103]

To this we may add a similar observation, also recorded in 1618: "Outside Riga, for miles and miles at a stretch, nothing but a vast wilderness and a dismal sight is to be seen."[104] Riga's surrender was by now only a matter of time, for the Swedish king had secretly obtained a fortification plan of the besieged city.

On September 9, 1621, Swedish forces captured a segment of the fortifications by the Sand Gate, whose nearby tower had guarded the eastern entrance to the town for centuries. Equipped with twenty-four barrels of gunpowder, the Swedes began to mine Riga's walls in preparation for their destruction.[105] Even the city's most stalwart defenders, worn down by five weeks of furious resistance, realized that the fight was over. Riga's fate was now in the hands of Sweden's young warrior-king.

Chapter 7

Star City: The Swedish Century

Christina meine Königin
In Schweden mich verehret hin
Der Stadt Riga zu ihrem Schutz
Und ihrer aller Feinde Trutz[1]

My Queen Christina
Had me dedicated in Sweden
Presented to the city of Riga for its protection
And defiance of all enemies[2]

—Inscription emblazoned on two bronze cannons in Riga, 1639

Lasting from 1621 to 1710, the Swedish era in Riga coincided perfectly with the age of the Baroque, remembered for its creative exuberance, aristocratic splendor, and pretensions to grandiosity. A time of experimentation and innovation in music and the arts, the seventeenth century was also an era of discovery, colonization, and commerce on a global scale. From southeast Asia and the New World, Dutch fleets carried a cornucopia of goods across the oceans to meet the growing demands of European consumers. The world was becoming smaller, its most distant ports now embedded in a vast commercial network that sustained the flow of goods across the globe. This was also a time when the planet—indeed, the observable universe—was becoming more comprehensible, for the Baroque era was also an age of science. As mathematics demystified the natural world, now shown to be governed by mechanical principles, the cosmos was revealed to be a giant clock, the circulatory system a pump. In the most highly developed parts of the continent, the Age of Reason began its inquisitive reign.

Despite these achievements, the seventeenth century was also an age of war, now conducted in a manner that made armed conflict more destructive than ever before. The new kind of combat featured bigger armies and more powerful weaponry, deployed across vast theaters by ambitious and vainglorious monarchs who sought for reasons of state and faith and pride to extend their power as far as their armies could reach. It was during this era, beginning with the Polish-Swedish War (1600–1629), a prolonged conflict that eventually merged with central Europe's Thirty Years' War (1618–1648), that Swedish power in the Baltic surpassed that of Poland, whose long and agonizing decline was just beginning.

The prize in the struggle between the Commonwealth and the rising kingdom of Sweden was the city of Riga, which all the region's great powers understood to be the key to the eastern Baltic. For Gustavus II Adolphus, Riga's conquest would make possible the realization of what became, whether by accident or by design, the creation of a Swedish empire that nearly encircled the Baltic Sea. In this endeavor the young king was ultimately successful, for by 1625 the territories north of the Düna, including what are now Estonia and northeastern Latvia (Vidzeme) had come into Sweden's possession.[3] If these territories were to be the empire's granary, then Riga was to become its indispensable port, a reliable provider of food for the army and revenue to the crown.

Latvian and Estonian historians have by and large taken a favorable view of the Swedish century, praising the absolutist state for its "strict legality" and its protections against maltreatment.[4] In contrast to the chaotic Livonian Confederation of the Middle Ages or the sprawling Polish-Lithuanian Commonwealth that imposed itself upon Riga in 1581, the centralized Swedish state could command the mobilization of resources necessary for making much-needed improvements in infrastructure—above all roads, which they equipped with horse-changing stations and taverns at regular intervals.[5] The Swedes built bridges, dug drainage ditches, and created a postal system that linked the capital to the empire's continental possessions. Everywhere they built mighty fortresses to protect their holdings. If Sweden imposed heavy burdens on Riga and its other possessions in the eastern Baltic, it gave in return a modern civil and ecclesiastical order that was missing during the Middle Ages.[6]

The Swedish era (*Schwedenzeit*) was especially promising for the Livonian peasantry, who in peaceful times had endured the abuses of serfdom and who starved, died, or fled during times of war. Sympathetic to the plight of Livonia's peasants, Sweden's relatively enlightened rulers took measures to mitigate serfdom's abuses from the beginning: as early as May 1601, Duke (later King) Charles IX urged the Livonian nobility to free their peasants. While nothing came of the duke's proposal, later Swedish monarchs instituted reforms that limited the rights that lords could exercise over Livonia's rural inhabitants, so that by the end of the seventeenth century the virtual enslavement of the Livonian peasantry appeared to be a thing of the past. Less overjoyed were the nobles, for under Swedish rule they were compelled like never before to accede to a powerful state's radical demands.

For the city of Riga, the Swedish era was, often for the better and sometimes for the worse, a time of transformation. As military engineers thoroughly remodeled the city's fortification system, builders introduced modern architectural styles into the walled Old Town, where Riga's industrious merchants built their homes, exchanged merchandise, and worshiped in the city's towering red-brick churches. Adding another layer to the city's security were the revamped and fortified suburban districts whose populations swelled with Latvians from the nearby countryside seeking employment and opportunities that only Riga, by far the largest of the Livonian towns, could offer.

Yet the dawn of the "good old Swedish times"—or rather the end of Polish dominion—was far from promising, as the transition began during a drawn-out war accompanied by all the usual disruptions. For an entire decade, Riga was blockaded by sea and activity at its once-bustling harbor practically ceased. Three times the wooden houses and churches of the suburbs were burned to the ground. Famine struck in 1601, causing desperate peasants to seek refuge and sustenance behind Riga's walls. Although the siege was at last broken in 1610, the hardships continued as Poland and Sweden took their wars into the Russian lands. Renewing his offensive in the Baltic in 1621, King Gustavus II Adolphus was determined to bring the Livonian metropolis to its knees.

1621: Capitulation to Sweden

Of the many tragedies that Rigans endured in the seventeenth and early eighteenth centuries—for Livonia this was an era of reform and progress but also of floods and famines, plagues and war—among the costliest was the Swedish siege of August and September of 1621. Its defenses battered by a long artillery barrage, its soldiers exhausted, its citizens weak from hunger, the city could hold out no longer. Negotiations between the crown and the Riga Town Council (Rath), now under increasing pressure from a citizenry that howled in protest against the unnecessary sacrifices—hadn't the city been practically abandoned by Poland?—began on September 14, lasting late into the night and achieving no result. Further negotiations followed.

Riga's absorption into Sweden's expanding realm was by no means a foregone conclusion. The city might have been used as a bargaining chip in a possible deal with Poland: Gustavus was even heard to suggest that if his cousin Sigismund III were to capitulate and renounce his right to the Swedish throne, then the Swedish king might, if the Rigans wished, be willing to return the city and the Livonian territories to Poland after a few years' time; for himself, the king would keep only Estonia.[7] But the monarch's far-sighted chancellor Axel Oxenstierna (1583–1654), an influential confidante who was later appointed the city's governor-general, was better able to appreciate the strategic and economic significance of a conquered

Riga. Indeed, the worldly chancellor recognized more clearly than his master that Sweden's acquisition of Riga would be the indispensable step in the consolidation of Sweden's Baltic empire.

Truces between the warring powers were made and then broken as Sigismund plotted to recover the city for the Commonwealth as late as 1629, when this phase of the Polish-Swedish conflict came to a conclusion. But the outcome for Riga had been decided long before the fighting ended in the rest of Livonia. According to the terms of capitulation that were hastily drawn up on September 25, 1621, Sweden's king agreed to confirm the city's ancient privileges, to maintain its separate status within the framework of the empire, and to return its Jesuit churches and properties to the Lutherans.[8] The capitulation was not without popular support, for the traumatized burghers longed for a return to normalcy after so much suffering and uncertainty. Many were willing serve a new master, provided that master brought security, promoted the Lutheran faith, and respected the city's ancient liberties. Indeed, as the war continued to rage across the Livonian lands, the conquered city would provide the Swedish military with the support and resources it would need to defeat Poland.

With the Düna estuary now in hand, along with the mouths of several other rivers (the Neva and the Oder) that emptied into the Baltic, all kinds of resources flowed into the coffers of the Swedish state—among them license fees, portage taxes, loans from the city. Yet the more Riga gave, the more the crown demanded: to maintain the Swedish garrison in Riga, in 1622 the king ordered the city to contribute 24,000 thalers—a sum that increased with each passing year, regardless of the city's ability to pay.[9] The Swedes' insistence on maintaining a garrison inside the city was an immediate source of friction, for during the Polish era the Commonwealth's military forces were expected to remain *outside* the city walls.

It is easy to appreciate Rigans' apprehension about having thousands of Swedish soldiers housed within the city walls, where they might come into contact with the burghers who lived there permanently. First, there was the matter of public health, for in the fall of 1621 a plague struck the garrison and quickly spread to the local population. The Swedes lost 13,000 of their soldiers to the epidemic; how many Rigans perished, and how many people living in the city's outskirts, nobody can say. A further cause for alarm was the behavior of the Swedish forces in Riga: for to feed themselves and make up for their lack of provisions, the soldiers (along with the many non-Swedish mercenaries who served in the king's army) would simply rob the peasants who approached the city, taking their horses, appropriating firewood, seizing barges and rafts.[10] Transgressions like these only reinforced the burghers' conviction that their city's traditional rights were being egregiously violated.

With the crown in a constant state of military preparedness and regularly increasing its demands for financial contributions, it was not long before the town council concluded that Swedish domination had, despite the king's earlier assurances, placed unacceptable limits on the city's independence.[11] Whatever the benefits of Stockholm's protection, the reality is that nearly every aspect of Swedish rule was shaped by the military needs of the absolutist state. More than any other city in Gustavus Adolphus's enlarged realm, Riga was to pay for the defense of Sweden's Baltic empire.

Swedish Port

As the king anticipated, but did not live long enough to witness for himself (the "Lion of the North" perished while fighting in Germany in 1632), Riga turned out to be a highly lucrative source of income for the Swedish Empire. Or at least it became such once the Latvian and Estonian lands ceased to be battlefields and foreign trade resumed. In matters of commerce, this was the height of economic "mercantilism," an outgrowth of the colonizing thrust whose defining feature was the active role played by central governments in promoting and protecting commercial activities. This they accomplished through the granting of monopoly rights, the establishment of colonies to be exploited, and the collection of a stream of revenues through taxation on imports and exports as well as the imposition of licenses and fees. As an economic counterpart to royal centralism, mercantilism aimed at building up the state. For the burghers of Riga, as well as for the landed aristocrats of Livonia, these were more than abstract theories: all realized that the imposition of a strong, centralized government would mean a diminishing of local control.[12]

The disruptions of the Livonian War and the long conflict between Sweden and Poland notwithstanding, the century between 1550 and 1650 was on the whole a busy time at Riga's bustling port, and thus a generally prosperous era for Riga's merchants and craftsmen. The city's thriving trade with the West was best reflected in its connections with the ports of Holland, then at the dawn of its own "Golden Age" and in need of basic foodstuffs to make up for the difficulties of farming in the Netherlands' marshy terrain. Practitioners of a religious tolerance that was truly exceptional in a continent then being ripped apart by confessional struggles, the enterprising Dutch constructed a massive fleet that carried their growing trade and stimulated Holland's burgeoning industries. The Republic simultaneously fostered an explosion of secular art whose leading masters were Breugel the Elder, and later Vermeer and Harmenszoon van Rijn, better known by his surname Rembrandt.

At the moment of the painter's birth in 1606, merchants from Holland had already emerged as the most significant buyers of goods shipped from Livonian ports. As trans-Baltic shipping passed from the hands of Hanse merchants to the aggressively enterprising merchants of Leiden, Haarlem, and Amsterdam, the last emerging as a vibrant center of world trade, so changed the kinds of goods stuffed into the holds of the Dutch *fluyts*, which offered more cargo space while minimizing the need for hired crewmen: whereas a comparable English ship needed a crew of thirty, a 200-ton Dutch *fluyt* could sail with a crew of only nine or ten.[13] At the height of its power at the end of the seventeenth century, when the Dutch fleet dwarfed all others with its 50,000 vessels (four thousand were active in the Baltic), Holland's shipping dominance was total: of the ships that passed through the Danish Sound, two-thirds were commanded by Dutch captains.[14]

Some 239 ships docked at Riga's port in 1639, most filled with ballast in the form of bricks, roof tiles, and salt for stability. Of these vessels, 151 had Dutch or Frisian owners, eleven were English, ten Danish, thirty-six were German, and twenty had arrived from Sweden and its provinces.[15] To Riga they carried goods from the Atlantic that were little different from the merchandise imported during previous centuries: mainly salt (for ballast and for preserving food), silk, French wine, German beer, and produce from the colonies (sugar, tobacco, pepper, spices)—in other words, luxury goods for Riga's most prosperous burghers.

But it was Riga's exports, always far greater than its imports, that brought the city and its foreign rulers the greatest profits. If during the Middle Ages so-called "light" goods (principally furs and wax from the Russian interior) had dominated Riga's exports to Holland and the West, by the end of the sixteenth century these had largely been supplanted by "heavy" goods from lands then belonging to the Polish-Lithuanian Commonwealth. Among the most common were linseed and hemp, grain and dairy products, as well as the traditional forest products. Especially valued in the West were ash and pitch from the eastern Baltic (typically coming from Danzig and Königsberg rather than Riga), essential for building the fleets that allowed Atlantic states like Holland and later England to take their place as great maritime powers.

By the time the Swedes took possession of Riga, the bulk of its "Russian trade" was less dependably connected to the Muscovite cities and more deeply linked to the lands possessed by the feudal magnates of the Commonwealth.[16] It was from the noble estates in what is today Belarus that Riga's merchants obtained the majority of their goods, which were loaded onto the small vessels called *strugas* that sailed up the Dnieper and Düna Rivers to the Polish and Livonian ports. In good years, some 1,500 or 2,000 of these small, flat-bottomed, wooden vessels would slowly make their way from the hinterlands to Riga, where Latvian transport workers unloaded them and transferred their goods to the larger Dutch galleons and *fluyts* that carried them to the ports of western Europe. Registration records at Kokenhusen, a mercantile town located inland up the Düna, shows that some 1,444 *strugas* passed through its port on their way to Riga in the year 1653. The main item they carried was hemp, but the *strugas* also delivered barley, wheat, hempseed, linseed, and potash. More than a few were weighted with barrels of vodka.[17]

For much of the Swedish era, the most important grain collected in Riga was rye. Between 1630 and 1656, an average of some 3,500 *lasts* of rye were exported to the West per annum, with the peak of the rye trade occurring in the early 1650s as Riga shipped more than 9,000 *lasts* in 1651 and 13,600 in 1652. Such quantities of rye would not be seen again in Riga until the early 1680s, by which time Riga had supplanted Danzig as an exporter of commodities from the eastern Baltic.[18] The city's forested hinterland also became a leading source of the heavy timber used in the construction of ship masts, collected in Riga for export to Holland and England.[19]

Once in Riga, the eastern goods immediately came into the hands of the city's profit-minded traders, for the customary restrictions on foreign traders remained in place. Indeed, the ban on "guests" trading with "guests" that had been introduced during the fifteenth century remained in force throughout the many decades of Polish and then Swedish rule. Although dozens of "Russian"[20] merchants arrived in Riga each year, and although they maintained a permanent presence in their own quarters (most stayed in the Russian yard in the Lastadia suburb) with their own Orthodox churches, these petty traders were obliged to conduct their exchanges exclusively with merchants approved by Riga's guilds. The more these ordinances were violated, the more strictly they were enforced. Indeed, Riga's commercial life remained subject to all kinds of regulations that were designed to ensure that the Livonian merchants remained the sole intermediaries in the Baltic trade.

The embodiment of this concentration of affluence and privilege was a Riga burgomaster named Jürgen Dunte (1599–1660), who owned a manor just north of the city in what is now called Sarkandaugava. Into the hands of this wealthy German merchant fell a full one-third (35.1 percent) of Riga's export trade for the year 1632. Although hundreds of traders did their business in Riga, a relatively small number of them reaped the lion's share of the rewards. In the year 1694, for example, more than half the goods acquired from Russia went through a mere ten of Riga's 375 registered long-distance merchants.[21]

The profits that accrued to Riga's merchants in good times might be considerable, but their earnings were jeopardized when conflict and crisis befell the eastern Baltic. A comparison of the peaceful and prosperous 1590s to the difficult decades that followed is revealing. During the sixteenth century's final years an average of some 228 ships per annum sailed from Riga and paid Sound dues as they drifted past Denmark toward their destinations in western Europe. In 1595 alone Riga exported goods valued at some 413,000 thalers—an amount more than four times as great as its imports and nearly twice the amount Riga had exported a decade earlier. But as the on-again, off-again war between Sweden and the Commonwealth took its toll, the number of vessels paying Sound dues plummeted: a mere seventy-nine ships per annum arrived during the century's first decade, and only fifty-two in the years between 1621 and 1630.[22] At their lowest point, in 1627, Riga's exports were barely sufficient to fill even three ships.[23]

In lean times the Riga harbor would descend into idleness as the merchants who for years had grown fat on their profits fretted for their livelihoods—and Latvian workers, consigned to their traditional roles as porters, warehouse workers, and linen weavers, struggled to feed their families even as they organized themselves into fraternities (*Zünfte*) whose members enjoyed certain rights and privileges.[24] Peace and stability, on the other hand, brought recovery and a return to prosperity. Such was the case in the early 1630s, when an average of some three hundred Western ships per annum docked at Riga's port. By the 1640s more than four hundred ships were entering the Bay of Riga each year. Sweden's decision in 1646 to exclude Dorpat from those Livonian cities enjoying the right of emporium redounded to the advantage of the region's largest city—Dorpat's trade losses became Riga's gains—and probably contributed to Riga's economic boom.[25]

Changing consumption patterns, often but not always related to war, also affected Riga's commerce with the outside world. We might consider, for example, the impact on Riga of the greatest calamity the continent suffered in these times—the Thirty Years' War (1618–1648). With the Holy Roman Empire's urban population plunging by one-third, so collapsed the German market for rye and other grains. Given the simultaneous increases in cereal production in southern and western Europe, a declining demand for food and other goods from the eastern Baltic was inevitable.[26] And when western Europe's need for eastern goods dipped, the usual bustle at the port of Riga dampened.

The 1660s and 1670s, for example, were relatively slow decades for Riga's merchants, the number of ships docking at Riga falling by half since the port's mid-century heyday. While Riga's commerce traditionally dwarfed that of competitor cities such as Reval, Narva, and Pernau, its degree of dominance had noticeably declined. Stagnation at Riga's port contradicted the interests of Stockholm, which depended on income from portage. To make up the difference between what was needed and what could actually be collected, the Swedish crown increasingly resorted to imposing license fees on the city's merchants and extorting loans from an increasingly resentful Rath.

The city of Stockholm, enjoying rapid growth during the seventeenth century, was the kingdom's official capital (since 1634), but Riga was the empire's crown jewel. Already Sweden's leading port, Riga was emerging as an important manufacturing center as well. Modest factories established in and around the city produced rope, leather goods, bricks, and various products from metal—that is, items typically used for the construction of ships or for military purposes. Concerns like these were typically founded not by Rigans but by foreigners, often from Holland.[27] For the city of Riga and for Livonia as a whole, this was an age of growth and transformation. Enjoying the protection of the powerful Swedish military, the Düna metropolis prospered and became more modern and also more strictly regimented. It was just as the century came to a close that Swedish Riga reached the peak of its affluence; but another great catastrophe was just around the bend. The "good old Swedish times," it would turn out, were not always so golden.

City and Crown

A practitioner of the art of realpolitik—in other words, a pragmatist less concerned with achieving moral or religious ends, but instead devoted entirely to the needs of the state—Gustavus II Adolphus confirmed Riga's ancient privileges in the *Corpus privilegorium Gustavianum*, whose underlying premise was the city's separate status within the Kingdom of Sweden. The Baltic provinces of Estland (under Swedish rule since 1561) and Livland (1629) were likewise considered the empire's strategic bastions but were not constitutionally integrated into it. Owing to this arrangement it is somewhat misleading to say that Riga was Sweden's largest city. From the perspective of Stockholm, the Baltic provinces were overseas colonies—even if very few Swedes settled in them apart from aristocrats who acquired large estates and bureaucrats who occupied key positions in the administration. It was in such fashion that Livonia and Riga, like the German provinces and the ones snatched from Denmark-Norway, were governed.

At first, the Swedes ruled their Baltic provinces with a relatively light administrative touch backed by a commanding military presence; it wasn't until the end of the seventeenth century that the crown's aim became the administrative Swedification of Livonia and its largest city. Himself the Lutheran ruler of a Protestant country, King Gustavus confirmed the Augsburg Convention,[28] while working to raise Lutheranism's profile in the Livonian countryside: if Riga had only five parish priests in 1623, by 1630 that number had increased to forty-eight.[29]

Yet much remained as before, for the Swedish administration preserved the town council's traditional right to issue laws and administer justice in the German language while allowing the city to take half the income from its portage customs. To the disappointment of the local nobility, the crown also confirmed a two-year limitation on any claims to peasants who had escaped serfdom—a condition that never existed in Sweden proper—and made their homes in Riga. The city had the right to forge its own money, but the coins had to be made with Swedish plates and impressed with the image of the Swedish king.[30]

Above all, Riga was to pay for its own defense, for which the crown supplied the mixed blessing of a garrison. In addition to being a source of financial distress, this burden also inconvenienced those burghers whose homes were commandeered to house Sweden's military forces. In such manner was an already-congested city made to feel still more uncomfortable for the Germans who still comprised a majority of Riga's citizens.

If at first Riga's German councilors acquiesced to the changes in the city's political arrangements as the price for security, the local elite soon came to feel that Swedish dominion was imposing unacceptable limits on the city's independence. The crown's reversal, in fact, took no time at all, for it was not long after he confirmed the city's privileges that the Swedish king then delimited them. In the future, Gustavus informed the city, when a new monarch was to be crowned, Riga would be required to send a delegation to Stockholm to render him (or her, as in the case of Queen Christina) an oath of loyalty. The city would also be required to make a contribution to cover the coronation expenses.[31] The arrangement was made all the more burdensome by the possibility that the new monarch might choose not to confirm the city's privileges.

This appeared to be the situation in the autumn of 1646 when a Riga delegation headed by the crown's appointed burgrave Melchior Fuchs (1603–1678) journeyed to Stockholm to negotiate Riga's privileges with state chancellor Axel Oxenstierna. As the discussions dragged on through the winter, a complete understanding eluded both sides: Rigans sought the crown's support in their efforts to squeeze out competitors in Narva and elsewhere, but Oxenstierna refused to grant the city an absolute monopoly on the Baltic trade. Although the never-married Queen Christina (r. 1632–1654), a highly educated daughter of Gustavus, was persuaded to confirm the city's privileges the following May,[32] Riga's burgrave was so irritated by the experience that he returned to the city and began to compile his work *Historia mutati regiminis et privilegiorum Civitatis Rigensium* (1654), a chronicle whose purpose was to justify the maintenance of Riga's traditional privileges.[33] Often finding it difficult to implement royal absolutism in their Livonian holdings, the Swedes were keenly aware of the suspicious attitudes of the local power-wielders and understood that under the right circumstances (e.g., the outbreak of war) the loyalties of the Livonian nobility and of Riga's burghers could easily shift to the Catholic monarch of Poland-Lithuania or even to the Orthodox tsardom of Muscovy.[34]

Stockholm's unwanted impositions notwithstanding, authority to govern the city still belonged to the Rath, consisting of fourteen or sixteen of the town's wealthier citizens, three of whom became *ex officio* assessors of the Supreme Court (*Hofgericht*) in Stockholm. Although invited to send delegates to the *Riksdag*, on only one occasion did the town council, concerned about damaging the prestige of what not long ago had been a "free city" of the Holy Roman Empire, avail itself of this privilege.[35]

Membership in the Rath remained a family affair, for when a member died he was typically replaced by a son or another close relative. Each councilor also retained an additional post in the city's administration. The words of Riga native Basilius Plinius, published in 1595 when Riga was under Polish dominion, still applied fifty and even a hundred years later during the Swedish era:

To some officials the duty of caring for the churches
is delegated, to others, custodianship of the schools.
Some are responsible for harmonious organization
in matters of maintenance, planning needed tasks:
Keeping the battlements and ramparts in good repair,
providing for the construction of public buildings.
To others the care and guardianship of orphans is entrusted,
Still others to see to it that the wealth of our country is not squandered.[36]

Thus one councilor might oversee church affairs and religious matters (even if the Swedes established a consistory for this purpose), another would lead the city chancellery. Still another was charged with organizing the city's defense, while a treasury master oversaw the collection of tolls and excises.[37] Council members also oversaw the city's graveyards and mills, its canals and wells, as well as its communal horse stalls, then located at the end of what is now Mārstaļu iela near the old city wall.[38]

A painting of the Riga Town Council from sometime in the 1650s—its creator unknown, it now hangs in the Museum of the History of Rīga and Navigation—shows sixteen identically dressed men sitting or standing around a table: each is adorned in a black robe and a white collar, and nearly all have shoulder-length hair and a mustache. It is the day before St. Michael's Day, when the council's newly elected members perform their old custom of reading the city laws (*Burspraken*) through an open window in front of the Town Hall Square.[39] To these men belonged the power to make law and to judge. That this group formed a more or less closed caste—nearly all were wealthy traders—can be seen in the family names of the Council membership.

Few exercised so much influence for so long as the Dreiling family. The first in the long line of Dreilings who served on the town council was Paul Dreiling (Dreilingk), who was born in Tyrol, Austria, in 1476 and eventually moved to Riga, where he was elected to the city's governing body in 1518.[40] That the Rath had two burgomasters with the same name toward the end of the Swedish era—Johan Dreiling—would have surprised no one, so small was the circle of patricians, and so respected was this clan within it.[41] The long line of Dreiling mayors would endure well into the Russian era, ending only when Theodore von Dreiling died in 1766.[42]

A similar longevity was enjoyed by members of the Zimmerman family (1551–1747) and the Rigemann family (1596–1803), for the fathers and sons of these families sat on the Rath nearly uninterrupted for two centuries.[43] During Swedish times they were joined by the Berenses, who made their fortune in the export of hemp and flax. The first of this family to serve on Riga's town council, Hans Hinrich Berens, was born in Rostock in 1643 and became a wholesaler in the trade that connected Lithuanian magnates (notably the powerful Sapieha family) to Dutch money. Having made his way to Riga, Hans Hinrich Berens loyally served his adopted city and the Swedish state as an alderman. Several of his sons and grandsons would go on to serve the Russian state in the same capacity.[44]

Such men hailing from old and respected families not only oversaw the city's internal affairs, but were also responsible for supplying their Swedish overlords with the revenues they required, often in the form of loans, to offset the expense of the kingdom's military adventures. It was not long before Riga became one of the Swedish crown's most reliable creditors and an indispensable supplier of grain for the consumption of the Swedish army.[45] This left Riga's local power holders—the Berenses and Dreilings and Zimmermans—to cope with the contradictions inherent in serving the needs of their Swedish masters while at the same time administering Riga on behalf of its burghers. Both the crown and the city required revenues and resources to function, and it was the town council's responsibility to secure them.

A consideration of the activities of Johan Skytte, a particularly energetic governor-general of Livonia,[46] brings the relationship between Stockholm and its colonial acquisitions into sharper relief. A former tutor to the future King Gustavus Adolphus and later an important educational reformer, the Swedish baron arrived in Riga in 1629 as a state centralizer: Livonia, in his view, must be completely integrated into the Swedish kingdom.[47] It was also Skytte's aim to rein in Livonia's greatest city by bringing Riga under the jurisdiction of the high court at Dorpat, which covered all Livonia except Riga.[48] Lacking the king's support in these matters (and opposed by the Riga Town Council), such plans were never realized in practice. Yet the governor-general achieved one notable success: by removing the nobility's legal authority to sit in judgment over their own peasants, whose cases would now be heard by one of Livonia's three district courts, Skytte dramatically weakened the hold of serfdom, an institution that was alien and repugnant to Sweden's rulers and administrators.[49]

The reign of Gustavus II Adolphus further witnessed the establishment of schools, hospitals, and poorhouses throughout Livonia. To this we may add the state's vigorous support for the Lutheran church, which sought to improve the moral condition of their subjects while bringing God's word to a peasantry that had long been indifferent to Christianity. Even as the reforms fell short of being comprehensive—serfdom was not entirely abolished in Livonia, and the usual abuses went unpunished—by the time Charles XI died in 1697 it can be said that the peasants, although still attached to the land, had acquired certain rights, including the right to dispose of their personal property and to inherit land. Royal decrees from the 1690s offered further protection to their status and possessions. Acquiring the right to petition the monarch directly, Livonian peasants of this era would sometimes be seen on the streets of Stockholm, so frequently did they take up this welcome practice.[50]

But it was in Riga that many of the migrating peasants settled permanently. In the Livonian metropolis they faced the challenge of earning their daily bread and finding a secure position in what was by any measure a segregationist society. While under Swedish rule the city's non-Germans experienced the beginnings of a cultural resurgence, the fact remains that they were an underclass with few legal protections. To this subject we shall later return.

The unfortunate plight of abused and migrating peasants notwithstanding, there is much to be said for the notion that the era of Swedish rule was something of a "golden age" for Livonia and for Riga. While hardly universal, education became far more widespread, with schools established in every Livonian parish. Books were published and German-language periodicals began to spread the news of the day. Swedish protection was also beneficial for trade, which Rigans would have agreed was a very good thing, and the citizens could rest more easily knowing how well defended their city had become. But few could deny the enormous burdens that the state's military requirements placed on their city. That the state's demands could never be satisfied by the empire's busiest port only added to the strains in the unbalanced relationship between Sweden and the city of Riga.

Confirmed in the Treaty of Altmark, Sweden's victory over Poland in 1629 had secured the country's position as a great Baltic power; but it was on the battlefields of Germany, where King Gustavus II Adolphus gave his life three years later, that the kingdom truly became an empire. Having forced into submission many of the principalities of the Holy Roman Empire, Sweden, now ruled by Gustavus's daughter Christina, emerged from the Thirty Years' War (1618–1648) in control of much of Pomerania on the southwestern Baltic coast, and with it the Hanseatic cities of Stettin and Stralsund. To these possessions the crown added the duchies of Bremen and Verden, located between the mouths of the Elbe and Weser rivers on the North Sea. As if to confirm Sweden's claim to imperial status, the kingdom also acquired overseas territories in the Caribbean and modest holdings in North America (part of Delaware) and West Africa. In this way Sweden joined the ranks of European powers possessing overseas colonies. But the most important achievement of Sweden's seventeenth-century rulers was the kingdom's complete control of the Baltic and of the trade that traversed this inland sea, for Sweden now possessed a larger navy than that of its rival Denmark-Norway and had freed itself from paying that country's Sound dues. The Baltic Sea had become, as it was often called, a Swedish lake.

As it attained supremacy over the Baltic, the kingdom learned to make war pay for itself—for in the Swedish system, the burdens of war, fought in large measure by soldiers recruited on the continent, were to be paid for by others.[51] That the great trading city of Riga was the goose whose golden eggs fed the Swedish military state was evident to its rulers, who exploited Riga's position as a collection point for food and raw materials. In 1641, for example, Riga supplied the Swedish capital with some two thousand barrels of grain, a practice that came to typify the relationship between the imperial center and the colonized periphery. The following year, as Sweden fought its wars on the continent, Riga loaned the crown 24,000 silver thalers, a sum that increased to 40,000 thalers in 1648. Such debts were secured against the crown's collection of portage on the city's exports and imports.[52]

The Swedish state maintained this advantageous position in the most trying circumstances, for in the middle of the seventeenth century the kingdom faced a coalition of the greatest powers of central and eastern Europe, above all a weakened Polish-Lithuanian Commonwealth and a resurgent Muscovy. Having recovered from its Time of Troubles (1598–1613), a calamitous era of civil war compounded by famine and foreign intervention, the Muscovite state ruled by Tsar Alexei (r. 1645–1676) was now in a position to renew its efforts to regain the old Rus' lands that had come under Polish-Lithuanian rule. Crippled by an uprising in the Cossack territories of Ukraine, the Commonwealth was particularly vulnerable to the tsar's predations. In 1654 the city of Smolensk fell to the Muscovites, who soon added to their expansive holdings the Cossack Hetmanate in Left-Bank Ukraine. In this way Russia acquired control over large parts of present-day Belarus and Ukraine.[53]

Anxious about the growth of Russian power in Poland-Lithuania, King Charles X Gustav, who acceded to the throne after his cousin Christina's abdication in 1654, invaded the Commonwealth, for Swedish interests dictated that there should be a preponderance of neither Polish nor Russian power in the hinterlands that fed the empire. Polish writers refer to the events of the mid-seventeenth century as the "Deluge," a catastrophe that has been seared into Poland's national consciousness, for this was a time (and it would not be the last) when a quarter of the population perished as the Polish state was nearly swept out of existence. Just as Sweden was ascending to the height of its power, the long decline of the vast and disunited Commonwealth had begun. Both blocked Russia's direct access to the Baltic Sea.

Now confronting Swedish power in Poland-Lithuania, the pious Alexei Mikhailovich Romanov, open to Western ideas and committed to recovering the territories that Muscovy had lost in earlier conflicts, focused on two objectives in the Baltic. One was to overturn the Treaty of Stolbovo that in 1617 had left Sweden in control of border territories on the Baltic—Kexholm, southwest Karelia, and the province of Ingria. The second was to take under his own power the Düna trade route. Sailing up the Düna in their modest barges and rafts, and bringing with them food, weapons, and cannons, the tsar's forces captured one fortress after another. On June 30, 1656, they seized Dünaburg (Daugavpils), a fortress on the upper Düna then lightly defended by Swedish forces. On August 14, the Russians took Kokenhusen (Koknese), and soon after that Kirchholm (Salaspils), whose three cannons were evacuated to Riga. By August 22, the Muscovites had arrived at the southern approach to Riga. Fearing that their city would fall to the tsar, some wealthy Rigans fled to Courland and Lübeck. Even the governor-general of Swedish Livonia, the Reval-born Magnus Gabriel De la Gardie, was tempted to abandon the city to the siege, threatening the councilors at one point to depart for Sweden with his wife.[54]

Defending the city of Riga were approximately 1,800 hired infantry, 2,000 cavalrymen, and 1,500 armed burghers. They were joined by peasants who fled to the city at the sight of the approaching Russians. Another seven thousand soldiers in the pay of Sweden were spread across garrisons in Livonia, Estonia, and Ingria.[55] The greatest challenge facing the tsar, however, was overcoming Riga's powerful fortifications. Although carefully renovated by the city's Swedish rulers, the new defenses were not yet complete when the Russian siege began on August 24, 1656.

Star City

If Holland during its seventeenth-century golden age is remembered for its vast commercial empire, its unsurpassed Renaissance masters, and a mass mania for tulips, Sweden's singular talent was its ability to make war for long periods of time on the basis of limited human and material resources. A "power state" (*Machtstaat*) in which military needs trumped all other considerations, Sweden aligned and mobilized all its institutions for the single purpose of maintaining its Baltic empire.[56] Riga was the linchpin of that empire.

Troubled by the inadequacies of the city's outdated medieval fortifications, Riga's Polish governors had accelerated their modernization, for the age of arrows and stone projectiles had passed: the sobering, not-so-new reality was gunpowder artillery. Towers were remodeled and reinforced, the aging masonry walls were strengthened and thickened. Ramparts fashioned from earth and sand were constructed around the city to create an additional protective shell.

The first ramparts predated the eras of Polish and Swedish rule and were built along Riga's vulnerable northern side between the Sand and Jacob Towers, for here there were no natural barriers against invasion, only an open pasture.[57] The system of ramparts was then extended from the Jacob Tower to the Riga Castle, which anchored the Düna embankment, and also along the city's eastern and southern edges (today's Vaļņu and 13 Janvara streets). So massive were these earthen barriers—intended to soften the impact of cannonballs, in some places the ramparts reached twelve meters in height—that the old masonry walls were in most places completely obscured.

Through the construction of these ramparts, the entire area between Riga's five new roundels acquired an additional line of defense. Offering another protective layer was the ditch that was dug around the ramparts. This moat became the basis for the present-day Riga Canal, which separates the medieval inner city from the newer residential districts. The limits of the moat's effectiveness were amply demonstrated in April 1582, when the city's new master, King Stephen Bathory, attempted to cross it on horseback. Legend has it that the ditch was so narrow and shallow that its water barely touched the steed's belly. The useless channel, the Polish king concluded, must be deepened and widened.

Indeed, as much as the Poles had worked to modernize Riga's defenses, the entire system would require another upgrade in order to withstand the powerful artillery of the seventeenth century. What was once an improvement eventually became a liability. Consider, for example, the five roundels that by 1612 formed the main defensive points around the inner city. Defended by men equipped with crossbows and cannons, these structures had two intrinsic flaws: one was the blind spot in the rear; another was the lack of space for cannons on the roundel's upper level. That Swedish forces were able to mine the ramparts right under the noses of the city's defenders during the siege of 1621 demonstrated exactly how vulnerable the defensive system had become. Once the war with Poland ended in 1629, Riga's new rulers committed themselves to its renovation.

All over Europe, the medieval fortifications that had long provided security for town-dwellers were being replaced by the star (or bastion) fort. As the revived learning of the Renaissance supplied engineers with the mathematics and geometry necessary for an effective defense, medieval fortifications everywhere were modernized to meet the demands of the new warfare. The result was the bastion—a protruding terraced platform that extended into the defensive moat and was situated low above the ground so as not to provide the enemy with an easy target. Designed to allow defensive artillery to cover all approaches to the city, the pentagonal bastion would prove to be far superior to the roundel.[58] First appearing in Italian cities like Florence, which gave the responsibility of improving the city's fortifications to its famed sculptor Michelangelo Buonarotti, the new star-shaped defensive systems gave employment to legions of Italian engineers whose skills were soon in demand across the continent. By the end of the sixteenth century, bastion forts had become especially common in Holland and had largely supplanted the older defensive systems in much of the rest of Europe, even if their astronomical cost sometimes bankrupted the very communities they were designed to defend.

Already in 1617 the city's Polish rulers had begun to rebuild Riga's roundels into Dutch-style bastions (*bolwerken*), which had the advantage not only of eliminating the roundel's "blind spot," but also of providing more room for cannons and for the soldiers who manned them. In front of this defensive line the Swedes created triangular-shaped detached outworks called ravelins. Covering the defensive works in the gaps between the bastions, the new ravelins functioned as fortified islands in the city moat, configured in such a way that an assault force would necessarily be divided. With this thorough upgrading and deepening of the city's defenses—along with their extension into the hitherto undefended suburbs—Riga was on its way to becoming one of northeastern Europe's best-fortified cities.

The revamping of Riga's defenses was a joint enterprise initiated by officials of the Swedish crown with the cooperation of local authorities. In this expensive endeavor Riga was not alone, for Reval and other strategically important locations in Sweden's Baltic empire also required a defensive upgrading at this time. If the "good old Swedish times" are remembered fondly for advancements in legality and popular enlightenment, what is sometimes understated is the colonial nature of the relationship. Indeed, as the Swedes established their dominion over Livonia, the crown wasted little time in taking over the estates that belonged to nobles (often Poles) who had sided with the Commonwealth.

But it was the crown-appointed governors-general, with their seat in Dorpat (now Estonian Tartu), who acted as the king's permanent representative in Livonia (Livland) and Estonia (Estland) and who were assigned responsibility for collecting contributions for the city's defense. The governors-general, beginning with Jakob De la Gardie (1622–1628), also determined the quantity of military forces inside Riga's walls.[59] In the late 1640s the governor's residence (formerly in Dorpat) became the Riga Castle, altered and extended in the 1640s to meet the needs of the Swedish administration.[60] A more substantial renovation of the castle took place during the rule of King Charles XI, who in 1682 added an armory, where the king delighted in showing his guests the armaments and uniforms that symbolized the power of the Swedish state.[61]

Swedish authorities began drafting plans for improving the city's defenses from the outset of the occupation. By 1640 much work had already been completed on the defenses in and around the inner city, where the main tasks were to deepen and widen the city moat, complete the transformation of roundels into bastions, and create ravelins in between them. The Swedes paid particular attention to the Sand Roundel (near the present-day Powder Tower, then known as the Sand Tower), which had revealed itself during the Polish-Swedish War as a weak point in city defenses, for enemy forces ensconced in the nearby Kube Hill could easily fire on the city from that position.

The modifications of the 1630s and 1640s also had the effect of altering the routes by which Rigans could enter and leave their city. Most significant were the changes by the Sand Gate. Its nearby roundel converted into a bastion, the old Sand Gate ceased to be an entrance into the city. This amounted to a major alteration to the flow of traffic in and out of Riga: for centuries the Sand Road leading to the gate and tower had been the only dry road by which merchants arriving

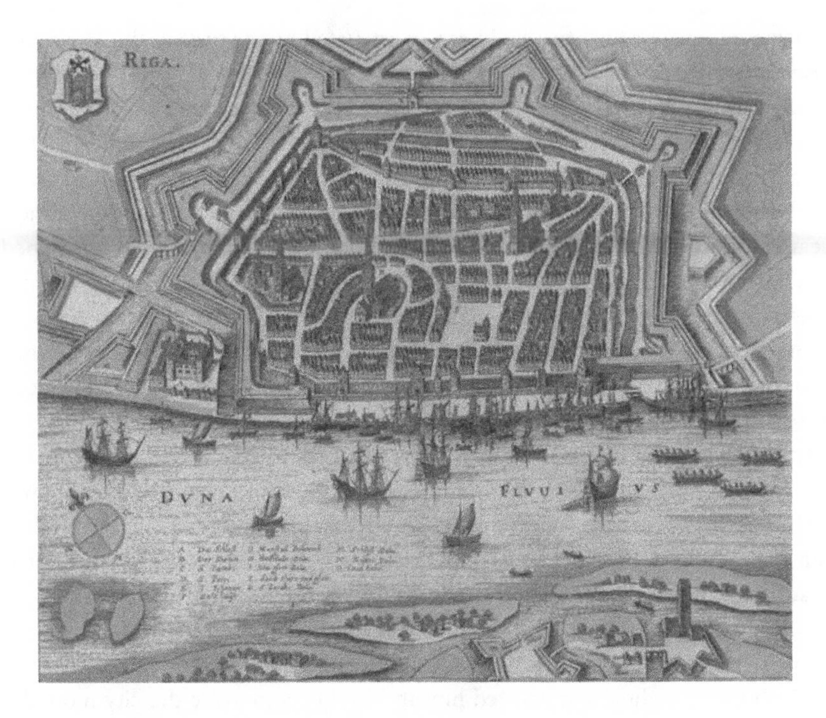

FIGURE 11. View of the town and harbor of Riga, ca. 1637. By Matthew Merian. Courtesy of Barry Lawrence Ruderman Antique Maps.

from the east could reach the town, but now a new way to allow entry into the city would have to be found. This would be the Lime Gate, named for the nearby lime kiln.[62] Passage through the portal that ran across the Lime Ravelin (1639) would then bring people to the Lime Road, a street that became one of the city's two main thoroughfares.[63] The other, Lords Street, ran perpendicular to the Lime Road but likewise led to the Town Hall Square where the main market was located.[64]

A second corridor that connected the city to its outlying districts was located near St. Jacob's Bastion at the city's northern approach. This artery can be seen on the left side of Matthew Merian's gorgeous illustration of the city layout, published in 1637. It was traditionally through the Jacob Gate, located in front of the spot where the National Theater is today, that Rigans reached the old road to the city pastures on the city's northern side.[65] Although a ravelin was added during the Swedish renovations, the renovations there did not, as Rigans feared it would, impede their access to the pastures.[66]

As extensive as the renovations to the inner city were around the margins and at its entry points, the city's core road network remained largely intact, and indeed the course of these arteries would change little until modern times. Of the anticipated ravelins only two had been constructed by the time of the Muscovite invasion of 1656. These would be known as the Sand Ravelin and the Charles (Karl) Ravelin, near which a third entrance to the city was later (in 1685) built, near what is now called the Moscow (or Latgale) suburb. Two more ravelins would eventually be added to provide the inner city with a more complete defense in the areas between the bastions. Although Riga's ravelins and bastions disappeared long ago, the Sand Tower, then rebuilt as an appropriately barrel-shaped container for storing gunpowder (henceforth it would be known as the Powder Tower), stands as a compelling reminder of the Swedish century.

It was in the *Vorstadt*—the suburb outside the fortified town—and in the lands opposite the city on the other side of the Düna where the Swedish renovations were still more dramatic. The planned development of these areas, largely for military purposes, occurred in two stages. The first projects were undertaken from the late 1630s through the first half of the 1650s, and then were resumed after the war with Muscovy. Two men supervised the first stage. One was the Dutchman Johan van Rodenburg (d. 1657), who as quartermaster-general for all the Swedish fortifications in Livonia, Estonia, and Ingria, as well as the island of Ösel, was responsible for supplying the army. A second was the Bavarian Francis Murer (Franz Murrer; 1609–1681), a medical doctor and fortifications engineer who married Rodenburg's daughter and assisted him in his efforts to make the city more defensible. A third engineer, the Swede Erik Dahlberg (1625–1703), would play the primary role in the improvements of the 1670s and 1680s and in the creation of the Citadel just north of the Riga Castle. To Dahlberg's work we shall return later.

Having supervised the construction of the nine-bastioned fortress at Rostov Velikii (Rostov the Great) while in the employ of the Muscovite tsar, Johan van Rodenburg entered into Swedish service in 1637, where he was put to work on the suburban fortifications at Narva on the Russian border. But it was the fortifications around Riga that commanded the greater part of his attention, such as the reconstruction of Fort Kobron.[67] The new defensive work was built on the Düna's left bank opposite the city of Riga, an area that was largely unsettled until modest numbers of Latvians gradually began to build homes there during the seventeenth century. Rebuilt on the Dutch model, the new Fort Kobron was given a star shape, formed by its five bastions and four ravelins, as well as a large defensive ditch.

But as with many of the Swedes' plans, the construction of Fort Kobron generated conflict with the town council, as Rodenburg's plan effectively blocked the traditional land route from Riga to Courland and Lithuania.[68] That the area on the land side of the fortress was declared an esplanade—an open and level area outside the fortress to provide a clear line of vision for the men who manned Kobron's guns—delayed a dense settlement of the area until the early years of the twentieth century. Later it was on this site that the Soviet regime would build a large park dedicated to the Red Army's victory in World War II.

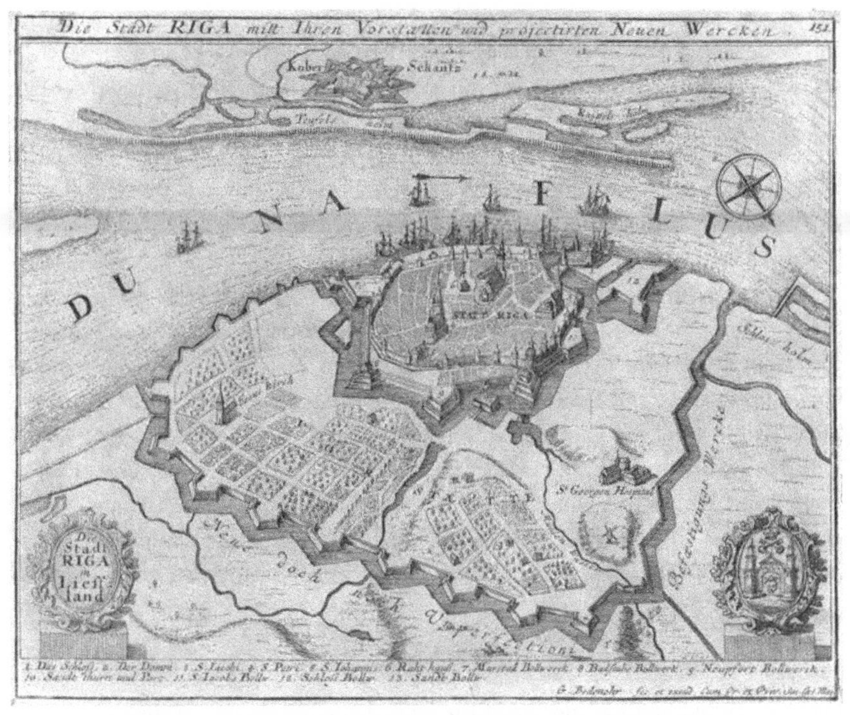

FIGURE 12. Riga with fortifications and Fort Kobron in the second half of the seventeenth century. Johann Stridbeck, ca. 1700.

By 1639 Rodenburg had also begun work on the remodeled Dünamünde[69] fortress near the mouth of the Düna.[70] First built by the Poles but now transformed into a pentagonal fortress in the Dutch style, the seaside fort bore the same name as an old monastery-castle, located several kilometers to the east, that had been destroyed in 1624 during the Polish-Swedish War.[71] At times the Dünamünde fortress would house as many as one thousand men, making it one of Riga's largest garrisons. With such improvements to the defensive works on the Düna's left bank in the vicinity of Riga, the city would now be better defended from enemies who approached by water.

Sometimes Swedish plans came into conflict with the interests of propertied Rigans. That is exactly what happened when Rodenburg announced his plan to unite the city of Riga and the Riga Castle into a united fortification system. As a possession of the Livonian Order before 1561, the Riga Castle had been legally and administratively separate from the walled city during the Middle Ages; only in 1582 did the Polish king Stephen Bathory transfer control of the former order castle to Rigan authorities. The aging castle was also physically separated from the city by ramparts and a moat. Rodenburg's renovations, therefore, would not only be expensive, but extensive. Concerned that the defensive system being rebuilt around the castle would destroy the townsfolk's gardens outside the city and obstruct their access to the city pastures, Riga's councilors dispatched an embassy to Stockholm for consultations with Queen Christina and other state officials. The results were mixed: while the burghers would retain access to the pastures outside the Jacob Gate, they would, as we have noted, be required to pass through a ravelin. As the crown simply dismissed other local concerns, Rigans learned to accept that the defensive system would now occupy a wider zone.[72]

In general, however, the changes inside the old walled city were not especially disruptive, for the dense network of irregular streets remained largely intact through the Swedish years and beyond. The more significant aspect of the work undertaken between the 1620s and the 1640s was the complete unification of the area between the city's medieval walls and its earthen ramparts into an integrated defensive system that was now juridically part of the city. In this arc stood the wooden warehouses and homes inhabited mostly by the city's non-Germans. The annexation of these areas meant that the city had reached the geographical limit of thirty-five hectares that it would maintain until the defensive walls were razed in 1857–1863.[73]

Riga's Suburbs

Once an individual had departed the walled medieval city through one of its gates, he immediately passed into Riga's open and vulnerable suburbs. The contrast with the enclosed inner city, darkened by its imposing walls and ramparts, its air befouled by the clogged and reeking rivulet that gave the city both its original shape and its name, must have been striking indeed. Just outside the town were its gardens and mills, as well as shelters and a hospital known as St. George's. Also in the suburbs were the city's cemetery and churches where services were conducted in Latvian: these were St. Gertrude's[74] along the Sand Road and the Jesus Church (original, 1638–1656; second, 1688–1710) in the south. To this ensemble the Swedes would erect in the wake of the 1677 fire a gallows located near the intersection of present-day Post Street and Freedom Street.[75]

It was in the suburbs, constructed almost entirely of wooden buildings so they could be burned in times of war, that the city's iron workers labored, for theirs was a trade that carried with it the threat of fire. With their noisy taverns and kilns, and their stinking slaughterhouses and tanneries, the sprawling, irregular suburbs had a vastly different character than the tightly knit inner city. Streets in the Lastadia area with names indicating the area's most significant objects—"road to the Jesus Church"[76] and "the path to the Lime kiln"[77]—nicely illustrate the region's undeveloped, almost rural nature.[78]

Taking a stroll through the suburbs, a visitor might encounter various non-German craftsmen and hired laborers, as well as the occasional doctor, apothecary, or barber. If he came across a merchant at all it would likely have been along the Great Sand Road that led to Russia; few Germans, except those who had the desire and means to imitate the lifestyle of the landed nobility, lived outside the walled city. Hermann Meyer owned an estate in the neighborhood of the Jesus Church (an area populated by Russian traders), and lands belonging to councilor Brand Marquart were located along the Great Sand Road on both sides of the outer palisades that were erected in 1692–93. But it was in the medieval core—Old Riga—that nearly all Riga's Germans resided and conducted their transactions, their leaders pursuing policies that increasingly isolated the city's privileged elements from its non-German populations.[79]

In the event of war, it was the *Undeutsche* living in the suburbs who were the most vulnerable. Even Lastadia, a shipbuilding center that was established in the fourteenth century—it was here that "Russian" traders maintained a yard that Germans called *die Ruße*—remained undefended into the 1620s. Among the harshest realities of life in the suburban districts was fire, for in the event of war it was the fate of the suburbs, whose modest structures were made of wood, to be sacrificed to save the city. One such occurrence, taking place during the Swedish-Polish War, is documented in a letter that the town council sent to Chancellor Radziwill in 1622:

> We had neither ships that could confront the enemy's fleet, nor land forces that could engage in battle outside Riga, and therefore we had to burn down the suburbs, which we had rebuilt three times, destroy its gardens and cut down its fruit trees.[80]

It was during this long conflict that the Swedes first attempted to equip the suburbs with defensive fortifications. Having captured Riga in 1621, the Swedes erected palisades—fences made from wooden stakes—to provide an additional line of defense against an anticipated Polish counterattack. Protecting an area of 191 hectares, the palisades followed a wide arc that ran from the Düna embankment to the Pasture Dike[81] just northeast of the inner city—a line that roughly corresponds to present-day Mill Street (Latv. Dzirnavu iela).[82]

Another twenty years would pass before the Dutchman Johan van Rodenburg began to draw up a more ambitious set of plans for Riga's suburbs. With the appointment of Francis Murer as his chief engineer in 1649, the stage was set for the extension of inner Riga's complex fortification systems into the districts on its northern, eastern, and southern frontiers.[83] In place of the old suburban palisades, Rigans would build ramparts paralleled by a deep moat. Along the moat the engineers imagined a series of bastions and half-bastions that, when combined with the other renovations, they expected would shield the suburbs from all potential invaders and thereby give the inner city another layer of insulation.

The suburban plans of Rodenburg and Murer were intended to serve another purpose as well: protection against the annual spring floods. All too often the flooding was severe, even catastrophic, devastating both the inner city and the suburbs about once a decade. Among the worst of these calamities was the great Düna flood of April 1649. As the spring thaw melted the frozen river, blocks of dislodged ice floated downstream where they created a dam that blocked the channel's flow. The waters rose and the city was inundated, causing extensive damage to the city walls and those of the Riga Castle. Still grimmer was the impact on the suburbs, as the deluge destroyed the homes and gardens of Latvians and washed away half the inhabited sand dune known as Kube Hill. Also wiped out were the new bridges located at the city's main entrances, as well as all the buildings on the islands of the Düna River.[84]

The tragedy also provided an opportunity to rebuild and improve. According to the plans of Sweden's engineers, the irregular suburban network of winding roads was to be replaced by a grid of parallel and perpendicular streets protected by an outer line of defense at a distance of several hundred meters from the inner fortifications. Exactly how much was accomplished in the suburbs at this time is hard to say, for when the Muscovites attacked in the summer of 1656 the outer districts were once again burned in order to free up an esplanade for the city's defense: such a dead zone would provide the enemy with little in the way of cover. It seems, however, that by the time of the Muscovite siege a ditch running from the Sand Road to the Düna—a line that corresponds to present-day Elizabeth Street—had been completed. Furthermore, the Speķupe rivulet (a now-disappeared tributary of the Düna) had by this time been widened into a defensive moat south and east of the city that was linked to the inner canal near the Sand Bastion.[85] To reach Riga by land, its enemies would now have to contend with a second line of defense.

By the time of the Muscovite siege, thirty years of Swedish efforts to improve the city's fortifications had transformed the city's defensive shell and its suburbs, but much work remained to be done, especially in the outlying districts. While the star-shaped Fort Kobron, opposite the old city on the other side of the Düna, had been completed and now garrisoned around one hundred soldiers, the larger fortress at Dünamünde at the river's mouth was still in the process of construction. The revamping of the suburban areas located east and south of the city, as well as the planned Citadel on the northern side, would not be completed until after the Russians were driven back.

1656: The Muscovite Siege

Tsar Alexei's attack on Riga in August 1656 was part of a larger campaign to overturn an arrangement that for nearly forty years had succeeded in creating a Swedish barrier between Russia and the West that was circumvented only by going through Russia's far northern White Sea port at Archangel. Having deprived Russia of direct access to the Baltic by seizing a thin strip of territory along the coast, Sweden had managed to divert much of Russia's export trade to the Baltic towns; in such manner, Stockholm was able to tax and control Russia's commercial interaction with the West. Russian officials continued to grumble about the unfairness of local commercial regulations, for the Muscovites were considered "guests" in Riga and the other Livonian ports and were not allowed to have direct contacts with merchants from western Europe; this was the prerogative of the authorized Livonian traders alone.

To facilitate their transactions with Riga's middlemen, Russian merchants were, in fact, permitted to stay in the city, but were treated shabbily. It was not until the 1640s that the Russians had their own guest house, and even then it was unsuitably small and located outside the city walls. Russian merchants in Riga were especially vexed by the house master, Jürgen Striess, whom they accused of abusing his position, notably by charging a 1 percent commission on all the transactions he brokered, while also collecting various fees from his guests.[86] Humiliations like these, the Muscovites believed, would come to an end only when Russia had established a military presence in the Baltic.

While one detachment of Tsar Alexei's army struck at Swedish Ingria, the main force marched along the shores of the Düna in the direction of Riga and the sea. As the outlet for an enormous and prosperous hinterland and a linchpin of commerce with the Dutch and English, Riga was the tsar's primary target, for control over the city would give Muscovy an important outlet for its fibers, grain, timber, tallow, and other goods. Indeed, it was through Riga, the most direct and nearest route to western Europe, that Russian goods would find their buyers. But first, the city had to be conquered.

After capturing a series of fortresses along the Düna River, the tsar's forces, many times larger than those commanded by the Swedes, set up camp around Riga in three groups during the fourth week of August.[87] The main group, headed personally by the tsar, decamped south of the city in the area around present-day Ķengarags. It was here that the Russians, possessing six cannons, concentrated their heavy artillery. Meanwhile, a second force set itself up opposite the city in Überdüna (Pārdaugava), and a third was positioned in the north in the pastures by what is now called Sarkandaugava.

Once the Russians received word on August 24 that the Swedes had rejected their demands, the siege began. To prevent the enemy from reaching the city's inner fortifications, the suburbs were burned to the ground, reduced to little more than a smoldering dead zone.[88] The arrival on August 26 of a small flotilla carrying war materials alleviated the siege, but the benefit to Sweden was only temporary, as commercial life in Riga nearly ground to a halt and deliveries of food and other necessities nearly ceased.[89]

The worst of the struggle came in September as the Russians strafed the besieged city with thousands of cannonballs, some weighing as much as two hundred pounds. A main target was the tower of St. Peter's, which was partially damaged, while many other buildings and homes were destroyed completely. Needing to feed their soldiers even as Riga's wealthiest citizens attempted to flee, Swedish authorities squeezed the city for supplies of food as hundreds of its residents succumbed to starvation. Among the siege's 1,600 victims were seven members of the town council, twenty-three merchants of the Great Guild, and three teachers of the Dome School. Bodies of the deceased were stacked in the city's churches, leaving little standing room for parishioners, and minimal space for more corpses. So great was the stench of death in Riga's houses of worship that for several months church services had to be conducted in the hall of the Great Guild.[90]

While the arrival on September 11 of a force of 1,400 Swedes might have given the burghers hope for a timely end to the siege—after all, Russia still lacked a navy capable of blockading the Düna—it was the spread of disease among the Muscovite soldiers that was perhaps the decisive factor behind Russia's failure to take Riga. Indeed, fifty days of being encamped outside the city walls had left the Russian forces in pitiable condition: by the time the siege ended on October 5, many had fallen victim to plague. For those still enjoying good health, an increasingly attractive alternative to a miserable death was desertion.[91]

With winter approaching and his armies suffering from the strain of having mounted three major campaigns in three years, the twenty-seven-year-old tsar pulled his forces back to Polotsk. Whereas the Muscovites had experienced success in Dorpat, whose neglected fortifications garrisoned a mere 750 soldiers, they had simply never encountered fortifications as sophisticated as the system the Swedes were perfecting in Riga. The struggle between Muscovy and Sweden continued elsewhere in Livonia, but there would be no further Muscovite attacks on Riga during the long rein of Tsar Alexei.[92]

Not only had the Russians failed to take Sweden's most important port, they had also failed to achieve Alexei's objective of improving trade links with the West, Riga's Muscovite house having burned down during the war. Although Russia's Baltic trade gradually recovered (and the Russian merchants were once again given a modest house in a Riga suburb), increasingly it was to the port at Narva rather than Riga that Russian merchants traveled to conduct their business. The problem could be chalked up in part to the municipality's own restrictions, for the "Regulations for the Muscovite Commercial Establishment in Riga," issued in 1663, only hindered the growth of the Russian trade.[93]

Eventually the Russians began to return to Riga. By the time Tsar Alexei died in 1676, the annual volume of Muscovy's exports to Riga regularly reached 40,000 thalers—evidence that Russian supplies of hemp, grains (hempseed, linseed), and naval goods (timber, potash, tallow) were responding to a rising demand for such products in the West. In 1700, at the height of Swedish power in the Baltic, Muscovite merchants owed debts of some 81,745 thalers to thirty-two Riga merchants, a clear indication that commerce between them had grown substantially by the end of the century.[94]

Having reoriented itself away from Siberian furs and toward the grains and naval supplies produced in northwestern Russia, the Muscovite state's breakthrough to the Baltic had already begun, despite Alexei's military failure and despite the uncertainties that followed his death at the age of forty-six. The mission of completing this process, and of fulfilling Russia's promise as a great military power, would fall to the youngest of Alexei's thirteen children, the sea-loving Westernizer Peter Alexeyevich Romanov.

Modernization

For their loyalty to the Swedish crown during the Muscovite siege, the men who controlled Riga's institutions were duly rewarded. As Alfred Bilmanis (Alfrēds Bīlmanis) wrote in his classic *A History of Latvia* (1951), "The valorous repulse of the Tsarist forces by the Riga militia in 1656 inspired Charles X to ennoble all sixteen of the city councilors and permit them to crown the lion of Riga's coat of arms."[95] While they might have appreciated the gesture, the citizens of Riga, no less than the Livonian nobility, could hardly ignore the absolutist tendencies of their Swedish rulers. To such men (and one woman) the adage "that which was once given can easily be taken away" readily applied.

This the landlords of Livonia and Estonia discovered when King Charles XI (Karl XI; r. 1672–1697), in an effort both to raise revenue for the crown and to force the nobility into submission, carried out a "reduction" of the great estates starting in 1680.[96] A program of confiscation disguised as state reform, the reductions meant that those fiefs that had been granted both to Swedish and local noblemen after 1632 were now to revert to the state. It was this act above all, affecting some five-sixths of all estates in Swedish Livland (and half those in Estland), that angered the German landowners and eroded their loyalty to the crown, for they saw the reductions as a violation of the local privileges that the monarch had agreed to uphold. While the legal and educational reforms of Charles XI, and perhaps most famously his then-radical proposal that serfdom be abolished,[97] earned him the local reputation of a "peasants' king," the Livonian nobility were far less smitten with a ruler whose untimely death in 1697 may have been the only thing that prevented the complete emancipation of the Latvian and Estonian peasantry. The loyalty of the local aristocracy would be put to the test during the Great Northern War.

To remark that defending Sweden's possessions was no less difficult than acquiring them is no slight to the successors of Gustavus II Adolphus, all of whom were committed to preserving the empire and were aware of Riga's value to the enterprise. Increasingly it was from Riga that Western countries purchased the masts and boards they required to build their ships, as well as the grain needed for daily sustenance. As money poured in from its surging exports during the 1670s and 1680s, Riga was at last in a position to challenge Danzig's status as the leading port of the eastern Baltic. The state's coffers swelling with revenues from the collection of portage taxes and license fees, Swedish authorities were able to resume the vital work of improving the city's defenses against three of Riga's most dangerous enemies: foreign aggressors, fire, and floods.

Of the building projects of the period, the most significant was the Citadel, located on an expanse of land on the northern side of the city where more modest fortifications had stood since the fifteenth century. Intended to house the city's military garrison as well as its high-ranking officials and officers, the Citadel would become the most heavily fortified part of Riga. The first plans for the Citadel appeared around 1650, but the Muscovite siege interrupted the initial preparations, and Rodenburg never got to carry out this project. Only in 1674 did the construction of the Citadel really get underway, by which time the work of fortifying and modernizing Riga was in the hands of an industrious Swede named Erik Dahlberg.

During the same years that his better-known contemporary, the aristocrat Sébastien Le Prestre de Vauban (1633–1707), was making his name by supervising the construction of a series of massive, star-shaped fortifications along the borders of King Louis XIV's France, the low-born Erik Dahlberg (1625–1703) was quietly earning a similar reputation by building more than fifty fortifications throughout the Swedish empire.[98] Ennobled in the 1660s for his distinguished military service, the "Swedish Vauban" rose to become an engineer, the governor-general of Swedish Livonia, and eventually a field marshal, a position he held at the time of his death in 1703. Keeping costs low on his many projects by employing gangs of soldiers who worked for a small supplement to their regular pay, it was Dahlberg who brought the Citadel project to completion in 1697.

Surrounded by moats and earthen ramparts, the Citadel was equipped with two ravelins and six bastions—each named after a member of the Swedish royal line. While the new fortification was separate from the Riga Castle, it was connected to it and to the city through a series of underground passages beneath the bastions. The same principles that had been applied to the Dünamünde fortress at the marshy mouth of the Düna were implemented at the Citadel: although geometrically precise and symmetrical, these Baroque fortifications were built with little thought to their topographical setting. The most radical idea, proposed by the engineer George Palmstruck in 1692, envisioned the creation of a fortified belt that united the Citadel not only to the castle and the city, but also to the Lastadia suburb in the south. This ambitious plan was never realized in practice.

Nevertheless, the century's last decades witnessed major improvements to the city's fortifications. All five of the city's bastions and both its ravelins received upgrades, and a new ravelin was built between the Pancake and Bath House bastions. The new construction meant that any buildings standing in the way would have to be razed—the fate of some forty-five structures in the incorporated areas that had formerly been suburban. Most affected by the renovations were the city's Latvians inhabitants, whose compensation rarely equaled their losses.[99] German and Swedish estate owners were also inconvenienced by the upgrades: with the erection of a new line of suburban palisades in 1692–1693 along what is now Dzirnavu iela, agricultural properties belonging to Balzer Fritsch, Olaf Bengtssonn, and Brand Marquart were incorporated into the outer defensive system.[100] Now Riga's suburbs were to be defended by two teams of soldiers, one with eleven companies and the other with ten, for a total of 122 men.[101]

The suburban project was continuous with the plans hatched by Rodenburg and Murer in the 1650s. As noted, their schemes envisioned the creation of a regular street grid that characteristically ignored the area's topographical features, in particular its wetlands and many small bodies of water. In general, however, the districts just outside the city retained their rural character through the end of the seventeenth century: it was only under Russian rule during the first half of the eighteenth century that the suburbs became more densely settled with wooden houses. Of the structures built in the suburbs during Swedish times, no church or manor house or hospital survives today, for these wooden districts were always burned when an enemy approached.

Like the rising waters that inundated the city about once every decade, fire was a sobering reality to Riga's inhabitants, especially during times of war. Sometimes the conflagrations were caused by bombardments, at other times the flames might be sparked by a lightning storm or a simple accident. The worst of the fires that occurred on Sweden's watch was the inferno of May 21, 1677, which not only damaged the churches of St. John and St. Peter, but reduced to ashes nearly all the buildings on present-day Grēcinieku, Peldu and Audeju ielas. The flames also consumed half the homes on Mārstaļu iela, Jauniela, and other nearby streets—areas that some historians believe had been continuously inhabited by Lettish and Livish salt and beer porters until the fire forced them to relocate.[102] Altogether some 250 domiciles and warehouses were burned to the ground.[103] Since random sparks could set homes ablaze even during times of peace, it was for good reason that the kilns used for baking bricks were allowed only outside the city walls. It was the misfortune of Governor General Krister Horn to inform the Swedish king that "on June 3, 1684 there was a fire in the suburbs: all of Lastadia burned, beginning with the limestone kiln . . . 140 houses altogether [were destroyed]."[104]

A third great fire broke out in 1689, this time in the belt between the earthen ramparts and the inner walls. Destroyed were 235 wooden homes and dozens of other structures that had been built into the city walls. Many homes belonging to Lithuanian residents were lost to the flames, as well the convent built by Riga mayor Francis Nienstedt during the Polish era. Catastrophe, however, was quickly followed by renewal. With the city now prohibiting wooden constructions in the area between the wall and the ramparts, the scorched zone became a new staging point for stone structures—that is, dwelling houses for its wealthier citizens. Gradually the distinction between the largely German inner city and the wall-rampart ring that hitherto had been the preserve of non-Germans disappeared as the poorer parts of the city were given over to a seventeenth-century version of gentrification.[105]

The examples cited above demonstrate an enduring facet of life in early modern Riga: while a great fire might wipe out an entire neighborhood, such a catastrophe would also provide a clean slate for city planners. Indeed, it was the great fire of 1812, set by Russian military officials in Riga's suburban districts in the mistaken belief that Napoleon's forces were on their way to Riga, that made possible the outer city's dramatic transformation after the 1850s.

Baroque Riga

The busiest time for Riga's construction workers was the decade that ended with the outbreak of the Great Northern War: of the fifty-seven domiciles built in Riga between 1660 and 1700, more than half appeared in the 1690s.[106] During these same years many existing homes were modernized and updated, in some cases taking on an appearance that would have been familiar to anyone who had set eyes upon Amsterdam or Holland's other bustling cities, for now it was Dutch influence that came to bear most strikingly on the architecture of inner Riga. Influence from southern Germany could also be seen in the new structures—for example, the reconstructed house of the Great Guild, the meeting place of Riga's wealthiest citizens, to which a richly decorated northern façade was added in the 1690s.

But it is with the name Rupert Bindenschu (1645–1698), the city's master builder during the last quarter of the seventeenth century, that the history of Riga's Swedish-era architecture begins. Born in Strasbourg and trained as a carpenter, Bindenschu arrived in Riga in 1671 and immediately began work on a variety of projects in the region. After assisting in the reconstruction of St. Olaf's in Reval, Bindenschu was called upon to reconstruct St. Peter's in Riga, whose Gothic tower had collapsed during a storm in 1666—and then, after being rebuilt, was consumed by the great fire of 1677. Placed in charge of rebuilding the Riga skyline's most iconic structure, between 1688 and 1692 Bindenschu and his team restored the church's façade and tower in grand fashion, creating a Baroque masterpiece that for a time was the tallest wooden structure in the world.[107]

Having also rebuilt the Jesus Church in the Lastadia suburb, Bindenschu was additionally connected with the construction of several significant dwelling houses built in the style of Dutch classicism, a genre notable for its restraint and simplicity. An exceptionally well-maintained example of the form, which flourished not only in the cities of the Netherlands, but also in the Dutch colonies and in the Protestant parts of northern Europe, is located at Mārstaļu iela 2/4, the site of a home that was built for the town councilor Johann von Reutern (1666–1714). A *kontor* house—that is, an edifice that functioned both as a domicile and a warehouse—that featured the highest ceilings and the tallest windows in Riga, the Reutern House was built to impress and entertain; as such, it was well suited to a wealthy merchant who was known for his extravagances. With its smooth façade contrasted by the detailed ornamentation that surrounds its portals, this Baroque palace, presently being used by the Union of Journalists, remains pleasing to the eye even as its main floor currently serves as an unremarkable rock-and-roll bar.

Far sadder is the condition of the Dannenstern House, which is located at the end of Mārstaļu iela and dates to 1696. The building's boarded-up windows and crumbling portals, not to mention the flourish of graffiti—one of the great shames of today's Riga—tell the tale of this structure's heartbreaking decline. Three centuries ago the Dannenstern House was one of the largest detached homes in all Riga and a perfect representation of the lifestyle of Riga's political, economic, and cultural elite at the height of Swedish power.

While its authorship is unconfirmed—all indications once again point to Bindenschu—the home's original owner was a Dutch merchant named Ernst Metsu (d. 1721). Relocating from Amsterdam to Riga around 1690, Metsu made his fortune in the lumber business and acquired a fleet of some 150 ships, many of which were built in Riga using the same shipbuilding materials that Riga exported to the West.[108] Ennobled by the King of Sweden, Riga's wealthiest man was granted the title "von Dannenstern" and enjoyed considerable status in his adopted city. Visible at the time from across the Düna, Metsu's grand house, a two-story building with a basement and five attic floors for the storage of goods, was intended to reflect the merchant's elevated status. Neglected for many decades and now sadly dilapidated, the building retains its original Baroque façade along with classical elements such as Corinthian pilasters, a frieze, and pediments crowning the bays that frame the house's two monumental entrances, built of dolomite and sandstone.[109]

Among those known to have visited the Dannenstern House were Count Ernst Johann von Biron—an unpopular Duke of Courland (r. 1737–1740, 1763–1769) whose influence on Empress Anna (r. 1730–1740) was so great that for a time he practically ruled the Russian Empire—and later the conductor Richard Wagner, who worked and lived in Riga in the 1830s. Earlier, of course, there had been Peter the Great: having conquered the city in 1710, he returned to Riga on several occasions and visited Metsu at his home, for the two men shared an interest in naval affairs, trade, and shipbuilding.[110] Such were the comings and goings at this stately house near the quay. More than just a domicile, the Dannenstern House

Figure 13. Dannenstern House, 2009. Once the largest domicile in Riga, the Dannenstern House belonged to the wealthy merchant Ernst Metsu. Photo by Sergey Alekseev.

was a palace for entertaining, where performances were staged in a grand hall. That such an important cultural landmark appears to be on the verge of collapse is a reminder of how much of old Riga has been lost to the ravages of fire and war—and to ordinary neglect.[111]

It is fortunate, then, that city authorities turned their attention to a decaying old home at Grēcinieku iela 18. Built by the town councilor and glazier Jürgen Helm in 1695 and restored as a museum in the early 1990s, the richly adorned Mentzendorff House, named for a merchant family that occupied the building until 1939, was both a family home and a pharmacy. (At one time it was known for selling the best coffee in Riga.) Its walls and ceilings covered with decorative and allegorical paintings from the eighteenth century, few homes in Riga give a clearer impression of how Riga's wealthier inhabitants lived at the end of the Swedish era and in the eighteenth century. While critics charge that faulty restorative work ruined the original façade, at least the Mentzendorff House, like the homes that once belonged to the Metsu and Reutern families, was saved; of the many other homes built in Riga during these times, only a handful remain.

But what of the more modest structures occupied by the less affluent? Less impressive than the *Stadtpaläste* (urban palaces) belonging to the city's wealthiest merchants were the side-gabled buildings inhabited by ordinary Rigans. As noted, after the fire of 1689 there was a building boom in the area between the wall and the ramparts, including much of the territory that had once been occupied by the stagnant Riga rivulet, a public nuisance that was gradually being covered and filled in. With the prohibition on wooden houses extended to what had once been Riga's suburbs, buildings of stone construction began to typify these areas. Thus, the modest expanse from today's Vaļņu iela (indicating the former location of the city ramparts) to Wagnera iela (named for Richard Wagner) was soon characterized by dense clusters of masonry houses with long façades that were three or more stories in height.[112]

But it was the warehouse building above all that typified the construction of the last third of the seventeenth century, for the older merchant homes were simply too small to accommodate the boom in Riga's exports. The city needed new storage facilities. Built of brick and stone and roofed with tiles, warehouses built in the seventeenth century were large and relatively unadorned except around the portals, whose decorations were typically indicative of the business activities of their owners. On some of these aging warehouses one can still see the old iron anchors and crosses as well as indications of the ancient lifting devices that hoisted merchandise up to the storage attic. Most were torn down during the renovations of the late nineteenth century, yet some two dozen of these aging buildings remain scattered about the Old Town in varying states of disrepair.

Notes on Culture, Enlightenment, and Nationality in Swedish Riga

The task of reconstructing Riga's physical transformation belongs to historians, cartographers, and archaeologists, who have at their disposal the many maps drawn by Sweden's military engineers, a documented record of events, and tools for digging. The challenges facing scholars of Riga's cultural history—its religious life and its music, theater, and entertainment—are perhaps more daunting. Aside from texts of a religious nature, dictionaries, the German-language newspaper *Rigische Novellen* (est. 1681), and some legal publications, historians have relatively few written records with which to reconstruct the cultural atmosphere in Riga during the "good old Swedish times."

To consider one example: in the absence of recordings, sheet music, drawings, or illustrations, what can be known with certainty about the popular music and entertainment enjoyed by Rigans of the seventeenth century? We last broached the topic of popular amusements in chapter 3, which examined the ways that city elites celebrated their festival holidays during the later Middle Ages. There we observed how such occasions were dominated by music, banquets, and the quaffing of copious amounts of beer. In the guild houses and in the House of Blackheads, hired musicians would bleat their horns and bang their drums before their processions spilled into the nearby streets and market square. That musical companies performed at the major feasts and above all during Carnival (Shrovetide) celebrations would not have distinguished Riga in the least, for such activities took place everywhere in Europe in the fifteenth and sixteenth centuries.

Perhaps the most significant development in Riga's musical culture after the Reformation was the appearance of the choir. As a Lutheran musical culture emerged in northern Germany, the singing of liturgical music by trained choirs became common throughout the Baltic world and gave rise to similar (and enduring) traditions in Riga and in the Latvian and Estonian lands.[113] Even as choral music developed a diverse array of characteristics, the arrival in Livonia of the Lutheran custom of singing hymns at church services was a clear demonstration of how the Baltic Sea was a transmitter of ideas and culture—in this case, a specifically Lutheran culture that was heavily promoted by the Swedish authorities.

The first choirs in Riga predated Swedish rule by a century, for it was during the Reformation that the boys of the Dome School were trained to sing. Often they would be called upon to perform at the funeral ceremonies of Riga's more distinguished citizens, as it was forbidden to bury the dead without funeral songs. The Dome School boys also performed in plays of a didactic character. Known as "school dramas," these performances were typically based on Biblical themes, and they provide just one example of the overwhelmingly religious orientation of popular entertainment at the end of the Middle Ages.

Liturgical music emerged as one of the most significant forms of cultural expression in Swedish Riga and Livonia, where German-language hymnals were published in 1615, 1631, 1660, and 1664. The appearance of Latvian editions suggests one method by which Livonia's Swedish authorities attempted to regulate liturgical worship in both congregations.[114] But it was only with the imposition of the Swedish Church Order in Livonia and Estonia in 1690—four years after it was introduced in Sweden proper—that the relationship between church and state was clarified.[115] Stipulating that all official correspondence be in Swedish, the regulations were aimed partly at getting the region's German nobility used to the Swedish language. Such efforts to impose top-down "Swedification" measures, appearing at the same time as the "reductions" proposed by Charles XI, doubtless played a significant role in the Livonian nobility's growing alienation from the Swedish crown.

If the new regulations aimed at imposing greater uniformity on religious practice in the empire, it seems there was ample room for individual artistic expression in the performance of the liturgy. This was especially true of church organists, whose job was to perform hymnal music by turns with (or accompanying) the choir, which had its own separate stall in every church.[116] In Riga the best-known performer of hymnal music at this time was Johann Valentin Meder (1649–1719). A singer, composer, and musical director who served as *Kantor* (organist and musical supervisor) in Riga from 1700 until his death, his works continue to be performed on the famous pipe organ at the Riga Cathedral.[117] Another major contributor to Swedish Riga's cultural heritage was Johannes Breverus (1616–1700). A Lutheran theologian, professor of poetry and rhetoric at the Riga gymnasium, and pastor at St. Peter's Church, Breverus compiled a collection of four hundred hymns that was repeatedly republished. So revered in Riga was Breverus that a later writer devoted a book to his life and works.[118]

But while we know that hymns were sung in church—thanks to Breverus, scholars even know *which* hymns were sung—what was chanted and performed in the streets by professional entertainers or ordinary people whilst amusing themselves and each other is far less clear. Also unclear is the influence of foreigners on Riga's cultural life. During an era remembered for ships and shipping, the Baltic Sea was also an agent of cross-cultural pollination—a highway that brought news, ideas, and fashions to Livonia as readily as it did salt, wine, and beer. Among the people who carried Europe's vibrant cultural life to Riga were touring companies of thespians and jokesters from England and Holland, Italy and Germany. Of the individuals who journeyed to Riga to sing and dance and spin stories we know almost nothing; such are the fates of the itinerant and illiterate. However, we do know something of their circumstances: for example, since theater was banned in England between 1642 and 1660, performing troupes from that troubled country would appear in other European cities to earn a living. Some came to Danzig and Riga, overcoming the language barrier by performing well-known stories (such as "The Prodigal Son") with the exaggerated use of gestures and mimicry. Some performed in German as well.[119]

Given these rather impressionistic observations of the street scene in Riga, it must be admitted that not a lot is known about the way Germans and Latvians living in Riga entertained themselves in their own homes or among friends and family in the seventeenth century. The simple fact is that little of what went on in the private world of premodern Rigans was ever written down. The scanty historical record in the area of secular entertainment—popular music, storytelling, and street performance; jesting and joking, gambling and games—continues to leave much to the imagination.

When writing about Old Livonia, the Baltic German writers of the nineteenth and early twentieth centuries preferred to focus on political, military, and religious developments, while demonstrating a notably positive attitude toward Swedish Protestantism. Yet the Baltic Germans had relatively little to say about cultural affairs in Riga during the Swedish era. Influenced by modern nationalism and sensitive to St. Petersburg's Russification policies, the Baltic Germans saw Old Riga as a fundamentally Teutonic city and showed mixed feelings for the "good old Swedish times," not least due to the centralizing efforts that inevitably undermined a local (German) administration that had always been in the hands of the Rath.

On the other hand, Latvian historians of the first republic, like their Estonian counterparts, tended to view the era of Swedish rule rather more favorably, in part because they saw in these times the first stirrings of local (Latvian) national consciousness and activism. After the establishment of a Latvian state, Latvian historians were especially keen to develop the Latvian grand narrative by demonstrating the existence of a *Latvian* culture in Riga during the Middle Ages and beyond.[120] Lending credence to this notion, and to the likelihood that a community of Latvian readers had emerged by this time, was the appearance in 1632 of the newspaper *Latweeschu awihse* (Latvian gazette) under the auspices of the Swedish postmaster; these years also witnessed the production of a few books in Latvian.[121]

To illustrate further the state of Latvia's literary culture during the Swedish years, let us consider the biographies of two churchmen who were active in and around Riga. The first is Johann Ernst Glück (1652–1705), a Lutheran pastor and educator who earned some fame in Livonia for his religious and scholarly endeavors. Born in Wettin (Saxony), Glück completed his studies at Wittenberg and Leipzig and soon thereafter became a missionary preacher in Livonia. While living in Riga and its environs, the German parson acquired a good knowledge of the peasants' languages and translated various religious works into Latvian. In the view of Latvian historians, Glück's most important achievement was his translation of the Old and New Testaments from Hebrew and Greek into Latvian. For this King Charles XI, who, like all Swedish rulers, supported the strengthening of Lutheranism in Riga and Livonia, allocated 7,500 thalers to offset the costs of printing.[122]

Here, then, is the story of how an educated German delivered to the Latvian people the written word by which they might come to know God—and ultimately themselves and their own history and destiny as a *tauta* (nation). Indeed, the history of Livonia in the eighteenth and nineteenth centuries was to be populated not only by cruel landlords who whipped and beat their serfs, but also with well-intentioned Baltic Germans who learned the local languages, compiled dictionaries, and collected Latvian stories and folk songs. While the very notion that Latvians benefited from a long period of German "tutelage" may elicit some vocal (and understandable) objections, it is in such a context that we may best appreciate Glück's contribution to the nation's history.[123]

Let us now turn to another man of God, one whose achievements have become known largely through the work of later Latvian scholars—which is to say that he was and remains virtually unknown outside the country. Johann Reuter (Jānis Reiters; ca. 1632–ca. 1697) was probably the first academically educated Latvian, and as such he is a unique reflection of the efforts that Livonia's Swedish rulers made to educate boys who came from all kinds of backgrounds. Not only did Riga have a gymnasium at the Dome School that prepared students for careers in theology and law, but after 1675 it also had a Swedish lyceum known as the Charles (Karl) School that admitted students without discrimination on the basis of nationality or social standing.[124] That Swedes, Germans, and others who had the means to educate their children were free to send them to Riga's schools—these now existed even for Latvians—opened up opportunities for a rather sizable number of non-Germans.

Born in 1632, Reuter could not have studied at the lyceum, as it had yet to open. Instead, this son of what we may presume to have been a rather well-to-do craftsman studied at the Dome School, where on September 10, 1650, he acquired a German surname and, as such, was effectively Germanized—the fate of all educated Latvian men in Riga.[125] Yet Reuter never lost touch with his Latvian roots. Having studied theology at the Academia Gustaviana in Dorpat (est. 1632),[126] he tried to get a stipend from the Riga Town Council for further education but was rejected—likely due to his Latvian background, for a highly educated Latvian was still rather exceptional during these times.[127] Undeterred, Reuter went on to study many languages and over the years he held numerous posts in various churches throughout Livonia—all while publishing an array of theological works, including a collection of prayers in forty languages (*Oratio Dominica XL linguarem*, 1662). Among them were prayers in Latvian.

It was Reuter's growing reputation as a "Latvian Moses," a lone prophet whose mission was to deliver his people from slavery, that earned him the enmity of Livonia's ruling class. While serving as the garrison pastor at Kokenhusen, the polyglot Reuter preached the Gospel not only in German and Swedish, but also in the Finnish and Latvian languages. It was, of course, his Latvian-language preaching that endeared him to the local peasants, who flocked from nearby parishes and from as far away as Courland to hear him speak, even as neighboring landowners forbade their serfs from attending his sermons. Hatred of Reuter among the nobility grew so great that when he tried to save his books and manuscripts in Riga during the great fire of May 1677, the pastor was arrested, accused of having started the fire himself.[128] Although he was not prosecuted, Reuter was forced to leave his homeland and ended up teaching in Swedish Ingria near the Russian border.

The fate of Reuter's literary work is arguably no less tragic than that of a life cut off from the place of one's birth, as many of his original works were lost for various reasons. Among them was the Book of St. Matthew that he had translated into Latvian in 1664, some twenty years before Glück completed his translation of the Bible. Although such losses were typical (the collection and preservation of writings had not yet become systematized in the eastern Baltic), the disappearance of Reuter's translations and commentaries were a great loss to Latvia's cultural heritage, for these were the first literary works by a true Latvian intellectual.

One historian who has made this point with some force is Jānis Straubergs. The early chapters of his *Rīgas vēsture* (1937; The history of Rīga), written after the founding of the first Republic of Latvia, are especially concerned with restoring the centrality of Latvians to the history of old Riga. In Straubergs's view, the first significant activist in the cause of the Latvian nation came not from the community of Baltic Germans but from a circle of relatively prosperous Riga Latvians. Johann Reuter, in other words, represents a group of Latvians living in Riga in the seventeenth century that had not yet lost its freedom, whose members were materially well off, and who were strongly dissatisfied with the elite's efforts to delimit the rights of Latvians in Riga.[129]

The case of Johann Reuter naturally raises the question of the legal and social status of "non-Germans" in Riga during the Swedish era. In earlier chapters we have seen how the distinctions between the Latvians (including the increasingly bilingual Livs) and Germans living in Riga sharpened between the fourteenth and sixteenth centuries. Germans and non-Germans had distinctive lines of work, wore different clothing, and de facto lived in separate parts of the city. Although far better off than the serfs in the countryside, the Latvians and Livs (to whom we may also add Lithuanians) of Riga were, due to their relative poverty, relegated to the city's physical and social margins. As German society isolated itself from Latvian society, it reserved for itself certain rights and privileges, some of which were once enjoyed by the non-Germans who joined one of the city's several dozen craft brotherhoods. It is in the brotherhoods of craftsmen that the social delineation between German and non-German becomes most evident in the documentary record of the seventeenth century.

The ethnic/social division was even more stark among Riga's merchants. Of the several hundred "great traders" of the Swedish era (i.e., merchants who did business with traders from the West), none are known to have been Latvian—after all, dealing with overseas trade was a privilege reserved for Germans and other Westerners. If there were among any of these merchant families one or two with a Latvian background, such men were of course no longer Latvian, for any Latvian who learned German and was accepted into German society was in fact now a German. Since those who spoke the German language typically believed that they belonged to a higher culture and civilization, one's identity as a "German" was as much an indicator of social status and cultural orientation as it was a marker of ethnicity. Thus, a person who was born into a Latvian family could, under the right circumstances, *become* a German. Such was the case, as we have seen, with the theologian Johann Reuter.

Although the historical record is less clear on this matter, it also seems likely that a German of humble social standing could, simply as a consequence of the type of labor he performed, become Latvianized. If one becomes the company one keeps, there is no reason to think that Germans who for whatever reason did transport or warehouse work would not have eventually merged into the Latvian population. Although social mobility was very limited in Riga at this time, even in the dark it was a two-way street.

The complexity of nationality in Riga is also revealed in property matters. Up to Swedish times, those Latvians who still possessed real estate in the city continued to enjoy "householder rights" that were the same as those belonging to any German; as such, these Latvians were legally distinct from those who possessed no real estate and therefore had no rights as householders. But such were the conditions in the seventeenth century that when the Latvians who lost their homes in the fire of 1677 moved to the suburbs, their loss of householder rights threatened the rights of all Latvians living in Riga.[130] In other words, the city's non-Germans did not lose all their rights at the moment of the German conquest or even during the three centuries that followed: despite the regulations that were introduced in the Middle Ages concerning guild membership and real estate ownership, it was only gradually that Latvians living in Riga lost their rights. Even as conditions for peasants improved dramatically in the countryside, in Riga the Swedish era saw the continuation of a process that would culminate in the total loss of rights for Latvians during the first century of Russian rule.

Still, when calamity came to the rural districts, it was to German Riga that the Latvian peasants would flock. Consider, for example, the impact on the city of the appearance at the city gates of thousands of peasant refugees in 1601. With the countryside in the midst of a famine, many settled on the outskirts of Riga, planted gardens, and resumed their traditional crafts. Some joined the ranks of Riga's beekeepers, for beekeeping was a traditional Latvian activity that was viewed with disdain by brotherhoods of craftsmen. Their members were forbidden from having social contact with the beekeepers, for the latter stood at the lowest rung of Latvian society. As the city swelled with peasants and craftsmen desperate to escape serfdom or hunger, the number of beekeepers—a socially marginalized group even among the Latvians—grew by a similar proportion.[131] One could not simply show up in Riga, take up a craft, and assimilate into urban life, for even when the population swelled with refugees, the non-German immigrants were still considered outsiders—a threat to the livelihood of Riga's predominantly German craftsmen.

Entry into the established craft guilds or brotherhoods was tightly controlled according to regulations known as *Schragen*. These were almost always written in Low German and were far more favorable to Riga's Germans than to its non-Germans.[132] To themselves the Germans reserved certain crafts—for example, only Germans were allowed to work with gold and other precious metals. Less desirable crafts and occupations were left to non-Germans—transportation and warehouse work, weaving, keeping bees, and so on. In some cases, however, there were separate brotherhoods for Germans and Latvians employed in the same craft: this was the case for carpenters, cobblers, and masons. As these crafts faced increasing competition not only from an influx of peasants but also from the outside world—wooden Dutch shoes were all the rage in the seventeenth century, as were Polish ceramics—restrictions were introduced that limited the number of masters and journeymen. To cite just one example: regulations introduced in 1640 in the parallel brotherhoods of German and Latvian masons limited each German master to having three journeymen; a Latvian master, however, could only have two. In some crafts Latvian masters could now employ only one journeyman—an arrangement that invariably worked to the detriment of the Latvian craftsmen.[133]

As the Swedish century wore on, then, opportunities for Latvians to work their way up from apprentice to journeyman to master diminished substantially. Such upward mobility, as limited as it was, collapsed altogether with the onset of the Great Northern War, when Latvians were mobilized en masse into the Swedish army to fight Russia. A clear example is the masons' guild: if four of the thirteen masters of the masons' guild were Latvians in 1706, by 1713 that number had shrunk to zero. No more Latvian apprentices would be taken on after Riga's surrender, for an exclusively German masons' brotherhood would be founded in 1731.[134] In this way a trade that had always been in the hands of Latvians was given over completely to Riga's German community.

The intersection of class and nationality in early modern Riga, like the evolving relationship between Germans and non-Germans, has yet to be explored in any systematic way. So significant are the blank spots in this period of Riga's history that even the number of people living in Riga at any given point in the seventeenth century remains a topic of speculation. Historians might have a good sense of *where* Latvians and other non-Germans lived in and around the city, and we know much about the roles each played in the local economy; but how *many* people lived in Riga and its environs can only be guessed at. Did the inner city house some twelve or perhaps even fifteen thousand people at the end of the seventeenth century?[135] If we include the suburban districts, is it possible that Swedish Riga had as many as 30,000 inhabitants?[136] And of these, how many were Latvian?[137] How many German? And what of the Lithuanians, and of the handfuls of Swedes, Dutchmen, Poles, and Russians?

Much remains unknown about the lives of ordinary people in Riga during the "good old Swedish times." In many respects, the century of Swedish rule was better for Rigans and for the people of Livonia than what came afterward—two hundred years of Russian domination, during which the social position of Latvians fell still further and the rights and privileges of the city's German elites were gradually eroded. But the judicious historian of Riga must exercise some caution when wading into the muddied waters of class and nationality, for Riga in the seventeenth century was a city in flux and all the old categories were under challenge. The medieval era now firmly in the past, Riga joined a modernizing world with which it was connected by the hundreds of ships that docked at her harbor each year, bringing European goods and fashions, European science and technology, European news and values.

If the values of seventeenth-century Europe were still premised on the traditions of monarchy, hierarchy, patriarchy, faith, honor, and service, much the same could also be said of Riga, which in 1699 was a bustling port of a Swedish empire then seemingly at the height of its power. But in all important respects the characteristics of Riga were neither Swedish—even if the city's coat of arms, like its coins, now featured the king's crown—nor entirely German, and they were Latvian only at the margins, for Riga had developed into a multinational yet quintessentially European city, albeit with its own distinctive personality and peculiarities. That it was a fortress town *par excellence* owes much to the organizational genius of Sweden's industrious officials and engineers. The crown's efforts to deter its enemies from attacking Riga by transforming it into an impregnable citadel would be put to the test in the Great Northern War, an epic, exhausting, and ultimately devastating struggle among northern Europe's great powers for mastery over the eastern Baltic Sea.

Chapter 8

"This Accursed Place": The Great Northern War

At church today, I heard a grievous sermon about the destruction of Jerusalem.
The same fate now threatens Riga in our own sorrowful time.
God, save us from the siege![1]

—Riga's surveyor, E. Tolk (1709)

May God grant us grace to avenge ourselves on this accursed place.[2]

—Peter the Great (1710)

The century of Swedish rule ended much the same way it had begun: with a long, drawn-out war whose end result was the death of many thousands and the transfer of authority over Riga to the region's ascendant power. After decades of political stability and commercial vigor, the final years of Swedish dominion over Livonia turned into a nightmare of plagues and floods, invasions and sieges, mass starvation and economic ruin. To say that the last moments of the Swedish century were apocalyptic is to exaggerate only slightly, for the miseries that rained down upon Riga and the eastern Baltic were Biblical in their scale and impact.

So catastrophic were the times that the devastated lands and hollowed-out towns that fell into Russia's hands during the Great Northern War (1700–1721) were depopulated and idle, their surviving inhabitants too weak and emaciated to be of much initial use. While Russia managed to acquire the ports it needed for its new Baltic navy, the war that transformed medieval Muscovy into the Russian Empire brought still greater misery to a region already in turmoil. That the overall population of the eastern Baltic littoral at the beginning of the eighteenth century was smaller than it had been in 1500 underlines the scope and intensity of the disasters.[3] By the time Riga submitted to the tsar in 1710, the city had been reduced to a ghost town, its starving inhabitants exhausted by so many years of war and famine, floods and disease. It was an inauspicious start to what would become two centuries of Russian imperial rule.

The latest crisis began with a great famine in northern Europe, the worst in the history of the eastern Baltic. How many victims it claimed cannot be known, for reliable population statistics did not exist before the introduction of the modern census. To the estimated one-quarter of Finland's population that is believed to have perished in 1696–1697, we may add a comparable proportion of Estonians and Latvians. As tens of thousands starved, grain from Sweden's Baltic provinces continued to flow: some 800,000 tons were exported in the crisis year of 1697.[4] That same year Riga's town council recorded the appearance of 2,250 beggars in the city looking for food.[5] Having endured eight sieges, two civil wars, and numerous outbreaks of pestilence during its first five centuries, Riga faced its greatest calamity to date. The end of what would later be remembered as the "good old Swedish times" was nigh.

The Swedish century was enormously consequential for the city of Riga. As we have seen, the city's submission to the crown in 1621, after twenty years of intermittent warfare between Sweden and Poland, brought with it the restoration of internal order and greater security from outside attack. At the same time, Riga's surrender also quashed any remaining hopes that the city might return to the semi-autonomous status it had enjoyed during the Middle Ages. Although slow to recover from the war that opened the seventeenth century, Swedish Riga eventually became one of Europe's strongest and most admired fortresses, now equipped with bastions and ravelins, its ramparts reinforced, its moats deepened and widened. Swedish military engineers even thought to fortify Riga's suburban districts, where additional lines of defense were created with the digging of "Rodenburg's moat" in the southeast and the erection of a line of palisades in the northeast.

To protect the city from enemies arriving by sea, the Swedes rebuilt an existing stronghold as a bastion-type fortress at the mouth of the mighty river that flowed past Riga, appropriately known as Dünamünde. Directly across the river from the city, they established Fort Kobron, one of several dozen defensive works the Swedish authorities built or rebuilt in the empire's Baltic territories. No expense was spared in perfecting Riga's complex system of fortifications, designed by Sweden's engineers to suit the requirements of a style of a style of warfare that was now based on large, mobile armies and heavy artillery. The port of Riga, the crown's Polish, Danish, and Russian rivals knew well, was the key to Stockholm's domination of the eastern Baltic. Having reached a peak in the middle decades of the seventeenth century, the limits of Swedish power were tested by the Scanian War (1674–1679), when the kingdom nearly lost its most recent territorial acquisitions to Denmark. No longer could Sweden's naval superiority be taken for granted.[6]

It was just at this time that Riga's Swedish authorities upgraded the city's defenses with the construction of the massive, star-shaped Citadel on its northern edge. Housing the Swedish garrison, the Citadel was connected to the old Riga Castle by underground passages and a drawbridge near the Charles (Karl) Gate. But no matter how meticulous and expensive the improvements to the city's fortifications, neither Sweden's overworked engineers nor its audacious military commanders would be able to save the city from its fate during the Great Northern War. Its dwindling population reduced to a few thousand starving burghers and refugees, Riga was to endure a long and harrowing siege only to surrender to Russia's powerful and boldly ambitious tsar.

Few individuals have exercised greater influence on Riga's history than Peter the Great.

The "Insult"

As the first-born child of Alexei Mikhailovich's second wife (she went on to produce twelve more children) and thus a potential threat to the ambitions of the family members of his father's first wife, Peter Alexeyevich Romanov (1672–1725) was raised in a fog of intrigue and danger that at times was not unlike the childhood experiences of Ivan the Terrible, a paranoiac who entertained similar notions about opening up the Baltic Sea to Russian shipping and power. Not to indulge in at least a few details of Peter's extraordinary life would be negligent, for Russia's first emperor was so commanding a figure in Riga's history that in the early years of the twentieth century a bronze equestrian statue of the city's conqueror stood in the city center.[7] That the very same spot has been occupied by the westward-facing Freedom Monument since 1935 constitutes an unmistakable rebuke of the two centuries of Russian domination that began with Riga's submission to the tsar in 1710.

Towering over his peers at more than two meters in height, Peter I was a force of nature who wielded his unlimited powers in a determined effort to overcome what he knew to be Russia's relative backwardness. That his goals were rational and materialist and progressive, while his methods were violent and coercive, has caused some historians to see him as a harbinger of Joseph Stalin, who shared with the tsar similar beliefs about the desired relationship between a powerful state and an acquiescent population.[8] Members of his entourage were subjected to angry blows and cruel humiliations; his eldest son was executed for treason. Pushing aside all resistance, Peter locked away in convents his first wife and a half-sister while taking for his second wife the foster daughter of Johann Ernst Glück, the Livonian pastor and translator who was among the thousands evacuated to Russia during the Great Northern War. The tsar's love of drink and merriment nearly matched his capacity for work and for waging war against Russia's enemies. With a verve and energy that exhausted his officers and servants, the stern and imposing ruler devoted more than half his life to modernizing the Russian state, for it was Peter the Great's ambitions to transform Muscovy into an empire and a great European power.

Peter was especially fascinated by the sea. This feature of his personality was closely connected to his youthful preference for whiling away the hours in Moscow's "German Quarter," where he became friendly with men from Holland, Scotland, England, and Germany. Foreigners were brought to Moscow to make up for what Russia lacked in engineers, craftsmen, technicians, army officers, and doctors, for a growing recognition of the importance of Western knowledge and skills had taken place during the reign of the pious Alexei Mikhailovich during the third quarter of the seventeenth century. A witness (and contributor) to Poland's decline, which he believed Russia should never be allowed to emulate, Tsar Alexei was a cautious modernizer who laid the foundations of a standing army, consolidated the power of the Romanov family, and augmented his patrimony by annexing parts of Ukraine.[9] As we have seen, his attempt to capture Riga in 1656 ended in failure.

The circumstances inherited by Peter, then, were rather fortuitous, for a vigorous demographic expansion during his father's long reign saw the Muscovite population approach eleven million by 1678 at the same time as serfdom was becoming more deeply entrenched. Together these developments gave the country the workforce it would require for an economic opening to the West. By the time Peter became fully sovereign in 1696,[10] Muscovy was on the verge of breaking out of its long isolation, already having begun to take its place as an important supplier of raw materials and semi-processed goods destined for markets in Holland and England.[11]

The groundwork for the country's Westernization having been laid by his predecessors, it was the curious and headstrong Peter who embraced without reservation the notion that Muscovy, increasingly dependent on trade-related revenues, should also adopt European manners and, more to the point, Western technology. Above all, Russia needed a fleet, for without one she would remain hemmed in by her neighbors, unable to project her power and cut off from direct commercial contacts with the West. Indeed, as much as Russia benefited from foreign trade, few of its merchants conducted their business abroad and the country's traditional outlets to the Baltic Sea were in Swedish hands. To end its isolation, Russia must have its own ships and direct access to the Baltic shoreline. Since it was in the shipyards of Holland and England that the world's finest vessels were crafted, these were among the young tsar's destinations when he set off on his "Grand Embassy" in late March of 1697.

Peter's embassy is directly connected to the history of Riga, for the Livonian port was his first stop on the way to the cities of western Europe. Indeed, Riga was the first European city the young ruler had ever seen. But even if the incidents that took place in Riga outraged the tsar and likely influenced the course of events, the

Grand Embassy initially had little to do with the city on the Düna. Its real purpose was to arrange an international solution for dealing with a traditional Muscovite enemy, the Ottoman Empire, for just as Sweden blocked Russia's maritime ambitions in the Baltic, so did the Ottoman Empire hinder Russia's access to the Black Sea and thence to the Mediterranean. To defeat the Turks, Peter began to build a modest navy in the winter of 1695–1696. Russia's conquest of the Turkish fortress at Azov in 1696 loosened Turkey's grip on the Black Sea, but to complete the job, Peter would need allies.

This was the main purpose of the Grand Embassy. Hoping to exploit his recent success against the Ottomans, the tsar intended to pay a series of courtesy calls to friendly European rulers in the hopes of gathering the allies he would need for an anti-Turkish crusade that was in fact of little importance to the European powers. It is possible that even at this early juncture he was pondering the creation of an anti-Swedish alliance with other countries who had territorial disputes with Sweden, but only later would that become the main goal of the tsar's foreign policy.[12]

Perhaps opportunism also played a part in Peter's grand design, for in April 1697, just after Peter's departure from Moscow, a fifteen-year-old who would become known as King Charles XII (Karl XII; r. 1697–1718) ascended the Swedish throne.[13] It was precisely at the time of Charles's accession that word had begun to reach the tsar about the frustrations of the Livonian nobility, some of whom were anxious to break free from Stockholm. To these propitious circumstances we may add the fact that the entire region had just been devastated by a famine. For Peter, the time would soon be ripe to end Russia's war with Turkey and focus on its Baltic ambitions.

It was as a member of this Grand Embassy that the adventuresome monarch, along with a contingent of some 250 men—among them soldiers, interpreters, physicians, musicians, cooks, coachmen, and even four dwarves—first set eyes on the bustling towns of Germany, Holland, and England, where the tsar was to witness for himself the technological advancements that accelerated the rise of western Europe. Traveling incognito to avoid the inconveniences of diplomatic protocol, "Peter Mikhailov" embarked on an expedition—the first such undertaking by any Russian ruler—whose principal destination was the Dutch Republic, where he took on an apprenticeship as a shipbuilder in Zaandam before the leering crowds forced him to move onto Amsterdam, where he labored at the world's largest shipyard. While mastering the craft of shipbuilding during his four months in Holland's restless capital, then Europe's leading center of trade and innovation, Peter also gained invaluable knowledge about how Westerners lived and worked, returning to Russia in 1698 determined to remake his country along western European lines.

The Grand Embassy was a turning point for Peter personally, for the Russian state, and indeed for the continent of Europe. It was also a turning point for Riga, for Peter would later claim as justification for starting the Great Northern War the "insult" he had suffered in Riga at the embassy's start. Even if the notion that such a minor incident was the proximate cause of the tsar's long and drawn-out war with Sweden is likely more fanciful than factual, one may be certain that the Russian ruler must have felt a certain satisfaction when he later conquered the city, for Peter's initial experience in Riga, his first significant stop beyond his country's western border, was miserable from the beginning.

The problems can partly be chalked up to simple misunderstandings. Erik Dahlberg, the aging fortifications engineer who had recently been promoted to governor-general of Swedish Livonia, was not expecting such a large contingent and had little idea what the appropriate protocol should be. After all, the tsar wasn't even part of the delegation, at least not in an official capacity; his stop in Riga served no diplomatic purpose; and, in any event, the stay was intended to be brief. Moreover, in Dahlberg's defense we may add that as Livonia was still in the grips of a famine and food was in short supply, the requirements of feeding an extra 250 visitors would surely have imposed a considerable burden on the embassy's hosts. For the most part, the confused guests were left to fend for themselves in Lastadia, the "Moscow suburb" located just south of the walled city.

In fact, the mix-ups began well before the embassy appeared in Riga. While the Swedish governor-general had made the proper preparations to bring the contingent to Riga in appropriate style by sending carriages escorted by cavalrymen to the frontier near Pskov, Peter missed this welcome, as he and some other important members of the embassy were traveling ahead of the main party. To make amends, the Swedes staged a second reception several kilometers outside Riga: the greeting party included all four of Riga's burgomasters, thirty-six Blackheads adorned in colorful garb, and some 140 armed citizens with horses and carriages, drums and trumpets.[14]

To Riga the tsar and his embassy brought some one thousand carts loaded with furs and other gifts intended for the various officials and royals they expected to encounter in the West that spring. Although the sojourn in Riga was intended to be brief, the ice on the Düna River broke earlier than usual that spring, thereby postponing the Russians' plan to cross the channel, six hundred meters wide where it passed the city. There was as yet no bridge, and no boat, raft, or ship could negotiate the ice floes that clogged the river where it flowed past Riga. For an entire week, Peter and his party waited with their carts and sledges in the suburb at Lastadia, where they accused the German merchants of exploiting their predicament by raising the prices for food and lodging.

On his second day in Riga, the young Peter Mikhailov, still maintaining a ruse that fooled nobody, mounted a gray horse and took off for a look around the city. Of special interest to the tsar were Riga's fortifications, which he decided to examine for himself. When the tsar and his companions were seen inspecting the ramparts and measuring the width of the city walls and the depth of its defensive ditch, the authorities rushed to intervene. Although the contingent's leader, Francis Lefort, a Swiss officer in Russian service who was also one of Peter's closest associates, apologized for the impertinent behavior, his graciousness did not change the decision of Riga's Swedish authorities: henceforth the guests would be accompanied by a small entourage of soldiers in their walks around the city.

The wound cut deep, for the insult at Riga was not only a question of the Swedes' intimation of espionage, but it was also matter of courtesy. Ignored by the stiff Dahlberg, the Russians were surprised to have to pay for their own expenses, horses, and fodder. No less disappointing, the unhappy guests were treated to no banquets or entertainments, no fun of any kind—and, whether he was the tsar of all the Russias or the humble Peter Mikhailov, the raucous and domineering autocrat did like to have fun.[15] In Riga, the irritated absolutist wrote to Moscow, "we lived like slaves and feasted only with our eyes."[16]

Still upset by the Swedes' strict supervision of their guests, Peter decided for reasons that remain unclear to leave Riga before the rest of the embassy. On the night of April 8, the tsar managed to cross the Düna on a barge. From the Überdüna area (Pārdaugava) on the river's west bank, he made his way to Libau (Liepāja) in the Duchy of Courland, and thence to Königsberg (Kaliningrad), where Peter found his hosts' offers of lavish banquets, fireworks, and hunting to be far more agreeable than the unpleasantness that had doomed his stay in Riga. While Peter schmoozed with the duke of Courland and the elector of Brandenburg, the rest of his companions were left behind to settle their financial disputes with Riga's merchants. When the embassy departed a few days later, the Swedes fired thirty-two gunshots in its honor; but the future "Peter the Great," then en route to the next stop on his eighteen-month journey, had already got into his head that the rude and low-born Dahlberg had badly mistreated his guests.

The governor-general himself must have been taken aback by the experience, for it was not long after the embassy's departure that Dahlberg asked Riga's councillors to pay close attention to any news from Moscow, to make preparations for further improvements to Riga's fortifications, and to register and observe all persons arriving in the city. Arriving Russians were to be confined to Lastadia; their small wooden *strugas*, carrying primary goods from the interior downriver to Riga, were to be carefully searched upon arrival. Later that spring, the governor-general ordered the liquidation of Kube Hill, the inhabited sand dune just beyond the ramparts and moat, for the enemy's occupation of this elevated position might prove fatal to the town. But the citizens never got around to carrying out these orders, even as the threat of war loomed over their city.[17]

It was just at this moment that Swedish officials and foreign dignitaries gathered for the funeral of King Charles XI, whose passing in early April brought to power the inexperienced teenager Charles XII. In Stockholm for the funeral, Dahlberg was heard to predict that Russia would soon make its bid to establish a foothold on the Baltic.[18] But the Russians would not be alone in waging war on Sweden, for the enemies of the Scandinavian monarchy smelled weakness. Denmark had a particularly strained relationship with Sweden, whose protectorate in neighboring Holstein vexed the Danish royal house. During his stop in Denmark, Peter discussed with King Christian V the possibilities for mutual support and aid in the event of war, but no concrete plans were made at that time.

The tsar's most important diplomatic achievement during his long trip abroad was his secret alliance with the reckless and lustful elector of Saxony, Friedrich-Augustus. Ascending to the Polish throne in 1697, this colorful figure is better known to history as Augustus II (r. 1697–1706, 1709–1733). A double-dealing collector of mistresses and a convert to Roman Catholicism (a requirement for anyone who aspired to rule the Commonwealth), Augustus earned the appellation "the Strong" on the basis of his raw physical power and perhaps also from his conviction that he alone could impose order on chaotic Poland-Lithuania, to whose throne he ascended in 1697.[19] Beholden to Peter for the Polish crown—the tsar had resorted to military force to ensure the election of a puppet who would be loyal to Russia—Friedrich-Augustus was a German who might have been expected to sympathize with the plight of the Baltic nobility; on the other land, the elector-king was also known to have designs on regaining Riga and the Baltic provinces for Poland. Such ambitions initially suited the tsar, for Peter's goals in the Baltic were still rather modest at this time. The main objective was to drive the Swedes out of Ingria and thereby open the Baltic Sea to Russian shipping. The pact was confirmed during a secret meeting the following summer in Rawa (in Galicia), where the sovereigns—Augustus acting in his capacity as elector of Saxony—met each other for the first time and decided to maintain a "close relationship" and form a military alliance against Sweden.

The behind-the-scenes organizer of this anti-Swedish league was an alienated aristocrat named Johann Reinhold von Patkul. Born in Stockholm in 1660, Patkul enjoyed all the advantages of noble birth, a good education, and extensive travel in Europe. Although he spent his twenty-seventh year in Riga, where he was an officer in the Swedish army, Patkul was not a burgher but the lord of a manor at a time when the crown was aggressively confiscating estates in Livonia and Estonia. A victim of Charles XI's reductions (see chapter 7), Patkul seethed with hatred for the Swedish monarchy—a feeling he shared with other Baltic Germans (who hoped to restore serfdom to the Livonian countryside) and perhaps a few members of Riga's town council.

For protesting the reductions in Livonia, Patkul was arrested and condemned to death, but the nobleman managed to flee the Swedish Empire empire for the relative safety of continental Europe. Bouncing from one place to the next, Patkul attended the fateful meeting at Rawa, where the elector-king and Tsar Peter planned an attack on Sweden. Indeed, not only did Patkul succeed in convincing Augustus that a conspiracy was afoot among the Livonian nobility, who he claimed would agree to recognize the king and his successors in the event of a Polish attack, he also gave the king detailed descriptions of the city's fortifications.[20] It was Patkul who became Augustus's messenger to the Danish king, who joined the alliance in July 1699. Later that November, Patkul attended the discussions at Preobrazhensky, a village located just outside Moscow. The outcome of this meeting was a secret treaty of alliance and a plan of action: Saxony was to invade Livonia in January or February 1700, and Denmark was to march on Holstein at the same time. Poland and Russia, meanwhile, were to keep Charles XII busy in the eastern Baltic. Although the tsar never committed to a precise date, he agreed to attack Swedish-held Ingria on Russia's northwestern frontier sometime in 1700. At this point, both Augustus II and Christian V regarded Peter as a junior partner.[21]

While perhaps junior to his allies, if only initially, Peter was by no means the youngest of the Great Northern War's belligerents. When hostilities broke out in 1700, King Charles XII was barely eighteen years old—a decade younger than Peter. A died-in-the-wool autocrat who was trained in the military arts, the aggressive Swedish monarch probably had little idea that he would spend the rest of his life on a horse doing battle with the tsar—after all, it was only a few months earlier, in October 1699, that Peter swore before a Swedish embassy in Moscow that Russia would continue to observe the disadvantageous settlement laid out in the Treaty of Cardis (1661) that had ended his father Alexei's failed war with Sweden.[22] If Peter's duplicity gave cover to his secret plans for aggression, Charles, so his biographers claim, avoided war as much as he could, maintaining in peacetime a mobile army of 36,000 conscripts (mostly peasants) alongside the paid troops, 23,500 in number, who garrisoned the ninety forts and castles of the empire. Mobilization of that army would take some time, and getting that army from one side of the Baltic to the other might prove impossible if the sea froze over.[23]

Riga being the Swedish army's main support point in the Baltic, the Düna city was critical to the empire's defense. In the instructions he prepared on November 29, 1699, the Livonian governor-general gave Rigans explicit orders for storing reserves of food. Dahlberg further insisted that the burghers prevent the Düna from being covered with a dense cover of ice: the frozen river must be continually broken so that it would become a natural ring of defense for the city.[24] As 1699 drew to a close and Saxon troops were positioned in Lithuania, everyone waited for Augustus to make his move.

1700: Opening Moves

Sometime during the bitterly cold weeks that opened the year 1700, Saxon forces belonging to Augustus the Strong, supplemented by some Polish units, crossed from Lithuania into the Duchy of Courland, then still a Polish possession. The objective of these 14,000 soldiers was to besiege Riga, for it was expected that the Livonian nobility would rebel against the Swedes and that the stunned Rigans would quickly capitulate and their city would be returned to Polish rule.

Impressed by the sophistication of Riga's fortifications, the Saxon commander, Lieutenant-General J. H. Fleming, issued his orders: the attack would take place on February 11–12, when Rigans would presumably be weakened from the excesses of the Carnival celebrations. Essential to the plan's success was the element of surprise. There would be no declaration of war.

In Riga the change of guard took place just after midnight. Spotted on the Düna's left bank, opposite the city, were sledges carrying weapons, ladders, pontoons, and everything else the Saxons would need to cross the river and reach the city. The ringing of Riga's church bells alerted the sleeping burghers to the danger, and soon enough the entire right bank of the Düna was alight. Bonfires were set by the city walls, making it practically impossible to see across the river; the city gates were locked and reinforced; the ice on the Düna was chopped so as to impede the enemy's hopes of getting to the Riga side on the right bank. If, as it seems, the Saxons had hoped to sneak into the city under the cover of darkness, such plans were scotched from the beginning, for the element of surprise was missing. Indeed, Augustus's secret plan had reached the Swedish administration in Riga long before the actual attack, giving the governor-general ample time to take the appropriate measures.[25]

For the moment, the Saxon-Polish forces focused on taking the Düna's left bank, capturing Fort Kobron (opposite Riga) on February 16 and then the area's islands. By the beginning of March, the entire left bank from Riga to Kokenhusen was in the hands of the Saxons. Two weeks later they captured the Swedish fortress at Dünamünde but at the cost of more than 1,500 men.[26] Nevertheless, so impressed were the Saxons by their victory that they promptly renamed the captured fortress "Augustusburg."[27] But even as the Saxon-Polish forces consolidated their position across the river from Riga, they lacked the artillery necessary for bombarding the city and the naval support required to maintain the siege. The attack was all for naught: Augustus's gamble had failed.

Although Riga remained beyond his reach, the king of Poland had at least managed to surprise his cousin, the king of Sweden, who learned of the attack while on a hunting trip. Now finding himself at war with Denmark over Holstein, Charles XII left the defense of Riga in the hands of the local garrison while he readied his field army to fight a war he did not want. As the city awaited reinforcements from Sweden, conditions in Riga, just then recovering from the famine of 1695–1697, worsened dramatically. In the peaceful and prosperous year of 1699, the last such until the 1720s, some 520 ships from western Europe docked at Riga's port, bringing with them a cornucopia of desired goods—French wine, German beer (Riga's beer was notoriously bad), English cloth, tobacco from the Atlantic

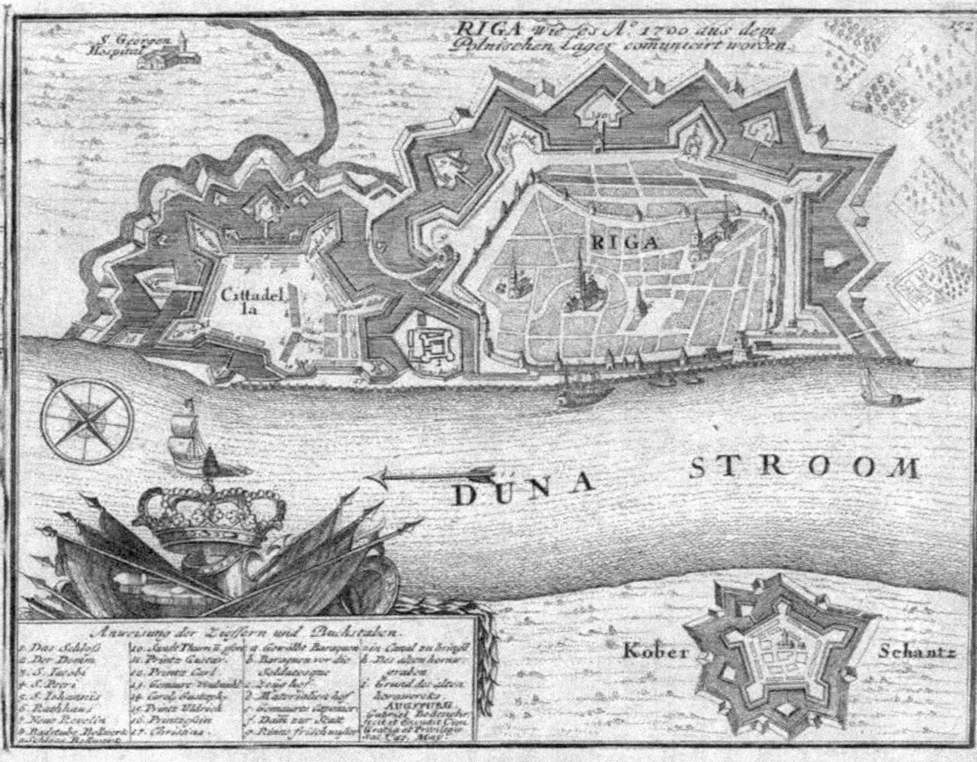

FIGURE 14. Riga in 1700 as viewed from the Polish camp. Gabriel Bodenehr, ca. 1720.

colonies.[28] The Saxons' conquest of Dünamünde, however, paralyzed the transit trade that in better times had brought prosperity to Riga's merchants, work and sustenance to its artisans, and daily bread to its laborers. As customs on the city's exports dried up, affluent Rigans learned to live without their accustomed luxuries. Poorer Rigans faced grimmer prospects.

As we have noted, leadership in the city was concentrated in the hands of Erik Dahlberg, the Livonian army's commanding officer and the territory's governor-general. Administering Livonia according to the Swedish principle that the provinces were to make do with their own resources, Dahlberg nevertheless expected their denizens, from the lowliest porters and peasants to the most distinguished families of the Baltic nobility, to carry out his commands without question. Thus, on the day after the Saxons first appeared in the vicinity in February 1700, Dahlberg called on all inhabitants of the land—owners of manors, their tenants, peasants, administrators, anyone capable of taking up arms—to rush to Riga and join the ranks of its defenders. The "non-Germans" of Riga and from nearby districts also answered the call, assigned to stand guard at the city's walls and blockhouses, armed with muskets and swords. But since it was not always easy to get the people under his jurisdiction to comply with his commands, the governor-general resorted to sterner measures: in July officials began to register all the city's inhabitants, house by house, to ensure that each person contributed to the city's defense.[29] Two years later, with the war still raging, the septuagenarian requested to be released from his military duties, citing his declining health. His replacement was to be General Otto Wellingk, until then the governor of Ingria, a Swedish-held territory on the Russian border.

The crown was uncertain of the loyalties of its Livonian subjects from the moment of the allied attack. After all, it was on behalf of the Livonian nobility and the burghers of the Swedish-occupied cities that Patkul had ascertained his right to negotiate when he met with the tsar in November 1699. But Patkul's claim that he had already formed a conspiracy in Riga was roundly rejected by the town council, for when Dahlberg got wind of Patkul's treachery, the governor-general demanded that Riga's leaders declare their allegiance to the crown. Soon all of Riga's town council members, the 556 members of the Great Guild, and the 364 members of the Small Guild unequivocally declared that they enjoyed no connections whatsoever with the "traitorous, oath-breaking, dishonorable" Patkul. With their signatures, Riga's leading citizens affirmed their loyalty to the Swedish monarchy.[30] Patkul's anticipated uprising of the Livonian nobility never materialized.

Upon receiving news that hostilities had begun in Riga, Charles XII demanded that reinforcements be sent to Riga and Livonia without delay. "I have resolved never to begin an unjust war," the king informed the Swedish *Riksdag*, "but also never to end a just war without overcoming my enemy."[31] This promise he was to pursue to the bitter end, for the only good defense, the king was convinced, was a vigorous offense. At this point, Charles would not have known that a third enemy, Peter I, was about to enter the anti-Swedish coalition.

In the war's early months, the Swedish cause benefited from the assistance of a fleet combined of Dutch and English warships, for these two trading giants—England's Baltic trade constituted some 10 percent of its imports—desired peace and the resumption of business as usual in the area of the Baltic Sea.[32] Charles XII's subsequent victory over Denmark, in July, forced the Danes to make peace with the Duke of Holstein and exit the war. But Sweden's victory would not save Riga from its fate, for on August 18, 1700, the announcement came that Russia and the Ottoman Empire had concluded a thirty-year armistice. That Russia declared war on Sweden the day after the treaty's announcement seems unsurprising, for the peace with Turkey freed the Muscovites from their war in the south so that the tsar might focus his attention on the north. Like Ivan the Terrible a century and a half before him, Peter the Great claimed that he was merely reclaiming what had been stolen from his ancestors. Whether at this early date the tsar eyed the Livonian capital as an object of permanent conquest is unclear. Peter's own correspondence, nevertheless, shows that at no time did he either forgive or forget his unpleasant stay in Riga.[33]

Although Russia spent much of the first nine years of the Great Northern War on the defensive fighting for goals that sometimes seemed unclear, in the end it was the tsar who triumphed, swallowing up Sweden's eastern Baltic territories and announcing Russia's entry into the exclusive club of great European powers. But was this Peter's goal from the beginning? Certainly he wanted a port on the Baltic Sea, probably having in mind Narva, a seaport near the border that fell into Russian hands during the Livonian War but stagnated under Swedish rule. If Narva was a likely target, the Neva was probably unfamiliar to Peter as this time. In 1700 the tsar simply could not have known that he would snatch its mouth from the Swedes and establish the city of St. Petersburg, intended to be a Russian "window on the West." Prior to this moment Peter's foreign policy had always had a southern orientation; but with the conclusion of peace with Turkey he no longer needed a Christian coalition to defeat it. Yet as early as the spring of 1700 the tsar had informed the Swedish ambassador to Moscow in no uncertain terms that "if the king of Poland should take Riga, it would not remain in his possession. I would tear it out of his hands."[34] What, in such an event, the tsar would do next with Riga was presumably left to his interlocutor's imagination.

Expecting what would later be known as the Great Northern War to last no more than two years, and having dangled the prospect of acquiring Swedish Livonia (with Riga) before Augustus II, it seems unlikely that the tsar's Baltic plans at the moment extended much beyond the acquisition of Karelia, Ingria, and Narva. But the more deeply involved he became in the region, the more the tsar's prodigious appetite grew. Some historians believe that only after the victory at Poltava in 1709 and the fall of Riga in 1710 did the tsar reveal still grander ambitions in the Baltic. Having sacrificed so much in what had become a much longer war than he had anticipated against an enemy that refused to make peace, Peter intended to keep what he had acquired.[35]

Of course, Peter's true intentions with regard to Riga cannot be known, and Russia's participation in the Great Northern War cannot be explained simply by the shabby treatment Peter and his companions endured during their stay a few years earlier. Yet the "insult" was a convenient *casus belli* for the tsar, even if it took some time before the Muscovites could be of much help to their Saxon-Polish allies, still encamped just outside Riga at the moment of Peter's declaration of war.[36] The Danish withdrawal from the alliance must have alarmed the aggressors Augustus and Peter, both of whom lacked a significant fleet. Now that troops from Sweden were preparing their descent on Livonia, Augustus needed a truce—a typical tactic of early modern warfare, according to whose unwritten rules hostilities could always be resumed at a more advantageous time and location. Breaking off the siege, the Saxons-Poles withdrew the bulk of their forces from the Riga area and burned their camp outside the city. The Saxon army's main winter base would now be upstream in Kokenhusen: from this castle[37] they could launch attacks in the direction of Livonia and Estonia, while smaller Saxon forces remained at Fort Kobron opposite Riga and at Dünamünde near the river's mouth.

The conclusion of a cease-fire and Riga's partial liberation from the siege gave its tired burghers the illusion of a coming peace. Such hopes must have grown in the wake of Sweden's great triumph at Narva on November 30, 1700, when an army of nine thousand Swedish soldiers defeated a Russian force more than four times its size. Although the odds were not in their favor, the Swedes could not have afforded a loss at Narva, for failure would have opened the door to a Russian conquest of Ingria, Estonia, and Livonia—and Sweden's eastern Baltic provinces would have been lost. Not only did the Swedes hold their ground against a much larger Russian army, they also picked up a treasure trove of war booty—artillery, thousands of cannonballs, and hundreds of barrels of gunpowder.

Even after his unlikely victory, King Charles XII, already shaping his legend as a soldier-king who had personally fought the Danes and who stood at the head of his outnumbered troops at Narva (Peter, on the other hand, departed the encampment for Novgorod on the eve of battle), did not hurry to Riga.[38] As late as the spring of 1701, the Swedish monarch was considering an invasion of Russia, but he was held back by the condition of his sick and hungry troops, for much of the king's army was unfit for action. The tsar, meanwhile, spent the winter of 1700–1701 recovering from the catastrophe at Narva, where some 8,000–10,000 of his recruits fell in battle and thousands more were captured. If the defeat initially gave him pause—he chalked it up to his troops' lack of experience[39]—Peter soon displayed his characteristic resolve in the face of adversity by rebuilding his armed forces. Twenty-seven new regiments were created in the winter of 1700–1701; church bells were melted down to make cannons; iron foundries were established, as well as factories for producing armaments and cloth. At the border town of Birze (Lith. Biržai) in February 1701, the tsar reaffirmed Russia's alliance with Augustus II. Hoping to encourage and reassure his ally, Peter offered the elector-king some 15,000–20,000 Russian soldiers and a substantial war subsidy. For the tsar, no price was too great when it came to taking revenge upon Sweden.

Without reinforcements from Sweden, Riga would scarcely be able to hold up against a force of such strength. Between the 2,800 soldiers stationed in the Citadel garrison and Riga's own forces, the governor-general could rely on some five thousand men—far too little for a serious defense of the city against the tens of thousands commanded by Peter and his Saxon-Polish allies. Watchmen were posted to the tower of the Riga Cathedral, from which they could see the entire Düna up to the Baltic Sea. From the Dome's steeple they observed the arrival of fresh Saxon units as they streamed into the forts on the river's left bank. As the Saxons set up artillery batteries protected by palisades, rumors began to spread of an imminent Russian attack on Livonia. Throughout the land, peasants, craftsmen—anyone capable of wielding a weapon, a shovel, or an oar—was called to arms.

In the spring of 1701, the news came to Riga that Sweden's young king would soon be arriving and that a great campaign to liberate the city from the siege would begin. All means of transportation were now registered, so that when the time came the city's barges and rowboats could be put into action. While Riga's ferrymen and fishermen were told to prepare their vessels, soldiers and citizens were ordered to covertly begin the construction of a bridge across the Düna that would convey the Swedish cavalry across the river: in this way, the Swedes planned to oust the enemy from its position opposite the city.[40]

While Peter toyed with the idea of a mediated peace, Charles sailed to Livonia, sending part of his Swedish forces up the Düna in the hopes of tricking his enemies into thinking that they were headed for the Saxons' main camp at Kokenhusen. All too easily did the Saxon commander, General Field Marshal von Steinau, fall for the ruse: by sending some of the heavy cannons from the Riga area to Kokenhusen, the Saxons weakened their position in Riga.

Spilve: The Crossing of the Düna

The Saxons' initial foray up the Düna in the winter of 1700 failed to produce the desired result: Augustus's soldiers managed to occupy several key installations across the river from Riga, but the combined Saxon-Polish forces failed to drive the Swedes out of the city.

In the summer of 1701, the adversaries braced for another confrontation in Riga. This was not the decisive contest that resulted in the city's capitulation to

Russia—nine years would pass before the end finally came. Yet the Battle of Spilve (in German it is known as the Battle of the Düna), fought in the shadow of the more famous campaigns at Narva (1700, 1704) and Poltava (1709), still commands the attention of Riga's historians, for on the morning of July 19, 1701, the city's fate once again hung in the balance.

Spread out along the river's left bank opposite Riga were some 28,000 Saxons, Poles, and Russians, now facing off against a Swedish army of 18,000 that had arrived in Riga after an exhausting march from Dorpat through Estonia and Livonia.[41] Making his appearance in the city on July 17, the Swedish king immediately climbed up the tower of the Riga Cathedral where, with the aid of a telescope, Charles observed his enemy's movements on the other side of the Düna River.[42] From his position of relative safety in Riga, its heavy artillery positioned all along the sophisticated defensive system the Swedes had built over the course of seven decades, the king prepared his landing.

The goal was to cross the Düna and drive the Saxon-Polish forces, including an army headed by Johann Reinhold von Patkul, from the Livonian forts. From the sparsely inhabited Überdüna (Pārdaugava) district, a minor force was to push the invaders back into the Duchy of Courland, a Polish dependency, while the bulk of the Swedish army was to be sent in the direction of Russia later that summer. The idea, as always, was to take the fight away from Sweden's territory and bring it to the enemy. To execute his strategy, however, Charles first needed to build a bridge across the Düna so that his infantry and cavalry might traverse the river's width of six hundred meters.

The date having been set for July 19, and with all his forces in place, on the eve of the attack the king suddenly shifted tactics. Frustrated by the delays and the stormy weather that impeded the construction of his floating bridge, Charles decided that the landing would instead be carried out on barges. Worked out by Dahlberg and the Swedish fortification engineer Karl Magnus Stuart, the plan called for the mobilization of some one thousand ferrymen, pilots, transport workers, and fishermen (these were typically Latvians) who secured some two hundred small boats and rafts of different shapes and sizes. In the wee hours of the designated morning, this flotilla filled the Düna: four were floating batteries, some were to transport artillery, others to carry the Swedish cavalry and infantry.

At 4 a.m. General Quartermaster Stuart gave the signal for his forces to embark on what he planned to be a quiet and unobserved passage across the river—a scheme that some of the Swedish officers saw as too risky in light of the river's daunting width, the growing strength of the enemies' forces, and the unfavorable weather. Knowing that success would favor the stealthy, the Swedes tried to obstruct the enemy's view by ordering that damp straw be placed in some of their small boats, which were then set alight and pushed out into the middle of the river so that the north-blowing wind would deliver the resulting smoke into the faces of the Saxons. Despite the haze, the vessels were quickly spotted and fired upon; but with the wind at their backs, the first boats reached the Düna's left bank in no more than fifteen minutes. When half this Swedish force of 7,600, led by their warrior-king, disembarked on the beach, it was met by an allied army of almost equal size under the command of the Saxon general Otto Arnold von Paykull.

The Swedes' primary objective was to take control of the area on the left bank where the floating bridge was to be completed, for soon the Saxon-Polish forces led by General Steinau would be arriving from Kokenhusen. Turning up as expected and immediately deploying his cavalry against the Swedes, Steinau and his officers swiftly came to the realization that their forces were too scattered along the Düna to prevent the Swedes from crossing the river. By 7 a.m. the Saxons had decided to withdraw. As they threw another wave of men at the Swedes to provide cover for their hasty retreat, Patkul, the injured Steinau, and their soldiers fled up the Düna, abandoning Fort Kobron and its storehouses of food and weapons. In this way a wealth of war booty—some heavy artillery as well as thousands of muskets and rifles—fell into the hands of the Swedes, who by now were too exhausted to chase their enemies.[43]

But what of the Russians who fought on the side of the Saxons? That a number of Russian soldiers, comprising an advance guard of Prince Repnin's regiment, panicked and fled even before the battle began only diminished Charles's low regard for Peter's army. Nevertheless, some four hundred Russians tenaciously clung to Lucas Island, where they were attacked by the Riga garrison, now bent on liberating the islands of the Düna.[44] It is believed that only twenty of these soldiers remained alive when Repnin's army belatedly reached Riga after the battle's conclusion.[45]

Occurring in the wake of his victories over Denmark and the rout of the Russians at Narva, the Battle of Spilve was a qualified success for King Charles XII. No doubt he was satisfied by the performance of his army: the Saxons lost some two thousand men, the Swedes fewer than one hundred. But his other objective, to capture his cousin Augustus, was stymied by the smoke and weather. Had they been able to complete their floating bridge, the Swedes might have unleashed the full strength of their cavalry on the treacherous elector-king. Their failure to do so would profoundly influence the course of events, for the Swedish monarch would spend the next several years fighting in Poland while trying to convince its nobles to depose a king who had drawn that troubled country into a war against one of Europe's most formidable armies.

Nevertheless, at this very moment, Sweden's daring, nineteen-year-old king must have seemed invincible. His victory at the Battle of Spilve meant that Riga would remain, for now, under the control of Stockholm.[46] The Swedes were also left in possession of Riga's floating bridge, which was completed in the wake of the battle and could now be used to defend the fortifications on the left side of the river. Located where the Stone Bridge (Latv. Akmens tilts) stands today, the pontoon bridge across the Düna, assembled each spring and taken down before the winter ice, became one of the great legends of old Riga.

With their city freed from the Saxon-Polish siege, many Rigans hoped that the war would soon be over and that they might soon enjoy the fruits of a long and stable peace. But this was not to be, for the Great Northern War was to rage, with long pauses, for another twenty years. The coming battles, however, would take place not in Riga but across a vast theater in northern and eastern Europe—in the weak and indefensible Kingdom of Poland, throughout the devastated lands of Livonia and Estonia, and deep within sprawling, endless Russia.

Riga in Wartime

The lover of numerous mistresses with whom he sired what was rumored to be hundreds of bastards, possessing a physical prowess that earned him the sobriquet "the Strong," and nurturing a passion for the arts that transformed the Saxon city of Dresden into a baroque cultural capital, Augustus II was one of the era's more flamboyant figures. But when it came to advancing the interests of Saxony and Poland, the notorious elector-king was a dud. While it was intended to earn him the admiration of his subjects and of the other European powers, his attack on Riga only provoked the Swedes, caused great hardship in the lands nominally under his control, and reinforced the perception "that his potency did not extend beyond the bedchamber."[47]

His army defeated at Riga in 1701, the "Saxon Hercules" withdrew from Livonia to focus on consolidating power in the messy Polish-Lithuanian Commonwealth. Poland, however, was to be no sanctuary, for the Swedish king, bent on avenging his cousin's sneak attack, wasted no time in moving his forces into Courland, then a Polish dependency. From there, Charles XII's army marched on Warsaw and Cracow in the spring, hoping to goad the Polish nobility into overthrowing an erratic king with whom it had an uneasy relationship in the first place. For the next several years the disunited Commonwealth was the main battlefield of the Great Northern War. Such were the results of Augustus's folly.

While Charles obsessed over punishing Augustus, the Russians advanced into the eastern Baltic, which the Swedes defended with whatever reinforcements the unfortunate Major-General Schlippenbach could piece together from Riga and elsewhere. The tsar's intention in Livonia was to ravage the region so thoroughly that the Swedes would not be able to support themselves by exploiting the ruined lands. This order General Sheremetev, the supreme commander of all Russian forces in the Baltic, duly carried out, writing to the tsar in 1702 that only Pernau, Riga, and Reval remained untouched; the rest of Livonia and Estonia had been reduced to a desert.[48] Among the many prisoners who fell into Russian hands at this time was the pastor Johann Ernst Glück, whose place in Latvian history was secured by his efforts to translate the Bible into the local vernacular, and his adopted daughter, a servant girl known to acquaintances as Marta Skavronskaya. Twenty-five years later, this illiterate and cheerful Lithuanian peasant would rule her late husband's vast Eurasian empire as Catherine I (r. 1727–1730).[49]

While blazing a trail of devastation across the Livonian lands, Peter's forces also attacked Swedish power on the lakes and rivers, achieving naval victories at Lake Ladoga and Kexholm that same summer. In 1704 the Russians destroyed the Swedish navy at Lake Peipus, while forces under the command of General Sheremetev besieged and captured Dorpat (July) and Narva (August). By acquiring a number of Swedish ships, Peter enhanced Russia's position in the Baltic; by imprisoning thousands of enemy officers and soldiers, the Russians weakened the Swedish military.

Perhaps the most consequential Russian achievement during the war's early years was the conquest of the Swedish fortress at Nöteborg. Under Swedish control for a century, Nöteborg guarded the Neva River and prevented Russia from reaching the Baltic Sea. Falling into the tsar's hands in the spring of 1702, the fortress was renamed Schlisselburg from the German word *Schlüssel*, or key; its conquest allowed the Russians to occupy the seventy-four-kilometer length of the Neva River and absorb the Swedish province of Ingria, then sparsely inhabited by Finns. It was here that the tsar, seizing his moment of triumph while Charles chased Augustus around Poland, established his new city on the Neva in 1703. Located on a flat and sandy marsh more than six hundred kilometers from Moscow, St. Petersburg was hardly an ideal spot for the hundreds of Russian nobles who were compelled to move there, or for the tens of thousands of laborers who perished while building what Peter intended to be his capital. What was important was that the new city be defensible. Protected by a naval base at Kronstadt that guarded all approaches to the Neva River, St. Petersburg was to become Russia's leading Baltic port and—much like Riga after the Russian conquest, but on a grander scale—its "window on the West."

The Baltic theater was secondary after 1703, the principal battlefields being in Poland and then in Russian Ukraine. Only after Peter's victory at Poltava in 1709 would Riga and its environs once again become a combat zone. But even if the fortress-city was enclosed in its own little world, its gates locked at night to bar the entry of enemies, beggars, and plagues, Riga was hardly immune to the effects of the fighting. Contrary to the allies' original assumption that the struggle against Sweden would be brief, the war turned into a long, tormented conflict that destroyed farmland, disrupted shipping and trade, undermined the local economy, and plunged Riga into instability.

Even during those months that the Baltic Sea wasn't blocked, Rigan traders still faced the challenge of getting the customary goods from the interior, for the Saxons' position further up the Düna at Kokenhusen positioned them to hinder the delivery of grain, hemp, and linseed from Lithuania and Belarus. The fall and destruction of Dorpat in August 1704 meant that the overland corridor from the Novgorod and Pskov regions was also blocked for a time. Trade that once went through the Livonian merchants was now rerouted to the tsar's far northern port of Archangel, thereby depriving Riga's traders of considerable revenue.

The Swedes' liberation of the Dünamünde fortress in December 1701 might have given Rigans hope that the Baltic trade would soon pick up, but the war's continuation made overseas shipping risky for everyone involved. Moreover, the new rules that Swedish authorities imposed upon the local merchants further depressed commercial activity in Riga and the other ports of the eastern Baltic. Special permission was now required to export grain, hemp, hops, oxhides, and many other items, and such permission was rarely given during this time of shortage.[50] Fewer ships came to Riga, and once the goods had been loaded, the vessels then departed for the West with their holds only partially full. In 1704 only 287 ships from western Europe docked at the port of Riga—a contraction by nearly half since the last year of peace.[51] As trade slowed to a crawl, the crown's income from excises dropped precipitously. In the last year before the war, the Swedes collected 38,000 thalers from Riga; in 1704 it was able to collect only 21,500.[52]

Yet the Rigans who endured so many trials and hardships during the Great Northern War were the same burghers who had resented Swedish taxes, who chaffed at the empire's continual demands for contributions and loans, and who loathed the centralizing tendencies that eroded local authority. Given the imperial nature of the crown's dominion over Riga, one may well ask the following question: did its burghers actually *desire* a war that promised to liberate the city from the burdens of Swedish rule? The Rigans' actual wartime behavior suggests that the answer is a qualified "no," for whatever their misgivings about the Swedes, Rigans remained prudently loyal to the crown for the entirety of the war's first decade. Surely there was unrest among the Livonian nobility—for example, the notorious Johann Patkul, who complained bitterly about the "reductions" policy of King Charles XI. Yet the noble uprising anticipated by Patkul never took place. Riga's councilors might have bristled at the demands of the Swedish governors, but instead of rebelling the burghers behaved cautiously. Rigans complied with wartime regulations. They joined Swedish regiments. They defended their city from the Saxons in the confrontations of 1700 and 1701. It was only after enduring much suffering and another long siege that the city at last succumbed to the Russians in the summer of 1710.

Setting aside the matter of the burghers' preferences, it may be argued that a closer economic relationship with Russia would have been more organic to Riga's geographical position than the colonial relationship it had with Sweden. After all, being located near the mouth of a major river whose source was in Russia had for centuries allowed Riga to collect the bounty of the forested interior for transport to the West. All Sweden did, some Rigans complained, was levy taxes on the goods that others had taken care to ship, float, or haul by sledge to and from the port of Riga. But while Rigans grumbled about the crown's abuses, the reality of 1700 was that the likeliest alternative to Swedish rule was not Russian power, but a return to Polish domination. Considering how the fortunes of the Polish state had fallen so dramatically since its sixteenth-century golden age, the city's absorption into the rickety Commonwealth was hardly a desirable outcome for Rigans. Despite the stresses and strains of the war, and despite Stockholm's efforts to squeeze all it could from the Baltic provinces during a time of crisis, Rigans remained true to their oaths.

This is not to suggest that their loyalty was not tested, for even as Livonia was being overrun by Russian forces in 1702, Swedish authorities did not hesitate to increase their demands on the city; Livonia, after all, was the indispensable granary of the absolutist, military state, and Riga was a leading source of cash income. In addition to the expected contribution of 20,000 thalers, in 1702 Riga was to loan the crown a further 12,000 thalers—even as the city collected grain to feed the Swedish army.[53] Over the following three years (1703–1705), the crown was to collect another 52,574 thalers from Riga for the maintenance of the city's defenses, the quartering and provisioning of the Swedish garrison, and the prosecution of the Great Northern War.

Another drain on the city's coffers was the replenishing of the Swedish regiments in Riga with new recruits. The addition of 4,000 new soldiers in 1708, combined with the economics of scarcity, drove the annual cost to the city of maintaining the garrison up to an astronomical 160,000 silver thalers.[54]

The people of Riga, as well as the foreign traders who did their business in the city, paid for the war in a variety of ways. Not only were merchants compelled to make loans to the crown and to pay excise taxes on the goods exchanged at the port, lower-class Rigans were required to labor on the city's fortifications, which were in constant need of repair. For example, it was during the Great Northern War that the moat surrounding the Riga Castle, for many years an island, was filled in so that the castle would be adjoined to the city's fortifications.

Meanwhile, hundreds of burghers, like thousands of Latvian peasants from nearby districts, were recruited into the Swedish army—some to fight, others to dig, haul, and build whatever needed digging, hauling, and building. Although few received the pay they were promised, many Rigans and Livonians defended Sweden's Baltic provinces at the cost of their lives. One battle in Estonia against Russian forces in the summer of 1702 saw the evisceration of a unit of Rigan recruits (i.e., Latvians). Meanwhile, as Sheremetev's army marauded across Livonia, the Swedes abandoned Riga's suburban districts as well as the Latvian families who inhabited them, for the authorities had decided to concentrate Riga's forces: infantry stationed in Lastadia and the suburbs were now moved into the city and the neighboring Citadel, leaving the areas beyond Riga's bastions and ravelins completely vulnerable to the enemy.

Indeed, as the danger of war returned to Riga, the city gates were overwhelmed by men, women, and children fleeing the unprotected countryside. Among the refugees were landlords with their families. Most, however, were simple peasants who brought with them their meager belongings—and sometimes even their cattle. Now exacerbated by the influx of country people, shortages persisted and the price of food skyrocketed. From time to time, the city's Swedish authorities imposed regulations to keep the price of food and other necessities within reach, but the town council received complaints about the city's bakers, butchers, and cobblers just the same. Another grievance was the garrisoning of reinforcements and local militias in the city: burghers had to admit into their modest homes not only officers and soldiers, but also their family members and sometimes livestock as well. Exceptions, of course, were made for Swedish officials and for Riga's town councilors; likewise for noblemen who owned property in the city, the aldermen of the guilds, and servants of the Church.[55] All Rigans were expected to shoulder the burdens of war, but not equally.

Rigans had greeted the outbreak of war with the presumption of Sweden's military (and cultural) superiority over both Poland and Russia. Having twice driven the Saxons and Poles from the city, the Swedes would surely triumph over their weaker and less-disciplined enemies. Confidence in Charles XII's army was sapped by the Russian army's shocking performance in Estonia and Ingria. The former was left in ruins; the latter fell to the Russians late in the spring of 1703, just as the tsar was laying the foundations for his new city on the Neva.

As hopes for a Swedish victory dwindled, Rigans dawdled. Letters and reports from the Rath to the governor-general suggested the burghers' growing habit of procrastination and avoidance.[56] Never ideal to begin with, the relationship between the Swedish administration and Riga's civic leaders descended into mutual distrust, and morale plummeted.

Scorched Earth

Before resuming the story of Riga during the Great Northern War, let us reflect upon the wider conflict as it spread across the eastern Baltic. After the Livonian and Ingrian campaigns of 1702–1704, Peter I took his army westward into Poland, where events began to turn in favor of the Swedes. If the principal aim of Charles XII at this time was to overthrow his cousin Augustus—the war was against the king, not his nation—his method was to make the Polish *Sejm* feel the consequences of Augustus's war. Following the Swedish conquest of the fortress town of Thorn, the *Sejm* formally deposed its king. In the place of Augustus, Charles installed his own puppet on the Polish throne, the twenty-seven-year-old Stanislas

Leszczynski, now ruling as Stanislas I (r. 1704–1709, 1733–1736). Even as he remained elector of Saxony, Augustus refused to accept his demotion, resolving to continue the fight and affirming his alliance with Russia. That the alliance was more of a dependency must have been evident to Peter, but the tsar also realized that in order to exercise influence in Warsaw, he would need his own Polish puppet. Such a policy would be perfected much later by Empress Catherine II (r. 1762–1796), who in the end found Poland to be such a headache that dismembering the restless Commonwealth was thought to be preferable to propping it up.

The Polish civil war left the country reeling, unable to defend itself against the Swedes, whose control over the eastern Baltic Sea allowed them to send a steady stream of equipment and provisions to the Commonwealth. Having chased the Russians out of eastern Poland, late in the summer of 1706 the Swedish army of Charles XII marched unopposed into Saxony and then Poland. Defeated on the battlefield, Augustus the Strong was at last compelled to yield the Polish throne, renounce his alliance with Russia (a temporary concession), and quit the war. The terms of the treaty, concluded in secret, also compelled Augustus to hand over to the Swedes the person who many believed had started all the trouble to begin with.

This was the Livonian nobleman Johann Reinhold von Patkul. Exiled from his manor for his opposition to royal absolutism, Patkul spent these years in the service of Peter the Great, who placed him in command of Augustus's troops in Poland during its civil war. Arrested by the Saxons and delivered into Swedish hands, on October 11, 1707 the presumed architect of the anti-Swedish alliance was condemned to death, his body beaten with a sledgehammer and his battered head severed from his neck in four sloppy blows.[57]

Even as the struggle between the northern powers raged in distant lands, the prospect of another Muscovite offensive in the direction of their city loomed over the burghers of Riga, for Russian soldiers were rarely far away. In the summer of 1705, a Russian detachment of ten thousand men besieged the castle of Mitau (Latv. Jelgava), located some forty kilometers south of Riga, in an effort to oust the Swedes from Courland. Knowing that Riga was Sweden's most important supply point, the tsar simply could not permit his enemy to retreat to the safety of its fortifications. But could Peter's army finally capture Sweden's greatest port? During the siege of Mitau, a small force under the tsar's command made its way to Riga to work out an answer to this very question.

From the area near Fort Kobron on the opposite side of the Düna River, the Russians were able to observe Riga's fortifications for three hours on the day of August 12. Convinced that the city was capable of withstanding a Russian assault, Peter decided not to besiege Riga and instead returned to Mitau, whose garrison capitulated on September 4 after eight days of resistance, ten hours of furious bombing, and the death or incapacitation of two thousand Swedish soldiers—twice the Russian losses.[58] While good fortune now seemed to smile on the tsar and his army at every turn (not least because the Russians had just acquired another two hundred cannons), Riga was spared another great siege, for at this moment it was more important to turn back the Swedish advance than it was to capture the Livonian capital.

Once Swedish troops had been cleared from Courland, the crown's significant possessions in the Baltic littoral were reduced to merely Riga, Pernau, and Reval. Still, Charles XII refused to discuss peace, even as his rival offered to return all of Livonia, Estonia, and Ingria except for St. Petersburg, the fortress of Nöteborg-Schlisselburg, and the Neva River that linked them. Indeed, now Charles was intent on pursuing Peter just as he had chased Augustus, taking the war to Russia and leaving the devastated and depopulated Baltic provinces weakly defended. The warrior-king's audacious plan was to strike directly at Moscow, in the expectation that such an attack would draw Russian forces away from the Baltic where General Adam Ludwig von Löwenhaupt, the military governor of Riga, had at his disposal 12,500 men and stores of food and military goods. These troops could then be used as the escort for a supply convoy that would move south from Riga through the devastated lands of Poland-Lithuania. At some point the convoy was to rendezvous with the Swedish army as it swept toward the Kremlin, now being readied for battle.

While Charles went on the offensive, moving his forces into Lithuania in December 1707, Peter played defense. After a clash the following month at Grodno (a Belarusian town today), the tsar retreated and ordered a broad belt of destruction nearly two hundred kilometers wide from Pskov to Smolensk. No matter which direction the Swedes marched from their winter quarters, they would be trudging through scorched earth: bridges were destroyed, farmland ravaged, food scarce. Altogether the Swedes had some 70,000 men preparing to descend on Moscow—in Finland, in the Baltic provinces, in Saxony, and in Poland. Peter now had at his own disposal an army of 110,000 men that he had remolded after the defeat at Narva (1704) and transformed into an effective fighting force. Charles's odds of defeating this substantially larger army on its own turf were abysmal to begin with. Without the materials and men arriving from Riga, the Swedes would be sunk.

But the single-minded king of Sweden, an unmarried man now in his mid-twenties, had a plan. In March 1708, Charles XII ordered General Löwenhaupt to collect whatever supplies he would need to provision his own men for three months and the entire Swedish army for six weeks. Once they had loaded the wagon trains with food, weapons, and ammunition, his soldiers were to escort the convoy through Lithuania/Belarus to join with the main army, which Löwenhaupt would replenish for a final attack on Moscow. Overwhelmed by the volume of materials he was expected to gather for this campaign, the general was delayed and stayed in Riga a month longer than anticipated. The plan was to rendezvous with the main army at the end of July. When the appointed time arrived, however,

Löwenhaupt had barely left Livonia; meanwhile, Charles's main army, after a victory over the Russians at the Battle of Golovchin (Pol. Holowczyn), had made it as far as Mogilev on the Dnieper River, some four hundred kilometers away from Löwenhaupt's convoy.

The success of Charles's plan hinged upon the timely arrival of Löwenhaupt's men and supplies, and now they were on their way. But fleet of foot this army was not. Forced to carry in sections a heavy and unwieldy portable bridge, the Swedes lumbered through the forests and swamps, pausing to take frequent rests.[59] Before him all Charles could see was scorched earth, and still Löwenhaupt had not appeared. An advance on Moscow was impossible, but retreat meant failure. As autumn approached, Charles decided to turn south into Ukraine. This would turn out to be one of the most second-guessed decisions ever undertaken by a military commander, with consequences of stunning magnitude for Sweden, for Russia, and for all of northeastern Europe.

But first: where were the supplies from Riga? Charles would never see them, for before Löwenhaupt and his troops could meet up with the king's main army, they first encountered a force of 14,000 Russians, led by the tsar himself. Trapped in a confrontation outside Mogilev against a superior force possessing far greater firepower, Löwenhaupt's exhausted units fell apart: a few of his soldiers plundered the officer's wagons, some disappeared into the forest with Cossacks and Kalmuks in pursuit as their commander ordered a retreat. Löwenhaupt lost half his forces at the Battle of Lesnaya; three thousand of these were taken prisoner by the Russians. Between six and seven thousand survivors of the campaign ended up joining Charles's army, but the supplies from Riga that the Swedes so desperately needed were lost. Rather than allow their two thousand wagons of food and war materials to fall into the laps of the Russians, Löwenhaupt ordered that they be burned. Having lugged sixteen cannons through eight hundred kilometers of swamps and forests, the Swedes now buried them in the earth.

If less famous than the Battle of Poltava the following summer, the Battle of Lesnaya must be considered a major turning point in the Great Northern War. Its upshot was that the Swedes had effectively abandoned the Baltic, leaving Riga practically undefended. Peter himself later referred to the battle as the "first day of our good fortune."[60] As the Swedish empire slipped from Charles's grasp, so did much of his army disappear: instead of a 16,000-man corps of soldiers and a supply train bulging with provisions, King Charles XII was now left with a demoralized army of 6,500 hungry stragglers who had just endured an unparalleled disaster. Having exhausted their own provisions and unable to find anything on the land, the desperate Swedes began to eat their own horses.

Undeterred from his goal of ending this "unjust war" with an outright victory, the warrior-king now planned to lead this pitiful force south into Ukraine—a problem area for Russia that Charles hoped to exploit. The Cossacks of Astrakhan had rebelled in 1705, the Don Cossacks in 1707. Now, in the autumn of 1708, it was the turn of the Cossacks under Ivan Mazepa, the grand hetman of left-bank Ukraine, who saw in Peter's efforts at centralization a threat to traditional Cossack autonomy. These circumstances Charles intended to use to his advantage. For Mazepa, coming under a Swedish protectorate would presumably secure his Cossacks' independence not only from Russia but also from Poland and Turkey. But if Charles expected the bountiful fields of Ukraine to be overflowing with milk and honey, he was mistaken. Not only was Mazepa unable to offer much in the way of sustenance, in terms of military aid all he could give the Swedes was three or four thousand men.[61]

While Charles and his army turned toward Ukraine, the weather that October grew colder. The winter of 1708–1709 would turn out to be one of the severest in centuries. In England they called it the Great Frost. In Venice the canals were frozen over, while the Baltic Sea hardened so deeply that Scandinavians could walk across it as late as April. As the temperature plunged, rivers and roads were blocked by ice and cities became cold, dark, and desolate, isolated from their sources of supply. In the vast, empty spaces of Ukraine, where Charles's dwindling army struggled to find shelter and warmth, three thousand Swedes froze to death.

Surrender

Plague had returned to the eastern Baltic. Originating in Central Asia, the disease caused by flea-infested rats carrying *Yersinia pestis* spread to eastern and central Europe, a giant battlefield whose conditions were conducive to the spread of other epidemics as well—spotted fever, dysentery, smallpox. Striking southern Poland in 1702, whose city of Lwów (now Ukrainian Lviv) was completely depopulated, the epidemic made its way north into Lithuania and the Baltic region. The city of Danzig lost half its population in the second half of 1709; the Duchy of Courland experienced similar losses.[62] While Riga's 563 cannons, 66 mortars, twelve howitzers, and thousands of soldiers prevented the enemy from capturing the city for an entire decade, Riga's defenses were useless against *die grosse Pest.*[63]

About the plague we will have more to say later, for when the first cases appeared in Riga in the spring of 1710, the city was still struggling to recover from the catastrophic deluge of 1709, the worst in Riga's eight hundred-year history. The cause of the cataclasmic flood was an ice jam at the mouth of the Düna: nearly two meters thick in some places, the ice had frozen into place some twenty-two ships in the vicinity of Riga. But when the spring thaw began in early April there was nowhere for the water to go but up, for the Bay of Riga was still frozen. As blocks of ice crowded the river's mouth, the water overflowed the riverbanks: the islands near Riga were flooded, houses on the left bank in the Überdüna region were washed away along with many boats that were docked at Riga's pier.

On April 6 the water breached the city gates: in a flash the streets were inundated and the homes, shops, and warehouses of Riga's burghers were knee-deep in water. Before long the rising tide reached the altar of the Dome Cathedral, which for a time resembled an aquarium where fish could be seen swimming. Nor were the suburban districts spared, for the roofs of the modest houses south and east of the inner city were completely submerged.[64] Even as Rigans drowned in their dozens and hundreds lost their homes, their pleas for assistance went unanswered. Having taken the war to Russia, King Charles was in no position to send further aid: Livonia would have to defend itself with its own resources.

Abandoned by the crown, how would the broken city manage its affairs and tend to the needs of its suffering inhabitants, much less supply and maintain its thousands of defenders? More to the point: what would Riga do if—*when*—the Russians came?

The *annus horribilus* was only to grow worse for the people of Riga, for the plague that was sweeping through northern Europe was soon to hit the city, the Swedish order in the Baltic was collapsing, and the Russians were indeed coming. At the end of June, the tsar's forces, lured toward the small Ukrainian town of Poltava by a Swedish siege, braced for a confrontation with the exhausted and overstretched army of the wounded Charles XII, who had been shot in the foot on June 17. After spending a severe winter eating whatever roots and berries they could find to supplement their meager bread ration, the Swedish army of 22,000–28,000 was neither strong nor healthy.[65] Encouraged by the news of his injured rival, the Tsar Peter led his entire army across the Vorksla River. Numbering at least 40,000 and enjoying a home-field advantage—it was far easier for the Russians to supply and replace personnel than it was for the Swedes—Peter's army was well positioned to destroy such a severely weakened enemy.

The day of the battle was July 8, 1709—the result a massacre: at Poltava the Swedes lost 6,901 dead and wounded, with thousands more captured.[66] After the battle, some 14,000 soldiers of the Swedish crown surrendered to the Russian commander, Prince Alexander Menshikov, while King Charles XII made his controversial escape across the Dnieper River into Ottoman territory, perhaps hoping to spare his countrymen the spectacle of being captured and paraded through Moscow. The soldier-king never returned to his homeland, instead spending the last four years of his life in semi-captivity in Turkey before falling in battle in 1718 at the age of thirty-six.

Having routed the enemy, the Russians simply followed the muddy trail blazed by the remnants of the Swedish army in the direction of the Baltic Sea. In October the Russians arrived at Dünaburg (Daugavpils). Courland was taken that same month. If Sweden's devastating defeat at Poltava failed to persuade Charles to discuss peace, then the tsar would simply snatch away his Baltic possessions. Riga was the main target.

In anticipation of a Russian siege, the Swedes appointed a new governor-general for Livonia. It was the task of Count Nils Stromberg to prepare the city's defenses while the clock ticked, the Russians advanced, an epidemic spread through northern Europe, and hundreds of traumatized peasants streamed into the hungry city. On October 26 Muscovite forces crossed the border into Swedish Livonia. The following day Sheremetev's army blockaded the port of Riga.

As the brief Latvian autumn gave way to a typically long and dreary Baltic winter, Stromberg ordered the concentration of Riga's forces inside the city's inner defensive ring, where they joined the citizen militia. The suburban military installations were abandoned as the Swedish garrison in Riga was reinforced with 12,000 soldiers. Although the Swedes managed to maintain their hold on the fortress at Dünamünde, at the time Riga's only source of food and ammunition from the outside world, they vacated the defensive works on the river's left bank opposite the city. On Stromberg's orders, the floating bridge across the Düna was removed in order to prevent a crossing by the Russians, who took the abandoned Fort Kobron in early November and renamed it in honor of their tsar. After meeting with the resurrected Augustus II in Thorn to renew their alliance, Peter arrived at the fortress on the afternoon of November 9 and immediately ordered the installation of the heavy artillery he had brought with him—some sixty cannons and twenty-four mortars. Positioned directly across the river from Riga, such weaponry had the capacity to destroy the city.

Having inspected the environment and judged conditions to be fair, the tsar's moment of revenge was at hand. "Today at five o'clock in the morning," he wrote to Menshikov on the evening of November 14, "the bombing of Riga began, beginning with three bombs sent into the city from my own hands. May God grant us grace to avenge ourselves on this accursed place."[67] Having gotten this much satisfaction—Peter did not have fond memories of Riga—and aware of the spread of the plague from Prussia to Livonia, the tsar realized that further efforts to bring the town to its knees would be pointless and costly: at that moment, the city still had sufficient men and weaponry to defend itself, at least for the time being. Concluding that it would be better to complete the construction of the siege works and let Generals Winter and Hunger do their work on the city, Peter ordered Count Sheremetev[68] to withdraw to his winter quarters in Courland so as not to expose his men to the severity of the climate. Command of all the Russian forces in the vicinity of Riga was transferred to General Anikita Repnin, whose seven thousand soldiers were to maintain the blockade and prevent food supplies from reaching either Sweden or its military outposts. On occasion the Russians would launch bombs into the city, leaving the scurrying Rigans to attend to the flames. Meanwhile, the tsar took off for St. Petersburg, where he dedicated a new church and a ship christened *Poltava* before traveling to Moscow, where he greeted the new year.

With Riga still in the grips of hunger and its suburban districts in misery, the desperate city was flooded by Lettish and Livish peasants seeking food and security behind Riga's walls, ramparts, and moats. The absorption of all these refugees swelled the city's population beyond its capacity to meet even their most basic needs. In December 1709 there were some 10,455 mouths in Riga (in addition to the 11,000 soldiers of the Swedish garrison) that had to be fed.[69] But grain from the manors wasn't arriving, little was being sent from Sweden, and another famine soon began.

Desperate Rigans consumed horse meat as the price of food escalated through the winter and following spring. A quantity of rye that cost 1.4 thalers in March 1710 soon cost four thalers; the price of a sheep that cost two thalers in late winter escalated to nine thalers in late spring. By June almost nothing was available, for money had practically lost its value.[70] Worst affected were the city's "non-Germans," who simply starved, while those on the verge of death stumbled through the city streets begging for sustenance.[71] So great was the lack of food—only fifteen ships docked at Riga's port in 1710[72]—that Governor Stromberg resorted to coercive measures. On May 25 the Swedish official detained Riga's councilors in the basement of their Town Hall, refusing to allow them outside until they had promised to hand over their stores of grain, goods, and money. The Swedes even sent teams to search the homes of Riga's wealthiest burghers, but inspections of the town's cellars and warehouses revealed that there were, in fact, no further resources in the city.[73] The siege had depleted Riga not only of resources, but of healthy leaders and hope.

In the absence of effective government, fear, terror, and hunger ruled the city. The wanton destruction of their homes and buildings shook and shocked the suffering burghers, who understandably had little wish to die on behalf of Swedish interests. With no way of knowing when the rumbling of cannons and the falling of bombs would begin, many Rigans were forced to live in vaults or basements.[74]

The blitz briefly came to a halt at the beginning of December 1709, but on the twelfth a tragedy occurred that shook the entire city. When a church in the Citadel was set ablaze by some Russian strafing, two nearby powder towers exploded—"as if it were the end of the world," wrote Joaquim Andreas Helms, a teacher at St. Peter's school and history's eyewitness to the nine-month siege. Militarily weakened by the loss of 1,200 barrels of gunpowder and much other war equipment, the Swedes' greatest casualties were human, for some eight hundred men met their fate that day.[75]

Facing a long winter in a starving city, the soldiers assigned to defend Riga voted with their stomachs and their feet, the number of deserters noticeably rising after the destruction of the Citadel. While there is merit to the notion that the Russians would have had a good chance at success had they decided to storm the city at that very moment, such speculation is countered by the fact that Sheremetev's main army was in Courland and the only Russian forces in Riga were some Cossacks and the artillery division under Repnin's command. The final assault would have to wait until the following spring.

On March 11, 1710, General Sheremetev returned from his winter rest in Moscow to reinforce the blockade of Riga. A few weeks later he and Repnin were joined by Menshikov, whose job was to strengthen the Russian-held fortifications between Riga and Dünamünde.[76] For more than nine months the battered city was completely shut off from the outside world, its residents and refugees starving and enfeebled by disease. Conditions were even worse in the ruined Citadel next to the city. One Swedish officer in Riga reported to the governor-general that the hunger among the garrison soldiers was so great that they had to be forcibly prevented from devouring the carcasses of dead animals. In the eyes of the desperate, the city's dogs and cats looked like food.[77] Indeed, all kinds of ingenious substitutions were made for provisions that were in short supply. A case in point is the absence of suitable materials for repairing Riga's ravaged fortifications: in the absence of cement, the Swedes resorted to using quick-drying horse manure.

The pandemic that was devastating northern Europe turned out to be the continent's deadliest since the Black Death of the fourteenth century. Having ravaged the Prussian cities of Danzig and Königsberg (where some nine thousand people were buried through February 1710), the plague made its way to Riga the following spring. When the first cases cropped up—town councilors were first informed on May 10 that a person had died at the Charles Gate of plague-like symptoms—doctors initially thought it was spotted fever. It was not long before Riga's besiegers, consigned to standing in water-filled trenches outside the city, also began to fall ill. On May 14 a group of dying Russian soldiers was escorted to a nearby forest: all that could be done was to isolate them from their healthier comrades.[78]

Once a few weeks had passed, all doubt was removed: *die grosse Pest* had come to Riga, where conditions for its spread were ideal. After all, Riga was a container, enclosed by a thick wall and surrounded by the stagnant waters of the city moat and what remained of the murky Riga River. To this environment we may add the odor, rats, and various insects that made Riga a perfect petri dish. While starving burghers and refugees perished in the tens and hundreds—their bodies were buried in the cemetery at St. Gertrude's outside the inner city—the epidemic spread from the Rigans to their besiegers and to the nearby fortress at Dünamünde.

The smell of decay filled the air in Riga that summer as the death toll climbed week after week. Rare days of calm were followed by a hailstorm of bombs that rained down on the city's frightened inhabitants, tore holes into St. Mary's Church (Dome), and destroyed hundreds of homes. Some of the projectiles were packed not with gunpowder but with propaganda advertising the recent successes of the

Russian army and reminding the burghers that the Swedish king was far away in Turkey, where he was helpless to do anything for Riga.

While the claim by the burgher Joaquim Helms that 7,084 cannonballs fell on Riga seems impossibly precise, one can hardly question the burghers' overwhelming feelings of paralysis and hopelessness. "God Almighty help us, since human help is of no use," confided the diarist during the worst of the bombing.[79] Least of all would there be help from Sweden's navy, its king detained in the Ottoman lands and its navy prevented from reaching Riga by the Russian blockade.

As Rigans sank into despair, the Russians grew more confident, for the end was now in sight. Vyborg surrendered to the tsar on June 13 even as the plague began to claim the health and lives of its attackers. Soon the Swedish forces, now reeling from a string of disasters from which they would never recover, would abandon their possessions in Finland. In Riga the weakening of the garrison's health and numbers was matched by its declining resolve. Intensifying their pressure on the city, the Russian commanders unleashed another massive bombing campaign during the last days of June. To augment their use of blunt force, the attackers were open to a diplomatic solution: if the Swedish garrison refused to surrender, Sheremetev was under orders to conclude a separate peace with the city, whose residents, having endured so much for so long, now clamored for relief. Thus the military assault was preceded by a propaganda campaign that promised the Livonian nobility (and the city of Riga) guarantees of their earlier privileges and the free exercise of their faith, as well as the return of the lands that had been confiscated as a result of Charles XI's reductions.[80] Frightened and friendless, Rigans begged the Swedish military governor to negotiate favorable terms of surrender with the Russians.

As the pandemic spread from burgher to burgher and the siege took its toll, Stromberg's hold on the weakened city slipped from his grasp. According to the diarist Joaquim Helms, in the ten-day period between June 14 and 24, 1710, some 3,389 shells fell on the ravaged city.[81] On July 2 Prince Repnin captured the ruined Citadel and planted a Russian flag. Rejecting Governor Stromberg's request for a ten-day truce, Sheremetev gave the Swedish commander forty-eight hours to respond to his demands. Stromberg's inescapable answer was delivered on July 4: Swedish troops would abandon the city.[82]

Even as parts of the damaged city continued to smolder, Repnin's force of six thousand Russians peacefully entered Riga, having been ordered by Sheremetev neither to plunder the city nor to molest its remaining inhabitants. Two thousand of his men settled in the ruined Citadel.[83] As the guns went silent, the shocked, sick, and grieving burghers trickled into Riga's streets. Helms's observation that "there were not enough people living to bury the dead," was no hyperbole, for most of the city's aristocrats, magistrates, merchants, guild members, and officials had fled in search of food and safety. Of the men belonging to Riga's upper and middle classes (i.e., Germans and Swedes), only 864 remained in the city, along with a few thousand laborers and service people—that is, Latvians and Livs. Their numbers, too, had been eviscerated by the plague: of Riga's 150 registered porters, only fifteen remained alive at the moment of Riga's capitulation.[84]

The occupiers quickly learned that surviving Rigans were too ill to be of any use at all. Their care was now the responsibility of General Sheremetev, who ordered the distribution of provisions that could meet the immediate needs of 4,500 people.[85] But the worst of the plague was yet to come, for "after the city was opened," wrote Constantin Mettig, the Baltic German historian of Riga, "the fresh air penetrating the city seemed to befoul the miasma of the plague, distributing it across the city."[86] If this dubious account lacks the virtue of scientific accuracy (much like Peter's belief that by setting alight piles of horse dung the disease might be prevented from spreading among his soldiers),[87] it suggests that there was much more suffering to come even after the surrender. As was nearly always true of the armed conflicts of the early modern era, during the years of the Great Northern War far more people died from hunger and disease than from wounds sustained in combat.

Aftermath

In their wartime correspondence the tsar and his subordinates playfully discussed the occupation in allegorical terms: the union between Russia and Riga was a "wedding" and the captured city was the "bride."[88] That the tsar's banter was a play on the custom of symbolic bride kidnapping, then common in areas around Russia's periphery, seems evident enough. Whether or not the act was consensual, Riga was now betrothed to Russia.

Thus, even as thousands of their own soldiers succumbed to the epidemic, the Russians announced the conclusion of their grueling siege by staging a triumph in Riga—a celebration of the city's conjugal bond with the tsar's swollen realm. The parade held for Sheremetev on July 12 reflected the grandeur of the occasion. Fetched into the smoldering and broken city at the Charles Gate by eight knights and prominent citizens of Riga, Sheremetev was awarded two symbolic gold keys to the city by the surviving members of the town council. Riding a white horse, the commander along with his procession (including Prince Repnin) entered Riga in grand style, with dozens of Livonian nobles and officers hailing the city's conqueror to the accompaniment of trumpets and drums. Cannons mounted in the city and in the Citadel were shot in the air as the party approached the entrance to the Riga Castle. A congregation heard sermons of gratitude at St. Peter's Church, where the assembled noblemen sang the traditional Christian hymn of praise, "Te Deum."

Sheremetev then rode to the Town Hall Square, where he approached a podium that was overlain with red cloth. At the center of the stage was a chair covered with red velvet cloth and golden pleats. Draped above the chair was a canopy, also made of red velvet. It was at this spot, then and now the heart of Old Riga, that the Russian commander accepted oaths of loyalty from the Livonian noblemen on the tsar's behalf. When the spectacle came to an end, Sheremetev climbed into his carriage and the procession departed for his main camp outside the city. Such were the events of July 12, 1710, as recorded by Joachim Helms.[89] It was the last entry in the schoolteacher's diary of the siege.

Having completed his mission, Sheremetev transferred his command to Repnin, who that autumn would be appointed the first Russian governor-general of Riga. The other transfer of power, from Sweden to Russia, took place without any major incidents. While Russians occupied the entirety of the devastated city, the surviving members of the Rath were stripped of their keys to the city gates. Many years would pass before the town council resumed its normal activities.[90]

All that remained of Swedish power in Riga was the garrison at Dünamünde, whose soldiers courageously resisted even as they fell victim to the plague. The garrison's final moments came in the last days of August, when the fortress at last fell to the Russian army. The coastal city of Pernau was taken in the middle of the month, and Reval's turn came in late September. "The enemy does not now possess a single town on the left side of the East Sea, not even an inch of land," the tsar wrote to his adviser Alexis Kurbatov, to which the latter enthused about the prospect of exporting the riches of Russia to the West without having to rely on the distant White Sea port of Archangel.[91]

Then there was the matter of exchanging personnel. Swedish officials were allowed to return to Stockholm, while captured Swedish soldiers were sent to Moscow so that they might be exchanged for the Russians taken at Narva in 1700. A similar fate befell Nils Stromberg: the former governor of Riga and Swedish Livland would be held in captivity for an entire year before he was exchanged for a captured general of the Russian army. Also seized by the Russians were some two hundred pieces of artillery, many of which had been cast in Riga. Although most of Riga's guns remained in the city castle after the capitulation, the most famous among them, the "Lion of Riga," presently adorns the entrance to the Museum of Artillery in St. Petersburg.

The plague continued to rage through the summer and autumn of 1710. Reduced to 5,132 men at the moment of their surrender, the soldiers of the Swedish garrison were already gravely ill when they were escorted to Moscow.[92] Some 9,800 Russian soldiers—one quarter of the tsar's forces—also fell victim to the epidemic.[93] By the time Peter I approved the "Points of Accord" that October, confirming all the traditional rights and privileges of the Baltic nobility and also of the burghers of Riga, more than half the councilors of the Rath had died. Illness had taken the aldermen of both guilds, every official of the local courts had perished.[94] All of Riga's leading families were robbed of precious lives. Of the men of the patrician Dreyling family, only one remained at the war's end; the Depkins, men of the church, lost all but two of their male kin.[95]

Caskets being in short supply, the dead remained in their beds or on the streets for days on end. Filled with the bodies of the deceased, churches reeked of death and myrrh, a sweet-smelling resin that was used to mask the scent of decay.[96] Even as they abandoned Livonia in defeat, the city's previous masters could not escape the plague, for when the 114 former members of the Swedish administration (and their families) in Riga arrived in Stockholm in the autumn of 1710, the Swedish capital was burying some 1,500 victims each week.[97] Riga, in the meantime, plunged into darkness, its buildings and domiciles in ruins, its warehouses abandoned, its inhabitants defeated by hunger and by the worst plague Livonia had ever known.

Throughout the eastern Baltic, the bodies piled up, the living too weak and ill to bury the dead. In the besieged city of Reval in Estonia, the plague claimed the lives of two-thirds of the population, reduced to a mere 1,732 souls by October 1711.[98] Lacking a similar set of records, it is impossible to say how many men, women, and children died in Riga during the cataclysmic years of 1709 and 1710. Claims that some 22,000 Rigans were killed during the Russian bombardment or that 30,000 or even 60,000 Rigans lost their lives to the plague stretch the limits of credulity, as it is unlikely that the city—even with its suburbs included—ever housed that many people prior to the Russian era.[99] No less extreme, but impossible to verify, is the estimation of J. Straubergs, who suggested that the misfortunes of the era—beginning with the famine of 1697—claimed the lives of perhaps 80 percent of the inhabitants of Riga and its outlying districts.[100] The survivors of this ordeal, especially the territory's rural inhabitants, lived in misery for many years thereafter, for serfdom, a condition that in many respects was little different from slavery, would return to Livonia with the Russian occupation. As the historian Arnolds Spekke observed, "After 1710 the Latvian and Estonian peasants became living machines—robots."[101]

When the Russians took control of Riga, all that remained in the city were perhaps six thousand scared and hungry souls, many of whom were peasant refugees who had barely put down roots. This was about half the city's population at the time of the war's outbreak a decade earlier. If Riga proper had become a tomb, then the undeveloped districts across the river in Überdüna (what is now Pārdaugava) had become little more than a desert zone, practically devoid of human inhabitants. It would take until the end of the 1720s before Riga's population returned to its prewar level.

Whatever the actual cost in lives and property, the era of the Great Northern War was for Rigans, and for Livonia as a whole, the very worst of times. From the vantage point of 1709–1710, the fat years of the 1680s and 1690s must have seemed like a faded dream. It is perhaps for this reason above all that the "good old Swedish times" came to enjoy such a fine reputation, for what followed was calamity. The early years of Russian rule were to become notorious for their hardships and deprivations; it would be many years before life returned to normal in the shattered city.

What is sometimes overlooked in the standard accounts of the Great Northern War is the demographic catastrophe that all but wiped out the Livs of war-ravaged Vidzeme, then Swedish Livland. Their farms devastated, many of the surviving Livs fled to Riga, where the refugees intermingled with larger numbers of Letts. Perhaps no event did more to accelerate the extinction of the Livish people than the catastrophic war that opened the eighteenth century. Already by the early 1600s their language had vanished in Riga and its neighboring districts, but it was the Great Northern War that accelerated the disappearance of the Livish language in eastern Latvia, until then a deeply bilingual environment.

If the arrival of German merchants, warriors, and priests in the thirteenth century inaugurated the subjugation and conversion of the Finno-Ugric tribes that gave Livonia its name, it was the Great Northern War that all but ensured their eventual extinction. The Livs' fate would be sealed during the era of Soviet rule in the twentieth century, when their last remaining villages in western Latvia came under Moscow's close military supervision. No longer able to make a living from fishing along the coastal waters of Courland, the last speakers of the Livish tongue moved to Riga or elsewhere, while a stubborn handful aged and died in their ancestral villages.[102]

Epilogue

One can hold the Russians responsible for the plague no more than one can blame the Saxons, the Poles, or the Jews—although in some European towns the Jewish populations were made to feel the brunt of popular fury: at the height of the plague, Jews were expelled from several of the afflicted population centers. But Jews had yet to settle in the city of Riga, at least not in any significant numbers.[1] The migration of Jews to Riga, and of Russian officials and laborers, are among the many developments that would take place during the two centuries that followed Riga's capitulation to the tsar. The city's renovation and the appearance of dozens of yellow-brick factory buildings in the suburbs—magnets for hundreds of thousands of Latvian peasants who joined the ranks of a swelling urban proletariat—were still to come. The ruined city that fell to Tsar Peter I in 1710 had none of the parks, canals, gardens, and urban villas that would transform Riga into one of northeastern Europe's most attractive and welcoming cities during the twilight years of the Russian Empire.

Even as Riga tore down its medieval walls in the 1850s and incorporated the suburban areas, where promenades and beautiful homes were built for the city's prosperous bourgeoisie, the oldest parts of Riga would retain many of their traditional features into present times. The old Order Castle near the Düna embankment, which became a seat of Russian power, remains in place, as have the city's great medieval churches and a handful of its public buildings, some of which, like the Town Hall and the House of Blackheads, were either upgraded or rebuilt in their entirety. If many of Riga's narrow, winding, and cobbled streets looked much the same in 1900 as they did in 1700, the symbols of Russian power in Riga gradually accumulated and communicated none too subtly the city's subordinate and permanent status in the empire. Among these were a Victory Column (1817) to commemorate Russia's triumph over Napoleon, an enormous Orthodox church (1883) to meet the spiritual needs of the city's growing Russian population, and an equestrian statue (1910) of Riga's conqueror, Peter the Great, his austere gaze fixed on the east. All were intended to remind Riga's burghers—Germans, Latvians, Russians, and Jews—of both the benevolence and the permanence of the tsar's authority.

The westward-facing Freedom Monument that since 1935 has towered over the spot that was previously occupied by the tsar's bronze likeness would surely have been inconceivable to the Rigans of the eighteenth century—not least because this location was at that time a bastion in Riga's complex system of fortifications. At the same time, one suspects that the Rigans of yesteryear might have appreciated the monument's underlying idea: Riga, after all, was founded as a "free city" of the loosely administered Holy Roman Empire. While this river city has always enjoyed links with foreign lands, a thorough examination of its first five hundred years of recorded history confirms that Riga's political, religious, and cultural roots were always in the West (Europe) and never in the East (Russia).

The love of liberty and self-governance had been central elements of Riga's civic identity from the beginning. To defend the city's autonomy, its burghers had twice fought the knightly orders of the Middle Ages; at other times they fought foreign powers. But now Riga's ancient privileges and liberties, although in principle protected by an unusually generous treaty, were in fact irretrievably lost, for the broken and burning city, its noxious air carrying the stench of decay as its desperate inhabitants scrounged for food and firewood in its darkened streets and empty warehouses, had become a possession of Russia's victorious tsar. Having eluded this fate for centuries, Riga under Russian power was torn from its Western roots.

It was not until the twentieth century that the Düna metropolis reinvented itself as a center of Latvian politics and culture. Today this city of 700,000, divided equally between Latvians and ethnic Russians,[2] is recognized as the capital of the Republic of Latvia—a Latvian nation-state that would have been inconceivable to Rigans of the eighteenth and nineteenth centuries, when Livonia and its greatest city were in the iron grip of St. Petersburg. Had they been able to enjoy a glimpse of Riga's future, how strange it all would have seemed to its German-speaking burghers. The notion that someday their proud and prosperous port would emerge as a beautiful and vibrant *Latvian* city, its *Latvian* president holding court in a castle built for German knights, is something that no Rigan, whatever his native tongue, could possibly have imagined at the conclusion of the Great Northern War.

Notes

Introduction

1. An updated and expanded edition is now available. Kevin C. O'Connor, *The History of the Baltic States*, 2nd ed. (Santa Barbara, CA: Greenwood, 2015).

2. Arvīds Jozaitis, *Rīga—cita civilizācija* (Rīga: Zvaigzne, 2014).

3. There have been several excellent studies of Riga at various historical moments in the twentieth century, among them Anders Henriksson, *Vassals and Citizens: The Baltic Germans in Constitutional Russia, 1905–1914* (Marburg: Herder-Institut, 2009); Mark Hatlie, *Riga at War: War and Wartime Experience in a Multi-ethnic Metropolis* (Marburg: Herder-Institut, 2014); Geoffrey Swain, *Between Stalin and Hitler: Class War and Race War on the Dvina, 1940–46* (London: Routledge, 2004).

4. Anders Henriksson, *The Tsar's Loyal Germans: The Riga Community: Social Change and the Nationality Question, 1855–1905* (Boulder, CO: East European Monographs, 1983), 68.

5. Wilhelm von Neumann, *Das mittelalterliche Riga: Ein Beitrag zur Geschichte der Norddeutschen Baukunst* (Berlin: Julius Springer, 1892); *Riga und Reval* (Leipzig: E.A. Seamann, 1908).

6. See Jakob G. L. Napiersky, *Die Quellen des rigischen Stadtrechts bis zum Jahr 1673* (Riga: J. Deubner, 1876). Among Georg von Bunge's many works on Riga's legal history is *Die Stadt Riga im dreizehnten und vierzehnten Jahrhundert. Geschichte, Verfassung und Rechtszustand* (Leipzig: Verlag von Duncker & Humboldt, 1878; repr. Amsterdam: E. J. Bonset, 1968). Citations herein are to the 1878 edition. Most of Bunge's collections have been digitized and are available online.

7. Johann Kristofs Broce [Brotze], *Zīmējumi un apraksti / 1. sējums Rīgas skati, ļaudis un ēkas* (Rīga: Zinātne, 1992); *Zīmējumi un apraksti. / 2. sējums Rīgas priekšpilsētas un tuvākā apkārtne* (Rīga: Zinātne, 1996). Translated into Latvian from the original German.

8. See Jānis Lejnieks, *Rīga, kuras nav* (Rīga: Zinātne, 1998).

9. Arveds Schwabe [Švābe], *The Story of Latvia: A Historical Survey* (Stockholm: NLF, 1949); Arnolds Spekke, *History of Latvia: An Outline* (Stockholm: M. Goppers, 1950).

10. Indriķis Šterns, *Latvijas vēsture, 1180–1290. Krustakari* (Rīga: Latvijas vēstures institūta apgāds, 2002); Indriķis Šterns, *Latvijas vēsture, 1290–1500* (Rīga: Daugava, 1997).

11. Alfred Bilmanis, *A History of Latvia* (Princeton, NJ: Princeton University Press, 1951). Edgars Dunsdorfs published many works of history, among them *Latvijas vēsture, 1500–1600* (Stockholm: Daugava, 1964) and *Latvijas vēsture, 1600–1710* (Stockholm: Daugava, 1962).

12. See, for example, Reinhard Wittram, *Baltische Geschichte: Die Ostseelande Livland, Estland, Kurland, 1180–1918* (Munich: R. Oldenbourg, 1954), whose works reflected a *völkisch* framework that emphasized the hegemony of the Baltic German communities in

Livonia. Also see the following edited collections: Matthias Thumser, ed., *Geschichtsschreibung im mittelalterlichen Livland* (Münster: LIT, 2011); Ilgvars Misāns and Horst Wernickje, eds., *Riga und der Ostseeraum: Von der Gründung 1201 bis in die Frühe Neuzeit* (Marburg: Herder-Institut, 2005); Udo Arnold, ed., *Stadt und Orden: Das Verhältnis der Deutschen Ordens zu den Städten in Livland, Preussen und im Deutschen Reich* (Marburg: N.G. Elwert, 1993).

13. Friedrich von Benninghoven, *Rigas Entstehung und der frühhansische Kaufmann* (Hamburg: August Friedrich Velmede, 1961).

14. Wilhelm Lenz, *Riga zwischen dem Römischen Reich and Polen-Litauen in den jahren 1558–1582* (Marburg/Lahn: Herder-Institut, 1968); Thomas Lange, *Zwischen Reformation und Untergang Alt-Livlands: Der Rigaer Erzbischof Wilhelm von Brandenburg im Beziehungsgeflecht der livländischen Konföderation und ihrer Nachbarländer* (Hamburg: Verlag Dr. Kovač, 2014).

15. Andreas Fülberth, *Riga: Kleine Geschichte der Stadt* (Cologne: Böhlau, 2014).

16. Other important works by William Urban include *The Teutonic Knights: A Military History* (South Yorkshire, UK: Frontline Books, 2003) and *The Baltic Crusade* (DeKalb: Northern Illinois University Press, 1975).

17. Walther Kirchner, *The Rise of the Baltic Question* (Newark: University of Delaware Press, 1954).

18. Anu Mänd, *Urban Carnival: Festive Culture in the Hanseatic Cities of the Eastern Baltic, 1350–1550* (Turnhout, Belgium: Brepols 2005).

19. Ojārs Spārītis, *Monuments and Decorative Sculpture in Rīga* (Rīga: Nacionālais medicīnas apgāds, 2001).

20. Andrejs Plakans, *The Latvians: A Short History* (Stanford, CA: Hoover Institute Press, 1995); *A Concise History of the Baltic States* (New York: Cambridge University Press, 2011).

21. Teodors Zeids, *Feodālā Rīga* (Rīga: Zinātne, 1978).

22. See, for example, Andris Caune, *Pētījumi Rīgas arheoloģijā* (Rīga: Latvijas vēstures institūta apgāds, 2007).

23. *Enciklopēdija Rīga* (Rīga: Galvenā enciklopēdiju redakcija, 1988).

24. The two volumes of Iuri Abyzov, *Ot Lifliandiia k Latvii: Pribaltika russkimi glazami* (Moscow: Arkaiur, 1993), demonstrate a Russian perspective on life in Riga during the interwar era. The recent works of local historian Igor' Gusev view Riga's history through a distinctly Russian lens. See his *Istoriia Rigi: V voprosakh i otvetakh* (Riga: Zoriks, 2016).

25. Andres Kasekamp, *A History of the Baltic States* (New York: Palgrave, 2009), x.

26. John Leighly, "The Towns of Medieval Livonia," *University of California Publications in Geography* 6, no. 7 (1939), 238.

Chapter 1

1. Although the Latvian spelling of Rīga has been in official use since 1919, this book uses the traditional German spelling. The same holds true for most other place names, although when referring to tribal territories and castles I have gone with their Latvian names (e.g., Turaida, Jersika, etc.). Throughout the German occupation, Latvians continued to use many of the old or Latvianized place names alongside the Germanized ones.

2. On the origins of the ancient Balts, see Endre Bojtár, *Foreword to the Past: A Cultural History of the Baltic People* (Budapest: Central European University Press, 1999); Marija Gimbutas, *The Balts* (New York: Frederick A. Praeger, 1963); Mara Kalnins, *Latvia: A Short History* (London: Hurst, 2015), 1–24.

3. *Sen to Rīgu daudzināja/ Nu to Rīgu ieraudziju/ Visapkārt smilšu kalni/ Pate Rīga ūdenī*. As appears in Šterns, *Latvijas vēsture, 1290–1500*, 307.

4. Matti Klinge, *The Baltic World* (Keuruu: Ostava, 1995), 18; Gusev, *Istoriia Rigi*, 53–54; I. Gusev, *Istoriia Rigi i okrestnostei* (Riga: Zoriks, 2008), 11–12.

5. Zeids, *Feodālā Rīga*, 14; Bojtár, *Foreword to the Past*, 21.

6. Bilmanis, *History of Latvia*, 7, 98–99; Mara Kalnins, *The Ancient Amber Route: Travels from Rīga to Byzantium* (Rīga: Pētergailis, 2013), 35.

7. Rus' merchants called this channel the Dvina, for its source is in Russia's Valdai Hills, located about midway between Moscow and St. Petersburg. The river's Latvian name is the Daugava, a word that may have been derived from the word "*daudz*" (much), suggestive of the water's wide expanse and strong current. Germans arriving via the Baltic Sea called it the Düna, and that is the name we shall use throughout this book, for this is how the river was indicated in the earliest maps and in centuries of record keeping and official correspondence—even if there are equally valid reasons for calling the river by its Latvian or Russian names.

8. *The Chronicle of Novgorod*, trans. Robert Michel and Nevill Forbes (London: Offices of the Society, 1914), http://faculty.washington.edu/dwaugh/rus/texts/MF1914.pdf.

9. Although the word "Rus'" (or "Rus") originally referred to the Norsemen of what is now Russia, Rus' generally refers to the East Slavic people who inhabited parts of modern-day Russia, Belarus, and Ukraine.

10. On the Baltic amber trade, see Arnolds Spekke, *The Ancient Amber Routes and the Geographical Discovery of the Eastern Baltic* (Stockholm: M. Goppers, 1957); Kalnins, *Ancient Amber Route, passim*; Bojtár, *Foreword to the Past*, 23–35.

11. Tacitus, *The Agricola and the Germania*, trans. H. Mattingly (New York: Penguin, 1948; reprint, New York: Penguin, 1986), 139–40.

12. Klaus Zernack, "The Middle Ages" in *The Germans and the East*, eds. Charles Ingrao and Franz A. J. Szabo (West Lafayette, IN: Purdue University Press, 2008), 10–11.

13. In recent decades, scholars have warmed to the concept of "otherness," which refers to the means by which Westerners since Plato have come to define themselves against cultural outsiders. For further insights into this idea, see, for example, Richard Kearney, *Strangers, Gods and Monsters: Interpreting Otherness* (London: Routledge, 2003).

14. See the outstanding collection of essays in Alan V. Murray, ed., *The Clash of Cultures on the Medieval Baltic Frontier* (London: Ashgate, 2009).

15. Eric Christiansen, *The Northern Crusades* (New York: Penguin, 1997), 56–57.

16. Robert Bartlett, *The Making of Europe: Conquest, Colonization and Cultural Change, 950–1300* (Princeton, NJ: Princeton University Press, 1993), 67. Here we should note that about 80 percent of the castles set up by the Normans were of the motte-and-bailey type—that is, a fort made of earth and timber and situated on a raised earthwork called a motte. By the time the German invaders began to build fortifications in Livonia, where many castles were built from bricks and stones, this type of construction had come to an end.

17. In the fourteenth century, the most active period of castle building in Latvia, fifty-four castles were established in the region. Andris Šnē, "The Emergence of Livonia: The Transformations of Social and Political Structures in the Territory of Latvia during the Twelfth and Thirteenth Centuries," in *The Clash of Cultures on the Medieval Baltic Frontier*, ed. Alan V. Murray (London: Ashgate, 2009), 67.

18. Another Latvian river, the Lielupe, was known as the Kurländische (Couronian) Aa. This book typically uses the terms Gauja and Lielupe to avoid confusion.

19. A related term is *Ostbewegung*, the "eastward movement."

20. Jan Piskorski, "Medieval Colonization in East Central Europe," in *The Germans and the East*, eds. Charles Ingrao and Franz A.J. Szabo (West Lafayette, IN: Purdue University Press, 2008), 28–29.

21. Lonnie R. Johnson, *Central Europe: Enemies, Neighbors, Friends*, 2nd ed. (New York: Oxford University Press, 2002), 38–42.

22. Urban, *Teutonic Knights*, 13.

23. On the "papal monarchy," the origins of the crusades, and the motives of the crusaders, see John France, *The Crusades and the Expansion of Catholic Christendom, 1000–1714* (London: Routledge, 2005), 23–60.

24. The Sorbs, descendants of the Wends, are the only remnants of the Slavic tribes of this region to retain their cultural identity. The Sorbian language is still spoken by approximately 60,000 people in Germany today.

25. See Timothy Reuter's introduction to Adam of Bremen, *History of the Archbishops of Hamburg-Bremen*, trans. Francis J. Tschan (New York: Columbia University Press, 2002), xi–xxi. Also see Urban, *Baltic Crusade*, 34–38.

26. On papal policy regarding the Baltic crusades, see Iben Fonnesberg-Schmidt, *The Popes and the Baltic Crusades, 1147–1254* (Leiden: Brill, 2007). The author argues that papal policy on the Northern Crusades "was not an evolving one," but varied from pope to pope.

27. On the Wendish conversions, see Christiansen, *Northern Crusades*, 27–34, 50–72.

28. Known to modern readers as the monk who accused Peter Abelard of heresy in the 1130s, Bernard also played a leading role in the development of the Virgin cult, which was one of the most important manifestations of popular Christianity in the twelfth century and was certainly exploited for propaganda purposes by Riga's first bishop, who returned to Germany every year to recruit pilgrims to fight in *Marienland*—the Land of Mary.

29. Fonnesberg-Schmidt, *Popes and Baltic Crusades*, 32–33, 40–41.

30. Writing centuries after the tragedy he describes, Johann Gottfried Herder, a German pastor who lived in Riga in the 1760s and who came to know the locals and their languages, was aghast: "Humanity shudders at the thought of the blood shed in the savage wars, in which the Old Prussians were wiped off the face of the earth, and the Kurs and the Latvians reduced to slavery." Quoted in Spekke, *History of Latvia*, 152.

31. Bartlett, *Making of Europe*, 251.

32. Even after the German conquest, Latvians continued to use their own designations for Latvia's towns, rivers, and other place names. While I have chosen in some instances to use the traditional Latvian place names, this study generally uses the German names instead.

33. Guntis Zemītis, "10th–12th Century Daugmale—The Earliest Urban Settlement along the Lower Daugava and Forerunner of Riga," in *Cultural Interaction between East

and West: Archaeology, Artefacts and Human Contacts in Northern Europe, ed. Ulf Fransson (Stockholm: Stockholm Studies in Archaeology, 2007), 279–84.

34. On Latvia's urban development prior to the thirteenth century, see Andris Šnē, "Emergence and Development of Early Urbanism in the Late Prehistoric Latvia," in *Riga and der Ostseeraum: Von der Gründung 1201 bis in die Frühe Neuzeit*, eds. Ilgvars Misāns and Horst Wernicke (Marburg: Herder-Institut, 2005), 24–36.

35. See, for example, Kalnins, *Latvia*, cited above; Aldis Purs, *Baltic Facades: Estonia, Latvia and Lithuania since 1945* (London: Reaktion Books, 2012), 25; Bilmanis, *History of Latvia*, 38–49. Eric Christiansen takes a different view, arguing that the developments of this period "were not necessarily leading to greater cohesion or solidarity between the tribes." Christiansen, *Northern Crusades*, 37.

36. Spekke, *History of Latvia*, 120.

37. Plakans, *Concise History*, 13–14.

38. Latin terms for the Latvian peoples are still commonly used in the Anglophone world. Latgallians (sometimes spelled "Latgalians" or "Letgallians") are called *latgaļi* in modern Latvian, but *latgalīši* in the Latgallian dialect. Couronians (Cours) are *kurši*, Semigallians (Semigalians) are *zemgaļi*, and Selonians (Sels) are *sēļi*. See Plakans, *Latvians*, 40–43.

39. Analyses of water names reveal that the ancestors of the modern Baltic peoples likely once occupied a far wider swath of territory, from today's Kaliningrad to the upper reaches of the Dnieper River, than the tiny nation-states into which the Latvians and Lithuanians are squeezed now. See Bojtár, *Foreword to the Past*, 50–55.

40. Exactly when the Latvian and Lithuanian languages began to differentiate is unclear. Some scholars suggest that the separation began some two thousand years ago; others suggest it began more than half a millennium later, around the eighth century. See Spekke, *History of Latvia*, 55–56; Bojtár, *Foreword to the Past*, 75–76.

41. Bilmanis, *History of Latvia*, 29.

42. While Estonia is one of the three "Baltic states" that appeared after World War I, the majority of its inhabitants are speakers of a Finno-Ugric language.

43. The etymology of the world "Baltic" remains unsettled. One possibility is that it is derived from the Lithuanian-Latvian root *balt-*, meaning "white." Endre Bojtár suggests a likely Germanic origin, positing that Adam of Bremen derived the Latin *balticus* from the Germanic *belt-* (meaning "belt" or "zone"), perhaps using it to indicate the inland sea's extension from west to east like a belt. Bilmanis, *History of Latvia*, 1–2; Bojtár, *Foreword to the Past*, 8–10.

44. Kalnins, *Latvia*, 18–19.

45. See Anti Selart, *Livonia, Rus' and the Baltic Crusades in the Thirteenth Century*, trans. Fiona Robb (Leiden: Brill, 2015).

46. That many Livs became bilingual, perhaps as early as the sixteenth century, speaking both Latvian and their ancestral tongue, lends credence to the notion that the Livs were gradually assimilated by the numerically superior Latvians. Plakans, *Latvians*, 42.

47. Courland's outline is currently reflected in the silhouette of Riga's glitzy and shockingly expensive national library, completed in 2014.

48. Cours also lived in the area around Riga at the time of the German conquest. Scholars once speculated that the Cours, whose tribal territories included parts of present-day

Lithuania, were speakers of a Finno-Ugric language, but it is now believed that they spoke a Baltic language that was close to Lithuanian but increasingly resembled the dialects spoken by the Latvian tribes. Following the German-Christian conquest, most Cours melded into the Latvian nation. Bojtár, *Foreword to the Past*, 117.

49. The wide geographical dispersion of the Wends in ancient times is also indicated by the place names for western France's Vendée region and the Italian city of Venice.

50. James A. Brundage, ed. and trans., *The Chronicle of Henry of Livonia* (New York: Columbia University Press, 1961), 66–67 (hereafter cited as *CHL*).

51. A local historian of Riga, Igor' Gusev, ardently defends the presence of Slavic influences in prehistoric Latvia. These are discussed in detail in his *Istoriia Rigi*, 25–51. On the basis of Slavic ethnonyms and archaeological evidence, Gusev presents research purporting that Wendish communities lived in northern Courland and the lower Düna since the eighth century CE, and that they lived in Riga's environs since at least the eleventh century. Gusev moreover advances the thesis that the Latvian Wends had a "Slavic identity." The politicization of Riga's prehistory can also be seen in the excavations authorized by Republic of Latvia during the Ulmanis dictatorship of the 1930s, for their purpose was to confirm the city's Latvian origins.

52. William L. Urban elaborates on this point in his essay "Victims of the Baltic Crusade," *Journal of Baltic Studies* 29, no. 3 (Fall 1998), 195–212.

53. A classic work on Baltic prehistory, including the Balts' mythology and spirituality, is Gimbutas, *Balts*. While Gimbutas's book was pioneering in that it introduced Baltic prehistory to the outside world, it projected documented evidence about paganism from the later Middle Ages and afterward onto the ancient Balts, a common but questionable practice. Also see Kalnins, *Latvia*, 27–37.

54. Spekke, *History of Latvia*, 59–70. More generally, see Vaira Vikis-Freibergs, ed., *Linguistics and Poetics of Latvian Folk Songs: Essays in Honour of the Sesquicentennial of the Birth of Kr. Barons* (Kingston, Ont.: McGill–Queen's University Press, 1989.

55. Marek Tamm, "A New World into Old Worlds: The Eastern Baltic Region and the Cultural Geography of Medieval Europe," in *The Clash of Cultures on the Medieval Baltic Frontier*, ed. Alan V. Murray (London: Ashgate, 2009), 28.

56. Ibid., 27.

57. Carsten Selch Jensen, "How to Convert a Landscape: Henry of Livonia and the *Chronicon Livoniae*," in *The Clash of Cultures on the Medieval Baltic Frontier*, ed. Alan V. Murray (London: Ashgate, 2009), 152. While not enough information is available about Henry to make even the slimmest biography a possibility, it seems clear that he was not a "Latvian" native, as some later Latvian historians have suggested, but a German who was probably born in Saxony in the 1180s. It is also likely that he was trained at the Segeberg Abbey, where he would have learned about Meinhard's mission and probably acquired a basic knowledge of Livish (thanks to Bishop Albert's abduction of thirty young Livish hostages in 1200) and perhaps Lettish and Estonian before traveling to Livonia with Albert of Buxhoeveden's brother Rothmar (a priest at Segeberg) and "the rest of Albert's household" in 1205. See James A. Brundage, "Introduction: Henry of Livonia, The Writer and His Chronicle," in *Crusading and Chronicle Writing on the Medieval Baltic Frontier: A*

Companion to the Chronicle of Henry of Livonia, eds. Marek Tamm, Linda Kaljundi, and Carsten Selch Jensen (Burlington, VT: Ashgate, 2011), 1–19. In the same volume, also see Alan V. Murray, "Henry the Interpreter," 107–34.

58. Tamm, "New World," 32.

59. Brundage, *CHL*, bk. 4, 91.

60. Written from a clerical point of view in support of the Livonian church, the chronicle was written in Latin between 1224 and 1227 and first appeared in print in 1740. Published in English translation in 1961, Henry's chronicle has received considerable scholarly attention in recent years and has done much to shape the historical image of the crusades to Livonia.

61. Mark R. Munzinger, "The Profits of the Cross: Merchant Involvement in the Baltic Crusade (ca. 1180–1230)," *Journal of Medieval History* 32, no. 2 (2006), 163–85.

62. Although it was originally written in German, Jānis Straubergs included a Latvian translation of this passage in his *Rīgas vēsture* (Rīga: Grāmatu draugs, 1937), 14–15. The translation from Straubergs's Latvian into the Queen's English, however imperfect, is my own.

63. Tenu Karma, "Septini Lībiski vietvārdi Daugavas krastos," in *Daugavas Raksti: No Rīgas līdz jūrai*, comp. Vaida Villeruša (Rīga: Zinātne, 1994), 152.

64. Munzinger, "Profits of the Cross," 166–67.

65. There are several excellent accounts of Meinhard's mission in Livonia available in English. See, for example, Carsten Selch Jensen, "The Nature of the Early Missionary Activities and Crusades in Livonia, 1195–1201," in *Medieval Spirituality in Scandinavia and Europe: A Collection of Essays in Honour of Tore Nyberg*, ed. Lars Bisgaard (New York: Oxford University Press, 2001), 121–38. Also see Munzinger, "Profits of the Cross," 163–72.

66. At the time "Livonia" referred only to the right bank of the downstream Düna; only later did Livonia come to be equated with the territory of present-day Vidzeme and southern Estonia.

67. Tamm, "New World," 22–23.

68. The extent to which the peoples of eastern Latvia had embraced the Orthodox faith is a subject of some dispute. Latvian medieval historian Indriķis Šterns takes the position that Orthodoxy was not widespread there at the time of the German invasion. See Šterns, *Latvijas vēsture, 1180–1290*, 723.

69. Manfred Hellmann, "Die Anfänge christlicher Mission in den baltischen Ländern," in *Studien über die Anfänge der Mission in Livland*, ed. Manfred Hellmann (Sigmaringen, Germany: Jan Thorbecke, 1989), 20–23; Munzinger, "Profits of the Cross," 168.

70. Brundage, *CHL*, bk. 3, sec. 10, par. 1, p. 54.

71. Tiina Kala, "Rural Society and Religious Innovation: Acceptance and Rejection of Catholicism among the Native Inhabitants of Medieval Livonia," in *The Clash of Cultures on the Medieval Baltic Frontier*, ed. Alan V. Murray (London: Ashgate, 2009), 175.

72. This practice of building small castles to secure the mission had earlier been undertaken by Swedish crusaders in Finland and soon became a common strategy along the borders of Latin Christendom. Jensen, "Early Missionary Activities," 126–27.

73. Constantin Mettig, *Geschichte der Stadt Riga* (Riga: Jonck & Poliewsky, 1897), 3.

74. Munzinger, "Profits of the Cross," 169.

75. The arrangement establishing Hamburg-Bremen's metropolitan rights over the new see remained in place until 1214, when the third bishop of Livonia, Albert of Buxhoeveden, obtained a letter declaring his see free of any metropolitan jurisdiction. As we shall see, Albert never would achieve his goal of elevating Riga's status to that of archbishopric. Fonnesberg-Schmidt, *Popes and Baltic Crusades*, 66, 85.

76. With the help of the Swedish duke Birger Jarl, Meinhard also sent an armed force to fight the Couronians, whom, like the Estonians of Ösel (now Saaremaa), the Germans regarded as notorious pirates. Munzinger, "Profits of the Cross," 171–72.

77. Although the letter has since been lost, the pope's authorization of a crusade in Livonia was reported by both Henry of Livonia and Arnold of Lübeck. Fonnesberg-Schmidt, *Popes and Baltic Crusades*, 73.

78. Šnē, "Emergence of Livonia," 55. Also see Iben Fonnesberg-Schmidt, "Pope Honorius III and Mission and Crusades in the Baltic Region" in *The Clash of Cultures on the Medieval Baltic Frontier*, ed. Alan V. Murray (London: Ashgate, 2009), 104–5.

79. Munzinger, "Profits of the Cross," 174.

80. Jensen, "Early Missionary Activities," 130–32.

81. As appears in Nils Blomkvist, *The Discovery of the Baltic: The Reception of a Catholic World-System in the European North (AD 1075–1225)* (Leiden: Brill, 2005), 626.

82. Urban, *Teutonic Knights*, 83.

83. Brundage, *CHL*, bk. 2, sec. 4–6, pp. 32–33. Meinhard's alleged killer, a Liv who became celebrated during Latvia's nineteenth-century "national awakening" for his resistance to the predations of outsiders, was named Imauts (later transformed into Imants). Andrejs Pumpurs, author of the Latvian epic *Lāčplēsis*, wrote a poem about him in 1874, titled "Imants Groans Not in Death." Several decades later, the Latvian dramatist and poet Rainis (Jānis Pliekšāns) wrote a play titled *Imants*. A modern suburb of Riga, formerly a pine forest but now a district comprised entirely of Soviet-era block housing, is named in honor of Latvia's (arguably) first national hero.

84. The bishop's remains, first transferred to a Christian cemetery in Üxküll, were returned to Riga by his successor, Albert, who had them interred at the Dome Cathedral.

85. Brundage, *CHL*, bk. 2, sec. 7–10, pp. 33–34.

86. Although it is doubtful that Henry ever met Meinhard, who had been a canon at Segeberg in the early 1180s, it is likely that his mission was known within the community while Henry was a student there.

87. Brundage, *CHL*, bk. 3, sec. 10, par. 15, p. 67.

88. Blomkvist, *Discovery of the Baltic*, 507.

89. See A. Caune, *Pētījumi Rīgas arheoloģijā*; A. Caune, "Kā radās un veidojās priekšstats par pirmsvācu Rīgu," in *Senā Rīga: Pētījumi pilsētas arheoloģijā un vēsturē /1. sēj.*, comp. Andris Caune (Rīga: Latvijas vēsture institūta apgāds, 1998), 73–104.

90. At the time, the Düna shoreline was seventy meters closer to the city than it is today.

91. Andris Caune, *Rīgas lībieši un viņu īpašumzīme* (Rīga: Jumava, 1998); A. Caune, *Pētījumi Rīgas arheoloģijā*, 135–53.

92. Jānis Straubergs, *Rīgas vēsture* (Rīga: Grāmatu draugs, 1937), 10–12.

93. Major flood events occurred in 1358, 1363, 1587, 1589, 1615, 1618, 1649 (see chapter 7), 1709 (see chapter 8), 1727, 1744, 1770, 1771, 1783, 1795, 1807, 1829, 1837, 1912, 1917, 1924, and 1929. Pauls Ludvigs, *Mūsu Latvijas ūdeņi* (Rīga: Grāmatu draugs, 1967), 230.

Chapter 2

1. Simon Sebag Montefiore, *Jerusalem: The Biography* (New York: Vintage Books, 2011), xxii.

2. Fonnesberg-Schmidt, *Popes and Baltic Crusades*, 138–43.

3. On the Virgin Mary as the patron saint of Livonia, see Anu Mänd, "Saints' Cults in Medieval Livonia," in *The Clash of Cultures on the Medieval Baltic Frontier*, ed. Alan V. Murray (London: Ashgate, 2009), 191–223.

4. See Christopher Tyerman, "Henry of Livonia and the Ideology of Crusading," in *Crusading and Chronicle Writing on the Medieval Baltic Frontier: A Companion to the Chronicle of Henry of Livonia*, ed. Marek Tamm, Linda Kaljundi, and Carsten Selch Jensen (Burlington, VT: Ashgate, 2011), 27.

5. Brundage, *CHL*, 37. Some have noted Henry's play upon the words "Riga" (the city) and "*rigo*" (irrigate), which appears in the chronicle on several occasions. "*Roma dictat iura, Riga vero rigat gentes*" ("Rome makes laws, while Riga irrigates the nations").

6. Jensen, "Convert a Landscape," 162.

7. The original wooden Dome burned down in 1215. A new cathedral was built of brick and stone in a different part of the city.

8. The town of Albert's birth has been spelled any number of ways: Bekeshovede, Bexhövede, Buxtehude, etc.

9. The Latvian diplomat and historian Alfred Bilmanis tells Albert's story in his *History of Latvia*, 53–69. Also see Gisela Gnegel Waitschies, *Bischof Albert von Riga: Ein Bremer Domherr als Kirchenfürst im Osten (1199–1229)* (Hamburg: A. F. Velmede, 1958).

10. With the creation of a diocese of Riga in 1202 (including present-day Vidzeme and Latgale), Albert became the first bishop of Riga.

11. A prince of the House of Haufenstofen, Philip ruled Germany from 1198 until he was murdered in 1208.

12. Munzinger, "Profits of the Cross," 177.

13. Brundage, *CHL*, bk. 3, par. 2, p. 35.

14. See the essays collected in John C. Moore, ed., *Pope Innocent and His World* (Aldershot, UK: Ashgate, 1999).

15. Munzinger, "Profits of the Cross," 163–85.

16. Brundage, *CHL*, bk. 3, sec. 4, par. 2, p. 36.

17. Razed at the end of the eighteenth century for defensive purposes, the sand hill where Berthold was killed later became a dusty parade ground for the armies of the tsar before being converted into a lovely city park that has at various times been (and is presently) known as the Esplanade.

18. It is possible that the Liv hostages ended up at the Segeberg monastery, where the young Henry appears to have acquired his knowledge of the Livish language.

19. This legend is not unique to Riga. Similar tales appear in Virgil's *Aeneid* and in cultures as disparate as those of China, India, and Iceland. See Viktor Schklovsky, *Bowstring: On the Dissimilarity of the Similar*, trans. Shushan Avagyan (Champaign, IL: Dalkey Archive Press, 2011), 257–59.

20. Lee Hohenberg and Lynn Hollen Lees, *The Making of Modern Europe, 1000–1950* (Cambridge, MA: Harvard University Press, 1985), 53.

21. Plakans, *Concise History*, 56; Benninghoven, *Rigas Entstehung*, 99–100.

22. Urban, *Baltic Crusade*, 41–43.

23. In modern German, *Burg Weißenstein*, but *Wittensten* in the Low German dialect then used along the southern Baltic shore.

24. Lewis Mumford, *The City in History* (New York: Harcourt Brace, 1961), 66.

25. Ibid., 251.

26. The Estonian island Saaremaa.

27. The old German name for Lääne County in Estonia.

28. Est. Järva.

29. Est. Nurmekun.

30. Est. Sakala.

31. Jerry C. Smith and William L. Urban, trans., *The Livonian Rhymed Chronicle* (Bloomington: Indiana University Press, 1977), 21, lines 1416–91.

32. Bartlett, *Making of Europe*, 266.

33. At a time when Albert strained to recruit reinforcements in Germany, the Teutonic Order in Prussia, which was closer to Germany than was Livonia, was inundated with knights seeking redemption in exchange for as little as a few weeks of fighting.

34. Urban, *Baltic Crusade*, 55–56. Also see Urban, *Teutonic Knights*, 14–17; Christiansen, *Northern Crusades*, 84–85.

35. Urban, *Baltic Crusade*, 56.

36. At that time the main branch of the Düna River drained into the Baltic Sea through a northern arm that is now known as the Vecdaugava. It was here that the original Dünamünde monastery-fortress—destroyed and rebuilt several times over the course of three hundred years—was built. By the end of the sixteenth century this estuary had become severely clogged as the southern branch deepened and became the main outlet to the Baltic Sea. The Vecdaugava having lost its strategic significance, in 1576 the region's Polish occupiers, followed by the Swedes, built a new Dünamünde fortress at the location of present-day Daugavgrīva on the river's left bank.

37. Caupo, or Kaupo, was among those prominent Livs whom Albert invited to a drinking party with the intention of forcing them to give up thirty of their sons as hostages.

38. Brundage, *CHL*, bk. 3, sec. 7, par. 5, p. 43.

39. Urban, *Baltic Crusade*, 52.

40. Brundage, *CHL*, bk. 3, sec. 10, par. 9, p. 60.

41. Ibid., bk. 4, sec. 12, pp. 92–93. Later accused of conspiring with the Samogitians against the bishop, Visvaldis was gradually divested of his remaining possessions. Bilmanis, *History of Latvia*, 62.

42. Bilmanis, *History of Latvia*, 61.

43. Brundage, *CHL*, bk. 3: sec. 11, par. 8–9, pp. 76–78; Torben K. Nielsen, "Sterile Monsters? Russians and the Orthodox Church in the Chronicle of Henry of Livonia," in *The Clash of Cultures on the Medieval Baltic Frontier*, ed. Alan V. Murray (London: Ashgate, 2009), 237.

44. Brundage, *CHL*, bk. 3, sec. 10, par. 1, p. 57.

45. Ibid., bk. 3, sec. 10, par. 10, p. 59.

46. Also converting at this time were the region's Wends, many of whom lived where the town of Cēsis (Ger. Wenden), the site of an old Wendish hill fort, is located today. It was at this advantageous location next to the Gauja River, from which the Germans could control the trade route to Novgorod, that the Swordbrothers established a stronghold that later (in 1237) became the master's residence.

47. Brundage, *CHL*, bk. 3, sec. 12, par. 2–3, pp. 79–81.

48. Ibid., bk. 2, sec. 10, par. 17, p. 68.

49. Livonia's relationship with the empire was always rather vague. While it never belonged to the Kingdom of Germany (Regnum Teutonicum), which had its own common institutions, Livonia was part of the more universal and abstract Holy Roman Empire (Sacrum Imperium Romanum). Heikki Pihlajamäki, *Conquest and the Law in Swedish Livonia (ca. 1630–1710): A Case of Legal Pluralism in Early Modern Europe* (Leiden: Brill, 2017), 4.

50. That same year Albert's uncle Hartwig, the Archbishop of Bremen-Hamburg and the godfather of the Livonian mission, passed away. Six years later, in 1213, Pope Innocent III decreed that the diocese of Riga, like the new one that had just been established in Estonia, would not be subordinated to any other metropolitan.

51. Brundage, *CHL*, bk. 3, sec. 11, par. 3, pp. 69–70.

52. The beginning of the end of the Semigallian resistance came in 1287, when they tried and failed to take Riga.

53. Brundage, *CHL*, bk. 4, sec. 14, par. 1, pp. 94–95.

54. Ibid., bk. 4, sec. 14, par. 5, pp. 98–99.

55. Thereafter the Germans would dominate the Bay of Riga with their cogs, which were much larger than the enemy's ships and which the Couronians could not build. Christiansen, *Northern Crusades*, 101.

56. Quote from Brundage, *CHL*, bk. 4, sec. 14, par. 9, p. 103.

57. Urban, *Baltic Crusade*, 101, 110.

58. A. Caune, *Pētījumi Rīgas arheoloģijā*, 155.

59. Brundage, *CHL*, bk. 3, sec. 17, par. 6, p. 139.

60. Straubergs, *Rīgas vēsture*, 114; Blomkvist, *Discovery of the Baltic*, 519.

61. Albert did not live to see the completion of his cathedral, whose construction dragged on until around 1270. When it was completed, the grandiose Riga Cathedral (later remodeled as a basilica) was surpassed in size only by the cathedrals of Mainz and Speyer. Tatjana Pavele, Lidija Rendele, and Karina Vitola, The *Dom Cathedral Architectural Ensemble in Riga* (Leningrad: Aurora, 1980), 9, 13.

62. The city's topography and its earliest configurations are discussed in A. Caune, *Pētījumi Rīgas arheoloģijā*, 155–87.

63. Neumann's *Mittelalterliche Riga* remains a useful source on the buildings of medieval Riga. On St. Jacob's, see 24–27.

64. Anti Selart, "Orthodox Churches in Medieval Livonia," in *The Clash of Cultures on the Medieval Baltic Frontier*, ed. Alan V. Murray (London: Ashgate, 2009), 278–79; Anti Selart, "Russians in Livonian Towns in the Thirteenth and Fourteenth Centuries," in *Segregation—Integration—Assimilation: Religious and Ethnic Groups in the Medieval Towns of Central and Eastern Europe*, ed. Derek Keene et al. (Burlington, VT: Ashgate, 2009), 40.

65. The nunnery at St. James survived the events of the Reformation only to be handed over in 1582 to the Jesuits, who established a convent school that taught in Latvian.

66. A. Caune, *Pētījumi Rīgas arheoloģijā*, 171.

67. Straubergs, *Rīgas vēsture*, 83.

68. In 1266 the monks dug a small ditch on the Düna's right bank and built a mill on it at present-day Mīlgrāvis (Ger. Mühlgraben).

69. Straubergs, *Rīgas vēsture*, 116–17.

70. Spekke, *History of Latvia*, 145.

71. Bunge, *Die Stadt Riga*, 10.

72. Blomkvist, *Discovery of the Baltic*, 525–27.

73. Manfred Hellmann, "Der Deutschen Orden und die Stadt Riga," in *Stadt und Orden: Das Verhältnis der Deutschen Ordens zu den Städten in Livland, Preussen und im Deutschen Reich*, ed. Udo Arnold (Marburg: N. G. Elwert, 1993), 6–11.

74. It is possible that it was the city's resistance to Albert's offer of Livonia to Valdemar II that paved the way for the emergence of the Rigans' main institution of self-government, the town council. See Benninghoven, *Rigas Entstehung*, 84–89.

75. Intending to make all the conquered lands property of the Roman Catholic Church, the pope did not make Albert into an archbishop but instead promoted the development of small bishoprics (each of which were states in their own right) whereby the bishops had both religious and secular power and were directly subordinate to the pope. In this scenario, the bishop of Riga was granted only religious supervision over the smaller bishoprics. Only in 1255 did the pope confer the title "archbishop" on Albert II Suerbeer.

76. Eva Eihgmane, "The Baltic Crusades: A Clash of Two Identities," in *The Clash of Cultures on the Medieval Baltic Frontier*, ed. Alan V. Murray (London: Ashgate, 2009), 41; Bilmanis, *History of Latvia*, 66.

77. Brundage, *CHL*, bk. 4, sec. 29, par. 3–5, pp. 231–35.

78. Bilmanis, *History of Latvia*, 69–70.

79. Kalnins, *Latvia*, 44. The case of Courland is telling: defeated in 1230, King Lamekins entered into agreements with the papacy whereby he accepted Latin Christianity and a bishopric in his lands; in this way, he would preserve his title and his power in northern Courland as a vassal of the pope. But the Swordbrothers, dissatisfied with the treaties concluded by another papal legate, Baldwin of Alna, went on the attack. When William of Modena returned to the region as the bishop of Courland in 1234, he granted the order two-thirds of the region's still rebellious lands. It was not until 1267 that this once independent Latvian kingdom submitted to its new masters. Bilmanis, *History of Latvia*, 73–74.

80. Straubergs, *Rīgas vēsture*, 58–61; Hellmann, "Der Deutschen Orden," 8. As a result of its arrangements with the region's other masters, Riga received scattered territories in Livonia, including parts of Semigallia and, for a time, one-third of the Estonian island of Saaremaa (Ösel).

81. Šterns, *Latvijas vēsture, 1290–1500*, 175. Peasants who settled in the city could obtain citizenship rights by paying this fee as late as 1530. Arveds Švābe, *Latvijas vēsture. I. Daļu* (Rīga: Avots, 1990), 127, 141.

82. Bunge, *Die Stadt Riga*, 20.

83. Brundage, *CHL*, bk. 4, sec. 30, par. 6, pp. 245–46.

84. Christiansen, *Northern Crusades*, 94–95.

Chapter 3

1. This saying describes urban liberty as a principle of German law in the Middle Ages. Once in a city for a year and a day, peasants could not be reclaimed by the manors to which they had belonged. The principle became part of city law in Reval in 1515 and in Riga in 1543. Wittram, *Baltische Geschichte*, 44.

2. Big Christopher is further discussed in chapter 6.

3. Arvids Pope, *Rīgas ostas devinos gadsimtos* (Rīga: Jumava, 2000), 179–80.

4. A typical example of a trading ship of this type is the "Bremen cog," whose remnants were dredged from the Weser River in Germany in 1962. Dated to about 1380, its assemblage from thousands of fragments completed in 1999, the Bremen cog is nearly twice the length of the older ship exhumed in Riga with a cargo capacity four times as great.

5. For a thorough analysis of Riga's early traders and the medieval city's social composition, see Benninghoven, *Rigas Entstehung*, 98–109.

6. The standard work on the subject remains Philippe Dollinger, *The German Hanse* (Stanford, CA: Stanford University Press, 1970).

7. Leighly, "Towns of Medieval Livonia," 242.

8. Edda Frankot, *"Of Laws of Ships and Shipmen": Maritime Law and Its Practice in Urban Northern Europe* (Edinburgh, UK: Edinburgh University Press, 2012).

9. Pihlajamäki, *Conquest and Law*, 45.

10. Today's Narva is an entirely Russian-speaking town in eastern Estonia.

11. Younger than the other Livonian towns—it was established in 1345—Narva was denied Hanseatic privileges despite its advantageous location next to a river on the Russian border.

12. Bunge, *Die Stadt Riga*, 145.

13. Janet Martin, *Treasure of the Land of Darkness: The Fur Trade and Its Significance for Medieval Russia* (New York: Cambridge University Press, 1986), 43–49, 52.

14. The discovery, beginning in 1951, of many hundreds of birch-bark documents in and around Novgorod dating from the eleventh to the thirteenth centuries has been a boon to scholars. They also suggest a degree of literacy in Novgorod that was unusual for the time.

15. Martin, *Treasure*, 65.

16. Zeids, *Feodālā Rīga*, 74.

17. A *birkav* is unit of measurement earlier used by Scandinavian traders in Birka (Björkö). One *birkav* was equivalent to about 165 kilograms or about 360 pounds. Šterns, *Latvijas vēsture, 1290–1500*, 187.

18. Martin, *Treasure*, 159.

19. Harry A. Miskimim, *The Economy of Early Renaissance Europe, 1300–1460* (Englewood Cliffs, NJ: Prentice-Hall, 1969), 138.

20. Martin, *Treasure*, 66.

21. Šterns, *Latvijas vēsture, 1290–1500*, 213.

22. Zeids, *Feodālā Rīga*, 73.

23. In the city's early years, the trading profession was not yet limited exclusively to Germans. Of the 1,397 merchants whose names were recorded in a register of debtors (D*as Rigaer Schuldbuch*) covering the years 1286–1352, Germans comprised 1,175; of the remaining 222 merchants, 100 were "Russians," and 107 were "non-Germans" (Livs, Letts, Estonians). Benninghoven, *Rigas Entstehung*, 32, 149.

24. Šterns, *Latvijas vēsture, 1290–1500*, 192, 211.

25. Ibid., 209.

26. Ibid., 211.

27. Dollinger, *German Hanse*, 155.

28. Martin, *Treasure*, 66.

29. Dollinger, *German Hanse*, 163.

30. While June 29 is St. Peter's chief feast day, February 22 marks the founding of St. Peter's see in Rome.

31. Dollinger, *German Hanse*, 146.

32. Lastadia is derived from the word "*last*," a unit of measure equivalent to about two tons.

33. Zeids, *Feodālā Rīga*, 18.

34. Martin, *Treasure*, 67–68.

35. Zeids, *Feodālā Rīga*, 77–79.

36. Ibid., 97.

37. Thomas Esper, "Russia and the Baltic, 1494–1558," *Slavic Review* 25, no. 3 (Sept. 1966), 460.

38. Benninghoven, *Rigas Entstehung*, 99.

39. See Šterns, *Latvijas vēsture, 1290–1500*, 235–42.

40. Zeids, *Feodālā Rīga*, 76.

41. Šterns, *Latvijas vēsture, 1290–1500*, 158.

42. Ger. Sandwegh; Latv. Smilšu ceļš.

43. Ger. Kaufstrasse; Latv. Tirgoņu iela.

44. Latv. Pulvertornis.

45. Latv. Grēcinieku iela.

46. Latv. Grēcinieku tornis. Latvian-language descriptions of all the city's medieval towers can be found in Andris Caune, *Rīga zem Rīgas* (Rīga: Zinātne, 1985), 87–104. Readers of Germans may consult Benninghoven, *Rigas Entstehung*, 146–48, and Neumann, *Mittelalterliche Riga*, 6–10.

47. Latv. Mārstaļu tornis or Maršalka tornis.

48. Benninghoven, *Rigas Entstehung*, 147.

49. Juhan Kreem, *The Town and Its Lord: Reval and the Teutonic Order in the Fifteenth Century* (Tallinn: Tallinna Linnaarhiiv, 2002), 65.

50. Straubergs, *Rīgas vēsture*, 22–23.

51. Selart, "Russians in Livonian Towns" (2009), 38–41.

52. Zeids, *Feodālā Rīga*, 94. A *pood* was equivalent to about twenty pounds or 8.4 kilograms. Šterns, *Latvijas vēsture, 1290–1500*, 187.

53. Latv. Ratslaukums.

54. By the end of the sixteenth century, many merchants were selling their wares at a marketplace near the Düna embankment, where the main market remained for more than three hundred years.

55. These roads are present-day Tirgonu, Kaļķu, Audēju-Grēcinieku, and Kungu ielas.

56. Leighly, "Towns of Medieval Livonia," 255.

57. Benninghoven, *Rigas Entstehung*, 82.

58. Šterns, *Latvijas vēsture, 1290–1500*, 164; Gunārs Jansons, "Rekonstruktion der Architektur des Rigaer Rathauses im 14.–18. Jahrhundert," in *The Hansa Town Rīga as Mediator between East and West*, edited by Andris Caune and Ieva Ose (Rīga: Institute of Latvia Publishers, 2009), 164–65.

59. Benninghoven, *Rigas Entstehung*, 81.

60. Skaidrīte Cielava and Z. Ērgle, *Old Riga Tales* (Rīga: Liesma, 1977), 90.

61. Ibid., 90–91.

62. Indriķis Šterns, "Viduslaiku Rīga ārpus Rīgas," in *Senā Rīga 1. Sēj.*, ed. Andris Caune (Rīga: Latvijas vēstures institūta apgāds, 1998), 376.

63. Pope, *Rīgas ostas deviņos gadsimtos*, 27.

64. Riga's inhabitants were originally forbidden from establishing guilds, likely because Albert was afraid of the potential they would offer Rigans for organizing against him. The prohibition lost its force in the 1220s when the city was de facto freed from its feudal seigneurs.

65. Benninghoven, *Rigas Entstehung*, 82. Recognized brotherhoods of craftsmen are listed in Šterns, *Latvijas vēsture, 1290–1500*, 253–56.

66. On the commemoration of Riga's deceased, see Gustavs Strenga, "Remembering the Dead: Collective Memoria in Late Medieval Livonia" (PhD dissertation, Queen Mary University of London, 2014).

67. Having acquired a magnificent Baroque façade during the renovations of the seventeenth century, the House of Blackheads was destroyed during World War II but has been rebuilt in recent times.

68. How many Blackheads there were in Riga at any given time fluctuated: in 1416 there were 63 brethren and in 1417 there were 105, as compared to the 100 to 120 long-distance merchants who enjoyed membership in the Great Guild. Strenga, "Remembering the Dead," 46.

69. Both guilds, as well as the Blackheads, had their meeting quarters in the New House. The Small Guild met in the Hall of Soest, while the Great Guild's meetings were held in the Hall of Münster. The Latvian brotherhoods of beer and salt carriers also rented rooms in the New House for their meetings. It was not until 1713, three years after its partial destruction in the Great Northern War, that the Blackheads became the New House's owners and sole tenants.

70. Michael North, *The Expansion of Europe, 1250–1500* (Manchester, UK: Manchester University Press, 2007), 369.

71. Zeids, *Feodālā Rīga*, 63–64.

72. Falling on November 11, old style, Martinmas, or St. Martin's Day, marked the town council's new calendar year.

73. Anu Mänd's scholarship on urban festivals in the main Livonian towns sheds much life on the social atmosphere of medieval Riga. This section draws heavily on her research. Anu Mänd, *Urban Carnival*. Also see Strenga, "Remembering the Dead," 57–58; Mettig, *Geschichte der Stadt Riga*, 208–12.

74. Mänd, *Urban Carnival*, 66.

75. Ibid., 79.

76. Ibid., 58, 59, 76, 249–52.

77. Ibid., 76–77, 262–66.

78. Zeids, *Feodālā Rīga*, 96.

79. In the area of present-day Miesnieku iela.

80. Audēju iela.

81. Between present-day between Peldu and Mārstaļu ielas.

82. Mänd, *Urban Carnival*, 190–200.

83. Ibid., 201–29.

84. Ibid., 60, 224.

85. Ibid., 80, 228; Zeids, *Feodālā Rīga*, 95.

86. Mänd, *Urban Carnival*, 235–37.

87. Ibid., 82; Mettig, *Geschichte der Stadt Riga*, 82.

88. Mänd, *Urban Carnival*, 238, 245; Zeids, *Feodālā Rīga*, 94.

89. Mänd, *Urban Carnival*, 163–69.

90. Ibid., 65, 254–55.

91. Zeids, *Feodālā Rīga*, 97.

92. The transformation of the Sun into the independent deity Jāņis (the Latvian version of "John"), who was believed to take over the sun's functions during the summer solstice and who in fact has no real connection to St. John, is a fascinating (if disputed) example of the syncretic practices of the non-German populations. See Jāņis Priede, "The Development of the Study of Religion in Latvia in the 20th Century," in *Studying Religions with the Iron Door Closed and Open: The Academic Study of Religion in Eastern Europe*, ed. Tomáš Bubík and Henryk Hoffmann (Leiden: Brill, 2015), 224–25.

93. Urban, *The Livonian Crusade* (Washington, DC: University Press of America, 1981, 21.

94. Šterns, *Latvijas vēsture, 1290–1500*, 279–80.

95. Concerning Riga's hospitals and table guilds, see Anu Mänd, "Hospitals and Tables for the Poor in Medieval Livonia," *Mitteilungen des Instituts für Österreichische Geschichtsforschung* 115, no. 3/4 (September 2007), 234–70; Strenga, "Remembering the Dead," 30–44.

96. Mumford, *City in History*, 267; North, *Expansion of Europe*, 395.

97. North, *Expansion of Europe*, 395.

98. Švābe, *Latvijas vēsture*, 146.

99. Here a caveat is warranted, for historians tend to view the medieval notion of *Undeutsch* less as an ethnic category and more as a social one. Strenga, "Remembering the Dead," 80–84; Plakans, *Latvians*, 41.

100. Šterns, *Latvijas vēsture, 1290–1500*, 269–70. Riga's medieval guild statutes are reproduced in Wilhelm Stiega and Constantin Mettig, Schragen der Gilden und Aemter der Stadt Riga bis 1621 (Riga: Alexander Stiega's Buchhandlung, 1896).

101. Zeids, *Feodālā Rīga*, 87; Bunge, *Die Stadt Riga*, 143–44; Šterns, *Latvijas vēsture, 1290–1500*, 171; Wittram, *Baltische Geschichte*, 48. A similar prohibition went into effect in Reval in 1403: henceforth it was only the city's most venerable families who had the right to brew beer.

102. Strenga, "Remembering the Dead," 84–90; Zeids, *Feodālā Rīga*, 70; Bilmanis, *History of Latvia*, 100.

103. He was also the father of Thomas Schöning, who became archbishop of Riga during the Reformation in the 1520s.

104. Strenga, "Remembering the Dead," 85–108.

105. Zeids, *Feodālā Rīga*, 68.

106. Straubergs, *Rīgas vēsture*, 83–84; Šterns, *Latvijas vēsture, 1290–1500*, 170.

107. In summertime the large of herd of cattle belonging to Riga's house-owners would pass through Jacob's Gate along the Pasture Road (Ger. Weidenstrasse; Latv. Ganību iela) to the pastures just north of the city.

108. Ger. Rikenstrasse; Latv. Bagāto iela.

109. Ger. Swinenstrasse; Latv. Cūku iela.

110. A. Caune, *Pētījumi Rīgas arheoloģijā*, 192–95; Šterns, *Latvijas vēsture, 1290–1500*, 218–23.

111. Jānis Straubergs, *Sen to Rīgu daudzināja* (Stockholm: Daugava, 1952), 25–26.

Chapter 4

1. Satirical verse by Hans Hasentöter, composed between 1574 and 1577 and translated by Kevin C. O'Connor. See Lutz Mackenson, *Baltische Texte der Früzeit* (Riga: Verlag der Akt.-Ges. Ernst Plates, 1936), 136–37.

2. Bilmanis, *History of Latvia*, 60.

3. Šterns, *Latvijas vēsture, 1290–1500*, 19–29.

4. Ibid., 29–33.

5. Bunge, *Die Stadt Riga*, 98–100; Kreem, *Town and Lord*, 62, 65.

6. H. J. Böthführ, *Rigische Rathslinie von 1226 bis 1886* (Riga: J. Deubner, 1877), 43–46; Ilona Celmiņa, ed., *Rīga's pārvalde: astoņos gadsimtos* (Rīga: Rīgas nami, 2000), 63–64; Benninghoven, *Rigas Entstehung*, 89.

7. Roman Czaja, "Das Patriziat in den livländischen und preußischen Städten. Eine vergleichende Analyse," in *Riga und der Ostseeraum: Von der Gründung 1201 bis in die Frühe Neuzeit*, eds. Ilgvars Misāns and Horst Wernicke (Marburg: Herder-Institut, 2005), 215. For a detailed list of town council members, see Böthführ, *Rigische Rathslinie*.

8. Šterns, *Latvijas vēsture, 1290–1500*, 195–207.

9. Kreem, *Town and Lord*, 102.

10. Ibid., 114, 126.

11. Ibid., 132.

12. Smith and Urban, *Livonian Rhymed Chronicle*, 36, lines 2589–90.

13. Ibid., 26–28, lines 1859–1992.

14. The definitive English-language work on the Teutonic Order is Urban's *Teutonic Knights.*

15. Ibid., 94–100.

16. S. C. Rowell, *Lithuania Ascending: A Pagan Empire within East-Central Europe, 1295–1345* (New York: Cambridge University Press, 1994), 64.

17. Modern-day Kurzeme, Tartu, and Saaremaa.

18. Urban, *Baltic Crusade,* 199.

19. Urban, *Teutonic Knights,* 101–3.

20. Anti Selart, *Livonia, Rus' and the Baltic Crusades in the Thirteenth Century,* tran. Fiona Robb (Leiden: Brill, 2015), 259.

21. In defeat, their land ravaged by the Germans, some 100,000 Semigallians migrated to Samogitia, where many continued to fight the order as soldiers of a Lithuanian militia. Bilmanis, *History of Latvia,* 83; Spekke, *History of Latvia,* 142–43.

22. Mettig, *Geschichte der Stadt Riga,* 45.

23. Ibid., 46.

24. Urban, *Livonian Crusade,* 21.

25. Ibid., 25.

26. Mettig, *Geschichte der Stadt Riga,* 44–45.

27. This chapter is heavily indebted to the scholarship of the Baltic German historian Constantin Mettig and especially that of William Urban, who has published extensively on the subject of the Teutonic Knights. See Mettig's *Geschichte der Stadt Riga* and Urban's *Livonian Crusade.* Also of value is *Grundriss der Geschichte Liv-, Est- und Kurlands* (Riga: Jonck and Poliewsky, 1918), written by another Baltic German historian, Leonid Arbusow. I have consulted the following Russian-language edition of this classic: Leonid Arbuzov [Arbusow], *Ocherk istorii Lifliandii, Estliandii i Kurlaniandii,* trans. Vladimir Buka (Moscow: Troitsa, 2009).

28. Bunge, *Die Stadt Riga,* 24–25.

29. October 11, according to the Gregorian calendar that replaced the old Julian calendar throughout the Western world at the end of the Middle Ages. Throughout this book I have rendered specific dates in the old style.

30. Mettig, *Geschichte der Stadt Riga,* 47; Urban, *Livonian Crusade,* 34

31. Urban, *Livonian Crusade,* 35; Zeids, *Feodālā Rīga,* 44.

32. Urban, *Baltic Crusade,* 261.

33. Mettig, *Geschichte der Stadt Riga,* 47.

34. Rowell, *Lithuania Ascending,* 76–77.

35. Mettig, *Geschichte der Stadt Riga,* 50.

36. July 11, new style.

37. Mettig, *Geschichte der Stadt Riga,* 50–51; Bunge, *Die Stadt Riga,* 29.

38. As appears in Urban, *Livonian Crusade,* 41.

39. Bunge, Die Stadt Riga, 33; Mettig, *Geschichte der Stadt Riga,* 52; Urban, *Livonian Crusade,* 43, 50.

40. Mettig, *Geschichte der Stadt Riga,* 52.

41. Urban, *Livonian Crusade,* 45–48.

42. This is a different castle from the Dünamünde fortress the Swedes later built in the Düna's left bank.

43. Zeids, *Feodālā Rīga*, 46.

44. Urban, *Livonian Crusade*, 56.

45. Hellmann, "Der Deutschen Orden," 20; Christiansen, *Northern Crusades*, 151.

46. Urban, *Livonian Crusade*, 66–67.

47. William Chester Jordan, *The Great Famine: Northern Europe in the Early Fourteenth Century* (Princeton, NJ: Princeton University Press, 1996), 18.

48. Ibid., 157.

49. Urban, *Livonian Crusade*, 67; Hellmann, "Der Deutschen Orden," 20.

50. 1323 was also the year of Vilnius's official founding.

51. Rowell, *Lithuania Ascending*, 197, 211–12, 216.

52. Ibid., 242.

53. Bunge, *Die Stadt Riga*, 41; Mettig, *Geschichte der Stadt Riga*, 62.

54. A *last* in Riga was equivalent to about 12–24 barrels. Mettig, *Geschichte der Stadt Riga*, 63.

55. The hospital was moved to the site of the first Order Castle and was renamed the Convent of the Holy Spirit. That the order and the archbishopric continued to quarrel over the exchange of territories suggests that the transaction was improperly carried out.

56. Bunge, *Die Stadt Riga*, 42–44; Mettig, *Geschichte der Stadt Riga*, 65; Hellman (1993), 20; Urban, *Livonian Crusade*, 84–85.

57. Zeids, *Feodālā Rīga*, 49. For many years after the war's conclusion, while the new castle was being built, the order would conduct its affairs in the meeting room of the Holy Spirit Guild on the main town square, thereby forcing the Great and Small Guilds to build new houses for themselves. (See chapter 3.)

58. Arbuzov [Arbusow], *Ocherk istorii*, 63.

59. Neumann, *Mittelalterliche Riga*, 45–46; Māra Caune, *Rīgas pils* (Rīga: Zinātne, 2001), 201–4.

60. Urban, *Livonian Crusade*, 85.

61. Ibid., 85–88.

62. Kreem, *Town and Lord*, 28–30.

63. Urban, *Livonian Crusade*, 113–14.

64. Hellmann, "Der Deutschen Orden," 22; Urban, *Livonian Crusade*, 121.

65. Urban, *Livonian Crusade*, 124–25.

66. Mettig, *Geschichte der Stadt Riga*, 76–78; Hellmann, "Der Deutschen Orden," 22–24.

67. Mara Kalnins asserts that "amber revenues *alone* paid for the entire cost of running the Teutonic Order." Kalnins, *Ancient Amber Route*, 163–64.

68. Urban, *Livonian Crusade*, 169.

69. It is also called the Battle of Grunwald, meaning "green forest" in German. In Lithuania it is similarly known as the Battle of Žalgiris.

70. Historians of every participating nation have composed their own narratives of this battle. Polish nationalist historians, for example, portrayed Tannenberg as a historic victory of the Slavs over the Germans. The battle's mythology assumed great significance during the wars of the first half of the twentieth century when they were used for propaganda purposes by the German/Nazi and Russian/Soviet governments. Operation Tannenberg, for example, was the code name Hitler gave for his plan to invade Poland in 1939.

71. Hellmann, "Der Deutschen Orden," 24.

72. In addition to organizing a general council whose goal was to heal the Papal Schism, Wallenrode also negotiated on the order's behalf a treaty with Poland after the knights' defeat at the Battle of Tannenberg in 1410. He additionally played important roles both in the condemnation of Jan Hus and in the deposition of the anti-pope John XXIII (r. 1410–1415).

73. Mettig, *Geschichte der Stadt Riga*, 92–95.

74. Urban, *Livonian Crusade*, 240–43.

75. Of the 195 knights who belonged to the Livonian Order in 1451, 161 were from Westphalia and 26 were Rhinelanders; only two were native to Livonia. Švābe, *Latvijas vēsture*, 147.

76. Hellmann, "Der Deutschen Orden," 26.

77. Urban, *Livonian Crusade*, 245.

78. Bilmanis, *History of Latvia*, 109.

79. Strenga, "Remembering the Dead," 188.

80. Mettig, *Geschichte der Stadt Riga*, 106–07.

81. Urban, *Livonian Crusade*, 259.

82. Ibid., 311–12.

83. Ibid., 314.

84. Mettig, *Geschichte der Stadt Riga*, 134.

85. As appears in Urban, *Livonian Crusade*, 317. Also see Mettig, *Geschichte der Stadt Riga*, 134–35.

86. Defeated in the Thirteen Years' War, the Teutonic Order agreed to the (second) Treaty of Thorn (1466), which divided the Teutonic state. The order was compelled to give up the western half of its territory, including Danzig, which became an important entrepot for the grain being exported to the West. The western areas would remain within the Kingdom of Poland, while the Teutonic rump state in East Prussia became a Polish fief. Urban, *Livonian Crusade*, 330–36.

87. Zeids, *Feodālā Rīga*, 54–55.

88. Urban, *Livonian Crusade*, 320, 322; Mettig, *Geschichte der Stadt Riga*, 139–40.

89. Mettig, *Geschichte der Stadt Riga*, 140.

90. Ibid., 143.

91. Ibid.; Hellmann, "Der Deutschen Orden," 28–29.

92. Mettig, *Geschichte der Stadt Riga*, 143.

93. Aija Taimina, "15. gadsimta metala griezuma jeb 'skrosu' graviras un Rigas patriciesa Reinholda Soltrumpa gramatu likteni" (15th Century Metal Engravings and Fortunes of the Riga Patrician Reinhold Soltrump's Books), *Makslas vēsture un teorija* (2004/2), 5–19.

94. Zeids, *Feodālā Rīga*, 56; Mettig, *Geschichte der Stadt Riga*, 144.

95. Richard Hellie, *Enserfment and Military Change in Muscovy* (Chicago: University of Chicago Press, 1971), 154.

96. Erik Tiberg, *Moscow, Livonia and the Hanseatic League, 1487–1550* (Stockholm: Acta Universitatis Stockholmiensis, 1995), 38.

97. Urban, *Livonian Crusade*, 381.

98. Ibid., 383–86.

99. Kreem, *Town and Lord*, 161.

100. Ibid., 90, 121–22, 161–62, 165.

101. Urban, *Livonian Crusade*, 387.

102. Hellmann, "Der Deutschen Orden," 29.

103. A chronicle written in Latin and Low German by Helewegh, covering the years 1158 to 1489 and intended to prove that the Kirchholm Treaty was unlawfully imposed upon Riga, was lost in Riga's great fire of 1677. Surviving fragments were translated into High German.

104. Urban, *Livonian Crusade*, 387–91; Hellmann, "Der Deutschen Orden," 30.

105. Urban, *Livonian Crusade*, 391–92.

106. Bilmanis, *History of Latvia*, 109.

107. Hellmann, "Der Deutschen Orden," 30.

108. John (Johann) Schöning (d. 1502) was the father of a later archbishop of Riga, Thomas Schöning. See Böthführ, *Rigische Rathslinie*, 110–11.

109. Urban, *Livonian Crusade*, 397–99; Hellmann, "Der Deutschen Orden," 30.

110. Hellmann, "Der Deutschen Orden," 30–31; Zeids, *Feodālā Rīga*, 109.

111. Carnival or Shrovetide.

112. Anu Mänd, "Signs of Power and Signs of Hospitality: The Festive Entries of the *Ordensmeister* into Late Medieval Reval" in *The Man of Many Devices, Who Wandered Full Many Ways . . . : Festschrift in Honor of János M. Bak*, ed. Balázs Nagy and Marcell Sebok (Budapest: Central European University Press, 1999), 284.

Chapter 5

1. Thank you to Monika Hanley for assistance with translation.

2. This phrase appears in a sixteenth-century song in Low German that affectionately refers to Reval as "the house of wax and flax" and to Visby as "the house of pitch and tar." See "Die Hansestädte" in Lutz Mackensen, *Baltische Texte der Früzeit*, op cit. (1936), 160.

3. For an enlightening discussion of the "Third Rome theory," see Janet Martin, *Medieval Russia, 980–1584* (New York: Cambridge University Press, 1995), 260–66. Quote from page 261.

4. Catherine Merridale, *Red Fortress: History and Illusion in the Kremlin* (New York: Picador, 2014), 36–65.

5. Šterns, *Latvijas vēsture, 1290–1500*, 234.

6. Zeids, *Feodālā Rīga*, 110–11.

7. Balthasar Russow, *The Chronicle of Balthasar Russow*, trans. Jeremy C. Smith (Madison, WI: Baltic Studies Center, 1988), 50–63.

8. See Tiberg, *Moscow, Livonia*, 36–43; Esper, "Russia and the Baltic," 460–63.

9. Tiberg, *Moscow, Livonia*, 137.

10. David Kirby, *Northern Europe in the Early Modern Period: The Baltic World, 1492–1772* (London: Longman, 1990), 43.

11. Tiberg, *Moscow, Livonia*, 75, 78.

12. Ibid., 75.

13. The sprawling state built by Gediminas (r. 1316–1341) and Algirdas (r. 1345–1377) reached its limits by 1500, at which time it was still the largest country in Europe.

14. J. L. L. Fennell, *Ivan the Great of Moscow* (New York: St. Martin's Press, 1961), 212–17.

15. Ibid., 224.

16. Kirby, *Northern Europe*, 54.

17. Fennell, *Ivan the Great*, 242.

18. Urban, *Livonian Crusade*, 419–21.

19. Bilmanis, *History of Latvia*, 111.

20. If one compares the sadistic tendencies of Muscovite rulers and soldiers to their counterparts in Tudor-era England, one comes to the inescapable conclusion that the cruel behaviors exhibited by Russian and Tatar forces in Livonia were hardly unique.

21. Kirby, *Northern Europe*, 54–55. Also see Matthias Thumser, "Antirussische Propaganda in der Schönen Historie von wunderbaren Geschäften der Herren zu Livland mit den Russen und Tataren," in *Geschichtsschreibung im mittelalterlichen Livland*, ed. Matthias Thumser (Berlin: Schriften der Baltischen Historischen Kommission, 2011), 133–54.

22. Tiberg, *Moscow, Livonia*, 96–98, 106; Kirby, *Northern Europe*, 55; Esper, "Russia and the Baltic," 464.

23. Tiberg, *Moscow, Livonia*, 174–75.

24. Šterns, *Latvijas vēsture, 1290–1500*, 290–91.

25. Urban, *Livonian Crusade*, 435.

26. See N. K. Anderson, "The Reformation in Scandinavia and the Baltic," in *The New Cambridge Modern History: Vol. 2, The Reformation, 1520–1559*, 2nd ed., ed. Geoffrey Rudolph Elton (New York: Cambridge University Press, 1990), 167–71.

27. Hus's jailer was John V Wallenrode, then the archbishop of Riga.

28. Perhaps because his earliest pastoral duties involved preaching to the Latvian brotherhoods of porters (the fraternities of salt, beer, and ale carriers, as well as fishermen, paid priests to maintain their altars in the city's churches), it has sometimes been suggested, a bit fantastically, that Knopken was a Latvian. Born in Pomerania, but educated in Ingolstadt and Frankfurt, Knopken did not appear in Riga, where his brother Jacob was already a canon at St. Peter's, until he was nearly fifty years old. Pēteris Vanags, *Luterāņu roksgramātas avoti: vecākā perioda (16 g.–17 g.s. sāmuma) latviešu teksti* (Rīga: Mantojums, 2000), 11–13.

29. Originally a small hall church, St. Peter's had been expanded in 1406–1409 under the supervision of the master builder Johann Rumeschottel of Rostock. In 1491, a 137-meter pyramidal tower in the Gothic style was completed, transforming the church into one of the tallest structures in Europe at the time. Destroyed in a storm in 1666, the tower was later restored in the Baroque style it retains to this day.

30. Ojārs Zanders, *Tipogrāfs Mollīns un viņa laiks: Pirmās Rīgā iespiestās grāmatas 1588–1625* (Rīga: Zinātne, 1988), 39; Urban, *Livonian Crusade*, 436–37. In 1529 Knopken also composed Riga's first Lutheran hymn book in Low German; some of these hymns were translated into Latvian. Vanags, *Luterāņu roksgramātas avoti*, 12.

31. Ojārs Spārītis, "Evidence of the Reformation and Confessionalization in Livonian Art," *Journal of Art History* 9 (September 2015), 37.

32. Mettig, *Geschichte der Stadt Riga*, 185.

33. Sergiusz Michalski, *The Reformation and the Visual Arts: The Protestant Image Question in Western and Eastern Europe* (London: Routledge, 1993), 9.

34. Ibid., 92–93.

35. Klaus Garber, "Die 'Bibliotheca Rigensis': Eine Stätte grosser Sammler und kommunaler Identitätstiftung," in *Schatzhäuser des Geistes: Alte Bibliotheken und Büchersammlungen im Baltikum*, ed. Klaus Barber (Cologne: Böhlau, 2007), 55.

36. Today it houses the city's Museum of Decorative Arts and Design.

37. Michalski, *Reformation and Visual Arts*, 80–81.

38. Mettig, *Geschichte der Stadt Riga*, 186–87.

39. Zeids, *Feodālā Rīga*, 119–20.

40. Diarmaid MacCulloch, *The Reformation: A History* (New York: Penguin, 2004), 155.

41. Urban, *Livonian Crusade*, 442; Kirby, *Northern Europe*, 84.

42. Böthführ, *Rigische Rathslinie*, 129–31; Juhan Kreem, "Der Deutschen Orden und die Reformation in Livland," in *The Military Orders and the Reformation: Choices, State Building, and the Weight of Tradition*, eds. Johannes A. Mol, Klaus Militzer and Helen J. Nicholson (Hilsverum, Netherlands: Verloren, 2006), 49.

43. Kirby, *Northern Europe*, 70–71.

44. Arbuzov [Arbusow], *Ocherk istorii*, 151.

45. Kirby, *Northern Europe*, 68.

46. The archbishop journeyed to the papal curia in Rome and then to Spain, where he hoped to secure the backing of the Holy Roman emperor. This is where he perished in 1527. Urban, *Livonian Crusade*, 443–50; Zeids, *Feodālā Rīga*, 122–23.

47. Spārītis, "Reformation and Confessionalization," 29–30.

48. Plettenberg's successor, Hermann of Brüggenei (r. 1535–1549) completed the break with the Teutonic Order in Prussia. The last masters of the Livonian Order ruled autonomously.

49. In the 1870s another statue of Plettenberg was erected on the façade of what is now the Saeima building (then it was the House of the Livonian Noble Corporation), but it was destroyed in a fire in 1921 and replaced by a statue of the Latvian mythological hero Lāčplēsis.

50. Bilmanis, *History of Latvia*, 118–20; Kirchner, *Rise of the Baltic Question*, 35–36.

51. Zeids, *Feodālā Rīga*, 124.

52. The last years of the archbishopric are extensively documented in Friedrich Georg von Bunge, *Die letzten Zeiten des Erzbisthums Riga, dargestellt in einer gleichzeitigen Chronik des Bartholomäus Grefenthal und in einer Sammlung der auf jene Zeiten bezüglichen Urkunden* (Riga: Eduard Frantzen's Verlags-Comptoir, 1847).

53. Lange, *Zwischen Reformation und Untergang*, 1:165–66; Andris Kolbergs, *Rīga for the Curious Traveler* (Rīga: SIA, 2003), 42.

54. The papacy nixed Riga's earlier efforts to establish a town school in the late fourteenth century. Kreem, *Town and Lord*, 142.

55. Zeids, *Feodālā Rīga*, 168.

56. See Egil Grislis, "Recent Trends in the Study of the History of the Reformation in Riga, Livonia," *Journal of Baltic Studies* 7, no. 2 (1976), 145–69.

57. See Straubergs, *Rīgas vēsture*, 256–76.

58. Straubergs, *Sen to Rīgu daudzināja*, 115–16.

59. Vanags, *Luterāņu roksgramātas avoti*, 13.

60. Švābe, *Latvijas vēsture*, 153. When the Poles took control of Riga in the 1580s, St. Jacob's was handed over to the militantly Catholic Society of Jesus, while a Latvian school was established at St. John's.

61. Zeids, *Feodālā Rīga*, 168.

62. Celmiņa, *Rīga's pārvalde*, 84.

63. Ojārs Zanders, *Senās Rīgas grāmatniecība un kultūra Hanzas pilsētu kopsakarā (13.–17.gs.)* (Rīga: Zinātne, 2000), 134; Fülberth, *Riga*, 68–69. Some historians claim Ramm was a Latvian. See Straubergs, *Rīgas vēsture*, 271–72.

64. Vanags, *Luterāņu roksgramātas avoti*, 14. The oldest surviving complete work in the Latvian language is a Catholic catechism published by Peter Canisius in Vilnius in 1585.

65. Ibid., 20.

66. See the introduction to Ludger Lieb, Jan Mohr, and Herfried Vögel, eds., *Burkard Waldis: Esopus: 400 Fabeln und Erzählungen nach der Erstausgabe von 1548* (Berlin: De Gruyter, 2011), 10–14; also Zanders, *Senās Rīgas grāmatniecība un kultūra Hanzas pilsētu kopsakarā*, 129–32.

67. Fülberth, *Riga*, 69.

68. MacCulloch, *Reformation*, 540.

69. Mänd, *Urban Carnival*, 271–75.

70. Michalski, *Reformation and Visual Arts*, 87.

71. Other forms of Protestantism like Calvinism had virtually no influence in Livonia.

72. Edgars Dunsdorfs and Arnolds Spekke, *Latvijas vēsture, 1500–1600* (Stockholm: Daugava, 1964), 459–62.

73. Russell Shorto, *Amsterdam: A History of the World's Most Liberal City* (New York: Vintage, 2013), 57.

74. During the sixteenth century almost half of Amsterdam's trade was with Danzig, which was especially valued for its rye exports. Kirby, *Northern Europe*, 9.

75. Zeids, *Feodālā Rīga*, 146.

76. In an effort to compel Riga to recognize the trade limits they tried to impose on the Dutch in the Baltic Sea, during these years Lübeck and other Hanse cities repeatedly (1509, 1524) closed the Sound to ships with Riga's goods. Such decrees were soon revoked. Pope, *Rīgas ostas deviņos gadsimtos*, 32.

77. Artur Attman, *The Struggle for Baltic Markets: Powers in Conflict, 1558–1618* (Göteborg, Sweden: Kungl. Vetenskaps- och Vitterhets-Samhället, 1979), 159.

78. Zeids, *Feodālā Rīga*, 145.

79. Benninghoven, *Rigas Entstehung*, 74–75, 100.

80. Zeids, *Feodālā Rīga*, 154.

81. Cielava and Ērgle, *Old Riga Tales*, 63.

Chapter 6

1. Unattributed quote as appears in Spekke, *History of Latvia*, 197.

2. Sebastian Münster, *Cosmographie oder Beschreibung aller Länder* (Basel, 1550). The first edition (with many more to come) also included a Latvian-language version of the

Lord's Prayer by Hans Hasentöter of Königsberg, who was then residing in Riga. It is the oldest preserved text written in the Latvian language.

3. A further fifty castles were under the control of the Archbishop of Riga and other bishoprics.

4. Broce [Brotze], *Zīmējumi un apraksti*, 1:43–44.

5. Pārdaugava fell under the administration of the city of Riga in 1786. The floating bridge of earlier times was replaced by a pontoon bridge in 1892 and then by the Stone Bridge (Latv. Akmens tilts) in 1957.

6. On the evacuation of Riga in 1915, see Hatlie, *Riga at War*, 43–51.

7. Returned to the Catholic Church in 1922, St. Jacob's, also called the Church of St. James, is today the seat of Riga's Roman Catholic archbishop.

8. For variations on this story, see Alma Ancelāne, "Rīga atviz Daugavas ūdeņos," in *Daugavas raksti: No Rīgas līdz jūrai*, comp. Vaida Villeruša (Rīga: Zinātne, 1994), 7–8. Today the old statue of Big Christopher is preserved in the Museum of the City of Rīga and Navigation, while an exact copy, made in 1997, has been placed in a hut on the embankment.

9. Kirchner, *Rise of the Baltic Question*, 201–3; Lange, *Zwischen Reformation und Untergang*, 1:176–77, 188–94.

10. Kirchner, *Rise of the Baltic Question*, 38, 203–6. On the scheme to install Christopher of Mecklenburg, also see Valda Kļava, "Mēklenburgas Kristofs hercogistes un arhibīskapijas interešu krustpunktā," *Latvijas Universitātes raksti* 764. sēj. (2012), 119–33.

11. See Johannes Renner, *Johannes Renner's Livonian History 1556–1561*, trans. Jerry S. Smith, William Urban, and J. Ward Jones (Lewiston, NY: Edwin Mellen Press, 1997), 20–30.

12. Ibid., 30.

13. An intriguing source on the Livonian War is Russow's *The Chronicle of Balthasar Russow*. A Lutheran minister in Reval, Russow viewed the conflict as God's punishment for the Livonians' moral laxity—a view he seemed to share with Johannes Renner, who recorded the events of the war's early years in his own chronicle, cited above. A strictly chronological account of events, Russow emphasized the general sense of helplessness as war, plague, and famine came to Livonia.

14. The epithet "Ivan Grozny" came into use many years after his death. A better translation is Ivan the Fearsome.

15. See the editor's introduction to Ruslan G. Skrynnikov, *Ivan the Terrible*, ed. and trans. Hugh F. Graham (Gulf Breeze, FL: Academic International Press, 1981).

16. Isabel de Madariaga, *Ivan the Terrible* (New Haven, CT: Yale University Press, 2006), 119.

17. Heinrich von Staden, *The Land and Government of Muscovy: A Sixteenth-Century Account*, trans. and ed. Thomas Esper (Stanford, CA: Stanford University Press, 1967), 72.

18. Renner, *Livonian History*, 56.

19. Esper, "Russia and the Baltic," 473–74.

20. See William Urban's introduction to Russow, *Chronicle*. Also see his "The Origin of the Livonian War, 1558," *Lituanus* 29, no. 3 (Fall 1983), http://www.lituanus.org/1983_3/83_3_02.htm.

21. One may be certain that the tsar had not forgotten about the events of 1525 in Dorpat, a city that housed a significant number of Russian merchants. There the religious antagonism of the Reformation resulted in a series of attacks on the city's Catholic churches, as well as an assault on the Orthodox church of St. Nicholas. When the Livonian War broke out in 1558, the tsar's propaganda justified his actions in part as a struggle against Lutheran iconoclasm.

22. Urban, *Livonian Crusade*, 467. Also see Urban's introduction to Russow's *Chronicle*, xiv.

23. Kirchner's *Rise of the Baltic Question* provides a fascinating account of the intricacies of the Livonian War.

24. In April 1560 Frederick's younger brother Duke Magnus of Holstein moved his forces into the Estonian island of Ösel (now Saaremaa) and was subsequently named its bishop. Later Magnus would allow himself to be a pawn in Ivan's game. As the tsar's vassal, Magnus became the titular "King of Livonia" from 1570 to 1578, only to spend the last years of his life in Courland as a ward of the Polish crown. Although story is not recounted here, Magnus appears frequently in Balthasar Russow's chronicle of the Livonian War.

25. Kryzystof Zajas, *Absent Culture: The Case of Polish Livonia* (Frankfurt am Main: Peter Lang, 2013), 95.

26. Renner, *Livonian History*, 69.

27. The wooden church was rebuilt in 1589. The present-day red-brick church is an entirely different edifice.

28. Renner, *Livonian History*, 96.

29. Quoted in Spekke, *History of Latvia*, 187. The handwritten journal that Padel kept from 1539 to 1557 has been lost, but parts of it have been reproduced elsewhere. Böthführ, *Rigische Rathslinie*, 134.

30. See the emperor's letters to the king of Poland and to the tsar, reproduced in Renner, *Livonian History*, 125–28.

31. Lenz, *Riga*, 13.

32. Renner, *Livonian History*, 169–70.

33. See Urban's introduction to Russow's, *Chronicle*, xv.

34. Renner, *Livonian History*, 110.

35. De Madariaga, *Ivan the Terrible*, 130.

36. Lange, *Zwischen Reformation und Untergang*, 2:381–84.

37. Among them were Dünaburg, Selburg, Ludza, Rositten, and Bauske.

38. In Polish he is known as Hrehory Chodkiewiczowie (1514–72); his Lithuanian name is Grigorijus Chodkevičius.

39. Zeids, *Feodālā Rīga*, 210–13; Lenz, *Riga*, 15–16.

40. Renner, *Livonian History*, 189–90.

41. Lenz, *Riga*, 17–18.

42. In Lithuanian his name is rendered Mikalojus Radvila (1512–84). In Poland he is known as Mikołaj "Czarny" Radziwiłł.

43. Lenz, *Riga*, 13–14.

44. Russow, *Chronicle*, 98.

45. Lange, *Zwischen Reformation und Untergang*, 2:566–77.

46. Zajas, *Absent Culture*, 62–63.

47. Lenz, *Riga*, 24–25.

48. The *oprichnina* has several meanings. It refers to Ivan's secret police organization, the state in which the *oprichniki*—his henchmen—operated, and this period in Russia's history (1565–1572).

49. Kirchner, *Rise of the Baltic Question*, 224.

50. Ibid., 225–26; Zeids, *Feodālā Rīga*, 129; Bilmanis, *History of Latvia*, 149.

51. Unattributed quote as appears in Spekke, *History of Latvia*, 197.

52. Robert I. Frost, *The Northern Wars: War, State, and Society in Northeastern Europe, 1558–1721* (Harlow, UK: Pearson, 2000), 150.

53. Russow, *Chronicle*, 200.

54. Dunsdorfs and Spekke, *Latvijas vēsture*, 464, 470.

55. Zeids, *Feodālā Rīga*, 129–30.

56. Pihlajamäki, *Conquest and Law*, 27.

57. Jerzy Radziwiłł (1556–1600) in Polish; Jurgis Radvila in Lithuanian. Few aspects of this period are more confusing for the uninitiated than trying to sort through all the Radziwills and Chodkiewiczes who were in one way or another connected to Riga.

58. Zajas, *Absent Culture*, 57.

59. The Jesuit college was terminated when the Swedes took control in Riga in 1621.

60. Russow, *Chronicle*, 224.

61. Daniel Boorstin, *The Discoverers* (New York: Random House, 1983), 303.

62. Zeids, *Feodālā Rīga*, 139.

63. Böthführ, *Rigische Rathslinie*, 145–46. Ecke was accused of embezzling funds while he was the city treasurer. It was perhaps for this reason that the town council established a shelter for the widows of Rigan craftsmen in a building that currently functions as an upscale guest house.

64. For a review of the historiography of the Calendar Upheavals, see Anna Ziemlewska, "The 'Calendar Upheavals' in Riga (1584–1589), *Acta Poloniae Historica* 96 (2007), 87–111.

65. Ibid., 110.

66. Zeids, *Feodālā Rīga*, 141.

67. Bilmanis, *History of Latvia*, 151–52.

68. Zeids, *Feodālā Rīga*, 144.

69. Bilmanis, *History of Latvia*, 152.

70. Celmiņa, *Rīgas pārvalde*, 107–8.

71. Ibid., 115.

72. These are now the Latvian cities Lielvārde, Koknese, and Daugavpils.

73. Now called Kaliningrad, a Russian city.

74. Zeids, *Feodālā Rīga*, 131–34.

75. Ibid., 135.

76. Ibid., 167.

77. Zajas, *Absent Culture*, 63.

78. Intended for the wives of Riga landlords who had fallen on hard times, the convent was founded after Ecke had fallen under suspicion of having squandered city funds.

79. Zanders, *Senās Rīgas grāmatniecība un kultūra Hanzas pilsētu kopsakarā*, 133–44. It was also Hilchen who compiled the code of Livonian law, a significant milestone in its own right, that encoded serfdom in Livonia in 1599. Having come into conflict with the Rath, which accused him of treason, Hilchen eventually had to flee Riga, but later proved his patriotism during the war against the Swedes and was rehabilitated shortly before his death in 1610.

80. Zanders, *Tipogrāfs Mollīns un viņa laiks*, 19, 29.

81. Nicholas Viksninš, "The Early History of Latvian Books," *Lituanus* 19, no. 3 (Fall 1973), http://www.lituanus.org/1973/73_3_02.htm; Zanders, *Tipogrāfs Mollīns un viņa laiks*, 51, 56–57. On the emergence of a Latvian literary culture at this time, see Spekke, *History of Latvia*, 213–20.

82. Zanders, *Tipogrāfs Mollīns un viņa laiks*, 108–15.

83. Mollin's press was taken over by Gerhard Schröder in 1625. On Schröder's work, see Meta Taube, "Die Arbeiten des Rigaer Buchdruckers Gerhard Schröder (1625–1657)" in *Stadt und Literatur im deutschen Sprachraum der Frühen Neuzeit*, eds. Jörg Jochen Berns et al (Tübingen: Max Niemeyer Verlag, 1988), 2:800–812.

84. Vivian Siirman, "Der literarische Nachlass des Hermann Samson," *Forschungen zur baltischen Geschichte* 5 (2010), 36–58.

85. Zanders, *Senās Rīgas grāmatniecība un kultūra Hanzas pilsētu kopsakarā*, 219–22. Also see Aija Taimiņa, "The Book Collection by Daniel Hermann, a Poet, a Diplomat and a Civil Servant, as a Source for Biography and Culture Studies," http://www.ahm2015.ambermuseum.ru.

86. Plinius is believed to be a Latinized formed of Plone, Plen, or Pleene.

87. Bazilijs Plīnijs [Plinius], *Slavas dziesma Rīgai* (Rīga: Jumava, 1997).

88. Pope, *Rīgas ostas deviņos gadsimtos*, 43–44.

89. The Polish fortress was destroyed in 1624 and was later rebuilt as a bastion by the Swedes. While it is sometimes permitted to tour parts of Daugavgrīva's ruins, where the Soviets erected some military installations, intrepid visitors would be wise to bring an adequate supply of mosquito repellent during the summer months.

90. The legendary Red Tower is the basis of the neighborhood's current name, Torņakalns (Tower Hill).

91. Charles IX was, in fact, only the third Swedish king to be called Charles.

92. Michael Roberts, *Gustavus Adolphus and the Rise of Sweden* (London: English Universities Press, 1973), 16–18.

93. Attman, *Struggle for Baltic Markets*, 171.

94. See Jan Glete, *Swedish Naval Administration, 1521–1721* (Leiden: Brill, 2010); Frost, *Northern Wars*, 116–25.

95. Švābe, *Latvijas vēsture*, 168.

96. Zeids, *Feodālā Rīga*, 177.

97. Frost, *Northern Wars*, 65.

98. Glete, *Swedish Naval Administration*, 389–90.

99. Attman, *Struggle for Baltic Markets*, 180.

100. Roberts, *Gustavus Adolphus*, 30–31.

101. Ibid., 57.

102. Zeids, *Feodālā Rīga*, 181; Bilmanis, *History of Latvia*, 164.
103. As appears in Spekke, *History of Latvia*, 210.
104. Ibid., 197.
105. Pope, *Rīgas ostas deviņos gadsimtos*, 38.

Chapter 7

1. Mettig, *Geschichte der Stadt Riga*, 330.
2. I'd like to thank some acquaintances who shared my puzzlement over this one: Katia Junghans, Ted Weeks, and Karsten Brüggemann. The author alone is responsible for any errors in translation.
3. The present-day Latvian lands of Courland (Kurzeme) and Semigallia (Zemgale), in the hands of the Kettler family since the dissolution of the Livonian Confederation in 1561, remained an appendage of the Polish-Lithuanian Commonwealth. Polish Livonia, then called Inflanty and largely overlapping with present-day Latgale in southeastern Latvia, remained a Polish possession until 1795.
4. See, for example, the section titled "Swedish Rule Brings Light" in Schwabe, *Story of Latvia*, 20, and Bilmanis, *History of Latvia*, 160–81. Likewise, see J. Aberbergs, "Rīga pilsētas vēsture," in *Rīga kā Latvijas galvas pilsēta*, eds. Teodors Līventāls and Valters Sadovskis (Rīga: Rīgas pilsētas valde, 1932), 30–37;
5. Plakans, *Concise History*, 105–6.
6. Leighly, "Towns of Medieval Livonia," 291.
7. Roberts, *Gustavus Adolphus*, 57.
8. For a summary of these provisions, see Straubergs, *Rīgas vēsture*, 328–32. Riga retained its autonomy with regard to internal justice. Unlike Livonia's other lower courts, the city was not under the jurisdiction of the High Court in Dorpat: its appeals went directly to the Sevea High Court in Stockholm. German remained the court language throughout Livonia during the Swedish era. Pihlajamäki, *Conquest and Law*, 13–15.
9. Zeids, *Feodālā Rīga*, 188.
10. Ibid., 187.
11. Celmiņa, *Rīga's pārvalde*, 103; Zeids, *Feodālā Rīga*, 187–97.
12. Plakans, *Concise History*, 102–3.
13. Maarten Prak, *The Dutch Republic in the Seventeenth Century*, trans. Diane Webb (New York: Cambridge University Press, 2005), 96.
14. Jill Lisk, *The Struggle for Supremacy in the Baltic, 1600–1725* (New York: Funk & Wagnalls, 1968), 18; J. T. Kotilaine, *Russia's Foreign Trade and Economic Expansion in the Seventeenth Century: Windows on the World* (Leiden: Brill, 2005), 65; Prak, *Dutch Republic*, 97.
15. Straubergs, *Rīgas vēsture*, 336.
16. Dunsdorfs, *Latvijas vēsture, 1600–1710*, 297–300.
17. Pope, *Rīgas ostas deviņos gadsimtos*, 39.
18. Straubergs, *Rīgas vēsture*, 334–35; Kirby, *Northern Europe*, 231. See also Elisabeth Harder-Gersdorff, "Riga als Handelsmetropole des Osteeraums in der Frühen Neuzeit (16.–18. Jahrhunderts)," in *Riga und der Ostseeraum: Von der Gründung 1201 bis in die Frühe Neuzeit*, eds. Ilgvars Misāns and Horst Wernicke (Marburg: Herder-Institut, 2005), 144–68.

19. N.J.G. Pounds, *An Historical Geography of Europe, 1500–1840* (New York: Cambridge University Press, 1979), 280.

20. The words "Russian" and "Muscovite" were catch-alls for various kinds of people who spoke East Slavic languages and observed the Eastern Christian faith.

21. Zeids, *Feodālā Rīga*, 217.

22. V. V. Doroshenko, *Torgovlia i kupechestvo cherez Rigi v XVII veke* (Rīga: Zinātne, 1985), 55; Zeids, *Feodālā Rīga*, 147–50, 208; Dunsdorfs and Spekke, *Latvijas vēsture*, 470.

23. Kotilaine, *Russia's Foreign Trade*, 36.

24. See Dunsdorfs, *Latvijas vēsture, 1600–1710*, 317–24.

25. Kotilaine, *Russia's Foreign Trade*, 165.

26. J. A. Faber, "The Decline of the Baltic Grain-Trade in the Second Half of the Seventeenth Century," in *From Dunkirk to Danzig: Shipping and Trade in the North Sea and the Baltic, 1350–1850*, ed. W. G. Heeres et al. (Hilversum, Netherlands: Verloren, 1988), 31–51.

27. Ralph Tuchtenhagen, "Riga im Rahmen des swedischen Merkantilismus," in *Riga and der Ostseeraum: Von der Gründung 1201 bis in die Frühe Neuzeit*, eds. Ilgvars Misāns and Horst Wernicke (Marburg: Herder-Institut, 2005), 317–18.

28. The Augsburg Convention of 1555 ended the confessional wars in the Holy Roman Empire and affirmed the prince's right, under the principle *cuius regio, eius religio* ("whose realm, his religion"), to choose either Catholicism or Lutheranism for the lands under his jurisdiction.

29. Bilmanis, *History of Latvia*, 171; Kalnins, *Latvia*, 74.

30. Zeids, *Feodālā Rīga*, 187; Aleksander Loit, "Die Stadt Riga im schwedischen Ostseereich. Die Privilienfrage," in *Riga and der Ostseeraum: Von der Gründung 1201 bis in die Frühe Neuzeit*, eds. Ilgvars Misāns and Horst Wernicke (Marburg: Herder-Institut, 2005), 321–32.

31. Celmiņa, *Rīga's pārvalde*, 103.

32. After a long regency during her childhood, Queen Christina was officially crowned upon turning eighteen in 1644. Riga was obligated to contribute 30,000 thalers for the occasion.

33. Zeids, *Feodālā Rīga*, 191.

34. Plakans, *Latvians*, 100.

35. Bilmanis, *History of Latvia*, 174, 179.

36. Plīnijs, *Slavas dziesma Rīgai*, 395.

37. Zeids, *Feodālā Rīga*, 195.

38. The stalls were set on fire during 1656 siege, and after that they were rebuilt on the new Kalēju iela (Smiths' Street), located near the city walls, and Staļļu iela (today's Vecpilsētu iela). Broce, *Zīmējumi un apraksti*, 1:269.

39. Anita Gailiša, "Rīgas rātes krēsli, 17. gadsimta otrā puse–18. gadsimta pirmā puse," in *Senā Rīga 5: Pētījumi pilsētas arheoloģijā un vēsturē*, ed. Andris Caune (Rīga: Latvijas vēstures institūta apgāds, 2005), 298.

40. A descendant, Melchior Dreiling, oversaw the creation in 1663 of Riga's first waterworks, which pumped water from the Düna (Daugava) through city pipes. These served the city for two hundred years. Celmiņa, *Rīga's pārvalde*, 116; Böthführ, *Rigische Rathslinie*, 121.

41. One of the men named Johan Dreiling gifted St. Peter's Church with a bell he had purchased in Holland for 8,000 thalers. Celmiņa, *Rīga's pārvalde*, 116.

42. Ibid.

43. Ibid.

44. One of his progeny, the medical doctor and botanist Reinhold Berens (1745–1823), composed a fascinating family history that eloquently explains the proliferation of Berenses. Reinhold Berens, *Geschichte der seit hundert und funfzig Jahren in Riga einheimischen Familie Berens aus Rostock* (Riga: Julius Müller, 1812).

45. Zeids, *Feodālā Rīga*, 195–97.

46. Also in the governor-general's bailiwick were Swedish Ingermanland and Karelia.

47. Instrumental in the founding of the University of Dorpat in 1632, Skytte encouraged it to open its doors to the Livonian peasants.

48. Pihlajamäki, *Conquest and Law*, 92, 130.

49. Bilmanis, *History of Latvia*, 172; Kalnins, *Latvia*, 75–76.

50. Spekke, *History of Latvia*, 235–36.

51. Frost, *Northern Wars*, 116–18.

52. Zeids, *Feodālā Rīga*, 195.

53. The Treaty of Pereyeslav (1654) has been controversial almost since its inception. The Cossack leader Bogdan Khmelnitsky understood the agreement with Muscovy as a means of helping the hetmanate secure its autonomy from Poland by placing it under the tsar's military protection. The long-term result, however, was the incorporation of a swath of Ukraine into the Russian state—a development whose ramifications are still being felt today.

54. Zeids, *Feodālā Rīga*, 204.

55. Frost, *Northern Wars*, 177.

56. Paul Douglas Lockhart, *Sweden in the Seventeenth Century* (New York: Palgrave/Macmillan, 2004), 2, 32–37, 123.

57. Ojārs Spārītis, "Schwedische Impulse im Städtebau im lettischen Teil Livlands im 16. un 17. Jahrhundert," in *Riga and der Ostseeraum: Von der Gründung 1201 bis in die Frühe Neuzeit*, eds. Ilgvars Misāns and Horst Wernicke (Marburg: Herder-Institut, 2005), 383.

58. Jean-Denis G. G. Lepage, *Castles and Fortified Cities of Medieval Europe: An Illustrated History* (Jefferson, NC: McFarland, 2002), 201. Also see Christopher Duffy, *Siege Warfare: The Fortress in the Early Modern World, 1494–1660* (London: Routledge & Kegan Paul, 1979).

59. Other men to hold this position during the first few decades of Swedish rule included the aforementioned Johan Bengtsson Skytte (1628–1634), Bengt Bengtsson Oxenstierna (1634–1643), Gabriel Bengtsson Oxenstierna (1645–1649), and the aforementioned Count Magnus Gabriel De la Gardie (1649–1652, 1655–1658).

60. Zeids, *Feodālā Rīga*, 194; M. Caune, *Rīgas pils*, 206–8.

61. Ojārs Spārītis, "Some Aspects of Cultural Interaction between Sweden and the Latvian Part of Livonia in the 17th Century," *Baltic Journal of Art History* 1 (2009), 98–99.

62. Ger. Kalktor; Latv. Kaļķu vārti.

63. Ger. Kalck Straße; Latv. Kaļķu iela. Nowadays this is the touristy corridor that leads from the Freedom Monument to Town Hall Square.

64. It wasn't until modern times that most street names were fixed in Riga. The street that is known to Latvians as Kungu iela had at one time been known as Bredebeka strate, taking its name from its owner. After 1550 the road was called Herringstrasse (Herring Street), after the fish that provided sustenance for Riga's burghers. From there it was a short leap to the street's new meaning (*Herr* = lord, gentleman) and name (Herrenstrasse).

65. Ger. Weg zur Weide; Latv. Ganību iela.

66. Margarita Barzdeviča, *Rīga zviedru laika kartēs un plānos, 1621–1710* (Rīga: Latvijas vēstures institūtes apgāds, 2011), 132–33.

67. Swed. Cobrons skans; Ger. Kobron Schanz; Latv. Kobronschanz. Kobron was named for the Scotsman Samuel Cockburn (a.k.a. Cobron), a colonel in the Swedish army who in the 1620s captured the Red Tower (which was later razed) and built next to it a fortress where he was commandant. A detailed history of this lost Swedish fort may be found in Ieva Ose, "Kobronskansts pārbūves 17. gadsimtā un 18. gadsimtā zviedru inženieru ieceres un to realizācija," in *Senā Rīga 7: Pētījumi pilsētas arheoloģijā un vēsturē*, ed. Ieve Ose (Rīga: Latvijas vēstures institūta apgāds, 2012), 406–43. Also see Andris Šnē and Rūdolfs Brūzis, "Kobronskansts veidošanās un attīstība 17.–20/ gs.: 2010. gada arheoloģiskās izpētes rezultāti," *Latvijas Universitātes raksti* 764 (2012), 63–81.

68. Barzdeviča, *Rīga zviedru laika kartēs un plānos*, 60.

69. At the time it was called Neumünde, or Nymynde in Swedish; now it is called Daugavgrīva.

70. Ieva Ose, "Daugavgrīvas cietokšņa pārbūves no 1622. līdz 1710. gadam," in *Senā Rīga 7: Pētījumi pilsētas arheoloģijā un vēsturē*, ed. Ieva Ose (Rīga: Latvijas vēstures institūta apgāds, 2012), 202–33.

71. In a sense the older fortress lived on even after its destruction. Having lost much of its military significance due to a change in the course of the Düna in the sixteenth century, the old Dünamünde fortress was dismantled on the orders of the new Swedish authorities, its remains transported by boat to the site of the new fortress the Poles had begun erecting on the other side of the Düna.

72. Barzdeviča, *Rīga zviedru laika kartēs un plānos*, 133. Another example of the way the improvements affected the city's residents (and guests) was the rebuilding of the wall on the city's northern side, where the present-day Ramer Tower (reconstructed as a tourist attraction in the 1980s) and Swedish Gate (1698) are located. Here the result was the near disappearance of Trokšņu iela (Ger. Große Lärmstraße; Noisy Street), the quarter traditionally inhabited by "Russian" traders. Ibid., 127.

73. See ibid., 126–31.

74. Churches have existed on the spot where St. Gertrude's is located since 1418. The church that existed at this location in Swedish times was destroyed during the Great Northern War. The red-brick church that stands on this site today was built in the 1860s.

75. Now Stabu iela and Brīvības iela.

76. *Straße nach der Jesus-Kircke.*

77. *Die Weg nach dem Kalck Offen.*

78. Barzdeviča, *Rīga zviedru laika kartēs un plānos*, 140–41.

79. Ibid., 141, 144; Straubergs, *Rīgas vēsture*, 359–60.

80. Irēna Bākule and Arnis Siksna, *Rīga ārpus nocietinājumiem: Pilsētas plānotā izbūve un pārbūve no 17. gadsimta līdz Pirmajam pasaules karam* (Rīga: Neputns, 2009), 28–29.

81. Now Ganību dambis.

82. Barzdeviča, *Rīga zviedru laika kartēs un plānos*, 131.

83. Appointed in January 1649, Murer took the place of Riga's previous main engineer, Heinrich Mühlmann, who held this post from 1632 or 1634 until 1648. Ibid., 58, 63.

84. Anna Ancāne, *Rīgas arhitektūra un pilsētbūvniecība 17. gadsimta otrajā pusē* (Rīga: Latvijas Mākslas akadēmijas Mākslas vēstures institūts, 2016), 67–74.

85. Barzdeviča, *Rīga zviedru laika kartēs un plānos*, 138.

86. Kotilaine, *Russia's Foreign Trade*, 320.

87. A detailed engraving by Adam Perelli that illustrates the siege was published in 1697. It shows the tsar's army numbering 118,000 men. Similarly large numbers are repeated in many secondary sources. The military historian Robert I. Frost suggests the more realistic figure of 35,000. Frost, *Northern Wars*, 177.

88. St. Gertrude's Church—a wooden predecessor of the present edifice that was located near the Sand Road east of the inner city—was, miraculously, unharmed; the invaders, however, took the church's organ and bells with them when they departed for Russia.

89. Zeids, *Feodālā Rīga*, 205.

90. Guntis Gerhards, "Epidēmijas viduslaiku un jauno laiku Rīgā," *Latvijas vēstures institūta žurnāls* 4 (2011), 48–49.

91. Zeids, *Feodālā Rīga*, 206.

92. In the autumn of 1657, a force of Poles and Lithuanians briefly attempted to blockade Riga.

93. L. V. Cherepnin, "Russian 17th-Century Baltic in Soviet Historiography," *Slavonic Review* 43, no. 100 (Sept. 1964), 16.

94. Kotilaine, *Russia's Foreign Trade*, 327–42.

95. Bilmanis, *History of Latvia*, 179.

96. Lockhart, *Sweden*, 123–35.

97. Bilmanis, *History of Latvia*, 175–78.

98. On Dahlberg, see Christopher Duffy, *The Fortress in the Age of Vauban and Frederick the Great, 1660–1789* (London: Routledge Library Editions: Military and Naval History, 1985), 182–97.

99. Barzdeviča, *Rīga zviedru laika kartēs un plānos*, 139.

100. Ibid., 143.

101. Ibid., 145.

102. Straubergs, *Rīgas vēsture*, 21–23.

103. Ancāne, *Rīgas arhitektūra*, 130.

104. Ibid.

105. Ibid., 131.

106. Ibid., 132.

107. Less well-known, partly because it has not survived, is Bindenschu's work on the wooden Jesus Church in the Lastadia suburb, the original version of which was built in 1638 but destroyed during the war with Russia in 1656. Bindenschu completed the new church in 1688, the same year he began work on St. Peter's.

108. Dunsdorfs, *Latvijas vēsture, 1600–1710*, 307.

109. These magnificent portals were adorned with various figures and decorative elements, including a coat of arms consisting of two fir trees (*Tannen*) and two stars (*Stern*) that identify its owner.

110. B. Shalfeev, "Petr I v dome Dannenshterna v 1714 g.," in *Ot Liflandiia k Latvii: Pribaltika russkimi glazami*, comp. Iu. Abyzov (Moscow: Arkaiur, 1993), 175–82.

111. That this once lovely building is now a dump has less to do with a lack of resources in Riga than one of simple neglect by the current city council, which has approved a number of tremendously expensive projects in recent years.

112. Ancāne, *Rīgas arhitektūra*, 198–99.

113. The choral traditions nurtured by the Latvian, Estonian, and Lithuanian peoples since the Reformation would later become associated with the creation of their modern national identities. The politicization of the Baltic choral tradition was particularly notable during the interwar era and was made known to the world during the "Singing Revolution" of 1988 to 1991.

114. Darius Petkūnas, *Russian and Baltic Lutheran Liturgy in the Nineteenth and Twentieth Centuries* (Klaipėda, Lithuania: University of Klaipėda, 2013), 17–21.

115. The spiritual regulations of 1686 defined Sweden as an evangelical nation, made the king the head of the Church, and with the establishment of parish registers called for the maintenance of church records on the births, baptisms, and deaths of the empire's inhabitants.

116. Ieva Pauloviča, "Garīgā mūzika vidzemē Zviedrijas lielvalsts vēlīnajā posmā (1660–1710)" (PhD diss., Latvijas kultūras akadēmija, 2009).

117. The first known Riga Dome organ was the largest in the world, but it was lost to the great fire of 1547. The Walcker organ that is currently housed in the cathedral was inaugurated in 1884 and even after extensive renovations in the 1980s retains its distinctive sound.

118. Christian August Berkholz, *Dr. Johann Breverus, Superintendent von Riga: Pastor, Professor und Inspektor: Eine Errinerun aus dem 17. Jahrhundert* (Riga: Bacmeister, 1869).

119. Zane Gailite, *Par Rīgas mūziku un kumēdiņu spēli* (Rīga: Pētergailis, 2003), 78–93.

120. See, for example, the relevant sections of Straubergs, *Rīgas vēsture*, and Šterns, *Latvijas vēsture, 1290–1500*.

121. Nicholas Vīksninš, "Some Notes on the Early Histories of Latvian Books and Newspapers, *Journal of Baltic Studies* 4, no. 2 (Summer 1973), 155–58; Bilmanis, *History of Latvia*, 180.

122. Heronims Tichovskis, "Provost Ernst Glück as Educator in Livonia and Russia," *Slavic Review* 24, no. 2 (June 1965), 307–13.

123. Glück also made important contributions to Russian history, first by translating much of the Bible into the Russian vernacular, and secondly by bringing his Lithuanian foster daughter to Russia during the Great Northern War. Having joined the household of Prince Menshikov, in 1703 Marta Skravonskaya was introduced to Tsar Peter I, who made her his second wife. Marta would later be known as Empress Catherine I (r. 1725–1727).

124. Straubergs, *Rīgas vēsture*, 361.

125. Zanders, *Senās Rīgas grāmatniecība un kultūra Hanzas pilsētu kopsakarā*, 269.

126. The academy would later be known as the University of Dorpat (Tartu). Riga would not have its own institution of higher education until the Riga Polytechnic was established in 1861.

127. Since the University of Dorpat was open to peasants, Latvians and Estonians were sometimes admitted. Some Latvians earned teaching appointments at Livonia's new schools.

128. Strangers and suspected enemies of Swedish power were the first to come under suspicion. An investigation revealed the culprit to have been a young German named Gabriel Franck (aided by a Swedish youth, Petrus Andersson, who was tortured during his confession), who had worked as a tutor in several Livonian cities and in Moscow—the assumption naturally being that Muscovites were behind the crime. The same year the city erected a pillory at an ancient execution site (this is where the arsonists were punished) in the city's eastern suburbs that gives present-day Post Street (Latv. Stabu iela; Ger. Säulenstrasse) its name. Intended to remind Rigans of the catastrophe of 1677—and of Rigans' inquisitional reaction to it—the pillory was removed in 1849. Fülberth, *Riga*, 85; Spārītis, "Cultural Interaction," 101.

129. Straubergs, *Rīgas vēsture*, 362–65.

130. Ibid., 359–60.

131. Zeids, *Feodālā Rīga*, 221–22.

132. The lone exception was the brotherhood of linen-weavers, whose *Schragen* of 1625–1644 were written in both Latvian and German. Dunsdorfs, *Latvijas vēsture, 1600–1710*, 322; Straubergs, *Rīgas vēsture*, 209.

133. Zeids, *Feodālā Rīga*, 222–24.

134. Dunsdorfs, *Latvijas vēsture, 1600–1710*, 324; Straubergs, *Rīgas vēsture*, 199.

135. Plakans, *Concise History*, 105.

136. Frost, *Northern Wars*, 103.

137. Andrejs Plakans estimates the Latvian population at forty to fifty percent. Plakans, *Concise History*, 105.

Chapter 8

1. Igor' Gusev, *Pyotr i Riga* (Rīga: Zoriks, 2011), 25.

2. Robert K. Massie, *Peter the Great: His Life and World* (New York: Random House, 1980), 208.

3. Plakans, *Concise History*, 124.

4. Kirby, *Northern Europe*, 257.

5. Plakans, *Concise History*, 123.

6. Lockhart, *Sweden*, 120–22.

7. Erected in 1910 to celebrate the two-hundredth anniversary of Russian power in Riga, and evacuated from the city in 1915, the statue was loaded on a ship that was torpedoed and sank to the bottom of the Baltic Sea. Rescued by Estonian divers in 1934, it was brought back to the surface in pieces and returned to Riga. At some point the monument ended up in a warehouse and was later reassembled, making a brief and unexpected reappearance in a public park during the city's eight-hundredth anniversary celebrations in

2001. The statue now stands in a private lot outside the city center. See Spārītis, "Cultural Interaction," 192; http://articles.latimes.com/2004/jul/13/world/fg-peter13.

8. See Evgenii V. Anisimov, *The Reforms of Peter the Great: Progress through Coercion in Russia* (Armonk, NY: M. E. Sharpe, 1993).

9. Philip Longsworth, *Alexis: Tsar of All the Russias* (New York: Franklin Watts, 1984).

10. Tsar Alexei was succeeded by Feodor III (r. 1676–1682), his eldest son by his first wife, Maria Miloslavskaya. For fourteen years, 1682 to 1696, Peter co-reigned with his half-brother Ivan V, who was Maria's youngest son and beset by various disabilities.

11. J. T. Kotilaine advances this argument in *Russia's Foreign Trade*.

12. Lindsey Hughes, *Russia in the Age of Peter the Great* (New Haven, CT: Yale University Press, 1998), 22–23.

13. Charles XII was, in fact, only the sixth Swedish king to be called Charles (Karl).

14. Zeids, *Feodālā Rīga*, 230–31.

15. Massie, *Peter the Great*, 171–72.

16. Gusev, *Pyotr i Riga*, 25.

17. Zeids, *Feodālā Rīga*, 231–32.

18. R. M. Hatton, *Charles XII of Sweden* (NY: Weybright & Talley, 1968), 102.

19. Tony Sharp, *Pleasure and Ambition: The Life, Loves and Wars of Augustus the Strong* (London: I. B. Tauris, 2001).

20. Eugene Schuyler, *Peter the Great: Emperor of Russia*, 2 vols. (New York: Russell & Russell, 1884), 1:369–70.

21. Hughes, *Russia*, 27.

22. Ibid., 24.

23. Hatton, *Charles XII*, 114–15.

24. Zeids, *Feodālā Rīga*, 232.

25. Ibid., 232–33; Schuyler, *Peter the Great*, 1:373–74.

26. Oleg Pukhliak, *Velikaia severnaia voina na territorii Latvii, 1700–1721* (Riga: Rizhskoe slavianskoe istoricheskoe obshchesvto, 2010), 5–6.

27. When it was captured by the Russians in 1709, it would be renamed in honor of Peter I.

28. Pope, *Rīgas ostas deviņos gadsimtos*, 40.

29. Zeids, *Feodālā Rīga*, 234.

30. Ibid., 235.

31. Massie, *Peter the Great*, 318.

32. Kirby, *Northern Europe*, 233.

33. Gusev, *Pyotr i Riga*, 31; Hughes, *Russia*, 28.

34. Schuyler, *Peter the Great*, 1:377.

35. Nikolai N. Petrukhintsev, "The Baltic Strategy of Peter the Great," in *Russland an der Ostsee: Imperiale Strategien der Macht und kulturelle Wahrnehmungsmuster (16. bis 20. Jahrhundert)*, eds. Karsten Brüggemann and Bradley D. Woodworth (Vienna: Böhlau, 2012), 169–89.

36. The tsar's proclamation of war was predicated "on the many wrongful acts of the Swedish King, and especially because during the journey of His Majesty through Riga,

much opposition and unpleasantness was caused him by the inhabitants of Riga." Schuyler, *Peter the Great*, 1:378.

37. The castle at Kokenhusen (Latv. Koknese), blown up by the retreating Saxons in 1701, once stood high on a hill. Its ruins are now partially submerged in the Düna (Daugava) River owing to the construction of a hydroelectric dam in 1965.

38. On Peter's departure prior to the Battle of Narva, see Aleksandr B. Kamenskii, *The Russian Empire in the Eighteenth Century: Searching for a Place in the World*, trans. and ed. David Griffiths (Armonk, NY: M. E. Sharpe, 1997), 70–71.

39. Oscar Browning, *Peter the Great* (London: Hutchinson & Co., 1898), 162–63.

40. Zeids, *Feodālā Rīga*, 236–37.

41. Lisk, *Struggle for Supremacy*, 161. As concerns the number of soldiers who participated in any given battle, the sources are contradictory and imprecise. The numbers offered here are in no way definitive; they merely provide a sense of scale.

42. Pukhliak, *Velikaia severnaia voina*, 8–9.

43. Zeids, *Feodālā Rīga*, 238; Pukhliak, *Velikaia severnaia voina*, 13; Frans G. Bengtsson, *The Life of Charles XII: King of Sweden, 1697–1718* (London: Macmillan, 1960), 115–16.

44. Lucas Island (Latv. Lucavsala) is now a popular place for swimming and relaxing.

45. Much later, when Riga had been under Russian rule for nearly two centuries and the regime was seized by a fit of Russification in the imperial borderlands, the fallen soldiers were commemorated with a monument that was erected near the spot where they had perished. Slated for destruction, the nearly forgotten monument, erected on Lucas Island in 1891, was restored on the initiative of local Russians in 2001.

46. The Saxons managed to hold onto the strategically important fortress at Dünamünde, but the installation fell back into the hands of the Swedes in December.

47. Robert Bideleux and Ian Jeffries, *A History of Eastern Europe: Crisis and Change* (London: Routledge, 1998), 142.

48. Wittram, *Baltische Geschichte*, 105; Pukhliak, *Velikaia severnaia voina*, 19–20.

49. Marta's story is as complicated as it is fascinating and unlikely. The future empress was born in present-day Estonia, but her last name had indisputably Polish origins. Orphaned at age three, Marta later moved to Marienberg in Livonia (present-day Aluksne, Latvia), where she became Glück's housemaid. While many believe that the future empress was a Lithuanian of Polish origin, some writers claim she was a Latvian. See, for example, Spekke, *History of Latvia*, 23; Kalnins, *Ancient Amber Route*, 386.

50. Zeids, *Feodālā Rīga*, 242.

51. In 1708 only 187 ships arrived. Doroshenko, *Torgovlia i kupechestvo*, 110, 114.

52. Ibid., 141.

53. Straubergs, *Rīgas vēsture*, 386.

54. Gusev, *Pyotr i Riga*, 66; Straubergs, *Rīgas vēsture*, 387.

55. Zeids, *Feodālā Rīga*, 243.

56. Ibid., 240.

57. Massie, *Peter the Great*, 408; Wittram, *Baltische Geschichte*, 104.

58. Zeids, *Feodālā Rīga*, 240.

59. Massie, *Peter the Great*, 446–47; Bengtsson, *Life of Charles XII*, 292.

60. Hughes, *Russia*, 34.

61. Later fighting on the Swedish side at the Battle of Poltava and dying soon afterward, Mazepa has been treated as a traitor by Soviet and Russian historians. Many Ukrainians, however, consider him a hero who fought for an independent Ukraine.

62. Karl-Erik Frandsen, *The Last Plague in the Baltic Region, 1709–1713* (Copenhagen: Museum Tusculanum Press, 2010), 20, 26.

63. Pukhliak, *Velikaia severnaia voina*, 29.

64. Ludvigs, *Mūsu Latvijas ūdeņi*, 231; Straubergs, *Rīgas vēsture*, 386–87.

65. Hatton, *Charles XII*, 273–75; Hughes, *Russia*, 38–39.

66. Hatton, *Charles XII*, 303.

67. Browning, *Peter the Great*, 87.

68. The field marshal had received this title in 1706.

69. Reinhard Wittram, *Peter I: Czar and Kaiser: Zur Geschichte Peters des Grossen in siener Zeit* (Göttingen: Vandenhoeck & Ruprecht, 1964), 1:334.

70. Straubergs, *Rīgas vēsture*, 386–87.

71. Zeids, *Feodālā Rīga*, 247.

72. Ludvigs, *Mūsu Latvijas ūdeņi*, 255.

73. Straubergs, *Rīgas vēsture*, 387–88; Zeids, *Feodālā Rīga*, 248.

74. Zeids, *Feodālā Rīga*, 246–47; Johans Andreass Ēzens [Oesen], *Rīga 18. gadsimtā. Zīmējumi* (Rīga: Latvijas valsts vēstures arhīvs, 2004), 39–40.

75. Zeids, *Feodālā Rīga*, 247; Pukhliak, *Velikaia severnaia voina*, 30.

76. Pukhliak, *Velikaia severnaia voina*, 30.

77. Frandsen, *Last Plague*, 42.

78. Zeids, *Feodālā Rīga*, 247.

79. Ēzens, *Rīga 18. gadsimtā*, 38–39.

80. Kirby, *Northern Europe*, 306–7.

81. Pukhliak, *Velikaia severnaia voina*, 31.

82. Actually, three capitulations were concluded at that time: one with the city and citizens, a second with the nobility, and the third with the Swedish army.

83. Gusev, *Pyotr i Riga*, 84; Zeids, *Feodālā Rīga*, 249.

84. Straubergs, *Rīgas vēsture*, 390.

85. Gusev, *Pyotr i Riga*, 85.

86. Mettig, *Geschichte der Stadt Riga*, 276, as appears in Frandsen, *Last Plague*, 43.

87. "Letters of Emperor Peter the Great to Prince Repnin for 1710," http://www.vostlit.info/Texts/Dokumenty/Russ/XVIII/1700-1720/PetrI/Almanachi_knigi/text1.htm.

88. Mariia Smorzhevskikh-Smirnova, "Riga—'Nevesta' v baltiiskikh zavoevaniiakh Petra I," *Scando-Slavica* 56, no. 2 (2010): 251–68.

89. Straubergs, *Rīgas vēsture*, 388–89; Ēzens, *Rīga 18. gadsimtā*, 39–40.

90. Straubergs, *Rīgas vēsture*, 390.

91. Schuyler, *Peter the Great*, 2:169.

92. Pukhliak, *Velikaia severnaia voina*, 31; Gusev, *Pyotr i Riga*, 85.

93. Frandsen, *Last Plague*, 41; Gerhards, "Epidēmijas viduslaiku un jauno laiku Rīgā," 49; Pukhliak, *Velikaia severnaia voina*, 33.

94. Frandsen, *Last Plague*, 43; Zeids, *Feodālā Rīga*, 252.

95. Wittram, *Baltische Geschichte*, 125.

96. Zeids, *Feodālā Rīga*, 253; Straubergs, *Rīgas vēsture*, 390.

97. Frandsen, *Last Plague*, 43, 134. Perhaps 40,000 died in Stockholm altogether. Kirby, *Northern Europe*, 352.

98. Frost, *Northern Wars*, 302.

99. Arbuzov [Arbusow], *Ocherk istorii*, 243; Pukhliak, *Velikaia severnaia voina*, 33; Neumann, *Riga und Reval*, 4.

100. Straubergs, *Rīgas vēsture*, 382, 389–90.

101. Spekke, *History of Latvia*, 195.

102. The woman who is thought to have been the last native speaker of the Livish language, Marija Kristiņa, died in Canada in 2013. Born during the twilight years of the Russian Empire, she was 103 years old at the time of her passing.

Epilogue

1. Although there had been a small Jewish presence in Courland since sixteenth century, it was only in 1638 that a sufficient number of Jews had settled in Riga to justify the creation of a guest house (*Judenherberge*) beyond the walls and ramparts for Jewish traders. See Leo Dribins, Armands Gūtmanis and Marģers Verstermanis, *Latvia's Jewish Community: History, Tragedy, Revival* (Riga: Publishers of the Institute of the History of Latvia, 2001), 11–13.

2. Called "home" to the Reich by Adolf Hitler, the Baltic Germans abandoned Latvia and Estonia during World War II. Few Germans live in Riga today.

Bibliography

Aberbergs, Jānis. “Rīga pilsētas vesture.” In *Rīga kā Latvijas galvas pilsēta*, edited by Teodors Līventāls and Valters Sadovskis, 30–37. Rīga: Rīgas pilsētas valde, 1932.

Abyzov, Iu., comp. *Ot Liflandiia k Latvii: Pribaltika russkimi glazami*. Moscow: Arkaiur, 1993.

Ancāne, Anna. *Rīgas arhitektūra un pilsētbūvniecība 17. gadsimta otrajā pusē*. Rīga: Latvijas Mākslas akadēmijas Mākslas vēstures institūts, 2016.

Anderson, N. K. “The Reformation in Scandinavia and the Baltic.” In *The New Cambridge Modern History: Vol. 2, The Reformation, 1520–1559*, 2nd ed., edited by Geoffrey Rudolph Elton, 144–71. New York: Cambridge University Press, 1990.

Arbuzov [Arbusow], Leonid. *Ocherk istorii Lifliandii, Estliandii i Kurliandii*, translated by Vladimir Buka. Moscow: Troitsa, 2009. Originally published in German in Riga in 1918.

Arnold, Udo, ed. *Stadt und Orden: Das Verhältnis der Deutschen Ordens zu den Städten in Livland, Preussen und im Deutschen Reich*. Marburg: N.G. Elwert, 1993.

Attman, Artur. *The Struggle for Baltic Markets: Powers in Conflict, 1558–1618*. Göteborg, Sweden: Kungl. Vetenskaps- och Vitterhets-Samhället, 1979.

Bākule, Irēna, and Arnis Siksna. *Rīga ārpus nocietinājumiem: Pilsētas plānotā izbūve un pārbūve no 17. gadsimta līdz Pirmajam pasaules karam*. Rīga: Neputns, 2009.

Bartlett, Robert. *The Making of Europe: Conquest, Colonization and Cultural Change 950–1300*. Princeton: NJ: Princeton University Press, 1993.

Barzdeviča, Margarita. *Rīga zviedru laika kartēs un plānos, 1621–1710*. Rīga: Latvijas vēstures institūtes apgād, 2011.

Bengtsson, Frans G. *The Life of Charles XII: King of Sweden, 1697–1718*. London: Macmillan, 1960.

Benninghoven, Friedrich von. *Rigas Entstehung und der frühhansische Kaufmann*. Hamburg: August Friedrich Velmede, 1961.

Berens, Reinhold. *Geschichte der seit hundert und funzig Jahren in Riga einheimischen Familie Berens aus Rostock*. Riga: Julius Müller, 1812.

Bilmanis, Alfred. *A History of Latvia*. Princeton, NJ: Princeton University Press, 1951.

Blomkvist, Nils. *The Discovery of the Baltic: The Reception of a Catholic World-System in the European North (AD 1075–1225)*. Leiden: Brill, 2005.

Bogov, Vlad, and Kirill Soklakov. *Mnogolikaia Riga: sbornik ocherkov po istorii Rigi*. Riga: Rizhskoe kraevedcheskoe obshchestvo, 2010.

Bojtár, Endre. *Foreword to the Past: A Cultural History of the Baltic People*. Budapest: Central European University Press, 1999.

Böthführ, H. J. *Rigische Rathslinie von 1226 bis 1886*. Riga: J. Deubner, 1877.

Broce [Brotze], Johann Kristofs, *Zīmējumi un apraksti / I. sējums Rīgas skati, ļaudis un ēkas.* Rīga: Zinātne, 1992. / *II. sējums Rīgas priekšpilsētas un tuvākā apkārtne* (Rīga: Zinātne, 1996).

Browning, Oscar. *Peter the Great.* London: Hutchinson & Co., 1898.

Brück, Thomas. "Zwischen Autonomie und Konfrontation—Bemerkungen Politik des Rates von Riga in der ersten Hälfte des 15. Jahrhunderts." In *Riga und der Ostseeraum: Von der Gründung 1201 bis in die Frühe Neuzeit*, edited by Ilgvars Misāns and Horst Wernicke, 144–68. Marburg: Herder-Institut, 2005.

Brundage, James A., ed. and trans. *The Chronicle of Henry of Livonia.* New York: Columbia University Press, 1961.

———. "Introduction: Henry of Livonia, The Writer and His Chronicle." In *Crusading and Chronicle Writing on the Medieval Baltic Frontier: A Companion to the Chronicle of Henry of Livonia*, edited by Marek Tamm, Linda Kaljundi, and Carsten Selch Jensen, 1–19. Burlington, VT: Ashgate, 2011.

Bunge, Friedrich Georg von. *Die Stadt Riga im dreizehnten und vierzehnten Jahrhundert. Geschichte, Verfassung und Rechtszustand.* Leipzig: Verlag von Duncker & Humboldt, 1878; reprinted Amsterdam: E.J. Bonset, 1968.

Caune, Andris. "Kā radās un veidojās priekšstats par pirmsvācu Rīgu." In *Senā Rīga: Pētījumi pilsētas arheoloģijā un vēsturē /1. sēj.*, compiled by Andris Caune, 73–104. Rīga: Latvijas vēsture institūta apgāds, 1998.

———. *Pētījumi Rīgas arheoloģijā.* Rīga: Latvijas vēstures institūta apgāds, 2007.

———. *Rīga zem Rīgas.* Rīga: Zinātne, 1985.

———. *Rīgas lībieši un viņu īpašumzīme.* Rīga: Jumava, 1998.

Caune, Andris, and Ieva Ose, eds. *The Hansa Town Riga as Mediator between East and West.* Riga: Institute of Latvia Publishers, 2009.

Caune, Māra. *Rīgas pils.* Rīga: Zinātne, 2001.

Celmiņa, Ilona, ed. *Rīga's pārvalde: astoņos gadsimtos.* Rīga: Rīgas nami, 2000.

Cherepnin, L. V. "Russian 17th-Century Baltic in Soviet Historiography." *Slavonic Review* 43, no. 100 (Sept. 1964): 1–22.

Christiansen, Eric. *The Northern Crusades.* New York: Penguin, 1997.

Cielava, Skaidrīte, and Z. Ērgle. *Old Riga Tales.* Rīga: Liesma, 1977.

Czaja, Roman. "Das Patriziat in den livländischen und preußischen Städten. Eine vergleichende Analyse." In *Riga und der Ostseeraum: Von der Gründung 1201 bis in die Frühe Neuzeit*, edited by Ilgvars Misāns and Horst Wernicke, 211–21. Marburg: Herder-Institut, 2005.

Davies, Norman, and Roger Moorehouse. *Microcosm: Portrait of a Central European City.* New York: Cambridge University Press, 2002.

de Madariaga, Isabel. *Ivan the Terrible.* New Haven, CT: Yale University Press, 2006.

Dollinger, Philippe. *The German Hanse.* Stanford, CA: Stanford University Press, 1970.

Doroshenko, V. V. *Torgovlia i kupechestvo cherez Rigi v XVII veke.* Rīga: Zinātne, 1985.

Dribins, Leo, Armands Gūtmanis and Marģers Verstermanis. *Latvia's Jewish Community: History, Tragedy, Revival.* Riga: Publishers of the Institute of the History of Latvia, 2001.

Duffy, Christopher. *The Fortress in the Age of Vauban and Frederick the Great, 1660–1789.* London: Routledge Library Editions: Military and Naval History, 1985.

——. *Siege Warfare: The Fortress in the Early Modern World, 1494–1660*. London: Routledge & Kegan Paul, 1979.

Dunsdorfs, Edgars. *Latvijas vēsture, 1500–1600*. Stockholm: Daugava, 1964.

——. *Latvijas vēsture, 1600–1710*. Stockholm: Daugava, 1962.

Dunsdorfs, Edgars, and Arnolds Spekke. *Latvijas vēsture, 1500–1600*. Stockholm: Daugava, 1964.

Eihgmane, Eva. "The Baltic Crusades: A Clash of Two Identities. In *The Clash of Cultures on the Medieval Baltic Frontier*, edited by Alan V. Murray, 37–51. London: Ashgate, 2009.

Esper, Thomas. "Russia and the Baltic, 1494–1558." *Slavic Review* 25, no. 3 (Sept. 1966): 458–74.

Ēzens [Oesen], Johans Andreass. *Rīga 18. gadsimtā.* zīmējumi Rīga: Latvijas valsts vēstures arhīvs, 2004.

Faber, J. A. "The Decline of the Baltic Grain-Trade in the Second Half of the Seventeenth Century." In *From Dunkirk to Danzig: Shipping and Trade in the North Sea and the Baltic, 1350–1850*, edited by W. G. Heeres et al., 31–35. Hilversum, Netherlands: Verloren, 1988.

Fennell, J. L. L. *Ivan the Great of Moscow*. New York: St. Martin's Press, 1961.

Fonnesberg-Schmidt, Iben. "Pope Honorius III and Mission and Crusades in the Baltic Region." In *The Clash of Cultures on the Medieval Baltic Frontier*, edited by Alan V. Murray, 103–22. London: Ashgate, 2009.

——. *The Popes and the Baltic Crusades, 1147–1254*. Leiden: Brill, 2007.

France, John. *The Crusades and the Expansion of Catholic Christendom, 1000–1714*. London: Routledge, 2005.

Frandsen, Karl-Erik. *The Last Plague in the Baltic Region, 1709–1713*. Copenhagen: Museum Tusculanum Press, 2010.

Frankot, Edda. *"Of Laws of Ships and Shipmen": Maritime Law and Its Practice in Urban Northern Europe*. Edinburgh, UK: Edinburgh University Press, 2012.

Frost, Robert I. *The Northern Wars: War, State, and Society in Northeastern Europe, 1558–1721*. Harlow, UK: Pearson, 2000.

Fülberth, Andreas. *Riga: Kleine Geschichte der Stadt*. Cologne: Böhlau, 2014.

Gailiša, Anita. "Rīgas rātes krēsli, 17. gadsimta otrā puse–18. gadsimta pirmā puse." In *Senā Rīga 5: Pētījumi pilsētas arheoloģijā un vēsturē*, edited by Andris Caune, 297–303. Rīga: Latvijas vēstures institūta apgāds, 2005.

Gailite, Zane. *Par Rīgas mūziku un kumēdiņu spēli*. Rīga: Pētergailis, 2003.

Garber, Klaus. "Die 'Bibliotheca Rigensis': Eine Stätte grosser Sammler und kommunaler Identitätstiftung." In *Schatzhäuser des Geistes: Alte Bibliotheken und Büchersammlungern im Baltikum*, edited by Klaus Barber, 51–84. Cologne: Böhlau, 2007.

Gerhards, Guntis. "Epidēmijas viduslaiku un jauno laiku Rīgā." *Latvijas vēstures institūta žurnāls* 4 (2011), 37–65.

Gimbutas, Marija. *The Balts*. New York: Frederick A. Praeger, 1963.

Glete, Jan. *Swedish Naval Administration, 1521–1721*. Leiden: Brill, 2010.

Grislis, Egil. "Recent Trends in the Study of the History of the Reformation in Riga, Livonia," *Journal of Baltic Studies* 7, no. 2 (1976): 145–69.

Gusev, Igor'. *Istoriia Rigi: V voprosakh i otvetakh*. Riga: Zoriks, 2016.

——. *Istoriia Rigi i okrestnostei*. Riga: Zoriks, 2008.

———. *Pyotr i Riga*. Riga: Zoriks, 2011.

Harder-Gersdorff, Elisabeth. "Riga als Handelsmetropole des Osteeraums in der Frühen Neuzeit (16.–18. Jahrhunderts)." In *Riga und der Ostseeraum: Von der Gründung 1201 bis in die Frühe Neuzeit*, edited by Ilgvars Misāns and Horst Wernicke, 144–68. Marburg: Herder-Institut, 2005.

Hatlie, Mark. *Riga at War, 1914–1919: War and Wartime Experience in a Multi-Ethnic Metropolis*. Marburg: Herder-Institut, 2014.

Hatton, R. M. *Charles XII of Sweden*. NY: Weybright & Talley, 1968.

Hellie, Richard. *Enserfment and Military Change in Muscovy*. Chicago: University of Chicago Press, 1971.

Hellmann, Manfred. "Die Anfänge christlicher Mission in den baltischen Ländern." In *Studien über die Anfänge der Mission in Livland*, edited by Manfred Hellmann, 7–38. Sigmaringen, Germany: Jan Thorbecke, 1989.

———. "Der Deutschen Orden und die Stadt Riga." In *Stadt und Orden: Das Verhältnis der Deutschen Ordens zu den Städten in Livland, Preussen und im Deutschen Reich*, edited by Udo Arnold, 1–33. Marburg: N.G. Elwert, 1993.

Henriksson, Anders. *The Tsar's Loyal Germans: The Riga Community: Social Change and the Nationality Question, 1855–1905*. Boulder, CO: East European Monographs, 1983.

Hohenberg, Lee, and Lynn Hollen Lees. *The Making of Modern Europe, 1000–1950*. Cambridge, MA: Harvard University Press, 1985.

Hughes, Lindsey. *Russia in the Age of Peter the Great*. New Haven, CT: Yale University Press, 1998.

Jansons, Gunārs. "Rekonstruktion der Architektur des Rigaer Rathauses im 14.–18. Jahrhundert." In *The Hansa Town Rīga as Mediator between East and West*, edited by Andris Caune and Ieva Ose, 163–71. Rīga: Institute of Latvia Publishers, 2009.

Jensen, Carsten Selch. "How to Convert a Landscape: Henry of Livonia and the Chronicon Livoniae." In *The Clash of Cultures on the Medieval Baltic Frontier*, edited by Alan V. Murray, 151–68. London: Ashgate, 2009.

———. "The Nature of the Early Missionary Activities and Crusades in Livonia, 1195–1201." In *Medieval Spirituality in Scandinavia and Europe: A Collection of Essays in Honour of Tore Nyberg*, edited by Lars Bisgaard, 121–38. New York: Oxford University Press, 2001.

Jordan, William Chester. *The Great Famine: Northern Europe in the Early Fourteenth Century*. Princeton, NJ: Princeton University Press, 1996.

Jozaitis, Arvīds. *Rīga—cita civilizācija*. Rīga: Zvaigzne, 2014.

Kala, Tiina. "Rural Society and Religious Innovation: Acceptance and Rejection of Catholicism among the Native Inhabitants of Medieval Livonia." In *The Clash of Cultures on the Medieval Baltic Frontier*, edited by Alan V. Murray, 169–90. Burlington, VT: Ashgate, 2009.

Kalnins, Mara. *The Ancient Amber Route: Travels from Rīga to Byzantium*. Rīga: Pētergailis, 2013.

———. *Latvia: A Short History*. London: Hurst, 2015.

Kamenskii, Aleksandr B. *The Russian Empire in the Eighteenth Century: Searching for a Place in the World*. Translated and edited by David Griffiths. Armonk, NY: M. E. Sharpe, 1997.

Kasekamp, Andres. *A History of the Baltic States*. New York: Palgrave, 2009.

Keene, Derek, Balázs Nagy, and Katalin Szende, eds. *Segregation—Integration—Assimilation: Religious and Ethnic Groups in the Medieval Towns of Central and Eastern Europe*. Burlington, VT: Ashgate, 2009.

Kirby, David. *Northern Europe in the Early Modern Period: The Baltic World, 1492–1772*. London: Longman, 1990.

Kirchner, Walther. *The Rise of the Baltic Question*. Newark: University of Delaware Press, 1954.

Kļava, Valda. "Mēklenburgas Kristofs hercogistes un arhibīskapijas interešu krustpunktā." *Latvijas Universitātes raksti* 764. sēj. (2012): 119–33.

Klinge, Matti. *The Baltic World*. Keuruu: Ostava, 1995.

Kolbergs, Andris. *Rīga for the Curious Traveler*. Rīga: SIA, 2003.

Kotilaine, J. T. *Russia's Foreign Trade and Economic Expansion in the Seventeenth Century: Windows on the World*. Leiden: Brill, 2005.

Kreem, Juhan. "Der Deutschen Orden und die Reformation in Livland." In *The Military Orders and the Reformation: Choices, State Building, and the Weight of Tradition*. Edited by Johannes A. Mol, Klaus Militzer and Helen J. Nicholson, 43–57. Hilsverum, Netherlands: Verloren, 2006.

———. *The Town and Its Lord: Reval and the Teutonic Order in the Fifteenth Century*. Tallinn: Tallinna Linnaarhiiv, 2002.

Lange, Thomas. *Zwischen Reformation und Untergang Alt-Livlands: Der Rigaer Erzbischof Wilhelm von Brandenburg im Beziehungsgeflecht der livländischen Konföderation und ihrer Nachbarländer*. Hamburg: Verlag Dr. Kovač, 2014.

Leighly, John. "The Towns of Medieval Livonia." *University of California Publications in Geography* 6, no. 7 (1939): 234–314.

Lejnieks, Jānis. *Rīga, kuras nav*. Rīga: Zinātne, 1998.

Lenz, Wilhelm. *Riga zwischen dem Römischen Reich and Polen-Litauen in den jahren 1558–1582*. Marburg/Lahn: Herder-Institut, 1968.

Lepage, Jean-Denis G. G. *Castles and Fortified Cities of Medieval Europe: An Illustrated History*. Jefferson, NC: McFarland, 2002.

Lieb, Ludger, Jan Mohr, and Herfried Vögel, eds. *Burkard Waldis: Esopus: 400 Fabeln und Erzählungen nach der Erstausgabe von 1548*. Berlin: De Gruyter, 2011.

Lisk, Jill. *The Struggle for Supremacy in the Baltic, 1600–1725*. New York: Funk & Wagnalls, 1968.

Līventāls, Teodors, and Valters Sadovskis, eds. *Rīga kā Latvijas galvas pilsēta*. Rīga: Rīgas pilsētas valde, 1932.

Lockhart, Paul Douglas. *Sweden in the Seventeenth Century*. New York: Palgrave/Macmillan, 2004.

Loit, Aleksander. "Die Stadt Riga im schwedischen Ostseereich. Die Privilienfrage." In *Riga und der Ostseeraum: Von der Gründung 1201 bis in die Frühe Neuzeit*, edited by Ilgvars Misāns and Horst Wernicke, 321–32. Marburg: Herder-Institut, 2005.

Longsworth, Philip. *Alexis: Tsar of All the Russias*. New York: Franklin Watts, 1984.

Ludvigs, Pauls. *Mūsu Latvijas ūdeņi*. Rīga: Grāmatu draugs, 1967.

MacCulloch, Diarmaid. *The Reformation: A History*. New York: Penguin, 2004.

Mackenson, Lutz. *Baltische Texte der Frühzeit*. Riga: Verlag der Akt.-Ges. Ernst Plates, 1936.
Mänd, Anu. "Hospitals and Tables for the Poor in Medieval Livonia." *Mitteilungen des Instituts für Österreichische Geschichtsforschung* 115, no. 3/4 (September 2007): 234–70.
———. "Saints' Cults in Medieval Livonia." In *The Clash of Cultures on the Medieval Baltic Frontier*, edited by Alan V. Murray, 191–223. London: Ashgate, 2009.
———. "Signs of Power and Signs of Hospitality: The Festive Entries of the Ordensmeister into Late Medieval Reval." In *The Man of Many Devices, Who Wandered Full Many Ways: Festschrift in Honor of János M. Bak*, edited by Balázs Nagy and Marcell Sebok, 281–93. Budapest: Central European University Press, 1999.
———. *Urban Carnival: Festive Culture in the Hanseatic Cities of the Eastern Baltic, 1350–1550*. Turnhout, Belgium: Brepols 2005.
Martin, Janet. *Medieval Russia, 980–1584*. New York: Cambridge University Press, 1995.
———. *Treasure of the Land of Darkness: The Fur Trade and Its Significance for Medieval Russia*. New York: Cambridge University Press, 1986.
Massie, Robert K. *Peter the Great: His Life and World*. New York: Random House, 1980.
Merridale, Catherine. *Red Fortress: History and Illusion in the Kremlin*. New York: Picador, 2014.
Mettig, Constantin. *Geschichte der Stadt Riga*. Riga: Jonck & Poliewsky, 1897.
Michalski, Serguisz. *The Reformation and the Visual Arts: The Protestant Image Question in Western and Eastern Europe*. London: Routledge, 1993.
Misāns, Ilgvars. "Riga—ein Vorort der Livländischen Städtei im Mittelalter?" In *Riga und der Ostseeraum: Von der Gründung 1201 bis in die Frühe Neuzeit*, edited by Ilgvars Misāns and Horst Wernickje, 169–79. Marburg: Herder-Institut, 2005.
Misāns, Ilgvars, and Horst Wernickje, eds. *Riga und der Ostseeraum: Von der Gründung 1201 bis in die Frühe Neuzeit*. Marburg: Herder-Institut, 2005.
Miskimim, Harry A. *The Economy of Early Renaissance Europe, 1300–1460*. Englewood Cliffs, NJ: Prentice-Hall, 1969.
Montefiore, Simon Sebag. *Jerusalem: The Biography*. New York: Vintage Books, 2011.
Moore, John C., ed. *Pope Innocent and His World*. Aldershot, UK: Ashgate, 1999.
Mumford, Lewis. *The City in History*. New York: Harcourt Brace, 1961.
Munzinger, Mark R. "The Profits of the Cross: Merchant Involvement in the Baltic Crusade (ca. 1180–1230)." *Journal of Medieval History* 32, no. 2 (2006): 163–85.
Murray, Alan V., ed. *The Clash of Cultures on the Medieval Baltic Frontier*. London: Ashgate, 2009.
Neumann, Wilhelm von. *Das Mittelalterliche Riga: Ein Beitrag zur Geschichte der Norddeutschen Baukunst*. Berlin: Julius Springer, 1892.
———. *Riga und Reval*. Leipzig: E.A. Seamann, 1908.
Nicholas, David. *The Northern Lands: Germanic Europe, c. 1270–c.1500*. London: Wiley-Blackwell, 2009.
Nielsen, Torben K. "Sterile Monsters? Russians and the Orthodox Church in the Chronicle of Henry of Livonia." In *The Clash of Cultures on the Medieval Baltic Frontier*, edited by Alan V. Murray, 227–52. London: Ashgate, 2009.
North, Michael. *The Expansion of Europe, 1250–1500*. Manchester, UK: Manchester University Press, 2007.

Ose, Ieva. "Daugavgrīvas cietokšņa pārbūves no 1622. līdz 1710. gadam." In *Senā Rīga 7: Pētījumi pilsētas arheoloģijā un vēsturē*, edited by Ieva Ose, 202–33. Rīga: Latvijas vēstures institūta apgāds, 2012.

———. "Kobronskansts pārbūves 17. gadsimtā un 18. gadsimtā zviedru inženieru ieceres un to realizācija." In *Senā Rīga 7: Pētījumi pilsētas arheoloģijā un vēsturē*, edited by Ieve Ose, 406–43. Rīga: Latvijas vēstures institūta apgāds, 2012.

Osipova, Sanita. "Riga's Stadtrecht in Laufe des 13. Jh." In *International Conference: Hanse Yesterday—Hanse Tomorrow: Riga, June 8–12, 1998*, edited by Ojārs Spārītis, 162–68. Rīga: Vārds, 2001.

Paulovičа, Ieva. "Garīgā mūzika vidzemē Zviedrijas lielvalsts vēlīnajā posmā (1660–1710)." PhD dissertation, Latvijas kultūras akadēmija, 2009.

Petkūnas, Darius. *Russian and Baltic Lutheran Liturgy in the Nineteenth and Twentieth Centuries*. Klaipėda, Lithuania: University of Klaipėda, 2013.

Petrukhintsev, Nikolai N. "The Baltic Strategy of Peter the Great." In *Russland an der Ostsee: Imperiale Strategien der Macht und kulturelle Wahrnehmungsmuster (16. bis 20. Jahrhundert)*, edited by Karsten Brüggemann and Bradley D. Woodworth, 169–89. Vienna: Böhlau, 2012.

Pihlajamäki, Heikki. *Conquest and the Law in Swedish Livonia (ca. 1630–1710): A Case of Legal Pluralism in Early Modern Europe*. Leiden: Brill, 2017.

Plakans, Andrejs. *A Concise History of the Baltic States*. New York: Cambridge University Press, 2011.

———. *The Latvians: A Short History*. Stanford, CA: Hoover Institute Press, 1995.

Plīnijs, Bazilijs. *Slavas dziesma Rīgai*. Rīga: Jumava, 1997.

Pope, Arvids. *Rīgas ostas deviņos gadsimtos*. Rīga: Jumava, 2000.

Pounds, N.J.G. *An Historical Geography of Europe, 1500–1840*. New York: Cambridge University Press, 1979.

Prak, Maarten. *The Dutch Republic in the Seventeenth Century*, translated by Diane Webb. New York: Cambridge University Press, 2005.

Priede, Jāņis. "The Development of the Study of Religion in Latvia in the 20th Century." In *Studying Religions with the Iron Door Closed and Open: The Academic Study of Religion in Eastern Europe*, edited by Tomáš Bubík and Henryk Hoffmann, 199–238. Leiden: Brill, 2015.

Pukhliak, Oleg. *Velikaia severnaia voina na territorii Latvii. 1700–1721*. Riga: Rizhskoe slavianskoe istoricheskoe obshchesvto, 2010.

Renner, Johannes. *Johannes Renner's Livonian History, 1556–1561*. Translated by Jerry S. Smith, William Urban, and J. Ward Jones. Lewiston, NY: Edwin Mellen Press, 1997.

Roberts, Michael. *Gustavus Adolphus and the Rise of Sweden*. London: English Universities Press, 1973.

Rowell, S. C. *Lithuania Ascending: A Pagan Empire within East-Central Europe, 1295–1345*. New York: Cambridge University Press, 1994.

Russow, Balthasar. *The Chronicle of Balthasar Russow*. Translated by Jeremy C. Smith. Madison, WI: Baltic Studies Center, 1988.

Schuyler, Eugene. *Peter the Great: Emperor of Russia*. Vols. 1 and 2. New York: Russell & Russell, 1884.

Selart, Anti. *Livonia, Rus' and the Baltic Crusades in the Thirteenth Century*. Translated by Fiona Robb. Leiden: Brill, 2015.

———. "Orthodox Churches in Medieval Livonia." In *The Clash of Cultures on the Medieval Baltic Frontier*, edited by Alan V. Murray, 273–90. London: Ashgate, 2009.

———. "Russians in Livonian Towns in the Thirteenth and Fourteenth Centuries." In *Segregation—Integration—Assimilation: Religious and Ethnic Groups in the Medieval Towns of Central and Eastern Europe*, edited by Derek Keene et al., 33–50. Burlington, VT: Ashgate, 2009.

Shalfeev, B. "Petr I v dome Dannenshterna v 1714 g." In *Ot Liflandiia k Latvii: Pribaltika russkimi glazami*, compiled by Iu. Abyzov, 175–82. Moscow: Arkaiur, 1993.

Shorto, Russell. *Amsterdam: A History of the World's Most Liberal City*. New York: Vintage, 2013.

Siirman, Vivian. "Der literarische Nachlass des Hermann Samson." *Forschungen zur baltischen Geschichte* 5 (2010): 36–58.

Skrynnikov, Ruslan G. *Ivan the Terrible*. Edited and translated by Hugh F. Graham. Gulf Breeze, FL: Academic International Press, 1981.

Smith, Jerry C., and William L. Urban, trans. *The Livonian Rhymed Chronicle*. Bloomington: Indiana University Press, 1977.

Smorzhevskikh-Smirnova, Mariia. "Riga—'Nevesta' v baltiiskikh zavoevaniiakh Petra I." *Scando-Slavica* 56, no. 2 (2010): 251–68.

Šnē, Andris. "Emergence and Development of Early Urbanism in the Late Prehistoric Latvia." In *Riga und der Ostseeraum: Von der Gründung 1201 bis in die Frühe Neuzeit*, edited by Ilgvars Misāns and Horst Wernicke, 24–36. Marburg: Herder-Institut, 2005.

———. "The Emergence of Livonia: The Transformations of Social and Political Structures in the Territory of Latvia during the Twelfth and Thirteenth Centuries." In *The Clash of Cultures on the Medieval Baltic Frontier*, edited by Alan V. Murray, 53–71. London: Ashgate, 2009.

Šnē, Andris, and Rūdolfs Brūzis. "Kobronskansts veidošanās un attīstība 17.-20/ gs.: 2010. gada arheoloģiskās izpētes rezultāti." *Latvijas Universitātes raksti* 764 (2012): 63–81.

Spārītis, Ojārs. "Evidence of the Reformation and Confessionalization in Livonian Art." *Journal of Art History* 9 (September 2015): 23–52.

———, ed. *International Conference: Hanse Yesterday—Hanse Tomorrow: Riga, June 8–12, 1998*. Rīga: Vārds, 2001.

———. *Monuments and Decorative Sculpture in Rīga*. Rīga: Nacionālais medicīnas apgāds, 2001.

———. "Schwedische Impulse im Städtebau im lettischen Teil Livlands im 16. un 17. Jahrhundert." In *Riga und der Ostseeraum: Von der Gründung 1201 bis in die Frühe Neuzeit*, edited by Ilgvars Misāns and Horst Wernickje, 380–99. Marburg: Herder-Institut, 2005.

———. "Some Aspects of Cultural Interaction between Sweden and the Latvian Part of Livonia in the 17th Century." *Baltic Journal of Art History* 1 (2009): 79–104.

Spekke, Arnolds. *History of Latvia: An Outline*. Stockholm: M. Goppers, 1951.

Staden, Heinrich von. *The Land and Government of Muscovy: A Sixteenth-Century Account*. Edited and translated by Thomas Esper. Stanford, CA: Stanford University Press, 1967.

Šterns, Indriķis. *Latvijas vēsture, 1180–1290. Krustakari.* Rīga: Latvijas vēstures institūta apgāds, 2002.

———. *Latvijas vēsture, 1290–1500.* Rīga: Daugava, 1997.

———. "Viduslauiku Rīga ārpus Rīgas." In *Senā Rīga 1. sēj.*, edited by A. Caune, 342–77. Rīga: Latvijas vēstures institūta apgāds, 1998.

Stiega, Wilhelm and Constantin Mettig. *Schragen der Gilden und Aemter der Stadt Riga bis 1621.* Riga: Alexander Stiega's Buchhandlung, 1896.

Straubergs, Jānis. *Rīgas vēsture.* Rīga: Grāmatu draugs, 1937.

———. *Sen to Rīgu daudzināja.* Stockholm: Daugava, 1952.

Strenga, Gustavs. "Remembering the Dead: Collective Memoria in Late Medieval Livonia." PhD dissertation, Queen Mary University of London, 2014.

Sharp, Tony. *Pleasure and Ambition: The Life, Loves and Wars of Augustus the Strong.* London: I.B. Tauris, 2001.

Švābe, Arveds. *Latvijas vēsture. 1. daļa.* Rīga: Avots, 1990.

Švābe [Schwabe], Arveds. *The Story of Latvia: A Historical Survey.* Stockholm: NLF, 1949.

Taimiņa, Aija. "15. gadsimta metala griezuma jeb 'skrosu' graviras un Rigas patriciesa Reinholda Soltrumpa gramatu likteni." *Makslas vēsture un teorija* (2004/2): 5–19.

Tamm, Marek. "A New World into Old Worlds: The Eastern Baltic Region and the Cultural Geography of Medieval Europe." In *The Clash of Cultures on the Medieval Baltic Frontier*, edited by Alan V. Murray, 11–35. London: Ashgate, 2009.

Tamm, Marek, Linda Kaljundi, and Carsten Selch Jensen. *Crusading and Chronicle Writing on the Medieval Baltic Frontier: A Companion to the Chronicle of Henry of Livonia.* Burlington, VT: Ashgate, 2011.

Tiberg, Erik. *Moscow, Livonia and the Hanseatic League, 1487–1550.* Stockholm: Acta Universitatis Stockholmiensis, 1995.

Tichovskis, Heronims. "Provost Ernst Glück as Educator in Livonia and Russia." *Slavic Review* 24, no. 2 (June 1965): 307–13.

Tuchtenhagen, Ralph. "Riga im Rahmen des swedischen Merkantilismus." In *Riga und der Ostseeraum: Von der Gründung 1201 bis in die Frühe Neuzeit*, edited by Ilgvars Misāns and Horst Wernicke, 295–320. Marburg: Herder-Institut, 2005.

Tyerman, Christopher. "Henry of Livonia and the Ideology of Crusading." In *Crusading and Chronicle Writing on the Medieval Baltic Frontier: A Companion to the Chronicle of Henry of Livonia.* Edited by Marek Tamm, Linda Kaljundi, and Carsten Selch Jensen, 23–44. Burlington, VT: Ashgate, 2011.

Urban, William. *The Baltic Crusade.* DeKalb: Northern Illinois University Press, 1975.

———. *The Livonian Crusade.* Washington, DC: University Press of America, 1981.

———. "The Origin of the Livonian War, 1558." *Lituanus* 29, no. 3 (Fall 1983). http://www.lituanus.org/1983_3/83_3_02.htm.

———. *The Teutonic Knights: A Military History.* South Yorkshire, UK: Frontline Books, 2003.

———. "Victims of the Baltic Crusade." *Journal of Baltic Studies* 29, no. 3 (Fall 1998): 195–212.

Vanags, Pēteris. *Luteráņu roksgramātas avoti: vecākā perioda (16 g.–17 g.s. sāmuma) latviešu teksti.* Rīga: Mantojums, 2000.

Vīksninš, Nicholas. "The Early History of Latvian Books." *Lituanus* 19, no. 3 (Fall 1973). http://www.lituanus.org/1973/73_3_02.htm.

———. "Some Notes on the Early Histories of Latvian Books and Newspapers," *Journal of Baltic Studies* 4, no. 2 (Summer 1973): 155–58

Villeruša, Vaida, comp. *Daugavas raksti: No Rīgas līdz jūrai*. Rīga: Zinātne, 1994.

Vitola, Karina. *The Dom Cathedral Architectural Ensemble in Riga*. Leningrad: Aurora, 1980.

Waitschies, Gisela Gnegel. *Bischof Albert von Riga: Ein Bremer Domherr als Kirchenfürst im Osten (1199–1229)*. Hamburg: A.F. Velmede, 1958.

Wittram, Reinhard. *Baltische Geschichte: Die Ostseelande Livland, Estland, Kurland, 1180–1918*. Munich: R. Oldenbourg, 1954.

———. *Peter I: Czar and Kaiser: Zur Geschichte Peters des Grossen in seiner Zeit*. Göttingen: Vandenhoeck & Ruprecht, 1964.

Zajas, Kryzystof. *Absent Culture: The Case of Polish Livonia*. Frankfurt am Main: Peter Lang, 2013.

Zanders, Ojārs. *Senās Rīgas grāmatniecība un kultūra Hanzas pilsētu kopsakarā (13.–17. gs.)*. Rīga: Zinātne, 2000.

———. *Tipogrāfs Mollīns un viņa laiks: Pirmās Rīgā iespiestās grāmatas 1588–1625*. Rīga: Zinātne, 1988.

Zeids, Teodors. *Feodālā Rīga*. Rīga: Zinātne, 1978.

Zemītis, Guntis. "10th–12th Century Daugmale—The Earliest Urban Settlement along the Lower Daugava and Forerunner of Riga." In *Cultural Interaction between East and West: Archaeology, Artefacts and Human Contacts in Northern Europe*, edited by Ulf Fransson, 279–84. Stockholm: Stockholm Studies in Archaeology, 2007.

Ziemlewska, Anna. "The 'Calendar Upheavals' in Riga (1584–1589). *Acta Poloniae Historica* 96 (2007): 87–111.

Zunde, Māris. "The Historical Waterfront Revetments of Rīga in the Light of Dendrochronological Dating." *Archaeologica Baltica* 21–22 (2015): 148–62.

Index

Ako, 54–55
Albert, Duke of Brandenburg, 141–43, 155
Albert of Buxhoeveden, ix, 10, 32, 34, 37 (photo), 269n8, 269n10, 270n33, 270n37, 271n61, 272n74, 272n75, 275n64
achievements, ix, 64–65, 69, 72, 268n75
brothers, 57, 65, 67, 103, 266n57
death, 47, 64
founding of Riga, ix, 15, 28, 30, 36, 45–46, 59–63, 266n57
Northern Crusades, 28, 32, 41, 45, 46, 47–48, 51–59, 65–67
and Swordbrothers, 48, 51, 53, 57, 97
Albert Square, 36, 95
Alexander, Grand Duke of Lithuania, 133, 134
Alexei Mikhailovich, Tsar of Muscovy, 197–98, 206–09, 226, 227, 232, 296n10
amber, 14, 116, 263n10
Amsterdam, 94, 188–89, 212, 213, 228, 284n74
archaeology (in Riga), ix, 9, 23, 35, 36, 59, 95, 106
Archangel (Rus. Archangelsk), 149, 157, 206, 243, 256
Archbishop Albert II Suerbeer, ix, 104–05, 272n75
Archbishop Frederick of Perlstein, ix, 110–12, 114
Archbishop Fromhold, 115–16
Archbishop Henning Scharpenberg, 119
Archbishop Isarnus, 109–10
Archbishop Jasper Linde, 136, 138, 146
Archbishop John I of Lune, 105
Archbishop John II of Vechta, 105
Archbishop John III of Schwerin, 107, 109
Archbishop John V Wallenrode, 117, 118
Archbishop John VI Ambundii, 117, 118
Archbishop John VII Blankenfeld, 140, 142
Archbishop Michael Hildebrand, 125
Archbishop Silvester Stodewescher, x, 119–23
Archbishop Stefan Grube,123, 124
Archbishop Thomas Schöning, 140, 142, 143, 277n103
Archbishop William of Brandenburg, x, 129, 143, 155–56
Archbishopric of Hamburg-Bremen, 20, 66, 268n75
Archbishopric of Magdeburg, 20, 42
Archbishopric of Riga, x, xi, 3, 66, 104 118, 156
properties belonging to, xv, 97, 143, 147, 165
architecture in Riga
Jugendstil (Art Nouveau), 1, 4
in medieval Riga, ix, xiii–xiv, 7, 17, 47–48, 59–63, 69, 80, 92–94
in pre-conquest Riga, 31, 36
in suburban Riga, 204, 259
in Swedish Era, 186, 210–15
See also Churches; Housing; Riga Castle
Arnold of Lübeck, 30, 33
Ascheraden (Latv. Aizkraukle), 53
Avignon papacy, 98, 110–14

Balk, Hermann, 103
Baltic, etymology of, 24, 265n43
Baltic crusade. *See* Northern Crusades
Baltic Germans, 6, 7, 24, 31, 219, 261n12
abandonment of Baltic states, 82, 299n1
historians, 6, 7, 31–32, 218, 255, 278n27
under Polish administration, 167, 173, 175
under Swedish administration, 220, 231
Baltic Sea
amber, 14
cultures of, 216, 217
and Great Northern War, 224, 232, 236–37, 242–43, 246, 249, 251–52
and Muscovy, x, 3, 121, 129, 130, 132, 158, 160, 197, 206, 207, 209, 226, 227, 228, 231, 236–37, 242
piracy in, 75, 100

Baltic Sea (*continued*)
Swedish dominance of, viii, 179, 181–82, 185, 187, 192, 196, 198, 200, 225, 246, 250, trade in, xi, 14, 28, 70–78, 112, 126, 149–50, 188–89, 191, 193, 196, 207, 208, 225, 236, 242–43, 284n76
during Viking age, 14, 23, 24, 35, 71
See also trade
baroque, 184, 212–13, 275n67
Bartholomew of England, 27
bastion system, xiii, 153, 192, 199–206, 210, 225, 245, 260, 288n89
Battle at Wilkomierz (1435), 117, 119
Battle of Kirchholm (1605), 180–81
Battle of Lesnaya (1709), 248
Battle of Narva (1700, 1704), 158, 166, 237
Battle of Poltava (1709), 250
Battle of Saule (1237), 102–103
Battle of Smolin (1502), 134–35, 148
Battle of Spilve (1701), 238–41
Battle of Tannenberg (1410), 117, 279n69–70
Battle of the Düna (1701). *See* Battle of Spilve
Battle of Wenden (1578), 165–66
Battle of Wilkomierz (1435), 117, 119
beer, 74, 76–77, 85–87, 91, 100, 137, 148, 233, 277n100
Belarus, 2, 129, 149, 189, 197, 243, 247, 263n9
Benninghoven, Friedrich, 8
Berens family, 194–95, 291n44
Bergen, 71–72
Bernard of Clairveaux, 20
Bernd von der Borch, Master of the Livonian Order, 121–24
Berthold of Hanover, Bishop of Livonia, vix, 28, 33
Big Christopher, 69, 154–55, 285n8
Bilmanis, Alfred, 8, 209, 269n9
Bindenschu, Rupert, vix, 212–13, 293n107
Bishop Albert. *See* Albert of Buxhoeveden
Bishop's Castle, xii, 49
Bishop's Yard, 49, 59
Bishopric of Courland. *See* Courland, Bishopric of
Bishopric of Livonia xi, xv, 28, 30
Bishopric of Dorpat. *See* Dorpat
Bishopric of Courland. *See* Courland
Bishopric of Ösel-Wiek. *See* Ösel-Wiek, Bishopric of
Black Death, 47, 253
Blackheads, Brotherhood of, xi, xiii, 82, 85–89, 127, 139, 140, 150, 229, 275n68, 275n69
Blackheads, House of, xiii, 63, 82, 83 (photo), 85, 216, 259, 275n67, 275n69
Black Sea, 14, 228
Bohemia, 17–18
Bonnit, Engelbrecht, 74
Brandenburg, Duchy of, 111, 141, 143, 165
Breverus, Johannes, 217
Briesmann, John, 147
Brinken, Hans, 170–71
Brotze, Johann Christoph, 7
Bruges, 71, 74–75
Bruno, Master of the Livonian Order, 107, 109
Bunge, Georg von, 7, 261n6
burgomasters, xi, 91, 99, 120, 122, 125, 126, 137, 169, 171, 190, 194, 229. *See also* Riga Town Council
Butter, 2, 28, 76–77, 87
Buxhoeveden, Albert. *See* Albert of Buxhoeveden
Byzantine Empire, 51, 73, 130

Calendar Upheavals (1585–1590), ix, 167–171, 172, 174, 175, 287n64
canons of the Riga Cathedral, 98, 104, 107, 108, 113, 114, 115, 117, 118, 119, 120, 121, 123, 136
Carnival holiday, 80, 84–87, 147
Catherine I, Empress of Russia, 242, 294n123, 297n49
Catherine II, Empress of Russia, 246
Catholic Church
and Archbishopric of Riga, 3, 104, 122, 123, 272n75
and Counter Reformation, 168, 179
in Lithuania, 108, 113, 116, 133
and Livonian Order, 101, 105, 109, 111, 114, 116, 125, 140–43, 163–64
and missions to Livonia, vii, x, 30–32, 42
and Northern Crusades, 5, 14–16, 19, 32–34, 53, 267n72, 272n79
and Orthodoxy, 25, 61, 103, 133, 172
and Reformation, vii, 129, 136–48, 286n21
and city of Riga, vii, ix, 3, 5, 66–67, 101, 110, 116, 136–40, 143–48, 163, 167–74, 283n54, 284n60, 286n21

See also Albert of Buxhoeveden; Archbishopric of Riga; churches (in Riga)
Caune, Andris, ix, 9
Caupo, 32, 46, 52, 55–58, 270n37
Cēsis. *See* Wenden
Charlemagne, 16–17
Charles Gate, 253, 255
Charles IV, Holy Roman Emperor, 116
Charles V, Holy Roman Emperor, 141–42, 156
Charles IX, King of Sweden, 179, 181, 185
Charles XI, King of Sweden, 195, 200, 209, 217, 218–19, 230, 231, 243
Charles XII, King of Sweden, viii, ix, 154, 228, 230–33, 235–42, 245–50, 296n13
Chodkiewicz, Gregory, 162
Chodkiewicz, Jan Karol, 180–81
choirs, 120, 216, 217
Christianization. *See* Catholic Church; Northern Crusade
Christina, Queen of Sweden, 193, 196–97, 204, 290n32
Christmas, 84, 86–88, 147, 169
Christopher of Mecklenburg, 156
churches (in Riga). *See* Jesus Church; St. Gertrude's Church; St. Jacob's Church; St. John's Church; St. Mary's (Riga Dome) Church; St. Nicholas's Church; St. Peter's Church
Cistercian Order, 20, 28, 32, 63, 64, 110
Citadel, xiii, 202, 206, 210, 225–26, 238, 245, 252, 253, 254, 255
civil wars (Riga), vii, xi
  Riga's first civil war (1297–1330), 80, 98, 106–14
  Riga's second civil war (1481–91), x, 1, 86, 123–26, 151, 152, 155
cloth. *See* textiles
clothing, 87, 129, 173, 180, 220
cogs. *See* ships
commerce. *See* Hanseatic League; merchants; trade
Constantinople, 19, 46, 51, 73, 130
Cosmographia (1550), 152, 153
Cossacks, 248–49, 252–53
Courland (Latv. Kurzeme), 14, 17, 18, 25, 29, 32, 57, 119, 121, 143, 148, 154, 160, 162, 258, 265n47, 266n51, 272n79, 286n24
  Bishopric of, 105, 119
  Duchy of Courland and Semigallia, 164, 172, 198, 202, 213, 220, 230, 232, 239, 241, 246, 247, 249, 250, 251, 252, 289n3
Couronians (Cours, Kurs), 3, 25, 26, 45–46, 47, 49, 51, 57, 58, 72, 265n38, 268n76, 271n55
Cours. *See* Couronians
Craft guilds. *See* craftsmen; Small Guild
craftsmen, 13, 15, 18, 35, 36, 46, 47, 55, 70, 81–82, 84, 88, 89, 90–92, 94, 113, 122, 124, 138, 144, 146, 168, 169, 173, 174, 188, 204, 220, 221–22, 227, 238, 274n65, 287n63
crusades (Near East), 18–20, 21, 40, 41, 51, 56, 264n23. *See also* Northern Crusades
currency (in Riga), 75, 100, 164

Dahlberg, Erik, vix, 202, 210, 229–32, 235, 239
dainas, 12, 27
Dannenstern, Ernst Metsu von, ix, xiii, 213, 215
Dannenstern House, xiii, 213
Danzig (Pol. Gdańsk), xiv, 47, 71, 75, 85, 91, 97, 111, 114, 120, 137, 166, 249, 253, 280n86
Danzig Treaty (1366), 116
Daugava River. *See* Düna River
Daugmale, 23, 30, 35, 45
De la Gardie, Magnus Gabriel, 198, 291n59
De la Gardie, Jakob, 200
Denmark
  and Estonian conquest, 42, 58, 65–66, 72, 101, 115
  and Great Northern War, 231, 232, 233, 236, 240
  and Livonian War, 143, 149, 157, 159, 165
  and Sweden, 181, 192, 196, 225, 231
  and Sound dues, 149, 166, 190, 196
Dnieper River, 133, 189, 248, 250, 265n39
Dole Island, 25, 64
Dome Cathedral (Riga Cathedral). *See* St. Mary's Church
Dome School (St. Mary's), 144, 174, 208, 216, 219
Dominican Order, xiii, 63
Dorpat (Est. Tartu), xv, 10, 25, 59, 71, 72, 82, 103, 134, 172
  Bishopric of, 59, 65, 67, 105, 110, 119, 123, 140
  and Great Northern War, 239, 242, 243

Dorpat (Est. Tartu) (*continued*)
and Livonian War, 152, 158, 159, 160, 161, 166, 167, 286n21
and Reformation, 137, 144, 147
under Swedish rule, 195, 200, 208, 219, 289n8
and trade, 72, 132, 172, 191
Dreiling, Johan, 194, 291n41
Dreiling, Melchior, 290n40
Dreiling, Paul, 139, 194
Dreiling, Theodore von, 194
Dreiling family, 194–95
drunke, 84–88
Düna River (Latv. Daugava; Rus. Dvina)
Battle of (1700), 238–41. *See also* Battle of Spilve
and Battle of Kirchholm, 180–81
Bridges over, 38, 154, 238, 239, 240–41, 251, 285n5
castles and cities on, xv, 17, 23, 30, 31, 48, 50, 53, 57, 106, 119, 124, 172, 180, 197–98, 242, 253
commercial traffic with Russia, 14–15, 65, 72, 74, 114, 154, 170, 189
embankment (Riga), 47, 49, 60, 69, 79, 86, 104, 114, 125, 169, 198, 205, 259, 268n90, 275n54
flooding of, 38, 94, 106, 206, 249–50, 297n37
and early German merchants, 22, 25, 29–31, 34
harbor on, 38, 47, 76, 81
islands of, 31, 35, 44, 47, 49, 64, 206, 233, 240, 249, 297n44, 297n45
left bank, xiv, 38, 64, 154, 202, 206, 207, 213, 233, 239, 240, 246, 249, 257, 278n42, 293n71. *See also* Überdüna
legends of, 154–55
Livish communities near, vii, x, 13, 15, 25, 29, 33–35, 41, 44–46, 54, 63, 94–95
mouth of, 13, 30, 33, 45, 52, 64, 76, 110, 112, 121, 125, 158, 165, 178, 182, 203, 206, 210, 237. *See also* Dünamünde
name, 263n7
shifts in course, 38, 270n36, 292n71
tributaries, 14, 35, 47, 81, 151, 187, 206
and Vikings, 14, 35
Dünaburg (Latv. Daugavpils), 119, 172, 182, 197, 250
Dünamünde, xiii, 270n36
Cistercian monastery at, 52, 54, 63, 64, 76, 110
in Great Northern War, 233, 235, 237, 243, 251, 253, 256, 297n46
Livonian Order castle at, 111, 112, 113, 121, 123, 124, 125, 126
in Livonian War, 158, 160, 162
Polish fortress at, 178, 181, 182
Swedish fortress at, 203, 206, 210, 225, 292n71
Dunsdorfs, Edgars, 8
Dunte, Jürgen, 190
Durkop, Konrad, 137–38
Dutch Republic
architectural influence of, 199, 202, 203, 212
and Baltic trade, 71, 74, 78, 149, 150, 179, 181, 189, 190, 194–95, 213, 227, 284n76
commercial rise of, 149, 184, 188–89
Golden Age, 188, 198
and Great Northern War, 236
and Peter I's Grand Embassy, 227, 228, 229
and Polish-Swedish War, 180, 181
printing in, 174
Dvina River. *See* Düna River

East Prussia, Duchy of, 141, 143, 147, 280n86
Eberhard of Monheim, Master of the Livonian Order, 113–14
Eck, Johannes, 145
Ecke, Nicholas, 169, 175
Education (in Riga)
during the Middle Ages, 136, 283n54
during the Polish era, 172, 174, 272n65, 284n60
during the Reformation, 139, 144, 145
during the Swedish times, 195, 196, 216, 219, 295n126, 295n127
Engelbert of Buxhoeveden, 48, 57
England, 17, 217, 228
and Baltic trade, 28, 71, 72, 149, 157, 190, 227, 236
entertainment. *See* choirs; music; theater
Eric XIV, King of Sweden, 160–61
Esplanade, xiii, 36, 260n17
Estonia (Estland)
and Catholic Church, xi, xv, 10, 31, 58, 65, 67, 110, 143, 271n50

during Great Northern War, 237, 239, 241, 242, 244, 245, 247, 257
Lithuanian raids of, 39, 50, 103, 109
and Livonian Confederation, xi, 119
and Livonian Order, 98, 103, 110, 115, 126, 152, 156
during Livonian War, 157, 159, 160, 163–66, 286n24
and Muscovy/Russia, 123, 130, 132, 159, 160
and Northern Crusades, 32–33, 42, 47, 51, 53, 56–59, 65, 66–68, 102, 268n76, 271n50
and Old Livonia, 10, 22, 267n66
and Kingdom of Poland, 179, 181
and Riga, 58, 121, 124, 172, 180, 272n80, 274n23
and Rus', 24–25, 58, 59, 103
and Sweden, xv, 163, 165, 167, 172, 179, 185, 186, 198, 200, 202, 209, 217, 225, 231
uprisings in, 102, 115, 147
See also Dorpat; Narva; Ösel; Pernau; Tartu
Estonian language, 13, 24, 145, 265n42
Estonian tribes, 13, 24–25, 26, 57, 66, 102, 268n76

Famine, 112, 122, 151, 159, 186, 197, 221, 225, 228, 229, 233, 252, 257, 285n13
feast days, 80, 84–88, 216, 274n30
feudalism, 17, 47, 57, 65, 71, 97, 99, 119, 155
Finland, 25, 72, 125, 130, 179, 225, 247, 254, 268n72
Finno-Ugric peoples, 10, 23–27, 258
fires (in Riga), 59, 60, 61, 63, 92, 94, 107, 124, 153, 204, 205, 211–12, 220, 221, 251, 281n103, 283n49, 290n38, 294n117
Flanders, 72, 74–75, 97, 107
floods (in Riga), 38, 69, 106, 154, 178, 205–06, 249, 269n93
fortifications (in Riga), x, xiii, 3, 17, 78–79, 106, 151, 152–54, 172, 178, 183, 186, 198–200, 202, 203 (photo), 205–07, 208, 210, 225, 229–33, 240, 244, 246, 253, 260, 263n16. *See also* bastion system; Citadel; Dünamünde; Fort Kobron; moats; ramparts; Riga Castle
Fort Kobron, xiii, xiv, 179, 202, 203 (photo), 206, 225, 233, 237, 240, 246, 251, 292n67
Franciscan Order, 63, 110, 138, 139, 146
Freedom Monument, 226, 259
Frederick III (Holy Roman Emperor), 123
Fuchs, Melchior, 120, 193
fur trade, xv, 2, 15, 72, 73–74, 108, 189, 209

Gauja River (Ger. Treider Aa; Livländische Aa), 17, 25, 50, 57, 65, 119, 264n18, 271n46
Gdańsk. *See* Danzig
Gediminas, Grand Duke of Lithuania, 113–13, 281n13
Gendena, Heinrich, 75
Gerhard II, Master of the Livonian Order, 112
Germanization, 18, 145, 219, 262n1
German language. *See* Low German
Germans. *See* Baltic Germans
Germany. *See also* Holy Roman Empire
Archbishoprics of, 31, 42, 64, 66
architectural influence of, 212
cultural influence of, 216
education in, 173–74
and Hanseatic League, 71, 84
and Livonian Order, 161, 270n33
merchants from, vii, 14, 15, 21, 22, 25, 28, 30–34, 36, 39–40, 44, 45, 47, 58, 59, 64, 67, 70–78, 82, 88, 90–92, 99, 100, 121, 123, 129, 258
and Northern Crusades, 9, 14, 17, 21, 27, 28, 30, 32, 39, 41, 42, 45, 46, 47, 48, 49, 51, 52, 53, 54, 56, 58, 60, 64, 70, 105, 258, 264n28
and Reformation, 129, 134, 137, 140, 146, 163
and Thirty Years War, 191, 196
Gerzika. *See* Jersika
Giese, Martin, ix, 170–71
Gimbutas, Marija, 266n53
Glück, Johann Ernst, 218–19, 220, 226, 241, 294n123, 297n49
Gotland, 29, 31, 32, 42, 44, 53, 57, 60, 71. *See also* Visby
Gotthard Kettler, Master of the Livonian Order, 161, 163
grain exports, 57, 72, 77–78, 100, 108, 134, 149, 150, 189, 190, 191, 195, 197, 208, 209, 225, 243, 280n86. *See also* hempseed; linseed; rye
Grand Embassy. *See* Peter I
Great Guild, xi, 82, 86, 89, 99, 145, 150, 168, 170, 171, 208, 212, 235, 275n68, 275n69

Great Northern War, viii, ix, xiii, xv, 3, 4, 38, 154, 209, 222, 223, 224, 226, 232–60
guest ban, 131, 150, 190, 207
guilds. *See* Great Guild; Small Guild
Gustavus II Adolphus, King of Sweden, x, 182, 185, 186, 192, 196, 209

Hamburg law, 71
Hamburg-Bremen. *See* Archbishopric of Hamburg-Bremen. 20, 31, 42, 66
Hanseatic League, vii, xi, xiv, xv, 70–77, 79, 80, 86, 91, 92, 99, 100, 108, 122, 124, 132, 140, 149, 150, 159, 161, 179, 188, 196, 273n11, 281n2, 284n76
Hartwig II, Archbishop of Bremen-Hamburg, 31, 32, 33, 42
Hasentöter, Hans, 277n1, 284–85n1
Helewegh, Hermann, 124
Helm, Jürgen, 215
Helms, Joaquim Andreas, 252, 254, 256
hemp, 2, 77, 91, 92, 129, 140, 149, 150, 189, 194, 208, 243
hempseed, 189, 208
Henry of Livonia, x, 13, 25–26, 27–28, 34, 35, 39, 41–42, 44, 45, 53–56, 58, 60, 67–68, 266n57, 267n60, 268n77, 268n86, 269n5, 269n18
Hermann of Buxhoeveden, 59
Hermann of Sundern, 78
Hilchen, David, 173–74, 288n79
Hohenzollern, House of, 59
Holland. *See* Dutch Republic
Holm. *See* Kirchholm
Holy Land (Palestine), 16, 18–19, 33, 39, 41, 51, 56
Holy Roman Empire
  and conquest of Livonia, 19, 20, 30, 42, 48, 56, 65, 67, 271n49
  and Livonian War, 160, 164
  and Reformation, 135, 142, 148, 283n46, 290n28
  and Riga, vii, 3, 67, 97, 105–06, 167, 193
  and Thirty Years' War, 191, 196, 260
hospitals, 59, 90, 195, 276n95
House of Blackheads, xiii, 63, 82, 83 (photo), 85, 216, 259, 275n67, 275n69
householder rights, 221
housing (in Riga). *See also* architecture
  pre-conquest, 36
  medieval Riga, 47, 92, 93 (photo), 94, 153, 154
  Soviet era, 4
  Swedish era, 186, 204, 211–13, 214 (photo), 215
Hus, Jan, 137, 280n72

Iconoclasm, 139, 286n83
Ikšķile. *See* Üxküll
Imants (Imauts), 55, 268n21
indulgences, 32, 33, 48, 137
Ingria, 181, 197, 198, 202, 207, 220, 231–32, 235, 236, 237, 242, 242, 247
Ivan III, Grand Prince of Muscovy, 122, 130, 132–35
Ivan IV, Grand Prince of Muscovy, 122–23, 136, 157–61, 165, 167, 169, 226, 236, 285n14, 286n24, 287n48
Ivangorod, 130, 132

Jāņi, 27, 89
Jelgava. *See* Mitau
Jersika (Ger. Gerzika), 23, 30, 35, 53, 54, 73
Jerusalem, 18, 19, 40–41, 48, 49, 51
Jesuits (Society of Jesus), 144, 168, 169, 170, 171, 173, 175, 179, 187, 272n65, 287n59
Jesus Church, ix, xii, 190, 204–05, 293n107
Jews, 6, 115, 259
John Freitag, Master of the Livonian Order, 124, 125
John of Fellin, 113
John of Mengden, Master of the Livonian Order, 121
journeymen, 84, 150, 222. *See also* craftsmen; Small Guild
Jugendstil. *See* Art Nouveau

Kaliningrad. *See* Königsberg
Karelia, 24, 120, 181, 197, 236
Kasekamp, Andres, 10
Kettler, Gotthard. *See* Gotthard Kettler
Kexholm, 181, 197, 242
Kiev, 13, 66, 73
Kievan Rus'. *See* Rus'
Kilns, 49, 89, 100, 204, 211

Kirchholm (Holm, Salaspils), xv, 31, 33, 44, 45, 47, 54, 120, 162, 180, 190, 198
Battle of. *See* Battle of Kirchholm
Treaty of. *See* Treaty of Kirchholm
knights. *See* Swordbrothers; Livonian Order; Teutonic Knights; Knights Templar
Knights Templar, 102, 111–12
Knopken, Andreas, x, 137–38, 144, 282n28, 282n30
Knut VI, King of Denmark, 42
Kobron. *See* Fort Kobron
Kokenhusen (Latv. Koknese)
Archbishop's residence at, xv, 110, 122, 139, 140, 143, 150
and Great Northern War, 233, 237, 238, 240, 242, 297n37
Latvian hill fort at, 53
as tax collection point, 172, 189
Koknese. *See* Kokenhusen
Königsberg (Rus. Kaliningrad), 91, 147, 172, 189, 230, 253, 285n2
Kube Hill (Ger. Kubsberg), xiii, 26, 34, 36, 38, 45, 153, 178, 200, 206, 230
Kurzeme. *See* Courland

Lāčplēsis, 268n83, 283n49
Lake Ladoga, 242
Lake Riga. *See* Riga River
Landtag, xi, 119, 125, 128, 141–43, 148, 158, 162
Lastadia, 190, 204, 205, 210, 211, 229, 230, 244, 274n32, 293n107
Latin Christendom. *See* Catholic Church
Latgale (Moscow) suburb, xiii, 2, 23, 76, 81, 202, 204
Latgallia (Latgale) region, 23, 25, 54, 269n10, 289n3
Latvian language, 13, 24, 61, 145, 174, 217, 218, 219, 220, 262n1, 263n7, 264n18, 264n32, 265n38, 265n40, 265n43, 265n46, 266n48, 272n65, 274n46, 282n30, 284n64, 284n2, 292n64, 295n132
Latvian tribes, 22–27, 35, 50, 65, 72
Latvianization, 7, 145–46, 221
Latvians (in Riga), xi, 6–7, 8, 9, 36, 59, 73, 74, 77, 80, 86, 89, 90, 91, 129, 137, 140, 144–45, 148–49, 151, 154, 173, 180, 182, 186, 206, 211, 218, 219, 220, 221–23, 224, 244, 255, 259–60, 266n51, 275n69, 284n60, 295n137
churches belonging to, xiv, 61, 136, 145, 189, 191, 204
Lennewarden (Latv. Lielvārde), 53, 110, 172
Lent. *See* Carnival
Letts. Refers originally to Latgallians and then to other Latvian-speaking peoples. *See* Latvians
Libau (Latv. Liepāja), 230
library, 112, 168, 174, 265n47
Lime Gate, 201
Lime Ravelin, 201
linen, 87, 90, 149, 150, 191
linseed, 208, 243, 189
Lithuania, Grand Duchy of. For events after 1569 *see* Polish-Lithuanian Commonwealth
and knightly orders, 115, 116, 117, 119, 122, 124, 129
and alliance with Livonia, 133–35, 156–57
and Muscovy, 121, 132–34, 135, 161, 172, 197
and Riga, 122
and trade, 149
union with Kingdom of Poland, 116–17, 119, 121, 159, 166
Lithuanians, 23, 24
conversion to Christianity, 104, 108, 109, 113
and crusades, 101, 102–03, 109–10, 112, 113
raids by, 13, 21, 31, 34–35, 39, 44, 53, 54, 104
and trade, 99, 104, 108–09
in Riga, 6, 47, 50, 57, 73, 80, 108, 109–10, 113, 114, 211, 220
Liv Square, 36
Livonia (Ger. Livland; Alt-Livland). *See also* Livonian Confederation
definition of, xv, 2, 10
Livonia, Bishopric of. *See* Bishopric of Livonia; Meinhard; Berthold of Hanover; Albert of Buxhoeveden
Livonian Aa (Livländische Aa; Treider Aa). *See* Gauja River
Livonian Brothers of the Sword. *See* Swordbrothers
Livonian Confederation
definition, xi, 10, 119

Livonian Confederation (*continued*)
demise of, 155, 156–59, 289n3
founding of, 118–19
weaknesses, 127, 128, 134, 141, 142
Livonian crusade. *See* Northern Crusades
Livonian Order (Order of Livonian Knights). *See also* civil wars; Livonian War; Northern Crusades
and Archbishop of Riga, ix, xi, 3, 101, 104–05, 107, 109, 110, 111–12, 115, 116, 117–26, 136, 142, 156
castles belonging to, xv, 98, 100, 106, 111, 113, 114, 115–16, 119, 121, 129, 152
demise of, viii, 164
and Estonia, 115
and Lithuania, 104, 108, 111, 113, 115, 116–17, 119, 122, 124, 129
and Livonian War, 157–64
membership of, 102
and Muscovy, 128–29, 130–35
and Northern Crusades, 103, 106
origins of, xi, 64, 101–02
and papacy, 111, 112, 116
and Reformation, 138, 139, 140, 142, 143, 144, 148
and Riga Town Council, xi, 86, 100, 113–14, 118, 121–26
and Teutonic Order, 102–03, 109, 116
and trade, 75, 100, 108, 111
wars with Riga. *See* civil wars
Livonian Rhymed Chronicle, 50, 102
Livonian War, viii, xv, 3, 5, 8, 129, 148, 151, 155, 157–67, 172, 173, 178, 188, 236, 285n13, 286n21, 286n24
Livonians (Livs). *See* Livs
Livs (Livonians)
conversions of, x, 28–32, 34, 45, 46, 55
and Great Northern War, 145, 239, 252, 255, 258
language, 10, 13, 23, 24, 27, 31, 258, 265n46, 266n57, 269n18
and Lithuanian raids, 34–35, 39, 44, 50
and Northern Crusades, ix, 14–15, 27, 32–34, 44, 49–58, 65
in modern times, 25, 258, 299n102
in Riga, 13–14, 23, 26, 34–36, 38, 39, 46, 47, 56, 60, 61, 69, 72–73, 74, 77, 79, 89, 92, 95, 150, 173, 211, 220, 258
and Rus', 30, 72, 274n23
of Turaida, 23, 32, 45, 46, 52, 54–55, 57
Lohmüller, John, 137, 141, 146
London, ix, 4, 71, 75
Low German, 9, 40, 71, 145, 146, 270n23, 281n103, 281n2, 282n30
Löwenhaupt, Adam Ludwig von, 247–48
Lübeck, xv, 30, 33, 40, 44, 47, 58, 60, 64, 70, 71, 74–75, 82, 107, 134, 145, 161, 198, 268n77, 284n76
Lucas Island, 240, 297n45
Luther, Martin, 136–37, 141, 155
Lutheranism. *See* Reformation

Magdeburg, 20, 42
Mänd, Anu, 9, 84, 89, 276n73
Marquart, Brand, 205, 211
Marienland, 22, 41, 65
Mazepa, Ivan, 249, 298n61
Meder, Johann Valentin, 217
Meinhard, Bishop of Livonia, x, 28, 30–34, 36, 42, 266n57, 267n65, 268n76, 268n83, 268n86
Menshikov, Alexander, 250, 251, 253, 294n123
Mentzendorff House, 215
merchants (of Riga). *See also* Great Guild
in early Riga, vii, ix, xi, xiii, 4, 8, 33, 34, 37, 39–40, 45, 47, 60, 64–65,67, 70, 72, 99
and fur trade, 73–75
in Hanseatic Riga, 71–89, 92, 99, 104, 109, 113, 118, 121, 125, 129, 131–32, 136, 138, 149, 150, 157, 274n23, 275n54, 276n68
during Polish era, 166, 168, 169, 170, 172, 173, 175
during Swedish era, 186, 189, 190–91, 200, 207, 208–09, 215, 221, 229, 230, 235, 243, 244
Mettig, Constantin, 6–7, 31–32, 255
Mindaugas, King and Grand Duke of Lithuania, 23, 50, 104
Mitau (Latv. Jelgava), 154, 246
moats (of Riga), 12–13, 79, 114, 151, 178, 198–99, 200, 203, 205, 206, 210, 225, 230, 244, 252, 253
Mollin, Nicholas, x, 174–75, 179, 288n83
Mongols, 66, 77, 103, 130, 135, 157
Montefiore, Simon Sebag, 40

Müller, Heinrich, 169
Münster, Sebastian, 152, 15, 284n2
Murer, Francis, 202, 205, 211, 293n83
Muscovy. *See also* Alexei Mikhailovich; Ivan III, Ivan IV; Livonian War; Great Northern War
 and Baltic trade, 77, 129, 130–32, 149, 189, 207, 227
 expansion of, xv, 6, 77, 97, 119, 121, 122–23, 130, 135, 157, 158, 197–98, 291n53
 and Lithuania, 121, 132–34, 135, 156–57, 161, 172, 197
 population of, 227
 and Riga, 4, 129, 150, 151, 158, 160, 167, 172, 189, 198, 202, 206–09, 243, 246, 247–48, 251–58
 during Time of Troubles, 181, 197
 and wars in Livonia, viii, 127, 128–29, 130–35, 142, 143, 148, 151, 155, 156–67, 232–58, 282n20
 Westernization of, 209, 227
Muscovy Company, 149, 157
Museum of Decorative Arts and Design, 61, 107, 283n36
Museum of the History of Rīga and Navigation, 36, 69, 95, 194
music, 27, 86, 163, 216–17, 218

Napiersky, Jakob G. L., 7
Narva. *See also* Battle of Narva
 in contemporary times, xv, 273n10
 during Great Northern War, 236, 237, 239, 240, 242, 247, 297n38
 Order castle in, xv, 130
 and Livonian War, 158, 161, 165, 167, 236
 during Swedish era, 167, 172, 191, 193, 202, 208, 236
 and trade, 71, 72, 132, 172, 191, 193, 208, 273n11
Netherlands. *See* Dutch Republic
Neumann, Wilhelm von, 7, 271n63
Neva River, 72, 187, 236, 242, 245, 247
Nicholas I, Bishop of Riga, 104
Nienstedt, Francis, 28, 169, 174, 211
non-Germans (of Riga). *See* Latvians
Northern Crusades, vii, x, 1, 2, 5, 8, 13, 15–21, 28, 32–34, 39–42, 44–45, 48–61, 64–68, 73, 102–04, 105, 106, 267n60, 268n77
Norsemen. *See* Vikings
Nöteborg (Shlisselburg), 242, 247
Novgorod
 Muscovite conquest of, 121, 123, 130, 133
 and Northern Crusades, 103, 105
 Peterhof, 71, 73, 77, 123, 132
 as Rus' city, 13, 15, 58, 59, 61, 82, 273n14
 and trade, xi, xv, 15, 59, 71–74, 76, 77, 131, 132, 135, 271n46

Old Livonia. *See* Livonia
Order of Livonian Knights. *See* Livonian Order
Order of Swordbrothers. *See* Swordbrothers
Order of Teutonic Knights. *See* Teutonic Order
Order Castle. *See* Riga Castle
Orthodox Christianity
 in the eastern Baltic, 5, 15, 25, 53, 103
 and Muscovy, 130, 132–33, 158, 160–61, 172, 193
 and pagan conversions, 30, 267n68
 in Riga, 61, 160–61, 163, 173, 190, 259, 286n21
Ösel (Est. Saaremaa), 50, 67, 110, 121, 202, 268n76, 272n80, 286n24
Ösel-Wiek, Bishopric of, 105, 110, 115, 119, 272n80
Ostkolonization, 15, 17
Ostsiedlung, 17, 71
Ottoman Empire, 97, 133, 222, 228, 236, 249, 250, 254
Oxenstierna, Axel, 187, 193

Padel, Jürgen, 160, 286n29
Palestine. *See* Holy Land
Palmstruck, George, 210
Papal Schism (1378–1417), 116, 280n72. *See also* Avignon papacy
Pārdaugava. *See* Überdüna
Paris, 4, 46
Patkul, Johann Reinhold von, 231–32, 235, 239, 240, 243, 246
Paykull, Otto Arnold von, 240
peasantry (of Livonia). *See also* Latvians; Livs; refugees
 and Christianity, 136, 144, 147, 148, 195, 220
 and Great Northern War, 235, 238, 244, 245, 251, 252, 257
 and Livonian War, 158, 173

peasantry (of Livonia) (*continued*)
and Riga, 7, 12, 35, 56, 67, 70, 77, 89, 94, 108, 148–49, 173, 180, 186, 187, 192, 198, 221–22, 232, 235, 245, 251, 252, 257, 259, 273n81, 273n1
rebellions of, 115, 144, 147, 148
and serfdom, 151, 167, 185, 192, 257
during Swedish era, 185, 195, 209, 221, 291n47, 295n27
Pernau (Est. Pärnu), 77, 131, 144, 172, 181, 191, 241, 247, 256
Peter I, Tsar of Russia
early life, 226–27, 296n10
and Grand Embassy, 227–31
and Great Northern War, x, 224, 231, 232, 236–38, 240, 242, 245–56, 294n123
and Riga, 5, 213, 224, 227, 228–30, 236, 237, 246–47, 248, 251–53, 256, 259
statue of, 226, 259, 295n7
Peterhof (Novgorod), 71, 73, 77, 123, 132
Philip II of Swabia, Holy Roman Emperor, 42, 56
piracy, 25, 71, 75, 100
pitch, 78, 148, 189, 281n2
plague, 38, 115, 118, 134, 145, 154, 166, 187, 208, 249–57, 259
Plakans, Andrejs, 9, 10, 295n137
Plettenberg, Walter von. *See* Walter of Plettenburg
Plinius, Basilius, x, 152, 175–76, 193–94, 288n86
Poland, Kingdom of (before 1569), 111, 117, 118, 121, 122, 134, 141, 280n72, 280n86
Polish-Lithuanian Commonwealth (after 1569)
and Augustus II (King of Poland), 231, 232, 241
decline of, 185, 197, 227
formation of, 156, 166
and Great Northern War, 231, 232, 236, 240, 241, 242, 243, 245–47, 249
and Livonian War, 143, 156–63, 165–66
occupation of Riga, 3, 8, 152, 165, 166, 167–79, 180, 185
and trade, 189, 194–95, 243
Polish-Swedish War (1600–29), 178–83, 185, 186, 187, 196, 197, 199, 225
Polotsk, xv, 30, 31, 36, 44, 45, 53, 54, 65, 72, 73, 74, 77, 131, 208
Poltava. *See* Battle of Poltava
Pomerania, 161, 196, 282n28
Pomerelia, 111
pontoon bridge (Riga), 154, 238, 240–41, 251, 285n5
Pope Alexander IV, 104
Pope Boniface VIII, 108–10
Pope Celestine III, 32–33
Pope Clement V, 110–11
Pope Eugenius III, 19–20
Pope Gregory IX, 66, 102
Pope Gregory XIII, 168
Pope Honorius II, 41, 66, 268n78
Pope Innocent III, 44–45, 51, 65, 66, 271n50
Pope Innocent IV, 104
Pope Innocent VI, 116
Pope John XXII, 112–13
Pope Nicholas V (anti-pope), 114
Pope Sixtus IV, 122
Pope Urban II, 19
population of Riga. *See* Riga, population of
portage, 171–72, 187, 191, 192, 197, 210
porters (in Riga), 67, 86, 91, 137, 144, 191, 211, 235, 255, 282n28
potash, 189, 208
Powder Tower. *See* Sand Tower
printing, x, 138, 148, 152, 154, 174–75, 219
Protestant Reformation. *See* Reformation
Prussia. *See also* Danzig; Teutonic Order
Archbishopric of Prussia, 104, 141
crusades in, xi, 18, 20, 50, 56, 66, 102–03, 109, 264n30
Duchy of Prussia (East Prussia), 141, 142, 143, 147, 148, 155, 280n86
Plague, 251, 253
And rebellion of Prussian cities, 110, 114, 120–21, 163
and Reformation, 137, 141–42, 147
Royal Prussia, 141
and trade, 75, 91, 172, 189
Prussian Confederation, 120
Prussian tribes (Old Prussians), 14, 20, 24, 145, 264n30
Pskov, 58, 72, 74, 77, 1–3, 123, 132, 134–36, 166–67, 172, 229, 243, 247

Radziwill, George, 167–68, 205, 287n57
Radziwill, Nicholas ("the Black"), 163, 164, 166, 167, 286n42
Ramm, Nikolaus, 145

ramparts (in Riga), 3, 79, 94, 145, 151, 153, 173, 175, 194, 198–99, 203, 204, 205, 210, 211–12, 215, 225, 229, 230, 252
Rath. *See* Riga Town Council
Rawa, 231
Reformation, vii, x, 136–37
  and the Livonian Confederation, 138, 141–44, 148
  and the Latvian peasantry, 144, 145, 147
  in Riga, x, xiv, 61, 88, 92, 129, 137–41, 144–47, 148, 174, 216, 272n65, 277n103, 286n21
  See also Martin Luther; Andreas Knopken; Silvester Tegetmeier
refugees (in Riga), 145, 221, 222, 226, 245, 252, 253, 267, 258, 273n1
Renner, Johannes, 157, 160, 285n13
Repnin, Anikita, 241, 240, 251–56
Reuter, Johann, 219–220, 221
Reutern House, 213
Reutern, Johann von, 213, 215
Reval (Est. Tallinn)
  and Baltic trade, 59, 71, 72, 77, 131–32, 191, 281n2
  and beer, 277n101
  Blackheads in, 82
  founding of, xv, 47, 51, 58
  and Great Northern War, 241, 247, 256, 257
  and Livonian War, 158, 159, 160, 161, 163, 165, 285n13
  and Reformation, 137, 140, 141, 142, 147
  and Riga, 107, 123–24, 132
  under Swedish rule, 179, 200, 212
Rīdzene River (Rigebach). *See* Riga River
Riga (city of)
  commerce. *See* trade
  etymology of, 13
  fortifications of. *See* bastion system; Citadel; Dünamünde; Fort Kobron; moats; ramparts; ravelins; Riga Castle
  founding of, 2–3, 5, 9, 12–15, 17, 25, 28–34, 36, 38, 41–42, 44–46
  legends of, 12, 45–46, 61, 154–55, 240–41, 270n19
  population of, xiii, 3, 7, 47, 59, 61, 63, 70, 77, 90, 163, 172, 173, 226, 252, 257, 295n137
  prehistory of, 14–15, 22–28, 34–36
  sieges of, x, 3, 5, 38, 49, 58, 109, 123, 124–25, 180, 181, 183, 186, 198, 199, 206, 207–08, 209, 210, 224, 225, 226, 233, 237, 238, 241, 242, 243, 251–55, 256, 290n38, 293n87
  streets of, xiv, 3–4, 35, 36, 40, 47, 49, 61, 63, 78, 79, 80, 81, 92, 94, 154, 198, 202, 204, 205, 206, 211, 213, 215, 259, 277n107, 290n38, 291n63, 292n64, 292n72, 295n128
  trade in, vi, xi, 2, 14–15, 30, 45, 47, 70–78, 94, 100, 148–50, 188–92, 225, 242–43
Riga Castle (Order Castle), xiv, 1, 43 (photo), 48–49, 59, 61, 79, 86, 98, 106–07, 114, 121, 123, 124–25, 126, 135, 140, 143, 151, 152, 162, 164, 169, 177 (photo), 179, 198, 200, 201 (photo), 203, 206, 210, 226, 244, 255, 259, 279n55
Riga Cathedral (Riga Dome). *See* St. Mary's Church
Riga River (Rigebach, Riesing, Rīdzene, Rīdziņa), xiv, 13, 41, 48, 49, 59, 63, 78, 79, 81
  archaeological discoveries, 69–70, 106
  bridge over, 81, 106–07, 109
  deterioration of, 38, 76, 94–95, 155, 215, 253
  Riga's first port (Lake Riga), xiv, 35–36, 38, 47, 60, 63, 76
Riga Town Council (Rath)
  and conflicts with knights, xi, 2, 97, 101, 107–14, 118, 121
  expenses and responsibilities, 79, 94, 99–100, 106, 129, 150, 167, 192, 193–95
  founding of, 65, 67, 100, 272n74
  Great Northern War, 230, 231, 235, 245, 253, 255, 256
  Membership of, xi, 99, 122, 150, 193–95
  Polish era, ix, xi, 162, 166, 167, 169–71, 174, 182, 186, 193–94, 287n63
  during Reformation, 138–43, 145
  Swedish era, 186, 192, 193, 194–96, 202, 205, 208, 219, 225
Rigebach. *See* Riga River
Rigeholm, 81, 106
Rigemann family, 194
Rigische Novellen, 216
Riksdag, 179, 193, 235
Rodenburg, Johan van, 202, 205
Romanovs. *See* Alexei Mikhailovich; Peter I
Rome, 32, 41, 44–45, 52, 66, 98, 105, 107–10, 118, 137–38, 140, 143–44, 146, 283n46

rondels, 178, 198–200
Rostock, 40, 144, 174
Rothmar of Buxhoeveden, 57, 266n57
Rumeschottel, Johann, 282n29
Rus' (Kievan Rus'), 263n9
  and eastern Baltic tribes, 24–25, 30, 35, 45, 51, 53–54, 267n68
  chronicles of, 13, 25
  and crusaders, 53–54, 65, 99, 103
  and Riga, 4, 30, 35, 38, 58, 75, 77
  and trade, xv, 13–15, 30, 38, 44, 61, 71–77, 79
Russian Empire, xv, 3, 6, 7, 194, 195, 212, 213, 221, 224–25, 259, 260, 295n7, 297n45, 299n102
Russians (in Riga), xiii, 2, 5, 9, 36, 61, 72, 77, 79, 89, 132, 163, 168, 172–73, 205, 207, 208–09, 230, 251, 252–53, 255–56, 257, 274n23, 292n72
Russow, Balthasar, 132, 163, 168, 285n13
rye, 57, 190–91, 252, 284n74

St. Catherine's Church, 63
St. George's Day Uprising (1343–45), 115
St. George's Castle. *See* Riga Castle
St. Gertrude's Church, xiv, 160, 180, 204, 253, 292n74, 293n88
St. Jacob's Bastion, 202
St. Jacob's Church (St. James), xiv, 61, 81, 124, 136, 137, 138, 144, 145, 152, 154, 168, 169, 171, 284n60, 285n7
St. James's Church. *See* St. Jacob's
St. John's Church, xiv, 139, 211
St. Mary's Church (Dome Cathedral, Riga Dome), xiv, 42, 43 (photo), 47, 48, 57, 59, 60, 69, 79, 86, 98, 104, 101, 118, 139, 144, 152, 153, 238, 250, 253, 268n84, 269n7, 294n117
St. Nicholas's Church, 173, 286n21
St. Peter's Church, ix, xiv, 59, 60, 61, 62 (photo), 80, 101, 122, 126, 136–39, 144, 152, 170, 174, 177 (photo), 208, 212, 217, 255, 282n28, 282n29, 291n41, 293n107
St. Peter's school, 136, 144, 252
St. Petersburg, 3, 218, 236, 242, 247, 251, 256, 260, 263n7
Salaspils. *See* Kirchholm
salt, 74, 76, 86, 149, 189, 211, 217, 275n69, 282n28
Samogitia, 53, 55, 102, 108, 116, 117, 278n21
Samson, Hermann, 174–75
Sand Gate, 86, 183, 200
Sand Ravelin, 202
Sand Road, xiv, 4, 61, 78, 200, 204–06, 293n88
Sand Tower, xiv, 78, 114, 151, 200, 202
Sapieha, Lew, 171
Sarkandaugava, 178, 190, 207
Saxons, 34, 232–33, 235, 237–40, 242, 243, 245, 259, 297n37, 297n46
Saxony, Duchy of, viii, 17, 20, 27, 33, 45, 47, 72, 267n57
Saxony, Electorate of, 218, 231, 241, 246, 247
Scanian War, 225
Schlippenbach, Gustav Wilhelm von, 241
Shlisselburg. *See* Nöteborg
Schöning, John (Johann), 91, 125–26, 281n108
Segeberg, 28, 57, 266, 268n86, 269n18
Sejm, 159–60, 179, 245
Selonians, 23, 25, 57, 72, 265n38
Semigallia (Latv. Zemgale), xv, 23, 55, 57, 73, 106, 121, 272n80, 289n3. *See also* Courland
Semigallians, 23, 25, 30, 35, 54–55, 57, 64, 72–73, 102–103, 106, 265n38, 271n52, 278n21
serfdom, 77, 91, 145, 151, 185, 192, 195, 209, 219, 220, 222, 227, 231, 257, 288n79
Sheremetev, Boris, 38, 241–42, 244, 251–56
Ships and shipping (commercial)
  caravels, 75
  cogs, 7, 14, 75, 271n55, 273n4
  and Dutch Republic, 188–89
  excavations of, 36, 69–70, 95, 273n4
  hulks, 75
  and Riga, 29–30, 33, 38, 47, 60, 64, 72–76, 112, 124, 129, 148–49, 165, 166, 181, 190–91, 213, 233, 243, 249, 252, 284n76, 297n51
  strugas, 38, 189, 230
  Viking vessels, 14–15
  See also Hanseatic League; trade
shipyards, 70, 76, 81, 100, 205, 227, 228
Schragen, 222, 295n132
sieges of Riga. *See* Riga
Siegfried Lander of Spanheim, Master of the Livonian Order, 118
Sigismund I, King of Poland, 141

Sigismund II Augustus, King of Poland, 156, 159-60, 162–63, 166
Sigismund III Vasa, King of Poland, 170, 172, 179–80, 181, 182, 186, 187, 235
Silesia, 17, 18
silver, 76, 100, 143, 150, 197, 244
Skavronskaya, Marta. *See* Catherine I
Skytte, Johan, 195, 291n47
Small Guild, xi, xiii, 82, 84, 90, 91, 122, 168, 169, 173, 235, 275n69, 279n57, 279n70, 288n89
Smolin. *See* Battle of Smolin
Smolensk, 15, 61, 72, 77, 131, 133–35, 197, 247
Šnore, Rauls, 95
Society of Jesus. *See* Jesuits
Soltrump, John (Johann), 122
Soltrump, Reinhold, 122
Soviet Union, 1, 2, 3, 4, 6, 9, 202, 258, 268n83
Spekke, Arnolds, 8, 23, 257
Staden, Heinrich von, 158
Stanislas I (Stanislas Leszczynski), King of Poland, 245–46
Staden, Heinrich von, 158
Steinau, Adam Heinrich von, 238
Stephen Bathory, King of Poland, xiv, 151, 166–67, 175, 199, 203
Šterns, Indriķis, 8
Stockholm, 3, 179, 188, 191, 193, 194, 204, 230, 231, 256, 257, 289n8, 299n97
Stolbovo. *See* Treaty of Stolbovo
Straubergs, Jānis, x, 8, 220, 257
streets (of Riga). *See* Riga
Stromberg, Nils, 251–52, 254, 256
Stuart, Karl Magnus, 239
suburbs (of Riga), xiv, 38, 76, 81, 89, 138, 153, 160, 178, 180, 186, 190, 200, 202, 204–06, 207, 208, 210, 211–12, 215, 221, 223, 225, 229, 244, 250, 251, 252, 259, 268n83, 293n107, 295n128
Suerbeer, Albert II. *See* Archbishop Albert II Suerbeer
Švābe, Arveds, 8
Sweden, Kingdom of
  administration of Livonia (Livland), xv, 182, 185, 192, 195–96, 200, 209, 216, 217, 218, 289n8, 291n59
  administration of Riga, viii, ix, x, 186, 192–96, 197–98, 200, 216, 220–23, 287n59
  architecture in Riga, ix, x, 212–15
  conquest of Riga (1621), 182–83, 185–88, 205
  fortifications in Riga, xiii, xiv, 78, 79, 154, 186, 198–207, 210–11, 225–26, 288n89, 292n67, 292n69, 292n71
  and Great Northern War, 228–58, 296n36, 297n46, 298n61
  and Livonian War, 143, 155, 158, 159, 160, 161, 163, 165, 166
  and Muscovite attack on Riga (1656), 197–98, 202, 206–08
  and Northern Crusades, 32–33, 57, 103, 267n72
  in Riga's civil wars, 125–26
  and trade, 72, 189–92, 207, 225
  wars with Poland (1600–29), 166, 172, 178–81, 185, 196, 199, 203, 225, 288n79
  See also Charles XI; Charles XII; Great Northern War; Gustavus II Adolphus
Swedish Gate, 79, 292n72
Swordbrothers (Livonian Brothers of the Sword; Order of Swordbrothers), xi, 18, 48–49, 51–52, 56–59, 63–67, 97–99, 101–03, 271n46, 272n79. *See also* Northern Crusades

Table Guilds, 89–90
Tallinn. *See* Reval
Tannenberg. *See* Battle of Tannenberg
Tartu. *See* Dorpat
Tatars, 130, 133–35, 157–60, 182
Tegetmeier, Silvester, x, 138
Templars. *See* Knights Templar
Teutonic Order (Order of Teutonic Knights), xiv, xi, 18, 48, 76, 102–03, 108, 110, 111, 114, 116, 118, 119, 120, 122–123, 141, 142, 148, 155, 158, 270n33, 279n67, 280n86, 283n48. *See also* Livonian Order
textiles, 28, 73, 76, 132, 149, 233, 238. *See also* clothing
Theodoric of Turaida (Treiden), 32–33, 45, 46, 48, 52–53
Thirteen Years' War (1654–67), 120–21, 280n86
Thirty Years' War (1618–48), 185, 191, 196
Three Brothers, 93 (photo), 94
Town Council (of Riga). *See* Riga Town Council
Town Hall (Riga), xiv, 59, 63, 80, 82, 86, 121, 126, 163, 169, 252, 259

Town Hall Square, xiv, 80, 88, 171, 194, 201, 255, 291n63
trade
  in Baltic Sea, xi, 14, 28, 70–78, 112, 126, 149–50, 188–89, 191, 193, 196, 207, 208, 225, 236, 242–43, 284n76
  Dutch Republic, 71, 74, 78, 149, 150, 179, 181, 189, 190, 194–95, 213, 227, 284n76
  England, 28, 71, 72, 149, 157, 190, 227, 236
  fur, xv, 2, 15, 72, 73–74, 108, 189, 209
  Lithuania, 99, 104, 108–09, 149, 189, 194–95, 243
  Livonian Order, 75, 100, 108, 111
  Muscovy, 77, 129, 130–32, 149, 189, 207, 227
  Narva, 71, 72, 132, 172, 191, 193, 208, 273n11
  Novgorod, xi, xv, 15, 59, 71–74, 76, 77, 131, 132, 135, 271n46
  Prussia, 75, 91, 172, 189
  Riga, vi, xi, 2, 14–15, 30, 45, 47, 70–78, 94, 100, 148–50, 188–92, 225, 242–43. *See also* merchants (Riga)
  Reval, 59, 71, 72, 77, 131–32, 191, 281n2
  Rus' cities. *See* Novgorod; Polotsk; Pskov; Smolensk
  Sweden, 72, 189–92, 207, 225
Treaty of Altmark (1629), 196
Treaty of Cardis (1661), 232
Treaty of Cracow (1525), 141
Treaty of Drohiczyn (1582), 167
Treaty of Kirchholm (1452), 120, 142, 281n103
Treaty of Pereyeslav (1654), 291n53
Treaty of Poswol (1557), 156–57
Treaty of Stolbovo (1617), 181–82
Treaty of St. Severin (1582), 171
Treaty of Thorn (1466), 280n86
Treaty of Vilnius (1323), 113
Treaty of Vilnius (1559), 162
Treaty of Yam-Zapolski (1582), 167
Treiden (Latv. Turaida), xv, 1, 23, 32, 45–46, 52, 54–55, 57, 58, 108
Treider Aa (river). *See* Gauja River
Turaida. *See* Treiden
Turkey. *See* Ottoman Empire
Turks, 19, 73, 158, 163, 182, 228. *See also* Ottoman Empire

Überdüna (Latv. Pārdaugava), xiii, xiv, 38, 154, 207, 230, 239, 249, 257
Ukraine, 135, 197, 227, 242, 248–49, 250, 263n9, 291n53, 298n61
Ulmanis, Kārlis, 7, 36, 95, 266n51
Union of Krewo (1385), 116
University of Dorpat, 219, 285n26, 285n27
Urban, William, 8, 51, 278n27
USSR. *See* Soviet Union
Üxküll (Latv. Ikšķile), xv, 28, 30–34, 42, 44–45, 47, 268n84

Valdemar II, King of Denmark, 58, 272n74
Valmiera. *See* Wolmar
Vasili III, Grand Prince of Muscovy, 135
Vecdaugava, 270n36
Ventspils. *See* Windau
Vetseke, 53–55
Vicelinuis, 31
Vidzeme, 10, 23, 185, 258, 267n66
Viestards (Viesturs), 54–55
Vitebsk, 72, 74, 131
Vikings (Norsemen), 14, 16, 23, 25, 35, 263n9
Vilnius, 124, 164, 279n50
Vilnius Treaty. *See* Treaty of Vilnius
Visby, 32, 42, 47, 71, 107, 281n2
Visvaldis (Vsevolod), 53, 55, 270n41
Vladimir, Prince of Polotsk, 31, 54
Volquin, Master of the Order of Swordbrothers, 102
Vytenis, Grand Duke of Lithuania, 108, 110

Wagner, Richard, 213, 215
Waldis, Burkard, x, 146–47
walls (of Riga), xiii, xiv, 2, 3, 36, 40, 58, 73
  during medieval era, 47, 48, 49, 56, 59–61, 63, 78, 79, 81, 89, 91, 92, 94, 100, 106, 109, 114, 118, 120, 129, 145, 151, 153, 154, 160, 203
  during Polish era, 152, 169, 173, 174, 178, 183, 187
  during Swedish era, 186, 187, 194, 198, 200, 204–08, 211–12, 215, 229, 233, 235, 252, 253, 292n72
  razing of, 3, 153, 259
Walter of Plettenberg (Master of the Livonian Order), viii, x, 10, 86, 125–27, 130, 134, 135, 136, 138, 140–43
wax trade, 15, 28, 29, 72, 73–74, 77, 108, 132, 189, 281n2

Wellingk, Otto, 235
Wenden (Latv. Cēsis), xv, 65, 71, 86, 108–09, 119, 122, 126, 129, 135, 142, 150, 165–66, 271n46
Wenden, Battle of. *See* Battle of Wenden
Wends, 13, 17, 19–20, 25–26, 30, 31, 36, 65, 264n24, 264n27, 266n49, 266n51, 271n46
Westphalia, 17, 33, 72, 280n75
widows, ix, 81, 109, 174, 287n63
Wilkomierz. *See* Battle of Wilkomierz
William of Fürstenberg, 156, 161
William of Modena, 24, 55, 64, 66–67, 98, 272n79
Windau (Latv. Ventspils), 26, 71, 199
wine, ix, 28, 76, 80, 86, 87, 91, 100, 127, 128, 131, 149, 170, 189, 217, 233
witches and witchcraft, 81, 139, 148, 174–75
Witte, Engelbrecht, 74
Wolmar (Latv. Valmiera), 1, 71, 143, 148
World War I, 2, 265n42
World War II, xiv, 1, 2, 8, 24, 202, 275n67, 299n1

Zeids, Teodors, 9, 173
Zemgale. *See* Semigallia
Zimmerman family, 194–195

Printed in the USA
CPSIA information can be obtained
at www.ICGtesting.com
LVHW091642250823
756268LV00025B/586/J